The African-American Family in Slavery and Emancipation

In *The African-American Family in Slavery and Emancipation*, Wilma Dunaway calls into question the dominant paradigm of the U.S. slave family. She contends that U.S. slavery studies have been flawed by neglect of small plantations and export zones and by exaggeration of slave agency. Using data on population trends and slave narratives, she identifies several profit-maximizing strategies that owners implemented to disrupt and endanger African-American families, including forced labor migrations, structural interference in marriages and child care, sexual exploitation of women, shortfalls in provision of basic survival needs, and ecological risks. This book is unique in its examination of new threats to family persistence that emerged during the Civil War and Reconstruction.

Wilma A. Dunaway is Associate Professor of Sociology at Virginia Polytechnic Institute and State University. She is a specialist in international slavery studies, Native American studies, Appalachian studies, and world-system analysis. Her first book, *The First American Frontier: Transition to Capitalism in Southern Appalachia, 1700–1860*, won the 1996 Weatherford Award for the best book about Southern Appalachia. Her interdisciplinary work has appeared in several history and social science journals.

Studies in modern capitalism · Etudes sur le capitalisme moderne

Editorial board · Comité de rédaction

This series is devoted to an attempt to comprehend capitalism as a world-system. It will include monographs, collections of essays and colloquia around specific themes, written by historians and social scientists united by a common concern for the study of large-scale long-term social structure and social change.

The series is a joint enterprise of the Maisons des Sciences de l'Homme in Paris and the Fernand Braudel Center for the Study of Economies, Historical Systems, and Civilizations at the State University of New York at Binghamton.

Other books in the series

MARIE-CLAIRE BERGERE: *The Golden Age of the Chinese bourgeoisie, 1911–1937*
IVAN T. BEREND AND GYORGY RANKI: *The European periphery and industrialization, 1780–1914*
SUSHIL CHAUDHURY AND MICHEL MORINEAU (eds.): *Merchants, companies and trade: Europe and Asia in the early modern era*
FERENC FEHER: *The frozen revolution: an essay on Jacobinism*
GEORGES HAUPT: *Aspects of international socialism, 1871–1914*
HURI ISLAMOGLU-INAN (ed.): *The Ottoman empire and the world-economy*
CAGLAR KEYDER: *The definition of a peripheral economy: Turkey, 1923–1929*
LUISA PASSERINI: *Fascism and popular memory: the cultural experience of the Turin working class*
LUCETTE VALENSI: *Tunisian peasants in the eighteenth and nineteenth centuries*
IMMANUEL WALLERSTEIN: *The capitalist world-economy: essays*
IMMANUEL WALLERSTEIN: *The politics of the world-economy: the states, the movements and the civilisations*
IMMANUEL WALLERSTEIN: *Geopolitics and geoculture: essays on the changing world-system*
STUART WOOLF (ed.): *Domestic strategies: work and family in France and Italy, 1600–1800*
CHARLES F. SABEL AND JONATHAN ZEITLIN (eds.): *World of possibilities: flexibility and mass production in western industrialization*

This book is published as part of the joint publishing agreement established in 1977 between the Fondation de la Maison des Sciences de l'Homme and the Press Syndicate of the University of Cambridge. Titles published under this arrangement may appear in any European language or, in the case of volumes of collected essays, in several languages.

New books will appear either as individual titles or in one of the series which the Maison des Sciences de l'Homme and Cambridge University Press have jointly agreed to publish. All books published jointly by the Maison des Sciences de l'Homme and Cambridge University Press will be distributed by the Press throughout the world.

The African-American Family in Slavery and Emancipation

Wilma A. Dunaway

*Virginia Polytechnic Institute
and State University*

MAISON DES SCIENCES DE L'HOMME

CAMBRIDGE
UNIVERSITY PRESS

CAMBRIDGE UNIVERSITY PRESS
Cambridge, New York, Melbourne, Madrid, Cape Town, Singapore,
São Paulo, Delhi, Dubai, Tokyo

Cambridge University Press
The Edinburgh Building, Cambridge CB2 8RU, UK

Published in the United States of America by Cambridge University Press, New York

www.cambridge.org
Information on this title: www.cambridge.org/9780521012164

First published 2003

UWE, BRISTOL LIBRARY SERVICES

A catalogue record for this publication is available from the British Library

Library of Congress Cataloguing in Publication data
Dunaway, Wilma A.
The African-American family in slavery and emancipation / Wilma A. Dunaway.
    p.   cm. – (Studies in modern capitalism)
Includes bibliographical references and index.
ISBN 0-521-81276-3 – ISBN 0-521-01216-3 (pbk.)
1. Slavery – Social aspects – United States – History.   2. African American
families – History.   3. Slaves – United States – Social conditions.   4. Slaves –
Emancipation – United States.   5. Freedmen – United States – Social
conditions.   6. African Americans – Social conditions.   7. African American
families – Appalachian Region, Southern – History.   8. Slaves – Appalachian
Region, Southern – Social conditions.   9. Appalachian Region, Southern – Race
relations.   10. Appalachian Region, Southern – Social conditions.   I. Title.
II. Series.
E443 .D86   2003
306.3′62′0973 – dc21

                                                                    2002071484

ISBN 978-0-521-81276-4 Hardback
ISBN 978-0-521-01216-4 Paperback

Transferred to digital printing 2010

In memory of
William Sherman Dunaway, Sr.
and
Della Elizabeth Newcomb Dunaway,
resilient parents
who maintained our family
despite the threats from sharecropping and low-waged
industrial labor.
The best of me I owe to them.

The companion website for this book is located at
http://scholar.lib.vt.edu/vtpubs/mountain_slavery/index.htm

Contents

Maps

Introduction

> We just prayed for strength to endure to the end. We didn't expect
> anything but to have to go on in bondage till we died.
>
> – Delia Garlic, northern Alabama ex-slave

When Amelia Jones told her story to a WPA interviewer in the 1930s, she
described her former eastern Kentucky owner as a man who routinely
traded black laborers. "Master White didn't hesitate to sell any of his
slaves. He said, 'You all belong to me and if you don't like it, I'll put you
in my pocket.' " When Jim Threat described his experiences as a northern
Alabama slave, he focused on the danger of permanent separation. "We
lived in constant fear," Jim said, "that we would be sold away from our
families." In her story, Maggie Pinkard gave us some clue how often black
families were disrupted. "When the slaves got a feeling there was going to
be an auction, they would pray. The night before the sale they would pray
in their cabins. You could hear the hum of voices in all the cabins down
the row." Other enslaved women focused more sharply on the mother's
perspective. Several of them lamented that they had "no name" to give
their children because they must use their masters' surnames, not those
of their husbands. "I haven't never had a nine months child," Josephine
Bacchus told the WPA interviewer. "I ain' never been safe in de family way." This former slave went on to say that she experienced chronic
hunger, sexual exploitation from white males, and quick return to the
fields after childbirth. As a result, all her babies, except one, were stillborn. Katie Johnson captured the vulnerability of parents when she said:
"During slavery, it seemed lak yo' chillun b'long to ev'ybody but you."[1]

These voices recount experiences that are representative of a majority of slaves of the Mountain South, a region characterized by a low
black population density and small plantations. What they have to say
is startling because they are reporting a past that contradicts the dominant paradigm. The conventional wisdom is that owners rarely broke up
slave families; that slaves were adequately fed, clothed, and sheltered; and
that slave health or death risks were no greater than those experienced

1

by white adults. Why have so many investigations come to these optimistic conclusions? U.S. slavery studies have been handicapped by four
fundamental weaknesses:
- a flawed view of the slave family,
- scholarly neglect of small plantations,
- limited analysis of Upper South enslavement,
- academic exaggeration of slave agency.

The Flawed View of the Slave Family

U.S. slavery studies have been dominated by the view that it was not
economically rational for masters to break up black families. According
to Fogel and Engerman, households were the units through which work
was organized and through which the rations of basic survival needs were
distributed. By discouraging runaways, families also rooted slaves to owners. Gutman's work established the view that slave families were organized
as stable, nuclear, single-residence households grounded in long-term
marriages. After thirty years of research, Fogel is still convinced that two-
thirds of all U.S. slaves lived in two-parent households. Recent studies,
like those of Berlin and Rowland, are grounded in and celebrate these
optimistic generalizations about the African-American slave family.[2]

None of these writers believes that U.S. slave owners interfered in the
construction or continuation of black families. Fogel argues that such
intervention would have worked against the economic interests of the
owners, while Gutman focuses on the abilities of slaves to engage in
day-to-day resistance to keep their households intact. Fogel and most
scholars argue that sexual exploitation of slave women did not happen
very often. Moreover, the conventional wisdom has been that slaveholders
discouraged high fertility because female laborers were used in the fields
to a greater extent than male workers. Consequently, the predominant
view is that most slave women did not have their first child until about age
twenty-one and that teenage pregnancies were rare. To permit women
to return to work as quickly as possible, owners protected children by
providing collectivized child care.[3]

Scholarly Neglect of Small Plantations

Those who have supported the dominant paradigm neglected small slaveholdings, the second methodological blunder of U.S. slave studies.
Gutman acknowledged this inadequacy of his own work when he commented in passing that "little is yet known about the domestic arrangements and kin networks as well as the communities that developed among

slaves living on farms and in towns and cities." Fogel stressed that "failure to take adequate account of the differences between slave experiences and culture on large and small plantations" has been a fundamental blunder by slavery specialists. Because findings have been derived from analysis of plantations that owned more than fifty slaves, generalizations about family stability have been derived from institutional arrangements that represented the life experiences of a small minority of the enslaved population. In reality, more than 88 percent of U.S. slaves resided at locations where there were fewer than fifty slaves.[4]

Revisionist researchers provide ample evidence that slave family stability varied with size of the slaveholding. Analyzing sixty-six slave societies around the world in several historical eras, Patterson found that slavery was most brutal and most exploitative in those societies characterized by smallholdings. Contrary to the dominant paradigm, Patterson found that family separations, slave trading, sexual exploitation, and physical abuse occurred much more often in societies where the masters owned small numbers of slaves. There were several factors that were more likely to destabilize family life on small plantations than on large ones. According to Patterson, small slaveholdings allowed "far more contact with (and manipulation of) the owner" and "greater exposure to sexual exploitation." Compared to large plantations, slave families on small plantations were more often disrupted by masters, and black households on small plantations were much more frequently headed by one parent. Stephen Crawford showed that slave women on small plantations had their first child at an earlier age and were pregnant more frequently than black females on large plantations. Steckel argued that hunger and malnutrition were worse on small plantations, causing higher mortality among the infants, children, and pregnant women held there.[5]

Scholarly Neglect of the Upper South

In addition to their neglect of small plantations, scholars who support the dominant paradigm have directed inadequate attention to enslavement in the Upper South. Instead, much of what is accepted as conventional wisdom is grounded in the political economy and the culture of the Lower South. Why is it so important to study the Upper South? In the United States, world demand for cotton triggered the largest domestic slave trade in the history of the world. Between 1790 and 1860, the Lower South slave population nearly quadrupled because the Upper South exported nearly one million black laborers. In a fifty-year period, two-fifths of the African-Americans who were enslaved in the Upper South were forced to migrate to the cotton economy; the vast majority were sold through interstate transactions, and about 15 percent were removed in relocations with owners.[6]

Because of that vast interregional forced migration, Upper South slaves experienced family histories that contradict the accepted wisdom in U.S. slave studies. Though their arguments still have not altered the dominant paradigm, revisionist researchers offer evidence that slave family stability varied with southern subregion. Tadman contends that, after the international slave trade closed in 1808, the Upper South operated like a "stock-raising system" where "a proportion of the natural increase of its slaves was regularly sold off." As a result, the chances of an Upper South slave falling into the hands of interstate traders were quite high. Between 1820 and 1860, one-tenth of all Upper South slaves were relocated to the Lower South each decade. Nearly one of every three slave children living in the Upper South in 1820 was gone by 1860. Among Mississippi slaves who had been removed from the Upper South, nearly half the males and two-fifths of the females had been separated from spouses with whom they had lived at least five years. Stevenson contends that Virginia slave families were disproportionately matrifocal because of the slave trading and labor strategies of Upper South masters. Clearly, the fifty-year forced labor migration of slaves must be taken into account in scholarly assessments of family stability and of household living conditions.[7]

Scholarly Preoccupation with Slave Agency

The fourth weakness in U.S. slavery studies has been a preoccupation with slave agency. As Kolchin has observed, most scholars "have abandoned the victimization model in favor of an emphasis on the slaves' resiliency and autonomy." Like a number of other scholars, I have grown increasingly concerned that too many recent studies have the effect of whitewashing from slavery the worst structural constraints. Because so much priority has been placed on these research directions, there has been inadequate attention directed toward threats to slave family maintenance. Notions like "windows of autonomy within slavery" or an "independent slave economy" seriously overstate the degree to which slaves had control over their own lives, and they trivialize the brutalities and the inequities of enslavement. Patterson is scathing in his criticism of the excesses of studies that assign too much autonomy to slaves.

During the 1970s, a revisionist literature emerged in reaction to the earlier scholarship on slavery that had emphasized the destructive impact of the institution on Afro-American life. In their laudable attempts to demonstrate that slaves, in spite of their condition, did exercise some agency and did develop their own unique patterns of culture and social organization, the revisionists went to the opposite extreme, creating what Peter Parish calls a "historiographical hornet's nest," which came "dangerously close to writing the slaveholder out of the story completely."[8]

In their haste to celebrate the resilience and the dignity of slaves, scholars have underestimated the degree to which slaveholders placed families at risk. Taken to its extreme, the search for individual agency shifts to the oppressed the blame for the horrors and inequalities of the institutions that enslaved them. If, for example, we push to its rhetorical endpoint the claim of Berlin and Rowland that slaves "manipulated to their own benefit the slaveowners' belief that regular family relations made for good business," then we would arrive at the inaccurate conclusion (as some have) that the half of the U.S. slave population who resided in single-parent households did so as an expression of their African-derived cultural preferences, not because of any structural interference by owners. If we push to its rhetorical endpoint the claim that there was an independent slave economy, then we must ultimately believe that a hungry household was just not exerting enough personal agency at "independent" food cultivation opportunities. Such views are simply not supported by the narratives of those who experienced enslavement. Nowhere in the 600 slave narratives that I have analyzed (within and outside the Mountain South) have I found a single slave who celebrated moments of independence or autonomy in the manner that many academics do. Some slaves did resist, but ex-slaves voiced comprehension that their dangerous, often costly acts of civil disobedience resulted in no long-term systemic change.[9]

The Target Area for This Study

In sharp contrast to previous studies, I will test the dominant paradigm of the slave family against findings about a slaveholding region that was *typical* of the circumstances in which a majority of U.S. slaves were held. That is, I will examine enslavement in a region that was *not* characterized by large plantations and that did *not* specialize in cotton production. Even though more than half of all U.S. slaves lived where there were fewer than four slave families, there is very little research about family life in areas with low black population densities. Despite Crawford's groundbreaking finding that plantation size was the most significant determinant of quality of slave life, this is the first study of a multistate region of the United States that was characterized by small plantations.[10]

This study breaks new ground by investigating the slave family in a slaveholding region that has been ignored by scholars. I will explore the complexities of the Mountain South where slavery flourished amidst a

Map 1. Where is the Mountain South?

nonslaveholding majority and a large surplus of poor white landless laborers. In geographic and geological terms, the Mountain South (also
known as Southern Appalachia) makes up that part of the U.S. Southeast
that rose from the floor of the ocean to form the Appalachian Mountain
chain 10,000 years ago (see Map 1). In a previous book, I documented
the historical integration of this region into the capitalist world system.
The incorporation of Southern Appalachia entailed nearly one hundred
fifty years of ecological, politico-economic, and cultural change. Beginning in the early 1700s, Southern Appalachia was incorporated as a peripheral fringe of the European colonies located along the southeastern
coasts of North America. During the early eighteenth century, the peripheries of the world economy included eastern and southern Europe,
Hispanic America, and "the extended Caribbean," which stretched from

the Atlantic colonies of North America to northeastern Brazil. As the geographical space for several wars, the Mountain South became one of the major frontier arenas in which England, France, and Spain played out their imperialistic rivalry. Within two decades, the region's indigenous people were integrated into the commodity chains of the world economy to supply slaves to New World plantations and to produce deerskins to fuel western Europe's emergent leather manufacturing. After the American Revolution, Southern Appalachia formed the first western frontier of the new nation, so it was quickly resettled by Euroamericans.[11]

On a world scale, Southern Appalachia's role was not that different from many other peripheral fringes at the time, including inland mountain sections of several Caribbean islands, Brazil, the West Indies, and central Europe. Incorporation into the capitalist world economy triggered within Southern Appalachia agricultural, livestock, and extractive ventures that were adapted to the region's terrain and ecological peculiarities. Yet those new production regimes paralleled activities that were occurring in other sectors of the New World that had been colonized by western Europe. Fundamentally, the Mountain South was a *provisioning zone*, which supplied raw materials to other agricultural or industrial regions of the world economy.[12]

On the one hand, this inland region exported foodstuffs to other peripheries and semiperipheries of the western hemisphere, those areas that specialized in cash crops for export. The demand for flour, meal, and grain liquors was high in plantation economies (like the North American South and most of Latin America), where labor was budgeted toward the production of staple crops. So it was not accidental that the region's surplus producers concentrated their land and labor resources into the generation of wheat and corn, often in terrain where such production was ecologically unsound. Nor was it a chance occurrence that the Southern Appalachians specialized in the production of livestock, as did inland mountainous sections of other zones of the New World. There was high demand for work animals, meat, animal by-products, and leather in those peripheries and semiperipheries that did not allocate land to less-profitable livestock production.

On the other hand, the Mountain South supplied raw materials to emergent industrial centers in the American Northeast and western Europe. The appetite for Appalachian minerals, timber, cotton, and wool was great in those industrial arenas. In addition, regional exports of manufactured tobacco, grain liquors, and foodstuffs provisioned those sectors of the world economy where industry and towns had displaced farms. By the 1840s, the northeastern United States was specializing in manufacturing and international shipping, and that region's growing trade/production centers were experiencing food deficits. Consequently, much of the Appalachian surplus received in Southern ports was reexported to the urban-industrial centers of the American Northeast and to foreign plantation zones of the world economy. In return for raw ores and agricultural products, Southern markets – including the mountain counties – consumed nearly one-quarter of the transportable manufacturing output of the North and received a sizeable segment of the redistributed international imports (e.g., coffee, tea) handled by Northeastern capitalists.

Beginning in the 1820s, Great Britain lowered tariffs and eliminated trade barriers to foreign grains. Subsequently, European and colonial markets were opened to North American commodities. Little wonder, then, that flour and processed meats were the country's major nineteenth-century exports, or that more than two-thirds of those exports went to England and France. Outside the country, then, Appalachian commodities flowed to the manufacturing centers of Europe, to the West Indies, to the Caribbean, and to South America. Through far-reaching commodity flows, Appalachian raw materials – in the form of agricultural, livestock, or extractive resources – were exchanged for core manufactures and tropical imports.[13]

Slavery in the American Mountain South

Peripheral capitalism unfolded in Southern Appalachia as a mode of production that combined several forms of land tenure and labor. Because control over land – the primary factor of production – was denied to them, the unpropertied majority of the free population was transformed into an impoverished *semiproletariat*. However, articulation with the world economy did not trigger only the appearance of free wage labor or white tenancy. Capitalist dynamics in the Mountain South also generated a variety of unfree labor mechanisms. To use the words of Phillips, "the process of incorporation . . . involved the subordination of the labor force to the dictates of export-oriented commodity production, and thus occasioned increased coercion of the labor force as commodity production became generalized." As a result, the region's landholders combined *free* laborers from the ranks of the landless tenants, croppers, waged workers, and poor women with *unfree* laborers from four sources. Legally restricted from free movement in the marketplace, the region's free blacks, Cherokee households, and indentured paupers contributed coerced labor to the region's farms. However, Southern Appalachia's largest group of unfree laborers were nearly three hundred thousand slaves who made up about 15 percent of the region's 1860 population. About three of every ten adults

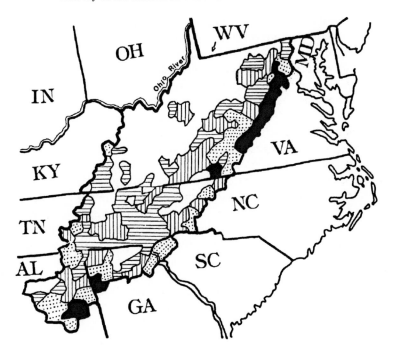

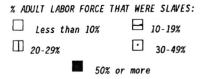

% ADULT LABOR FORCE THAT WERE SLAVES:

☐ Less than 10%   ⊟ 10-19%

⊞ 20-29%   ⊡ 30-49%

■ 50% or more

Map 2. Slaves in the Appalachian labor force, 1860. *Source:* Aggregated from NA, 1860 Census of Population.

in the region's labor force were enslaved (see Map 2). In the Appalachian zones of Alabama, Georgia, South Carolina, and Virginia, enslaved and free blacks made up one-fifth to one-quarter of the population. In the Appalachian zones of Maryland, North Carolina, and Tennessee, blacks accounted for only slightly more than one-tenth of the population. West Virginia and eastern Kentucky had the smallest percentage of blacks in their communities. The lowest incidence of slavery occurred in the *mountainous* Appalachian counties where 1 of every 6.4 laborers was enslaved. At the other end of the spectrum, the *ridge-valley* counties utilized unfree laborers more than twice as often as they were used in the zones with the most rugged terrain.[14]

Consisting of 215 mountainous and hilly counties in nine states, this large land area was characterized in the antebellum period by nonslaveholding farms and enterprises, a large landless white labor force, small plantations, mixed farming, and extractive industry. Berlin's conceptualization of a *slave society* caused us to predict that slavery did not dominate the Mountain South because there were not large numbers of plantations or slaves. I contested that assumption in a previous book. A region was not buffered from the political, economic, and social impacts of enslavement simply because it was characterized by low black population density and small slaveholdings. On the one hand, a Lower South farm owner was twelve times more likely to run a large plantation than his Appalachian counterpart. On the other hand, Mountain slaveholders monopolized a much higher proportion of their communities' land and wealth than did Lower South planters. This region was linked by rivers and roads to the coastal trade centers of the Tidewater and the Lower South, and it lay at the geographical heart of antebellum trade routes that connected the South to the North and the Upper South to the Lower South. Consequently, two major slave-trading networks cut directly through the region and became major conduits for overland and river transport of slave coffles (see Map 3 in Chapter 1). No wonder, then that the political economies of all Mountain South counties were in the grip of slavery. Even in counties with the smallest slave populations (including those in Kentucky and West Virginia), slaveholders owned a disproportionate share of wealth and land, held a majority of important state and county offices, and championed proslavery agendas rather than the social and economic interests of the nonslaveholders in their own communities. Moreover, public policies were enacted by state legislatures controlled and manipulated by slaveholders. In addition, every Appalachian county and every white citizen benefited in certain ways and/or was damaged by enslavement, even when there were few black laborers in the county and even when the individual citizen owned no slaves. For example, slaves were disproportionately represented among hired laborers in the public services and transportation systems that benefited whites of all Appalachian counties, including those with small slave populations. Furthermore, the lives of poor white Appalachians were made more miserable because slaveholders restricted economic diversification, fostered ideological demeaning of the poor, expanded tenancy and sharecropping, and prevented emergence of free public education. Moreover, this region was more politically divided over slavery than any other section of the South. Black and poor white Appalachians were disproportionately represented among the soldiers and military laborers for the Union Army. The Civil War tore apart Appalachian communities, so that the Mountain

South was probably more damaged by army and guerilla activity than any other part of the country.[15]

In an earlier work, I identified six indicators that distinguish the Mountain South from the Lower South.[16]

- One of every 7.5 enslaved Appalachians was either a Native American or descended from a Native American. Thus, black Appalachians were 4.5 times more likely than other U.S. slaves to be Native American or to have Indian heritage, reflecting the presence of eight indigenous peoples in this land area.
- Mountain slaves were employed outside agriculture much more frequently than Lower South slaves. At least one-quarter of all mountain slaves were employed full time in nonagricultural occupations. Thus, slaves were disproportionately represented in the region's town commerce, travel capitalism, transportation networks, manufactories, and extractive industries.
- In comparison to areas of high black population density, mountain plantations were much more likely to employ ethnically mixed labor forces and to combine tenancy with slavery.
- Compared to the Lower South, mountain plantations relied much more heavily on women and children for field labor.
- Fogel argued that "the task system was never used as extensively in the South as the gang system." Except for the few large slaveholders, Mountain South plantations primarily managed laborers by assigning daily or weekly tasks and by rotating workers to a variety of occupations. Moreover, small plantations relied on community pooling strategies, like corn huskings, when they needed a larger labor force. Since a majority of U.S. slaves resided on holdings smaller than fifty, like those of the Mountain South, it is likely that gang labor did not characterize Southern plantations to the extent that Fogel claimed.[17]
- Mountain slaves almost always combined field work with nonfield skills, and they were much more likely to be artisans than other U.S. slaves.

Several findings about the Mountain South cry out for scholarly rethinking of assumptions about areas with low black population densities and small plantations.

- On small plantations, slave women worked in the fields, engaged in resistance, and were whipped just about as often as men.
- Mountain masters meted out the most severe forms of punishment to slaves much more frequently than their counterparts in other Southern regions. Appalachian ex-slaves reported frequent or obsessive physical punishment nearly twice as often as other WPA interviewees. There was greater brutality and repression on small plantations than on large plantations. Moreover, areas with low black population densities were

disproportionately represented in court convictions of slaves for capital crimes against whites. As on large plantations, small plantations punished slaves primarily for social infractions, not to motivate higher work productivity.

- As Berlin observed, "the Africanization of plantation society was not a matter of numbers." Thus, slaves on small plantations engaged in much more day-to-day resistance and counter-hegemonic cultural formation than had been previously thought.[18]

Methods, Sources, and Definitions

As in my previous work, this study avoids the socially constructed regional definitions that emerged in the 1960s around the War on Poverty. Instead, I define the Mountain South in terms of *terrain* and *geological formation*, resulting in a target area that stretches through nine states from western Maryland to northern Alabama. The vast majority of the Mountain South is not mountainous. Hill-plateaus and valleys adjacent to long ridges make up more than 80 percent of the acreage. Most of the highest, longest ridges of the mountain chain lie in the Appalachian counties of Virginia, a zone that some scholars would exclude because it was characterized by such a high incidence of slaveholding. Geologically, these counties are part of the Appalachian Mountain chain, so it requires some artificial, nonterrain construct to justify their ejection from the regional definition. Indeed, it is crucial to include Appalachian Virginia because the prevailing view has been that terrain like the Blue Ridge Mountains prevented the expansion of slavery in North America. Thus, one could reasonably ask why slavery was so entrenched in Appalachian Virginia if rough terrain precluded the use of slave labor. Obviously, it is important to include all the subsections of the Mountain South to draw comparisons between zones characterized by diverse terrain, differently sized slaveholdings, and varied economic specializations. The reader will find discussions of *West Virginia* throughout the book, even though it did not achieve statehood until 1863, and those references are not an historical error on my part. Because that area formed a separate state in the midst of the Civil War, it is crucial to examine how enslavement differed in the eastern, western, and far western sections of Virginia. To ensure that my statistical analysis would not be corrupted by either an overestimation of slavery in Virginia's most western counties or an understatement of the extent of plantations in Blue Ridge and southwestern Virginia, I have separated out quantitative data and slave narratives for those counties that became West Virginia during the Civil War.[19]

To research this complex topic, I have triangulated quantitative, archival, primary, and secondary documents. I derived my statistical analysis from a database of nearly twenty-six thousand households drawn from nineteenth-century county tax lists and census manuscripts. In addition to those samples, I relied on archived records from farms, plantations, commercial sites, and industries. A majority of the slaveholder collections utilized for this research derived from *small* and *middling* plantations. However, I did not ignore rich Appalachian planters, like Thomas Jefferson or John Calhoun. Never to quote or cite an Appalachian planter is to deny that they existed and to ignore that they were the richest, most politically powerful families in Appalachian counties. Indeed, I present information about them to demonstrate that they are similar to their Lower South counterparts and, therefore, very different from the typical farmers in their communities. It is also necessary to draw upon planter documents to show that larger plantations implemented different crop choices, surveillance strategies, and labor management practices than did smallholdings. Still, those rich planters account for less than 1 percent of all the citations and details provided in this study.[20]

Throughout this book, I have used the term *plantation* consistently to refer to a slaveholding enterprise. I have purposefully done this to distinguish such economic operations from the nonslaveholding farms that characterized the Mountain South. Far too many scholars confront me at meetings with the mythological construct that the typical Appalachian slaveholder was a benign small farmer who only kept a couple of slaves to help his wife out in the kitchen. By using *plantation* to distinguish all slaveholding farms, I seek to erode the stereotype that small plantations might be the social, political, and economic equivalent of small nonslaveholding farms in their communities. On the one hand, small plantations could not have owned black laborers if those families had not accumulated surplus wealth far in excess of the household assets averaged by the majority of nonslaveholding Appalachians. On the other hand, planters and small-holders alike controlled far more than their equitable share of the political power and economic resources in their communities. Because small slaveholders aspired to be planters, they did not often align themselves with the political and economic interests of nonslaveholders. According to Berlin, "what distinguished the slave plantation from other forms of production was neither the particularities of the crop that was cultivated nor the scale of its cultivation.... The plantation's distinguishing mark was its peculiar social order, which conceded nearly everything to the slaveowner and nothing to the slave." That social order was grounded in a racial ideology in which chattel bondage and white supremacy became entwined. For that reason, it is crucial to distinguish a nonslaveholding farm from a slaveholding farm. In the Mountain South, a slaveholder did not have to reach planter status to be set apart from neighbors whose antagonism to enslavement would cause them to align themselves with the Union in greater numbers than in any other region of the American South. To distinguish plantations by size, I utilize the definitions that are typically applied by U.S. slavery specialists. A *planter* or *large plantation* held fifty or more slaves, while a *middling plantation* or slaveholder owned twenty to forty-nine slaves. Thus, a *small plantation* was one on which there were nineteen or fewer slaves.[21]

Slave Narratives from the Mountain South

History does not just belong to those who are reified in government and archival documents. The past is also owned by survivors of inequality and by those who live through injustice at the hands of powerful elites. As Trouillot recognized, "survivors carry history on themselves," and care must be exercised in the construction of knowledge from their indigenous transcripts. "Silences enter the process of historical production at four crucial moments: the moment of fact creation (the making of *sources*); the moment of fact assembly (the making of *archives*); the moment of fact retrieval (the making of *narratives*); and the moment of retrospective significance (the making of *history* in the final instance)." To be as inclusive as possible in the final moment of history production, I grounded this study in analysis of narratives of nearly three hundred slaves and more than four hundred white Civil War veterans. I spent many months locating Appalachian slave narratives within the Federal Writers Project, at regional archives, and among published personal histories. Beginning with Rawick's forty-one published volumes of the WPA slave narratives, I scrutinized every page for county of origin, for interregional sales or relocations that shifted slaves into or out of the Mountain South, and for occurrences during the Civil War that displaced slaves. After that process, I identified other archival and published accounts, finding several narratives in unusual locations, including archives at Fisk University and the University of Kentucky. In this way, I did not ignore the life histories of slaves who were born outside the Mountain South and migrated there or those who were removed to other regions. Ultimately, I aggregated the first comprehensive list of Mountain South slave narratives.[22]

How representative of the region are these narratives? In comparison to the entire WPA collection, Appalachian slave narratives are exceptional in the degree to which they depict small plantations. By checking the slave narratives against census manuscripts and slave schedules, I established that the vast majority of the Appalachian narratives were collected from individuals who had been enslaved on plantations that held fewer than twenty slaves. Consequently, Blue Ridge Virginia is underrepresented while the Appalachian counties of Kentucky, North Carolina, and West Virginia are overrepresented. Thus, those areas that held the fewest slaves in this region are more than adequately covered. Appalachian slave narratives are not handicapped by the kinds of shortcomings that plague the national WPA collection. Large plantations, males, and house servants are overrepresented among the entire universe of respondents. In addition, two-fifths of the ex-slaves had experienced fewer than ten years of enslavement. The most serious distortions derived from the class and racial biases of whites who conducted the vast majority of the interviews. Most of the mountain respondents had been field hands, and very few were employed full time as artisans or domestic servants. In terms of gender differentiation, the Appalachian sample is almost evenly divided. In contrast to the entire WPA collection, three-quarters of the mountain ex-slaves were older than ten when freed. Indeed, when emancipated, one-third of the respondents were sixteen or older, and 12 percent were twenty-five or older. Thus, nearly half the Appalachian ex-slaves had endured fifteen years or more of enslavement, and they were old enough to form and to retain oral histories. Perhaps the greatest strength of this regional collection has to do with the ethnicity of interviewers. More than two-fifths of the narratives were written by the ex-slaves themselves or collected by black field workers, including many Tennessee and Georgia interviews that were conducted under the auspices of Fisk University and the Atlanta Urban League. Because the mountain narratives were collected over a vast land area in nine states, this collection offers another advantage. The geographical distances between respondents offer opportunities for testing the widespread transmission of African-American culture.[23]

I have come away from this effort with a deep respect for the quality and the reliability of these indigenous narratives. When I tested ex-slave claims against public records, I found them to be more accurate than most of the slaveholder manuscripts that I scrutinized, and quite often much less ideologically blinded than many of the scholarly works I have consulted. Therefore, I made the conscious intellectual decision to engage in "the making of *history* in the final instance" by respecting the indigenous knowledge of the ex-slaves whose transcripts I analyzed. That means that I did not dismiss and refuse to explore every slave voice that challenged conventional academic rhetoric. In most instances, I triangulated the indigenous view against public records and found the slave's knowledge to be more reliable than some recent scholarly representations. In other instances, I perceived that Appalachian slaves are a *people without written history* and that it is important to document the oral myths in which they grounded their community building. Because mountain slave narratives present a view of enslavement that attacks the conventional wisdom, I recognized that they and I were engaging in a process that Trouillot calls "the production of alternative narratives." When contacted by a Fisk University researcher in 1937, one Chattanooga ex-slave comprehended that he possessed a knowledge about slavery that was different from the social constructions of the African-American interviewer. "I don't care about telling about it [slavery] sometime," he commented cynically, "because there is always somebody on the outside that knows more about it than I do, and I was right in it." Clearly, this poorly educated man understood that historical facts are not created equal and that knowledge construction is biased by differential control of the means of historical production. On the one hand, I set myself the difficult goal of avoiding the kind of intellectual elitism the ex-slave feared while at the same time trying to avoid the pitfall of informant misrepresentation. On the other hand, I heeded the advice of C. Vann Woodward and did not view the use of slave narratives as any more treacherous or unreliable than other sources or research methods.[24]

Organization of This Research Project

This study seeks to answer several important questions about the impact of enslavement and emancipation on the African-American family.

- To what extent did slave trading disrupt slave families?
- In addition to slave sales, what other labor migrations endangered the stability of slave families?
- Did Mountain South slaveholders provide better living conditions for slave families than Lower South plantations?
- To what extent did slaveholders intentionally interfere in slave marriages, reproduction, and child rearing?
- What was the role of the slave household in producing its own subsistence?
- What were the family roles of black Appalachian women, and were fathers a stable part of households?
- What threats to black family survival resulted from the Civil War, the emancipation process, and Reconstruction policies?

Publication of all the information from sources, methods, and quantitative evidence would require a separate monograph. To make those materials available to other researchers as quickly as possible, I created a permanent electronic library archive. That site provides the tables that support the findings throughout this study, as well as a detailed discussion of methodological issues. A comprehensive list and a descriptive analysis of the collection of Mountain South slave narratives can also be found there. In addition, antebellum photographs and drawings have been put online for use by other researchers. Throughout the notes, you will see references to sources that can be accessed at this website: **http://scholar.lib.vt.edu/vtpubs/mountain_slavery/index.htm**.

1   Slave Trading and Forced
       Labor Migrations

> Master White didn't hesitate to sell any of his slaves, he said, "You
> all belong to me and if you don't like it, I'll put you in my pocket,"
> meaning of course that he would sell that slave and put the money in his
> pocket.   – Amelia Jones, eastern Kentucky slave

In the United States, the European demand for cotton triggered the
largest domestic slave trade in the history of the world. In the seventeenth
and eighteenth centuries, tobacco production absorbed two-fifths of the
U.S. slaves. By the end of the American Revolution, however, prices for
tobacco, indigo, and rice (the three major Southern exports) had declined in the world economy. Simultaneously, cotton was required to fuel
expansion of the English textiles industry, so prices for that commodity
escalated and underwent fewer cyclical drops. Between 1810 and 1840,
U.S. cotton production increased nearly tenfold, as plantations pushed
westward to become concentrated in a long belt stretching from South
Carolina through Texas. In almost every decade from 1810 to 1860,
Lower South cotton production expanded three times faster than the
agricultural output of the Upper South.

As a result, the Lower South demand for slaves expanded 1,800 percent, more than twice the rate of increase in the U.S. slave population.
Between 1790 and 1860, U.S. enslavement underwent a major transformation such that two-thirds of the country's slaves were reconcentrated
in the region producing the most profitable staple for the world economy.
Over this seventy-year period, the Lower South slave population nearly
quadrupled because the Upper South exported two-fifths of its African-
Americans, the vast majority sold through interstate transactions, about
15 percent removed in relocations with owners.[1]

The Forced Migration of Appalachian Slaves
   to the Cotton South

As part of this interregional forced labor migration, there is conclusive
evidence in the census returns of the movement of slaves into and out of

Southern Appalachia. In 1860, the Upper South counties of the Mountain South were populated by only 71 percent of the slaves who would have been there if no forced outward migrations had occurred. During this period, western Maryland lost half its slave population to interregional transfers, while one-third of the slaves disappeared from eastern Kentucky, West Virginia, and Appalachian Virginia. There was a sharp contrast in the Lower South counties of the Mountain South where cotton production had expanded. Because new settlement areas opened after the forced removals of the Cherokees and Creeks in the late 1830s, the populations of northern Alabama and northern Georgia more than doubled between 1840 and 1860; and the slave populations in these zones nearly tripled to support the rapid expansion of cotton and tobacco production. Between 1810 and 1860, the slave populations of northern Alabama and northern Georgia ballooned to 1.5 to 1.8 times the level that would have obtained if no migration into these zones had occurred.[2]

By tracking age cohorts from the 1840 census, it is possible to estimate the rate at which slaves disappeared from the Mountain South. By 1860, two of every five slaves counted in the 1840 cohort aged birth to nine had disappeared from Southern Appalachia. Between 1840 and 1860, western Maryland lost more than half of this age cohort of slaves. Eastern Kentucky, western North Carolina, Appalachian Virginia, and West Virginia lost about two of every five slaves from this cohort. Similarly, 2.2 of every 5 slaves counted in the 1840 cohort aged ten to fifty-nine had disappeared from Southern Appalachia by 1860. During this period, for example, western Maryland lost more than two-thirds of this age cohort of slaves. Eastern Kentucky and West Virginia lost about one of every two slaves from this cohort, while two of every five slaves of this cohort were removed from the Appalachian counties of North Carolina, South Carolina, Tennessee, and Virginia. Males were exported from the region at a slightly higher rate than were females. In the ten to fifty-nine age group, 1.1 males were exported for every female, most probably leaving the region before the age of twenty-nine.[3]

In addition to surplus foodstuffs, salt, whiskey, timber, and iron, Southern Appalachians exported surplus laborers to the cotton South. Scholars continue to debate whether this interregional diaspora was produced by the exportation of slaves through interstate sales or by the forced migration of slaves with their masters. Earlier studies estimated that sales accounted for less than 40 percent of all slaves transferred between states. Very recently, Tadman has more closely analyzed slave trader's transactions and demographic data to conclude that only about 15 percent of this interregional diaspora occurred because migrating masters carried their own slaves with them. In similar fashion, only 15.3 percent of the

Appalachian slaves who had been transferred across state lines were removed by their migrating masters. Instead, interstate sales caused the vast majority of the interstate relocations of Appalachian slaves. Consequently, Southern Appalachians contributed significantly to the interstate traffic in slaves. Between 1840 and 1860, more than sixty-three thousand Appalachian slaves were exported from the region through interstate sales. Thus, black Appalachians were the victims of nearly one-fifth of all the interstate sales that occurred between 1840 and 1860. To put it another way, Appalachia was home for one of every eight of the slaves involved in the interregional black diaspora between 1840 and 1860.[4]

The chances of a slave from the Upper South falling into the hands of interstate traders were quite high. According to Tadman, "teenagers from this area would have faced rather more than a 10 percent chance of being traded, and those in their twenties perhaps an 8–10 percent chance. By their thirties, the danger of falling into the grasp of interregional speculators would have eased to about 5 percent." Nearly one of every three slave children living in the Upper South in 1820 was "sold South" by 1860. Each decade between 1820 and 1860, traders transported one-tenth of all Upper South slaves to the Lower South. After 1840, Appalachian slaves were being exported at a rate slightly higher than the Upper South average. Slaves in the Appalachian counties of Alabama, Georgia, Maryland, North Carolina, Virginia, and West Virginia were more likely to be moved as part of the interstate trade than were their Upper South counterparts. For example, nearly one-fifth of the slave population left Loudoun County, Virginia, between 1850 and 1860; the vast majority shifted southward through interstate sales. Slaves were being exported from the Appalachian counties of Kentucky, South Carolina, and Tennessee, but at rates slightly below the Upper South trend. In addition to laborer exports from the region, large numbers of slaves were imported into the Appalachian counties of Alabama and Georgia. What, then, accounts for this strange phenomenon? The forced removals of the Cherokees and Creeks were completed by 1839, spurring state lotteries that opened new lands to resettlement. Subsequently, slaveholders moved northward from within the two states, southward from Virginia and Tennessee, and eastward from South Carolina. Due to corruption and wealth inequality, public lands were concentrated into the hands of planters. Subsequently, cotton cultivation expanded rapidly into northern Alabama and uplands Georgia in this era. One of every twenty-one of the African-Americans moved through the interstate slave trade was imported into the Appalachian counties of Alabama and Georgia. In fact, the mountain sections were importing one-half to two-thirds of the slaves that were being relocated into those two Southern states between 1840 and 1860.[5]

Map 3. U.S. slave-trading routes, 1820–65. Approximate Locations of Appalachian Towns: 1, Wheeling, West Virginia; 2, Staunton, Virginia; 3, Knoxville, Tennessee; 4, Rome, Georgia. *Source:* Adapted from Fox, *Harper's Atlas of American History,* p. 42.

Interstate Slave Trading in the Mountain South

The Mountain South lay at the geographical heart of the interstate slave trade (see Map 3). This region was linked by rivers and roads to the coastal trade centers of the Tidewater and the Lower South. Across those transportation networks, local communities shipped agricultural and extractive exports, and Southern planters frequented 134 mineral spas scattered throughout the mountains. Two major slave-trading roads cut directly through the Appalachians, while the Ohio River linked the counties of western Maryland and West Virginia to New Orleans. Out of Baltimore and upper Virginia, slave traders followed a route that cut across western Maryland, utilizing canal and river connections to Wheeling (see point 1, Map 3). Seated at the top of the Ohio River, Wheeling grew into a major regional slave-trading hub, an ironic economic role for a town situated in an area with such a low black population density. On the one hand, Wheeling served as a collection point for slaves to be hired or sold to the West Virginia salt industry. On the other hand, Wheeling traders could follow the Ohio River southward to capitalize on major regional slave markets at Louisville, Memphis, Natchez, and New Orleans.[6]

A second major route emanated out of Tidewater Virginia, which was served by slave-trading hubs at Alexandria, Danville, and Norfolk. Using river, canal, and overland connections, traders moved southward through Richmond, a major national slave trading center. Across this route between 1810 and 1860, Virginia masters exported 441,684 slaves to other states. Out of Richmond, traders proceeded southwest through Appalachian counties, triggering a small subregional trading nucleus. Abingdon (north of point 3, Map 3) provided market access for east Kentucky, southwest Virginia, and upper east Tennessee buyers and sellers. To attract slave trader business, the East Tennessee and Virginia Railroad carried slave children free of charge. Down the route southward through the Tennessee River Valley, speculators were served by an east Tennessee trading hub around Knoxville (point 3, Map 3). Further south near the triangular conjuncture of Tennessee, Georgia and Alabama, they could take advantage of major subregional markets in Chattanooga and Rome, Georgia (point 4, Map 3).[7]

On the eastern boundary of Southern Appalachia, a third significant trading route linked Norfolk inland to Richmond, then south through the North Carolina piedmont via Salisbury. One ex-slave recalled that western Carolina owners "took hands in droves 150 miles to Richmond to sell them." Because they had been considering "selling property of that description," a Burke County, North Carolinian informed his family that "Negro property ha[d] taken a very considerable rise in Norfolk ... in consequence of the number of purchasers for the Louisiana market." In addition, the counties of western North Carolina were connected to a transportation network which transferred slaves from the Upper South through middle North Carolina, to terminate either at Charleston or via Montgomery to Mobile or Natchez.[8]

On the western boundary of Southern Appalachia, a fourth trading route ran southward from Louisville via Lexington and Nashville to terminate in the Vicksburg and Natchez markets. Because of their geographical proximity, middle Tennessee and eastern Kentucky counties linked into this trading network. When middle Tennessee slaves were not bought by itinerant speculators, they were sent to the "slave yards" at Nashville or Memphis where they often waited two weeks or longer to be auctioned to Mississippi, Texas, or Arkansas buyers. Secretly financed by prominent

GREAT SALE

of

SLAVES

JANUARY 10, 1855

THERE Will Be Offered For Sale at Public Auction at the SLAVE MARKET, CHEAPSIDE, LEXINGTON, All The SLAVES of JOHN CARTER, Esquire, of LEWIS COUNTY, KY., On Account of His Removal to Indiana, a Free State. The Slaves Listed Below Were All Raised on the CARTER PLANTATION at QUICK'S RUN, Lewis County, Kentucky.

3 Bucks Aged from 20 to 26, Strong, Ablebodied

1 Wench, Sallie, Aged 42, Excellent Cook

1 Wench, Lize, Aged 23 with 6 mo. old Picinniny

One Buck Aged 52, good Kennel Man

17 Bucks Aged from twelve to twenty, Excellent

TERMS: Strictly CASH at Sale, as owner must realize cash, owing to his removal to West. Offers for the entire lot will be entertained previous to sale by addressing the undersigned.

JOHN CARTER, Esq.
Po. Clarksburg   Lewis County, Kentucky

Because he was migrating westward, this eastern Kentucky slaveholder sold twenty-three slaves. Note that seventeen teenagers are being separated from their parents, and there is no indication that spouses are being sold together. *Source:* J. Winston Coleman Papers, University of Kentucky.

elites, Lexington slave dealers circulated throughout eastern Kentucky, buying up coffles of slaves directly from owners or at local auction blocks. As a result, Kentuckians sold more than six thousand slaves annually to southern markets, occasionally in large lots like the Lewis County sale described in the illustration. In 1829 Menefee County, Kentucky, a clergyman encountered "a company of slaves, some of them heavily loaded with irons, singing as they passed along." Because they were headed west to be auctioned at Lexington, the traveler was informed by the speculators that the slaves engaged in their march songs as "an effort to drown the suffering of mind they were brought into, by leaving behind their wives, children, or other near connexions and never likely to meet them again in this world." An eastern Kentucky slave remembered that Bluegrass dealers

made a business of buying up Negroes at auction sales and shipping them down to New Orleans to be sold to owners of cotton and sugar cane plantations.... [T]hey would ship whole boat loads at a time, buying them up 2 or 3 here, 2 or 3 there, and holding them in a jail until they had a boat load. This practice gave rise to the expression "sold down the river."[9]

Why Appalachian Slaveholders Exported Slaves

Phifer claimed that "no stigma attached to strictly local trades in which buyer and seller were both residents.... [B]ut a local seller who sold slaves to a buyer from another state was often censored." Similarly, Inscoe contended that few western North Carolina masters "violated the community norm of selling slaves only locally." Such romantic notions may accurately reflect slaveholder manuscripts, but the assumption that mountain communities ostracized slave traders is *not supported* by census data presented in this chapter or by evidence from regional slave narratives. In reality, two-thirds of the Appalachian sales were transactions in which the slaves were exported out of their counties of residence. Indeed, slave exporting offered five important advantages over intrastate sales. Locally, slaves could bring as little as one-third to one-half of the value they drew in the Lower South. Moreover, slaveholders might be handicapped by devalued local currencies. For instance, the Gwyn family favored interstate transport of slaves because their "customers want[ed] to pay them off in Tennessee money. The best of it [wa]s only worth eighty cents on the dollar North." Thus, selling to local buyers "would be a ruinous business." Third, slaves must be sold on credit to local buyers, with long-term arrangements for payment while interstate sales generated quick cash. Fourth, distant exchanges shielded financially embarrassed slaveholders from local gossip. Burdened by debts during his tenure in the Washington cabinet, Thomas Jefferson decided several times to sell slaves from his Albermarle and Bedford estates. "I do not (while in public life) like to have my name annexed in the public papers to the sale of property," the Monticello master cautioned his agent. Consequently, he "conclude[d] it w[ould] be best to carry them to some other sale of slaves" at Richmond. Fifth, it was advantageous for mountain owners to arrange slave sales through the same distant commission merchants who handled their agricultural exports. In this way, they centralized their accounting, banking, import orders, and insurance.[10]

Consequently, one of every four sales required the transport of Appalachian slaves to one of the towns that operated a large auction market along the national routes. From the Appalachian counties of Maryland, parts of West Virginia, and Virginia, mountain masters shipped farm products and slaves to Baltimore, Washington, D.C., Alexandria, Richmond, and Lynchburg. West Virginians could export directly via the Ohio River to New Orleans. Eastern Kentuckians frequented slave trading facilities in Lexington and Louisville, while middle Tennesseans sent surplus laborers to Nashville and Memphis. In the Southeast, Appalachian masters could trade slaves in Georgia's Augusta or Savannah or in South Carolina's Columbia or Charleston. Northern Alabama and northern Georgia slaveholders could ship surplus slaves via Montgomery to the Mobile market.[11]

Itinerant Speculators

However, two of every five of the Appalachian owners sold slaves to traders engaged in interstate trafficking, many of whom made regular annual or biannual circuits throughout the Upper South. According to Tadman, traders tended

to be semi-itinerant and to rove over one or two counties (and perhaps the fringes of others). They usually worked from a base in a particular town or village from which they attended public auctions and directly sought out clients in the countryside. This practice, no doubt, stemmed from the advantages of developing local knowledge and of offering sellers the least troublesome and hazardous way of disposing of their slaves.

Itinerant traders also regularly purchased free blacks from state and local governments after they had been condemned to "absolute slavery" for offenses "punishable by confinement in penitentiaries."[12]

Winchester, Virginia, attracted several itinerant traders in the 1820s. One newspaper announced that roving slave traders had for several days been wandering the streets of that town "with labels on their hats

exhibiting in conspicuous characters the words 'Cash for Negroes.' "
John Williamson offered to give cash "for fifteen or twenty likely negroes" to any local slaveholders who sought him out at Bryarly's Tavern.
Thomas Dyson did business in McGuire's Hotel while he bought up
twenty or thirty slaves. In the 1850s, the Baltimore-based Campbell firm
employed a regular agent in Winchester, one of the sites selected to keep
a steady supply of "large lots of the choicest Negroes" for export to New
Orleans. Marshall Mack reported that itinerant traders were a common
sight in Bedford County, Virginia. From there, coffles of slaves were "took
to Lynchburg, Va. to the block to be sold." The Louisiana-based firm
of Franklin and Armisted contracted regularly with Appalachian busi-
nessmen who collected slaves for consignment to the company's New
Orleans auctions. Their agents included J. M. Saunders and Company of
Fauquier, Virginia; western Maryland's George Kephart and Company;
Newton Boley of Winchester, Virginia; Thomas Hundley of Amherst,
Virginia; plus several smaller traders in western Maryland, southwest
Virginia, and eastern Tennessee. Beginning in the early 1800s, one such
Warrenton, Virginia, speculator opened business to "purchase slaves for
the Southern market." By exporting black Appalachians until the Civil
War, he subsequently "made a large fortune."[13]

In the early antebellum period, Samuel Carey appeared regularly to
buy up slaves in small western Maryland towns. Between 1832 and 1860,
an agent for an Alexandria firm frequently sought out buyers by setting
up operations at taverns in small Maryland communities. In the 1830s,
he offered "CASH IN MARKET. I wish to purchase FIFTY LIKELY
YOUNG NEGROES, of both sexes, from ten to thirty years of age. Persons wishing to dispose of slaves, would find it to their advantage to give
me a call, as I feel disposed to pay the highest market price." Interested
parties could leave messages for him at one of three tavern locations, including the Union Tavern in Frederick County. In fact, advertisements
appeared regularly in regional newspapers.[14]

Itinerant traders even situated themselves in counties with few slaves.
In the 1820s, speculators traveled regularly into the isolated mountains
of the Cherokee Nation. In the 1830s, Jeremiah Giddings advertised in
Monongalia County to "purchase FIFTY LIKELY YOUNG NEGROES
from 12 to 28 years old." Distant commission speculators also employed
resident agents who operated in many out-of-the-way Appalachian communities. In eastern Kentucky where there was the region's smallest slave
population, "traders came into the county to buy up slaves for the Southern plantations," taking them by boat or overland "down the river or
over in Virginia and Carolina tobacco fields." Lexington-based slavers
L. C. Robards and William F. Talbott employed local representatives in

Negroes Wanted.

WE want to buy from
100 TO 500
LIKELY NEGROES,
for whom we will pay the highest cash prices.

CHUNN & PATTON

Asheville, Feb. 10, 1859.

In the 1850s and throughout the Civil War, western North Carolina slaves were bought and hired for railroad construction. *Source: Asheville News, 10 February 1859.*

several eastern Kentucky towns. Betty Cofer "saw some slaves sold away from [her] Wilkes County, North Carolina plantation" to traders who "sold 'em down to Mobile, Alabama." Slave coffles were seen routinely on the main roads of eastern Tennessee where local and itinerant traders went from farm to farm buying slaves; the speculator paid a cash deposit and signed a note to complete payment when he resold them to cotton planters in Alabama or Mississippi. Itinerant traders "travel[ed] around the country" regularly in middle Tennessee. Handbills, like the one in the illustration, appeared throughout Appalachian counties, attached to storefronts, jails, courthouses, mills, and churches.[15]

Appalachian slaveholders could conceal their interstate trafficking by utilizing local lawyers. For example, a Monroe, West Virginia, master sent a slave to the Summers law firm in Charleston for export to New Orleans. The agent was advised to keep the slave "in jail for greater Security" and not to tell him that he was being sold out-of-state as he would "be disposed to run." Appalachians also maximized their family linkages with Lower South and Southwestern traders. For instance, the Walkers were urged to rent their slaves in Missouri "at double the Virginia rates." A South Carolinian wrote to his Madison, Virginia, relatives that "the cholera has thinned the Negroes much on the Coast and the South generally and they are then said to be selling very high." In early 1850, a Norfolk trader wrote his Appalachian kin that prime male slaves were "selling in Georgia or Florida at $1,000 to $1,200." A Fauquier, Virginia, owner decided to sell a slave family west after encouraging news from relatives there.[16]

Even though it was primarily rural in character, Appalachian slave trading was highly organized by roving speculators who made direct transactions with owners. According to the slave narratives, it was very common in the fall and spring for itinerant traders to appear in the countryside. Penny Thompson of Coosa County, Alabama, remembered that "de speculation waggin (negro traders) come by often. Dey stops 'cross de road f'om de Marster's place an' all de Marsters come dere for to trade." In Jackson County, Alabama, "de speckulaters was white men dat sometimes comes around buyin', sellin' or tradin' slaves.... Dem speckulaters would put de chilluns in a wagon ... and de older folks was chained or tied together ... and dey would go from one plantation ter another all ovah de country."[17]

To avoid any threat of runaways, Appalachian masters tried to disguise their plans. In Floyd County, Georgia, a twelve-year-old boy "was fooled out of [his] mammy's house by dem speculators wid an apple. When [he] went out, two or three white men grabbed [him]." Another Buncombe County, North Carolina, master sent all his slaves to their regular work in the fields. Then "Ole Marse he cum t'ru de field wif a man call de specalater. Day walk round jes' lookin', jes' lookin'. All de [slaves] know whut dis mean. Dey didn't dare look up, jes' wok right on. Den de specalater he see who he want. He talk to Ole Marse, den dey slaps de han'cuffs on him an' tak him away to de cotton country." When the speculator was ready to leave with his purchases, "effen dey [was] enny whut didn' wanta go, he thrash em, den tie em 'hind de waggin an' mek um run till dey fall on de groun', den he thrash em till dey say dey go [wi]thout no trouble."[18]

Appalachian Slave Traders

In addition to itinerant traders, some Appalachian entrepreneurs engaged in the practice of buying up local slaves for export. In reality, about one of every 154 Appalachian households acquired part of its income from slave-trading activities. Ten percent of them averaged $79,333 in assets, and they reported primary occupations like merchant, land speculator, farmer, or commercial wagoner. Some of these slave traders were among the region's most respected economic elites, like attorneys and judges who regularly handled slave transactions for distant clients. As a routine service, country stores advanced to bounty hunters the advertised rewards for runaways and then received larger commissions from the slave owners.[19]

Four respected community leaders acted as professional slave traders in Loudoun County, Virginia, often representing large interstate traffickers. Between 1839 and 1841, William Holland Thomas of western North Carolina bought and resold eight to twelve slaves every year. A

Coffee County, Tennessee, master worked on commission for his neighbors to carry "a bunch of the field hands down in Louisiana" every year.
Hamilton Brown earned a commission for arranging interstate sales for
his neighbors. When prices were lower than he desired, he withheld the
laborers for a better profit. In one instance, he advised the owner, "I think
the opportunity will be much better for selling them in the fall. I have
no doubt but I shall be able to sell for a much better price then than at
this time." Over a ten-month period in 1835 and 1836, Floyd Whitehead
of Nelson County, Virginia, exported to Mississippi seventy-three slaves.
Obviously, Whitehead's slave trading was extensive and continual, for
he formed a business partnership with a Lynchburg agent. Moreover,
he empowered a trusted slave to seek out prospective purchases in the
countryside. Still, Whitehead's involvement in the "abominable trade"
did not prevent him from being elected to positions as county sheriff and
representative to the state legislature.[20]

In Wilkes County, North Carolina, the partnership of Gwyn and
Hickerson aggressively engaged in land and slave speculation from 1845
through the Civil War. Gwyn initiated the lucrative business when a
Missouri relative proposed a venture in which Hickerson would buy up
military bounties, resell the lands to Missouri settlers, and then contract
to procure slaves for them. Within a few months, Gwyn was buying field
hands at bargain prices from neighbors who were burdened by debt. In
addition, Gwyn and his agents frequented estate auctions after owners
died, colluded with sheriffs, and bribed overseers for information about
troublesome slaves. Gwyn went so far as to use the courts to have a local
widow declared "a fit subject for the Asylum" when she tried to prevent
the sale of her slaves to speculators who would "scatter them." Friends
testified that "if she had no nigrose, they would not care what became of
her." Still the court declared Gwyn "guardian," giving him legal right to
dispose of her property. When they had accumulated enough for export to
Missouri, Gwyn sent the slaves off in overland caravans. In one instance,
his driver notified him that "tonight we have pitched our tents within ten
miles of Knoxville.... The negroes all seem to do as well as they know
how." In eastern Tennessee, Gwyn's slaves were put on Tennessee River
flatboats for the second stage of their westward journey.[21]

As the Staunton agent for the Lynchburg Hose and Fire Insurance
Company, John McCue wrote policies on the lives of slaves and supervised medical examinations. Using confidential information about his
clients' property, McCue acted as a commissioned middleman. In one
instance, he secretly evaluated the slaves of a client for a third party. He
informed the potential buyer that he "had Several Conversations with the
parties," but that there could be "no Compromise" unless "all [should]

be Strictly Confidential." McCue also reminded the secret buyer that he "Could get a fare chance" for him, for which assistance he expected to receive "a Small mite." Two West Virginia speculators regularly transported slaves via Charleston, down the Ohio River to Kentucky markets. One of their coffles of seventeen laborers landed at the Maysville steamboat wharf in the spring of 1849. The local newspaper reported that citizens had spotted the cohort "being conducted," in handcuffs and chains, inland to Lexington. Another West Virginia elite offered to buy up local slaves for resale. He responded to an inquirer: "Negroes always rise in the Spring. It is the time the traders are making out their companies for the South. January and February are the months to make purchases advantageously.... It would require some weeks to pick up such negroes as you want at the county about. It would be better to authorize me to purchase them for you."[22]

In addition to Appalachians who dabbled in the business as a sideline, there were many merchants who specialized in "the abominable traffic." Slave trading occurred often enough that most Appalachian towns charged such capitalists a special business tax. Recognizing the amount of revenue involved in the enterprise, Chattanooga taxed slave traders $500 annually. A Knoxville entrepreneur notified potential Bluegrass buyers that he would "carry slaves on speculation" and that he "intend[ed] carrying on the business extensively." Another eastern Tennessee merchant boasted that he had "bought and sold in [his] day over 600." In the tiny town of Chattanooga, two companies (F. A. Parham and A. H. Johnston and Company) operated slave exchanges on Market Street near the railroad depot. Frederick, Maryland, slavers Kephart and Harbin invested in a ship to export slaves, and they maintained a marketing agency in New Orleans. Augusta Countian J. E. Carson regularly bought up Shenandoah Valley slaves for export. One of Carson's typical newspaper advertisements declared that he would pay high cash prices for "500 likely YOUNG NEGROES of both sexes, for the Southern market." In addition, Carson searched down runaways and then purchased them cheap from their owners. A flourishing slave trade was centered in the Surry County, North Carolina, area where the notorious slave driver, Kit Robbins, carried on his operations in a six-county vicinity. Similarly, Tyre Glen was active in slave buying in the counties west of him; he exported laborers to southern Georgia and South Carolina. Calvin Cowles, a Wilkes County, North Carolina, merchant, purchased and hired slaves from whom he earned profits by contracting them out on annual hires. Frank White and William Beasley gathered coffles of slaves from Wilkes County, North Carolina, for the Charleston market. In White County, Tennessee, Daniel Clark and W. H. Matlock bought and resold about one hundred fifty slaves per year through their dealings in Tennessee, Virginia, North Carolina, Alabama, and Mississippi.[23]

Forty-five percent of the Appalachian slave traders were middling households, averaging $13,175 in assets. A land/Negro speculator of Cass County, Georgia; a Frederick County, Maryland, merchant; and traders of Giles County, Virginia and Randolph County, West Virginia, were typical of this segment. For example, Frank White and David McCoy of Page County, Virginia, engaged in intermittent slave trading as a sideline to farming and livestock. McCoy purchased Bethany Veney from a neighbor, "thinking he could make a speculation" on her at Richmond. Between 1835 and 1845, Britton Atkins and William Manor regularly transported overland coffles to the Mobile market from the small towns of Blount County, Alabama. Charlie Merrill bought up Franklin County, Tennessee, slaves for export to Nashville and Memphis. North Georgian H. M. Cobb regularly transported slaves from Virginia to auction at his firm in Rome, Georgia. Even in eastern Kentucky, local traders were active. Floyd County, for example, had two speculators. County Judge Houston and his son-in-law "gathered up all the slaves that were unruly or that people wanted to trade and housed them in an old barn until they had enough to take to New Orleans on a boat." Cherokee elites also accumulated part of their wealth from slave trading. Several Indian dealers, including planter James Vann, made regular trips to New Orleans, Savannah, and Charleston. In addition, the federal Indian agent collected bounties from masters for slave runaways and arranged transactions between Cherokees and whites.[24]

Surprisingly, nearly half the Appalachians who identified themselves to census enumerators as slave traders or speculators were men of very limited assets. One-third of those who engaged in the human traffic were farm owners or retail operators who averaged $244 or less in total wealth. Another 15 percent of them owned neither land nor any other personal assets. How, then, could these poor Appalachians be actively involved in slave trading? First, such a person may have had dreams of future fortunes, like two "Negro traders" from Franklin County, Virginia, and Tyler County, West Virginia, who invested in cheap slave children in order to earn significant profits when they reached prime marketable age. However, most of these poor whites were involved in slave trading through activities that directed a great deal of violence toward black Appalachians. For instance, a landless laborer may have thought of himself as a slave trader because he worked for a commercial speculator, helping to transport coffles or acting as intermediary to buy up local slaves for export. In many Appalachian communities, poor laborers managed special jails that housed runaways or slaves awaiting the auction block.

Customarily, slaveholders paid these jailers 30 cents to $1 per day for each slave housed.[25]

Some poor whites were "slave catchers" who trained and used bloodhounds to track and capture runaways. When "bounty hunters" spotted blacks "working about as free men" who fit the description of runaways, they contacted owners and offered to return them for a fee. After a Wilkes County, North Carolina, master advertised a reward for a truant, he was contacted by such a slave hunter. "I have noticed him closely since I have seen your reward," he wrote. "He is hired out by the month, and he has every opportunity of running away, if he should suspect a discovery. The man who has him hired has agreed with me to keep him in his employ until you can come and get him." In another instance, B. W. Brooks offered to assist an owner if he came "in the night" to check the identity of a black who was "working about as a free man" who had not "yet obtained any Certificate of freedom from the Court." Brooks thought "it most prudent not to take him up and commit him to jail as he would in that event be certain to break jail and escape." John P. Chester wrote to an owner that "if there is no other hand I will kidnap them." Fearing that someone else would interfere and collect the reward, Chester added: "I am compelled to keep this secret from the world."[26]

Finally, poorer Appalachians dabbled directly in the human export business through the violent practice of kidnapping blacks. Nearly 4 percent of the Appalachian slave narratives describe incidents in which individuals were captured and sold illegally in this manner. This activity occurred often enough for regional newspapers to coin the term *blackbirding* when they reported such cases. Two poor whites in a buggy lay in wait on an isolated country road for fourteen-year-old Benjamin Washington. "One jumped out and tied his hands together," and the pair sped off to sell him to an itinerant speculator who was collecting a coffle for export to Mississippi. In McMinn County, Tennessee, free blacks were kidnapped and sold at Chattanooga. In Grayson County, Virginia, "five white men undertook to take five negroes." When the free blacks resisted, "two white men and two or three negroes were killed." While driving a wagon to an isolated West Virginia field, teenager Peter Wych "was overtaken by a 'speculator' and brought to Georgia where he was sold." Similarly, two middle Tennessee slave children "wuz stole" and exported to Georgia and Mississippi. Because middle Tennessee children "were often stolen by speculators and later sold at auctions" in Nashville, one Warren County master constructed "a tall lookout on the roof" of his mansion. From that vantage point, a "watchman" kept guard over "the carefree children who played in the large yard of the nearby quarters." Cherokees were also kidnapped and sold into slavery. Near Lookout Mountain, Tennessee,

Sarah Red Bird, "a pureblood Indian," was sold to a Mississippi slave-holder after her family was killed "in an uprising wid de whites" who were "trying to drive dem out." Free Cherokees of mixed-Negro heritage were sometimes captured, and free blacks could be kidnapped in the Cherokee Nation and sold to traders.[27]

At Lexington, Virginia, an eight-year-old boy "was taken from the lower end of town by kidnappers, and carried off in a row boat." In West Virginia, blackbirders kidnapped slaves who had been hired out to the salt works, then sold them at Wheeling or Richmond. Promising their captives a march to freedom, Floyd County, Kentucky, "slave rustlers" stole blacks at night and "hid them in Campbell's Cave." When their trail had cooled, the kidnappers exported the black laborers to Clarksville, Tennessee, where they would "sell them again on Mr. Dunk Moore's slave market." Similarly, Lewis Robards, a Lexington slave dealer, used the services of "slave stealers" in rural eastern Kentucky. Some black-birders formed regional networks for their illicit traffic. In Rutherford County, North Carolina, for example, William Robbins colluded with poor whites to "rustle" slaves. In one instance, Robbins even convinced a free black that, by "stealing slaves," he could "make money much faster than he was doing" as a blacksmith. In Surry County, North Carolina, "a number of colored people" were "illegally held in bondage" after they were kidnapped and sold by a group of blackbirders. One company of slave and horse rustlers was made up of several men scattered through a four-county area along the eastern Tennessee and northwestern Georgia border.

They had stations in various parts of the country, at convenient distances, and when a member of the club succeeded in stealing away a negro or pony, he would pass him on as quickly as he could to the nearest station, from which point he would be forwarded to another, and so on, till the negro or horse was quite safely disposed of.

By promising them freedom, another gang was able to attract slaves to leave with them voluntarily. In northern Georgia, Buck Hurd "used frequently to come round to [the] quarters of a night," to "try to entice" slaves away. This kidnapper bragged in his community that he "had got slaves to run from one master, and after selling them to another, would induce them to run from him, and then sell them to a third." In that way, "he had been known to sell the same [slave] three or four times over."[28]

Overland Slave Coffles

The traffic in Appalachian slaves was dominated by *coffles* lasting as long as seven to eight weeks. Antebellum journalists observed that Lower

South firms preferred overland transport because it was "attended with less expense." Moreover, "by gradually advancing [slaves] into the climate, it in a measure preclude[d] the effect which a sudden transition from one state to the other might produce." The son of a western Maryland slaveholder reported in the 1830s that he had "seen hundreds of colored men and women chained together, two by two, and driven to the South." West Virginians sent slave coffles overland to the Ohio River for steamboat transport to New Orleans. When a West Virginia master sent twenty-four slaves to the Richmond slave mart, he cautioned his son to "be discreet ... so as not to excite a runaway slave." Over a five-year period in the 1830s, Samuel Hall spotted twelve or fifteen such coffles, averaging forty slaves each, passing along the road near his home in Greenbrier County. Hall's description of "a drove of 50 or 60 negroes" twelve miles west of Lewisburg presents testimony that such caravans were not a rare occurrence in the Appalachian countryside.

They usually 'camp out,' but as it was excessively muddy, they were permitted to come into the house [at Remley's Tavern].... '[D]roves,' on their way to the south, eat but twice a day, early in the morning and at night. Their supper was a compound of 'potatoes and meal.' ... [A] black woman brought it on her head, in a tray or trough two and a half feet long.... The slaves rushed up and seized it from the trough in handfulls, before the woman could take it off her head.... They slept on the floor of the room which they were permitted to occupy, lying in every form imaginable.... There were three drivers, one of whom staid in the room to watch the drove, and the other two slept in an adjoining room.... Six or eight in the drove were chained; all were for the south.

Distant speculators, like Franklin and Armisted, sent consigned slaves "overland but once a year – in midsummer." One traveler described the organization of such coffles leaving western Maryland for the cotton South.

A train of wagons, with the provisions, tents, and other necessaries, accompanies the expedition, and at night they all encamp.... Not more than three or four white men frequently have charge of a hundred and fifty slaves. Upon their march, also, they are usually chained together in pairs, to prevent their escape; and sometimes, when greater precaution is judged necessary, they are all attached to a long chain passing between them. Their guards and conductors are, of course, well armed.

In 1830, a West Virginia newspaper documented the frequency with which slave coffles were spotted in regional towns. During the past year, lamented the *Kanawha Register:*

the roads passing through Charleston have been crowded with travel of every sort.... [T]he demon in human form, the dealer in bones and sinew, driving hundreds ... clanking the chains of their servitude, through the free air of our

Because the Mountain South lay at the geographical heart of the domestic slave trade, overland coffles like this one crossing the New River in southwestern Virginia were not unusual in the region. *Source:* Featherstonhough, *Excursion*, vol. 1, p. 121.

valley, and destined to send back to us from the banks of the Mississippi the sugar and the cotton of that soil moistened with sweat and blood.[29]

Slave traders traversed the same roads as the massive livestock drives through the Mountain South. Hundreds of camping spots, like those near Bean Station or in Warren County, Tennessee, became well known as intermediate stopping points for coffles. One southwestern Virginia camp (probably located in Montgomery County) was described by an 1834 traveler who encountered the trading caravan depicted in the illustration. Just as they reached New River in the early morning, they came upon

a camp of negro slave-drivers, just packing up to start; they had about three hundred slaves with them, who had bivouacked the preceding night *in chains* in the woods; these they were conducting to Natchez on the Mississippi River to work upon sugar plantations in Louisiana.... [T]hey had a caravan of nine waggons and single-horse carriages, for the purpose of conducting the white people, and any of the blacks that should fall lame, to which they were now putting the horses to pursue their march. The female slaves were, some of them, sitting on logs of wood, whilst others were standing, and a great many little black children were warming themselves at the fires of the bivouac. In front of them all, and prepared for the march, stood in double files, about two hundred male slaves, *manacled and chained to each other.*

[Once the caravan was packed and ready to move], a man on horseback selected a shallow place in the ford for the male slaves; then followed a waggon and four horses, attended by another man on horseback. The other waggons contained the children and some that were lame, whilst the scows, or flatboats, crossed the women and some of the people belonging to the caravan.... The slave-drivers ... endeavor[ed] to mitigate their discontent by feeding them well on the march, and by encouraging them to sing "Old Virginia never tire," to the banjo.

As the traveler proceeded southward by stage coach, he encountered a second coffle encamped north of Knoxville, Tennessee. "Long after sunset," he reported,

we came to a place where numerous fires were gleaming through the forest.... There were a great many blazing fires around, at which the female slaves were warming themselves; the children were asleep in some tents; and the males, in chains, were lying on the ground, in groups of about a dozen each. The white men ... were standing about with whips in their hands.[30]

Local Slave Selling by Appalachian Masters

Fewer than one-third of all Appalachian slave sales were transacted locally. Only about 8 percent of the region's slaves were sold within the counties of origin each year, and mountain masters sold slaves locally only about half as often as other Upper South owners. During 1860, Appalachian masters marketed more than twenty thousand slaves in their local communities, grossing more than $17 million. Owners who were situated in out-of-the-way rural areas were not disadvantaged because there were numerous marketing strategies. Advertisements to buy and sell slaves appeared regularly in the region's newspapers. Routinely, slaves were used as collateral for loans, tendered as payment for unpaid debts, or traded for land or merchandise. In addition, slaves were regularly exchanged between owners who effected "court day" sales on the auction blocks erected near every regional county courthouse.[31]

Lawyers and merchants acted as middlemen to locate slaves on a commission basis for buyers or sellers. For example, a "Negro Book" details the slave transactions made by a Nelson County, Virginia, store. The Mennis family of Bedford County, Virginia, and the Summers family of Monroe County, West Virginia, regularly utilized lawyers to buy or sell slaves, to hire out laborers, and to offer runaway bounties. Knoxville attorney O. P. Temple arranged exchanges between slaveholders. In one instance, he located slaves and sent them overland to a plantation owner who had relocated to the Iowa frontier. Temple regularly communicated with outlying rural merchants who could locate surplus slaves. According to Temple's records, both the attorney and the store owner earned commissions in these transactions. Temple paid a small fee to the store owner after the trade was effected, but the lawyer earned commissions from both buyer and seller.[32]

Of all slaves sold locally, however, three-fourths of their owners disposed of them through public sales, most often conducted by sheriffs at auction blocks erected in courthouse squares. No matter how limited its slave population, every Appalachian county sold slaves on the same auction blocks where they disposed of other commodities. Winchester and Warrenton, Virginia, and Cumberland and Fredericktown, Maryland, were hubs of intense slave trading activity. Smaller towns like Hagerstown, Maryland; Asheville and Huntsville in North Carolina; McMinnville, Tennessee; or Uniontown, Alabama, offered monthly slave auctions. Virginians could trade at auction blocks located in small towns like Abingdon, Roanoke, Bristol, or New Market, in addition to regular public sales in every county having larger slave populations. At the tiny town of Christiansburg, "dey kept de slaves in de jail, an' dey would bring 'em out one at a time to be sold. Dere was a huge tree dat had been . . . shaped into a big block 'bout six feet tall." On the monthly court day in December 1858, "slaves sold enormously high" from the Fauquier County auction block. A month later on New Year's day, "a Negro man brought $1,275, and one woman $1,300, and a girl, fourteen years old, $1,150."[33]

Weekly slave auctions were held in Wheeling and Charleston, West Virginia; Knoxville and Chattanooga in Tennessee; and Rome, Georgia. At Rome, slaves were kept in a house "built just like cow's stalls" until they were "sold on a high block." In Talladega County, Alabama, commission firms or the sheriff would "cry slaves off to the highest bidder" on the first Tuesday of every month. "Buyers from all ober the country would be there," including itinerant speculators from Mississippi and Louisiana.

Jim Threat recalled that the Talladega auction block "was about three feet high and had two steps leading up to it. . . . The slave would stand up and turn slowly round while the buyers inspected them. They'd even look at their teeth. The owners would tell what kind of disposition they had and the kind of work they was best at."[34]

Even when their own slave populations were small, Appalachian towns provided the locus for the congregation of buyers and sellers; the pens, jails, and depots; the exchanges and auction blocks that supported the slave trade. For instance, an eastern Tennessee slaveholder advertised in local newspapers that he was "offering for sale 5 Negro slaves in pursuance of the Circuit Court . . . sitting at Tazewell," a tiny rural village. Despite the low black population density in that area, ex-slaves described auction blocks sprinkled all over eastern Kentucky, including sites in the counties of Laurel, Clay, Floyd, Knox, and Bell. In addition to sales at courthouses or specialized businesses, auction blocks were a routine component of river wharves. According to Fannie Tipton, Reed Landing on the Ohio River in Greenup County, "was a warehouse with a gravel road down to the river bank. Between the ware house and the river was the trading block. It was a platform 20 × 30 feet. Slaves was bought and sold there, or auctioned off or swapped." Even many of the region's smaller crossroads villages operated regular slave auctions that were handled by the local sheriff. Off the beaten path in the Virginia Blue Ridge, the small hamlet of Luray sold slaves on an auction block that measured five feet high and only seventeen inches across. Despite their very small slave populations, the eastern Tennessee villages at Rogersville, Andersonville, Robertsville, and Crab Orchard were gathering points for public sales on court days. In McDowell County, North Carolina, four slaves were "exposed to Public Sale at the Court House door" in the little town of Marion.[35]

Slave Hiring by Appalachian Masters

Much more often than selling, Appalachian masters engaged in commercial trading by hiring out their slaves on a profitable basis. For the Southern slave labor force as a whole, "about 7.5% were on hire at any moment of time." Judging from regional primary documents, Appalachian masters hired out slaves at rates that far exceeded the rest of the South. Of those mountain slaves whose narratives appear in Still's *Underground Railroad,* one-quarter had been hired out by their masters. One-fifth of the Appalachian narratives record instances of slave hiring. Appalachian slaveholders in Virginia, western Maryland, and South Carolina were leasing two-fifths to one-half of their slave laborers every year. In the Appalachian counties of Tennessee, one of every three slaves was being hired out. In

Mountain masters hired out a high percentage of slave artisans, like this Waynesville, North Carolina, carpenter. Through such annual contracts, owners structured the absence of fathers from families most of the year. *Source: Scribner's*, March 1874.

rare instances, it is possible to document the extent of slave hiring in the 1860 manuscript Slave Schedules. In two Appalachian counties, census enumerators systematically documented those slaves who were employed by persons other than their owners. In mountainous McMinn County, Tennessee, nearly 17 percent of the county slave population was hired out. Nearly two-thirds of those McMinn County slaves were males aged fifteen to forty-nine. The rest were slaves younger than fourteen who were primarily hired out as servants and nurses for white children. Similarly, Loudoun County, Virginia, masters hired out 1,060 of their laborers, nearly one-fifth of that county's slave population.[36]

Slave hires were regularly conducted by auction on court days in December and January. In 1858, for instance, 12 percent of the slaves of Fauquier County were hired out at such a January courthouse auction. To buffer themselves through middlemen, buyers could utilize lawyers, stores, or traders, like Gwyn and Hickerson of Wilkes County, North Carolina. Owners consigned laborers to a Nelson, Virginia, general store, so the merchant could arrange annual leases for sizable commissions. Hire-outs could be arranged by the owners themselves through two strategies. Locally, they could hire surplus laborers to nearby neighbors. For example, Wylie Nealy's "mother was a field hand" whose master "hired her out" to an adjacent farmer when he "didn't need her to work." For distant hiring, they published advertisements like this one in an 1840 Charleston, West Virginia, newspaper:

Negroes for hire. There will be offered for the ensuing year on Tuesday 29th, inst., at Leetown, a number of slaves, consisting of men, women, boys and girls. Persons who hired negroes of me the present year are requested to return them with the requisite clothing stipulated in their bonds. Punctual payment of the bonds will also be expected. Bonds and approved security will be required before delivery of the slaves to the hirer.[37]

In addition, slaveholders could rely upon the services of agents who specialized in slave hiring. Through a Lexington agent, Mississippi River steamboat companies hired eastern Kentucky slaves to work as deck hands and levee laborers. The Virginia and Tennessee Railroad used its own hiring agent to contract slave hires, as did the Bath Iron Works. In 1849, Colonel L. Partlow charged $1 per slave he procured for a Botetourt, Virginia, iron furnace. Similarly, Appalachian slaveholders could call upon reputable slave-hiring brokers located in large Southern cities. For example, one Kentucky firm boasted in handbills that their "experience of many years business with the citizens of Louisville and vicinity render[ed them] competent of judging and picking good homes and masters" for slaveholders seeking to hire out surplus laborers. Robert Hill of Richmond advertised that he charged "the usual terms, $7\frac{1}{2}$ per cent for hiring out, bonding, collecting the same, and attention during the year in cases of sickness. Medical attention c[ould] be had at $3 each – medicine gratis." In fact, Shenandoah Valley and Blue Ridge Virginia slaveholders could take advantage of "several hiring sections" at Richmond where employers could choose from "crowds of servants, men, women, boys and girls, for hire." Using a commercial agent, one western North Carolinian hired out several slaves to nonagricultural employers in Virginia, Tennessee, and Georgia.[38]

Using local agents, slaveholders in Appalachian Virginia arranged for their surplus laborers to be hired out at public auctions held at regional stores and hotels or "before the tavern door." Appalachian newspapers regularly publicized in December the annual hiring auctions of large lots of slaves. For example, agent Maurice H. Garland advertised "HIRING OF NEGROES. On Saturday, the 29th day of December, 1838, at Mrs. Tayloe's tavern, in Amherst County, there will be hired thirty or forty valuable Negroes. In addition to the above, I have for hire 20 men, women, boys, and girls – several of them excellent house servants." Some Appalachian masters hired slaves to distant employers and renewed their annual contracts so long as conditions were favorable.[39]

Motivations for Appalachian Slave Trading

About one-third of all slave narratives in the WPA collection report that masters sold slaves. Similarly, an Upper South slave risked a one-in-three chance of being sold before the age of forty. In the slave-exporting states, larger slaveholders sold slaves about once every three years. Smallholders of fewer than five slaves engaged in slave trading only about once a decade. Significantly, the Appalachian narratives reported slave selling by masters twice as often as narratives in the WPA collection as a whole. Nearly one-half of the Appalachian slaves whose narratives appear in Still's *Underground Railroad* ran away when their masters threatened to sell them or their family members. Three-fifths of the Appalachian narratives in the WPA collection reported that their masters engaged in slave selling. Only three indicated precisely that their Appalachian master never sold slaves. However, these three Appalachian slaveholders – who believed selling to be "against de law ob God," ridded themselves of unmanageable slaves by "givin' 'em away," not by emancipating them.[40]

By gleaning details from slave narratives, it is possible to deconstruct the economic motivations of mountain masters who engaged in slave trading. Three-fifths of the Appalachian slaveholders who engaged in slave trading did so to gain profits. Indeed, Tadman emphasized that for Upper South slaveholders, "tempting speculative opportunities, not 'necessities' and 'emergencies'" were the primary motivations for slave selling. The region's most extreme speculators vended slaves almost annually, like a McDowell, North Carolina, master who sold twelve of the sixteen children of one of his slave women "fas' as dey got three years old." Others were more like a Madison County, Virginia, master who separated a woman from her husband and seven children and sent her to the Richmond auction block. Upon inquiry about why her master was selling her, she replied, "He wants money to buy some land."[41]

Sale of Social Risks and Unhealthy Slaves

Two of every twenty-five mountain masters sold slaves who were considered "social risks" to the community or to the master. A few Appalachian slaveholders only disposed of "social embarrassments"; that is, they only sold "free-issue" slaves who were their own descendants. Some slaveholders "never sole a slave iffen dey acted halfway right, but iffen dey gits unruly [t]he[y] always carries dem off ter sells dem." After repeated infractions, a southwestern Virginia iron manufacturer decided that drunkenness would necessitate sale of one of his most productive laborers, even though loss of the slave "would be painful" to him. After two slaves escaped from a Kanawha, West Virginia, owner, the slaveholder "shiped all the residue of his slaves to Natches and the lower markets." A Russell County, Virginia, slave summed up the emphasis of Appalachian masters upon economic return from their investments. If an Appalachian slave was labeled "bad" in behavior, attitude, or temperament, "they'd sell him." Stealing triggered swift action from some owners. The Cowles family sold one "mean negro" who had a reputation for thievery and a second male who was described as "a scamp" and a "miserable drunkard." A southwestern Virginia iron manufacturer and the western North Carolina Lenoirs did "not care to be troubled with dishonest ones," so they sold slaves caught stealing. When a Blue Ridge Virginia slave was caught pilfering chicken and hogs, the "reckless scoundrel" was "taken out of the country as a matter of safety to the community." James Gwyn "had to sell" a teenage slave when "she got too far along in the sleight of hand to keep." Despite her weakness of character, Gwyn "got $1250 for her."[42]

If a slave was believed to be guilty of "conspiring" in a rebellion, the laborer was sold quickly. Habitual runaways were considered risks to the community and to the slaveholder, so they were held in jail until they could be exported. Slaves were routinely sold when their masters found them to be "troublesome" about resisting overseers or fighting other slaves. Robert Falls' father "was so bad to fight and so troublesome he was sold four times." Thomas Jefferson's reaction to a fight among laborers in his Monticello nailery is typical of the venom that Appalachian slaveholders displayed when slaves exhibited physical resistance toward their supervisors. He instructed his Albermarle manager that "it will be necessary for me to make an example of him in terrorem to others, in order to maintain the police so rigorously necessary among

the nail boys. [T]here are generally negro purchasers from Georgia passing about the state, to one of whom I would rather he be sold than to any
other person. . . . I should regard price but little in comparison with so
distant an exile of him as to cut him off compleatly from ever again being
heard of."[43]

When a slave was suspected of perpetrating violence against whites,
Appalachian masters retaliated with brutal vengeance. When his son died
suddenly, famed abolitionist Cassius Clay charged that one of his house
servants induced the "infant of tender age, to drink and swallow down"
a pint of arsenic. Even though the jury found insufficient evidence and
acquitted the slave, the eastern Kentucky master sold her to a Mississippi
speculator. His revenge did not end there; for he also separated by sale
the accused slave's mother, brother, and sister. "I sent them to New
Orleans and sold them there," rationalized Clay, "because I knew them
to be the abettors of the crime." When his actions were condemned by
abolitionists, Clay retorted in his antislavery newspaper: "I have never at
any time in my life sold any slave except for crime or by their own desire."
His slaves were part of a trust established by his father, he continued,
whose will instructed that if any of his slaves "should behave amiss, they
shall be sold, and the money settled in land."[44]

However, slaves did not have to be so provocative in their unruly behavior. "Unproductive" or "slow worker" were dangerous labels. For example, Mary Bell warned a slave cooper and his pregnant wife that "if
they d[id] not make [her] crib full of corn that [she] w[ould] sell them
in the fall for enough to fill it." The Brown family thought "there [wa]s
no end to [the] tongue" of one of their male slaves. The owner "told him
plainly he must quit it, and also told him that if he did not conduct himself correctly . . . that [he] would not be troubled with him; but sell him
and wife the very instant they cease to conduct themselves properly."[45]

Another one in twenty mountain masters only sold physically infirm
laborers, so slaves feared being sold away from their families when they
could no longer work. A western North Carolina slaveholder was quick to
sell "a great big strong likely woman" simply because "she stammer[ed]
badly at times." When one of his hired slaves died suddenly, Thomas
Jefferson learned that he suffered from a case of untreated, complicated
hiatal hernia, "which he had for several years. Because he feared being
sold due to illness, "he had concealed it from everybody even his wife."[46]

Because they could be marketed for medical testing, slaves could be
sold even after they were old or diseased. Medical colleges located at
Lexington, Louisville, Memphis, Baltimore, New Orleans, Charleston,
Augusta, Mobile, and Richmond regularly advertised to recruit chronically ill slaves, which their owners might wish to "dispose of" profitably.

For example, an 1838 Charleston newspaper carried an offer to pay "[t]he highest cash price" for fifty slaves "affected with scrofula or King's evil, confirmed hypochondriasm, apoplexy, diseases of the liver, kidneys, spleen, stomach and intestines, bladder and its appendages, diarrhea, dysentery, &c." For medical training and testing, some Southern schools hired slaves to purchase bodies from country owners. Slaves feared being allowed to die of curable illnesses because their bodies could be so easily marketed for dissection and autopsies. A European traveler reported in the 1830s that "the bodies of coloured people exclusively are taken for dissection, because the whites do not like it, and the coloured people cannot resist."[47]

Debt Payments and Estate Settlements

Only about one-fifth of the Appalachian slaveholders could be described as "reluctant" sellers. About 5 percent of the slaves reported that their masters did not engage in trading until their estates were settled or dissolved. Local courts regularly ordered the sale of slaves to satisfy the claims of the debtors of deceased slaveholders. For example, eleven slaves belonging to John Fairfax of Monongalia County, West Virginia, were sold as part of the estate appraisement after his death. One elderly Talladega, Alabama, master advertised his plantation and slaves for sale because he had "no family, but blacks" left in the county, and he was "growing too infirm to manage the supervision." Another 16 percent of the owners "did not like to let [slaves] go" unless they "needed de money bad." In the 1830s, ex-President James Madison was "obliged to sell a dozen of his slaves" to generate a cash flow to offset the debts of his Albermarle County, Virginia, plantation.[48]

As evidenced in archival records, the disposal of slaves to settle debts was not necessarily an infrequent occurrence among Appalachian slaveholders. When notes came due at their Richmond banks, the Wilson family of Kanawha County or the Hollands of Franklin County would offer several slaves for sale. To pay his debts, General Joel Leftwich of Bedford County, Virginia, marketed slaves several times between 1796 and 1826. To settle debts between 1788 and 1794, the Augusta County Dawsons marketed slaves several times at Richmond. When cash could not be found to meet looming loan deadlines, mountain masters routinely received slaves from their debtors. For instance, Katie Johnson recalled that her southwestern Virginia master was a poor businessman, so he was always "selling [slaves] because he had 'drank [them] up.' "[49]

When his estate debts became unmanageable, Thomas Jefferson reasoned that he could not "decide to sell lands. I have sold too much of them already, and they are the only sure provision for my children, nor would I willingly sell the slaves as long as there remains any prospect of paying my debts with their labor." To remain solvent, he rented out his lands, but he exported twenty slaves. Four years later, he marketed another forty slaves. Jefferson used this strategy repeatedly as his fiscal safety net. In fact, he sold 161 slaves between 1784 and 1794. Between 1787 and 1793, Jefferson sold slaves once every eight months. On average between 1803 and 1820, the Albermarle Countian sold groups of slaves once every four-and-one-half years – every time excusing his actions as being caused by the "pressure of mounting debts."[50]

Averring that he "loath[ed] the vocation of slave trading," Amherst Countian William Waller marched twenty slaves overland to Natchez, Mississippi, in the fall of 1847. "I still think it was my duty," he wrote home. "I care not for my exposure . . . or for *the privation of my usual comforts* if I can effect my purpose – if I can return all *freed from my bondage* [of debt] which has been for some years more awfully galling to my feelings." There is a bitter irony to his choice of words since there is no comment in his letters about the *bondage* of his black laborers or the *privation* he was causing by disrupting their families. After trying unsuccessfully for six weeks to dispose of his cargo, Waller worried "without effecting my purpose, what will become of our children?" Still he saw no paradox in his failure to empathize with the slave children he had separated from their parents. Finally in March 1848, the Appalachian slaveholder wrote home cheerfully that he had "sold out all [his] negroes" to one buyer. "I have not obtained as much as I expected," he complained, "but I try and be satisfied – the whole amount of the sales for the twenty is $12,675."[51]

When a western North Carolina man failed to repay a debt, the Brown family took court action to force the sale of his slaves. After "passing through many financial trials requiring much philosophy," William Holland Thomas began to require individuals to provide slaves as security against default on their loans. Thomas George Walton "placed in Thomas McEntire's possession a Negro woman Unity" as security against an overdue debt; the slave was to be hired out until the amount of the debt had been accumulated. Some debtors settled their problems by signing away part interest in their slaves. When the Spring Hill Plantation defaulted on a loan, the Fauquier County, Virginia, owner overcame his financial troubles by exporting slaves. "Sorry crops, added to the extremity of the times, has really heretofore rendered it impossible for me to raise money," he wrote to his Kentucky lender. "I have some likely Negroes . . . any of whom you shall have at fair moderate prices . . . in order to pay the debt. I expect they would sell well in [Kentucky] country, whereas they will not sell here, in consequence of the great scarcity of cash." It was not unusual for small and middling masters to sacrifice young slave children when sheriffs appeared to serve court orders about unpaid debts. For example, the Morganton, North Carolina, sheriff confiscated and sold "a small negroe Boy ... aged about 4 years old." Similarly, Jerry Eubanks was "brought away over night, when [he] was 12 years old by a speculator. Dr. Sam Hamilton of Rome, Ga.... lived in a fine house but couldn't meet the debt, and then's when [he] fell into the speculator's hands and was brought to Columbus Mississippi."[52]

Slaves as Investment Commodities

Appalachian farms exceeded Southern averages in their per capita production of food crops, livestock, and tobacco. However, the region's plantations produced crops at levels far below southern averages. Obviously, mountain masters were not maximizing the labor of their slaves to produce agricultural cash crops. In 1860, Southern Appalachia produced more than thirty million pounds of tobacco. However, that was less than one-quarter of the output that could have been generated if all its slaves had been applied toward crop cultivation. Most Appalachian masters applied less slave labor time toward staple production than was typical of the rest of the country's slaveholders. With the exception of northern Alabama where masters exceeded the national average in their application of slaves to cotton production, Appalachian slaves were utilizing only one-quarter as many staple crop labor hours per hand as slaves in other parts of the country.[53]

In reality, there were many more slaves in the Mountain South than were required to cultivate the agricultural surpluses of the region. Consequently, it was more profitable for masters to sell or hire out slaves than to apply their labor toward the production of export crops. "I could not make the interest of the money I would pay for them by farming here," James Gwyn rationalized about his frequent trading of Wilkes County, North Carolina, slaves. Because they were valued as "human capital" to be sold as workers for enterprises integrated into the commodity chains of the world economy, Appalachian slaves took on an added dimension as "objects of financial investment – a capital good, a store of wealth, and an object of speculation." Because they were viewed by their masters as commodities who were more valuable as investments than as laborers, more than one-third of the Appalachian slave population was involved in trading transactions in 1860. One-half or more of the slaves in the Appalachian counties of Maryland, South Carolina, and Virginia were hired out or sold. Appalachian Tennesseans were trading nearly two-fifths of their slaves per year. In the Appalachian counties of Alabama,

Georgia, and North Carolina, one-fifth to one-quarter of the slaves were traded every year. Even in those two zones with the fewest slaves in the region, eastern Kentuckians and West Virginians were selling and hiring out one-quarter of their slaves every year.[54]

Why, then, did Appalachians invest in slaves when they specialized in crops that were less labor-intensive than the cotton and sugar being produced in the Lower South? Nearly one-half of Mountain South households were landless whites, so there were 1.2 free laborers to every owner of farms, shops, stores, or industries. So why did Appalachians purchase slaves when there was a surplus of free landless laborers in the region? The answer lies in the profits owners netted from slave trading. Because they could gain lower profits from applying their labor to crop production, Appalachian masters hired out slaves three times more often than Lower South slaveholders.[55]

Slaves were sometimes a mountain master's most marketable commodity because they were more profitable than tobacco, grains, or livestock. Even though Monticello produced fifty hogsheads of tobacco in 1785, Thomas Jefferson commented that "the profits of the few house servants & tradesmen hired out were as much as those of the whole estate." When a Maryland planter migrated to eastern Kentucky in 1808, he decided to relocate twenty-five slaves, "out of which 19 may be hired" to effect greater profits than he could accumulate by raising crops. During a drought year, a small eastern Tennessee plantation hired out five of its prime hands rather than allocate them to financially risky field labor. When crop prices fell, a West Virginia slaveholder removed his slaves from the fields and hired them out, instructing his son: "Inasmuch as we need money I think you had better hire George, Ben and Daniel at salt works. . . . I wish my hands so employed as to yield me at least a moderate hire. . . . I will need the money as soon as you can collect it."[56]

Even though Appalachia had a smaller concentration of slaves than other parts of the South, slave trading formed a significant part of the region's local commerce. Southern Appalachians accumulated $1.60 through domestic slave trading for every dollar accrued through local marketing of agricultural commodities. Indeed, slave trading accounted for three-fifths of the value of local commerce. In the Appalachian counties of Alabama, Georgia, North Carolina, South Carolina, Tennessee, and Virginia, the gross value of 1860 domestic slave trading actually exceeded the value of locally sold grains and livestock. In the Appalachian counties of Alabama, Georgia, and South Carolina, nearly $2 were generated from local slave trading for every $1 earned from local agricultural sales. In the Appalachian counties of North Carolina and Tennessee, local slave trading accounted for 1.2 times the value of local agricultural marketing. In the Appalachian counties of Virginia, slave trading was three times more significant to local commerce than local agricultural marketing.[57]

Even in those Appalachian zones where local marketing of crops generated greater income, slave trading was still an important segment of local commercial activity. In eastern Kentucky, local slave trading generated nearly half the value of local commerce, and eastern Kentuckians generated 82 cents in local slave trading to every $1 acquired from local marketing of agricultural produce. Domestic slave trading was of least significance to western Maryland and West Virginia. Even there, however, local slave trading made up one-third of local commerce, and Appalachians accumulated $1 in local slave trading to every $2 acquired from local agricultural sales.

There was an important reason that Southern Appalachians engaged in slave trading more frequently than their Southern counterparts. Between 1840 and 1860 when the value of Southern cotton was escalating on the world market, Mountain South exports (tobacco, pork, beef, flour, cornmeal, salt and coal) declined significantly or remained stagnant in value. Early in the nineteenth century, Appalachian salt producers were shielded from foreign competition. After Lower South planters lobbied Congress to remove the protective tariff on salt imports, West Virginia manufacturers experienced a 50 percent drop in prices. In the mid 1840s, there was a resurgence in European demand for tobacco, triggering expanded production by the Upper South, the U.S. Southwest, and several other plantation economies. The oversupply had a depressing effect on the world price. Similarly, the Mountain South exported other agricultural and extractive commodities that became increasingly redundant and unprofitable on the world market after 1840.[58]

In contrast, slave prices rose steadily from 1840 through the Civil War, but cotton was the only agricultural commodity that showed any significant increase over this time period. In the face of the declining trade position of their agricultural and extractive exports, Appalachians watched their slaves appreciate in value as the Lower South demand for cotton laborers increased. In their records and documents dated in the 1840s and 1850s, Appalachian masters recognized their precarious economic condition. As early as 1842, one western North Carolina slaveholder lamented: "cattle, hogs, sheep, corn, oats, or small tracts of land, they are in no demand at all – negroes are the only property that is wanted." When he encountered depressed prices for cattle in 1844, another Appalachian reported that "the prospect of getting cash at even a reduced price is bad, and I have no property, but Negroes, that will command money." In the late 1850s, a third regional commentator worried that hogs were "not worth so much as they used to be," but prime field hands could be exported for "cash, quick" at prices three times higher than in 1849. Little wonder, then that so many mountain masters opted to sell the labor of their slaves rather than apply them toward the production of crops. This trend was in sharp contrast to the cotton- and sugar-producing sections of the South where "slaves were generally purchased for use, rather than speculation."[59]

In the South as a whole, slave sales accounted for less than 1 percent of all agricultural outputs. However, Mountain South slave trading was equivalent to more than half the gross value of marketed agricultural commodities. In the Appalachian counties of South Carolina and Virginia, slave trading was more economically significant than all local and external sales of agricultural commodities, including cotton and tobacco. Even though cotton production had expanded dramatically in the Appalachian counties of Alabama and Georgia, slave trading was still equivalent to about half the value of agricultural marketing. Surprisingly, West Virginians accumulated one slave trading dollar for every $2 in crop sales. Even though the Appalachian counties of Maryland and North Carolina were exporting tobacco, slave trading generated about $1 to every $3 accrued from marketing of crops. For every $4 collected from the marketing of agricultural commodities, the Appalachian counties of Tennessee generated a dollar from slave trading. Slave trading was least economically significant to the Appalachian counties of Kentucky. Even there, however, slave trading generated $1 for every $5 accumulated from agricultural commodities.[60]

Comparisons with industrial outputs are even more striking. In 1860, proceeds from slave trading rose to more than 80 percent of the gross value of all Mountain South industrial products. In the Appalachian counties of Alabama, Georgia, North Carolina, South Carolina, and Virginia, proceeds from slave trading exceeded the gross value of all extractive and manufactured commodities. In those areas, nearly $2 accrued from slave trading to every $1 produced by industries. Despite the high levels of extractive exports from the Appalachian counties of Kentucky and Tennessee, slave trading generated 50 cents to every $1 earned from industry. Extractive industries and manufacturing were much more economically significant than slave trading in West Virginia and western Maryland. Even there, however, $1 in slave trading was accumulated to every six industrial dollars.[61]

Slave trading was nearly as economically crucial to the Appalachian counties of South Carolina and Virginia as all their sales of agricultural and industrial products combined. The mountain counties of Alabama and Georgia were generating only $3 to $4 from marketing farm and factory products to every $1 involved in slave trading. Western North Carolina accumulated about one-fifth of its economic proceeds from slave trading. Even though it accounted for less than 15 percent of the value of all economic activities in eastern Kentucky, western Maryland, and Appalachian Tennessee, slave trading was not an inconsequential economic sector. Overall, the Mountain South generated $1 in slave trading to every $4 accumulated from the sale of agricultural, extractive, or manufactured commodities.

2   Family Diasporas and Parenthood Lost

> We lived in constant fear that we would be sold away from our
> families.   – Jim Threat, northern Alabama slave

Like their Southern counterparts, Appalachian owners verbalized a social mythology in which they idealized themselves as "trying to keep their
people together." For example, in their family papers and letters, slaveholders of western North Carolina espoused a "widespread reluctance . . .
to split up slave families." Some slaveholders disguised their slave selling
to their community peers. After the Brown family exported a popular
field hand to western Tennessee, they told neighbors that the slave had
simply been sent "to carry some shirts" to a son attending college. Two
months later, the master received a letter from his distant agent reporting that the absent slave had been "sold for eleven hundred dollars." A
few mountain masters sold slaves locally "to one person, as the object
[wa]s not to separate the family," as one West Virginia slaveholder advertised. Yet there were few such public announcements in antebellum
Appalachian newspapers, and these kinds of decisions were rare in the
slaveholder collections utilized by this researcher.[1]

Some masters did try to make arrangements to keep slave families
together, but in a vast majority of cases, owners only did so after deter-
mining that no economic sacrifices were involved. Conscience-stricken
statements about the well-being of slaves or their families did not pre-
dominate among the entries in Appalachian slaveholder records. Hidden
from the scrutiny of neighbors in their journals, letters, and diaries, the
words of the masters themselves give us the true measure of the degree to which they depersonalized their slaves. One example will make
the point. James Hervey Greenlee, a deeply religious western North
Carolina master, made this daily entry in his diary: "Considerable frost.
Sent the wagon to haul up the rent from Young and Martin. Leander
and Peter in the shop. Warrick mending harness. Sold Uncle Ephraim
a black man for $50.00." Judging from his placement of the slave sale
at the bottom of the list, the small slaveholder was less worried about

any damage he might do to this human being than he was about the weather.[2]

The Racist Mystique About Slave Families

Southern novels and slaveholder letters constructed a paternalistic mystique in which slaveholders very rarely separated slave families. Public affirmations by Appalachian slaveholders that "we only do what's best for our people" were "ideological camouflage," cultural myths relied upon to shroud their oppressive practices with decency and morality. However, these cultural myths are called into question in the face of Appalachian slave recollections and of statistical data. To maximize labor productivity and slave-trading profits, most Appalachian masters sold, moved, and relocated slaves in reaction to economic pressures. Thomas Jefferson's pragmatism with respect to slave family separations was typical of the attitudes of Appalachian masters. Because he was "endeavoring to purchase young & able negro men," Jefferson sold an older slave away from his family. He rationalized that while he was "always willing to indulge connections seriously formed by those people," he could only protect slave families "where it c[ould] be done reasonably." When it came to the long-range stability of slave families, mountain masters showed no more "heightened sense of duty toward their slaves" than other American slaveholders.[3]

Quite the contrary, Appalachian slaveholders grounded their maximal reproduction strategies in "an ideological framework of oppressive humiliation" that consisted of two racial stereotypes. On the one hand, Appalachian masters devalued the human characteristics of their slaves and convinced themselves that they had been "destined by Providence" to capture the labor of this "inevitable" class of "the lower sort." The wife of a Winchester, Virginia, slaveholder wrote this summary of their paternalistic ideology.

The men I most honored and admired, my husband among the rest, [w]ould constantly justify [slavery], and not only that, but say that it was a blessing to the slave, his master, and the country; and . . . that the renewal of the [international] slave trade would be a blessing and benefit to all. . . . [I]f it was legitimate [Africans] would be far happier if brought away from their own country, even as slaves, than they could be if they remained in freedom and barbarism.

One northern Georgia slave experienced intimate conflict with this ethnocentrism. When told by his master that it was "best to bring [him] from Africa to be a slave" so he would not have to live "like a wild animal," Wylie Nealy retorted dangerously that "freedom was de best anywhere."[4]

On the other hand, Appalachian masters stereotyped slaves as weaker beings who did not establish the same kinds of family bonds or loyalties as whites. Regional manuscripts are filled with comments that attest to the significance of family ties to mountain slaveholders. Marriages, births, illnesses, and deaths make up a disproportionate share of letter and diary content. John Johnston of Abingdon, Virginia, celebrated the expansion of his new family with the pronouncement that "the birth of a first-born is in a family what the discovery of a continent is in a world." West Virginia slaveholder Henry Bedinger thought that his new little daughter was "destined doubtless to be the smasher of many hearts." Rockbridge Countian William Lacy boasted that his wife "intend[ed] to give [him] another little boy" who would be "much finer and smarter" than his first child. Facing the birth of "the last" of his offspring, western North Carolinian William Lenoir pondered "calling it after its mother." One Talladega mistress thought of her one-year-old child as her "little bud of promise." Another southwest Virginia mistress enjoyed the "thousand little capers" and the "bright rosy face" of her "little angel." Despite their own family ideals, Appalachian masters and mistresses constructed an ethnocentric ideology grounded in the assumptions that slaves did not construct permanent marriages, did not establish strong emotional ties to their children, or did not value extended kinship networks. In addition, the disadvantages to disrupted families were denied since the slave's "strongest affection" was purported to be "love of his master, his guide, protector, friend," not ties to black kin. Like their Southern counterparts, Appalachian masters dispassionately rationalized that any family disruption could be ameliorated by the slave's quick remarriage or pregnancy. Perhaps most of the region's slaveholders shared the condescending ideology of the Appalachian mistress who assessed "darkey" marriages as "comical, mirthful and hilarious," not family connections to be respected.[5]

Forced Labor Migrations and Family Breakups

Within such a dehumanizing system, the emotional needs or kinship ties of slaves were not even recognized as anything like those experienced by their white oppressors. While espousing fierce loyalty to their own white kinship networks, Appalachian masters destroyed black families in great numbers. To maximize profits from their investments, the region's slaveholders routinely removed slaves through forced labor migrations. Using racial stereotypes to justify their ruthless actions, mountain owners terminated two of every five of the marriages among their slaves. Sixteen percent of the two-parent families were disrupted because the father was owned by a different master. When Appalachian masters emigrated, sold slaves, gave slaves to their children, or hired out laborers, they disrupted one of every four slave marriages. Appalachian narratives recount numerous instances in which the slaves were separated, often permanently, from their families. Whether masters were sorrowful or reluctant about their actions is irrelevant, for they held the legal power to dispose of slaves as "commodities," and that is precisely what they did. In their disruption of slave families, mountain masters replicated national trends, for small slaveholders broke up families much more frequently than large plantations. Smaller slaveholdings had a higher incidence of one-parent households and of children separated from parents. There were fewer children in two-parent households on farms with one to fifteen slaves than on those with sixteen or more. While smallholdings with fewer than sixteen slaves contained 43 percent of the slave population in 1850, they accounted for nearly two-thirds of all slaves living in divided residences and for over 60 percent of the slave children in one-parent residences. Like other areas with low black population densities, Mountain South plantations disrupted slave families through six types of forced labor migration.[6]

- Sales of slaves (59 percent of family disruptions)
- Long-term hire-outs (16 percent of family disruptions)
- Abroad marriages (15 percent of family disruptions)
- Owner migrations (4 percent of family disruptions)
- Estate settlements and presents to kin (3.5 percent of family disruptions)
- Labor allocation to an owner's distant work site (less than 3 percent of family disruptions)

Consequently, breakup of slave families by masters and the structured absence of black fathers occurred in the Mountain South more often than in the Lower South or on large plantations.

Permanent Family Separations

Gutman contended that all slave marriages were insecure.

No slave could predict when an owner would die and how his estate would be divided. No slave could affect the vicissitudes of the business cycle. And no slave could shape an owner's decision to reallocate his investments in human or other capital. That is why slave marriages – however long they lasted – cannot be characterized as stable. And that is why slave parents everywhere had good reasons to socialize their children to prepare for either the possible breakup of their marriages or sale from an immediate family.

One of every three slave marriages was broken by a master who removed adult males through forced labor migrations. Black Appalachian
husbands separated through interstate sales rarely were able to reunite
with wives and children after emancipation. *Source:* Library of Congress.

For the South as a whole, slave trader records have been used to estimate
that one of every three or four sales triggered the separation of spouses.
E. Franklin Frazier fostered the misperception that stable familial arrangements existed among most slaves living on small plantations. However, Appalachian slaves reported marriage breakups more often than
the national average. Of the 205 Appalachian masters described in the
WPA narratives as selling slaves, more than one-third of them disunited
husbands and wives.[7]

Appalachian slaves were more likely to be sold away from their spouses
than were their Lower South counterparts. "So 'tis dat de womens have
fust one, an' den tudder man," to apply the words of a middle Tennessee
ex-slave. In reality, most separated slave families permanently lost contact

with their kin because their masters removed them too far away for contact to be maintained. A Nelson County, Virginia, husband unsuccessfully begged his master to keep his wife. "Don't worry you can get another one," a Laurel County, Kentucky, master quipped to a man whose wife had just been sold. Sales of family members, out-of-state migrations of masters, and gifts to distant children accounted for two-thirds of the forced labor migrations that disrupted families. Four percent of these families were broken when masters migrated. For instance, one young Harper's Ferry couple was moved to Arkansas and "never heard from their kinfolks no more." When mother and children migrated west with the wife's master, Ben Chambers "ain't never seed" his father "no mo'." Appalachian slaves also lost contact with kin when they were given away to their masters' distant children. When the son of a northern Georgia master opened a frontier plantation in Florida, he selected the most valuable laborers and artisans, without any attention to preserving their kinship ties.[8]

In reality, one of every three Appalachian slave marriages was destroyed by the masters' structural interference to maximize profits from forced labor migrations. Family separations like the following cases were common. In the 1820s, the Carr family of Albermarle County, Virginia, separated several slave families by selling members to new owners in different parts of the Lower South. A Staunton, Virginia, father "was trafficked away from his woman and children to another state." Maggie Stenhouse and her two children never saw her husband again after he was sold. Anna Lee of Scott County, Tennessee, never knew what became of her parents because they "were sold to another man before I'se old enough to remember." An Amherst, Virginian soothed his conscience by rationalizing that he had not sought a higher price by separating a female slave from her young children. However, the slaveholder was not troubled that he had severed wife and offspring from their husband and father.[9]

Slaveholders carefully planned marriage breakups. Masters kept control by effecting removals without the knowledge of their kin. Abroad marital relationships were very particularly vulnerable to separations. One Appalachian slave recalled that his "uncle wuz married but he wuz owned by one master and his wife wuz owned by another. He wuz 'lowed to visit his wife on Wednesday and Saturday." When the husband returned for one of his visits, "his wife had been bought by the speculator and he never did know where she wuz." When he was arranging the separation of one married couple, the Buffalo Forge operator contrived to have a slave trader pick them up simultaneously. While the husband was to be hired out locally, the speculator assured the master that "if you wish your woman to go out of the country I will send her off." Similarly, a

Winchester, Virginia, mistress wrote in her diary of the manner in which the owner ripped apart the family of the slave she was renting. In her diary, Mrs. McDonald recorded: "The owner of Lethea has been several times to persuade me to give her up. . . . He does not tell her there is a negro trader coming for her." She continued, "I cannot endure the thought of her grief; to be torn from her husband and perhaps from her children." Still, the white mistress never forewarned the slave. A week later, "Poor L. [w]as gone. When she saw there was no hope, she submitted humbly and quietly. . . . Margaret was with her, but her other child was not to go."[10]

Even when Appalachian masters thought of themselves as preserving family units, they rarely sold fathers with their spouses and children. For instance, a western North Carolina slaveholder advertised his intent to market an "entire" family consisting of "a woman 27 years old, five children and another hourly expected . . . all one man's children." The fate of the father is never mentioned when North Carolina planter Nicholas Woodfin smugly commended a neighbor who had "very properly directed that a woman and her four children be sold together." A Franklin County, Tennessee, slave remembered that his mother had to remarry several times "because they would carry her husband off to one state or another." When slaves were sold on the Rome, Georgia, auction block to settle an estate, numerous families "never seed their fo'ks after they was sold at the 'dividement' of the property." In Albermarle, Virginia, Maria Perkins wrote to alert her "abroad" husband that their family would be broken up if he could not find a way to prevent it.

My master has sold albert to a trader on Monday court day and myself and other child is for sale also. I want you to tell dr Hamelton and your master if either will buy me they can attend to it. . . . I don't want a trader to get me they asked me if I had got any person to buy me and I told them no. . . . [A] man by the name of brady bought albert and is gone I don't know where. . . . I am quite heartsick.[11]

Sixty percent of the Appalachian slave narratives describe trading incidents. To justify their exploitation, slaveholders constructed an "ideological inversion of reality," which placed the blame for the actions of the masters upon the victims. As Tadman observed, slaveholders could

separate families and still see themselves as paternalists – since they could deceive and flatter themselves with the view that only they, the whites, really worried about black families. They could readily persuade themselves that . . . separations were only incidental to the system – for in their view the whole relationship of slavery was of primary benefit to the slaves, any temporary "hardships" of separation easily being overcome. . . . To have believed that the black family was really anything like as important as the white family would have meant permanent moral crisis for whites. Without that belief, the system was infinitely capable of

In addition to losing half their children to premature deaths, Appalachian slave mothers lost one of every three offspring to sales. *Source:* Library of Congress.

combining a vicious program of speculation and separation with a comforting, paternal self-image for masters.

According to the mystique, "the negro and negress, with new partners and another marriage [we]re quite as happy as if they had never been separated." Appalachian masters may have comforted themselves with such self-righteous mythology, but the auction block and traveling speculators loomed like ever-present shadows over black Appalachians. Jim Threat remembered that his Talladega, Alabama, quarters "lived in constant fear that they would be sold away from their families." Southwest Virginia slaves originated a hymn entitled "Massa's Gwyne Sell Us Termorrer" to document the annual "shippin' the slaves to sell 'em" that occurred between Christmas and early January. Maggie Pinkard of Coffee County, Tennessee, describes the recurrent trauma most poignantly: "When the slaves got a feeling there was going to be an auction, they would pray. The night before the sale they would pray in their cabins. You could hear the hum of voices in all the cabins down the row." More significantly, impending family separation was the underlying reason that Appalachian slaves verbalized most frequently for physical attacks on their masters or for running away.[12]

White Inheritance and Family Fragility

Fewer than 10 percent of Upper South slaveholders maintained and protected slave family ties in their wills. Instead, white inheritance practices structured barriers to the survival of slave families. On the one hand, the deaths of Appalachian masters disrupted families, as slaves were sold to settle estate debts. When Thomas Jefferson died, the families of 130 slaves were permanently separated. The five days of auctioning were so traumatic that it reminded one of Jefferson's grandchildren of "a captured village in ancient times when all were sold as slaves." A large extended Lumpkin County, Georgia, family was disunited forever when slaves were sold to settle the estate of Tom Singleton's dead master. Tom's grandparents, his mother, and his ten siblings were divided among several new masters. "My pa, my sister, and me wuz sold on de block at de sheriff's sale," Tom lamented. "Durin' de sale [Tom's] sister cried all de time, and' Pa rubbed his han' over her head an' face." The will of one Sevier County, Tennessee, master underscores the racist nature of these inheritance practices. Upon his demise, John Brabson commanded that his slave inventory be subdivided into seven lots, "the said lots to be as near equal value as may be." To make matters more destructive toward his slave families, Brabson instructed "the rite to the respective lots to be determined by drawing." When their Jackson, Alabama, owner died, Thomas Cole's slave community "cried jest lak it was one of der own family." They were not mourning the loss of the "dear departed," however. Instead, these slaves were afraid that "maybe [they] would all be sold. [They] didn't know what was goin' ter happen ter [them]."[13]

White inheritance practices endangered slave families in three other ways. Wills provided no guarantee about the treatment of elderly slaves at the hands of beneficiaries. Some offspring balked at the prospect of continuing the support of elderly slaves, so they moved quickly to sell them. In other instances, sons discontinued the promises that their fathers had made. When his father died, one Blue Ridge Virginia son decided to charge nonproductive "Granny Miller" for "the Lott" that she had been granted as "consideration for her maintenance." Another son calculated the high cost of "the burthen of four old negroes," one of whom "was a Loathsome cripple with a sore leg." Second, Appalachian masters and mistresses routinely awarded to their minor children slave infants, and those allocations ensured future black family breakups when the master's adult children were married or relocated. On the day she was born, Filmore Hancock's grandmother "was given" to her one-year-old "missus." Thirty years later, the mistress was forcibly relocated westward as part of the government's removal of the Cherokee Nation from Southern Appalachia. By then, the enslaved female was a thirty-three-year-old parent and wife, so she left behind two children and her husband. Third, Appalachian masters structured the futures of the unborn children of some young female slaves through their inheritance methods, for they routinely bequeathed to their kin their "slaves and their future increase." Mary Burton instructed her lawyer to hold in trust for her minor daughter "a certain female slave George Anna aged about 15 years." If her daughter died, "the said slave with her increase" were to "go in fee" to her yet-unborn grandchildren. When May Calhoon died, her will instructed the executors to utilize one of her teenage slave mothers to support her descendants into the future. To ensure the financial security of her kin, Calhoon's "woman Margaret and her [infant] son . . . and all her increase and there increase" were to be separately "hiered out as long as they live," and this strategy was to be "done yearly so long as the generation of the negroes last[ed]."[14]

Abroad Spouses and Kin

Because Lower South plantations sought to capture and manage labor tightly, masters on large plantations generally placed strict limits on marriage across plantations. In contrast, small and middling plantations permitted fewer marriage choices. So as not to circumscribe their reproduction capacities, small slaveholders more often encouraged "abroad spouse" arrangements. Consequently, about 15 percent of all Appalachian slave family separations occurred when women had "abroad" husbands who were owned by neighboring slaveholders. We must be careful not to romanticize abroad kin arrangements as day-to-day resistance in which slaves forced upon their masters family linkages that worked against the owners' economic interests. In the words of one mountain master, abroad marriages were necessary if small plantations were to maintain high fertility among their slave women. Thomas Jefferson Massie wrote to an inquiring friend that "the small fry (and 99 of every 100 are small fry) class of owners can't think" of prohibiting such marriages. "Old Amy without a husband," he continued, "would scarcely have been the 'goose which laid the golden egg' had she been denied a husband 'from home,' seeing her master had none at home for her." Clearly, such relationships offered other definite advantages to slaveholders. New births added to the inventory of those who owned the mothers, but someone else fed and clothed the fathers. Moreover, family ties rooted males to the geographical areas of their white masters, thereby deterring runaways to the North.[15]

To create bonds between local women and males who had been hired away from distant families, the Buffalo Forge operator took a direct role in structuring new marriages for his workers. Having local familial ties deterred slaves from running away to visit wives. "Andy asks me to drop you a line in relation to him," the ironmaster wrote to a neighboring plantation. "He is my property – has many good traits, is a good hand at work – has never been detected . . . in anything mean or dishonest – is rather high tempered, yet not unmanageable. . . . He has my consent to get married provided the girl is what she should be." Under these conditions, the families were granted visiting privileges at the whim of their masters. Anna Lee and her husband were owned by two small eastern Tennessee plantations. Anna recalled: "If our men lived on some other plantation my Maser and his Maser would have to agree for us to be married, and if that was the case his Maser would let him come stay with me one night out of a week, sometimes it would be two weeks before he would be allowed to come." Similarly, Jim Threat's Talladega County father only saw his family between Saturday night and Monday dawn.[16]

However, masters routinely restricted or withdrew family visiting privileges when distant slave rebellions occurred, when nearby slaves escaped, when slave kin were about to be sold, and during times of unrest. Masters also curtailed weekly visits when they needed to maximize the labor time of abroad husbands. One western North Carolina slave described the "confusion, mix-up, and heartaches" that resulted because his "pa b'longin' to one man and my mammy b'longin' to another, four or five miles apart." The husband came to visit his family "sometimes widout de pass. Patrollers catch him way up de chimney hidin' one night; they stripped him right befo' mammy and give him thirty-nine lashes, wid her cryin' and a hollerin' louder than he did." Sometimes family members were sold to "accommodate" neighbors, with the verbal understanding that the slave would not be sold out of the county. When Randolph Lewis relocated to Kentucky in 1807, he urged Thomas Jefferson to purchase one of his slave women who had married a Monticello male slave. After his bankruptcy, a Rockbridge County, Virginia, master advertised his desire to sell a slave woman "privately, as she has a husband in the county." However, there was nothing to prevent the subsequent resale of the slave by the new owner, as occurred in a case in Madison County, Kentucky. When the new owner broke his word and sold a slave into the cotton South, the seller sued for having been "deceived and defrauded." Subsequently, the court system awarded the seller $100 in damages and helped him save his reputation in the community, but the slave remained far away from family.[17]

Almost one-fifth of the family disruptions resulted from forced labor migration of members, disproportionately males, to distant sites that kept them away most of the time. When they were hired out on a yearly basis or when they were assigned at their owners' distant enterprises, family members were reunited only a few times each year. For instance, a Virginia slave woman was hired away from her family to work on construction of the James River and Kanawha Canal, but her master contracted for her husband to visit her only "once in the course of the year." One northern South Carolina ex-slave recalled that his parents lived in different counties, and the husband's master "didn't 'low" her father to visit his family "'cept twice a year." At the same time, her father's owner "want[ed] young healthy slaves," so he pressured her father to "g[e]t him another wife." That was "'zactly why" her father had two large families. Eli Davison belonged to a West Virginia master who "had three plantations," so he was isolated from the rest of his family when they were sent to work at different locations. The Cloverdale Furnace returned an injured husband to his owner three counties away, keeping on its payroll the man's hired wife. Because the couple had originally been hired together, this owner had made no provision to guarantee visitation privileges to either spouse.[18]

The Structured Absence of Husbands and Fathers

Despite forced labor migrations and intergenerational family diasporas, slaves developed persistent family ties. At least half of all U.S. Southern slave families were permanently headed by two parents. In another 12 percent to 15 percent, one of the two parents was absent part of the time. In such instances, one spouse was owned by another master or hired out. Most of these "abroad spouses" visited on some schedule determined by their masters. As a result, nearly two-thirds of ex-slaves may have been raised by both parents. Only about one-fifth of all slave families were headed by one parent, and another 15 percent of households consisted of children and single adults who were unrelated by kinship. At emancipation, both parents were present in most Virginia and North Carolina slave families, and many older couples had lived together in long-lasting unions. Long before the Civil War, however, at least one-third of all U.S. Southern slave marriages had been terminated by an act of force on the part of masters. In the Upper South states, one in every three slave marriages was broken by a master's intervention. One in every five slave marriages was terminated when masters sold spouses away from their families. Moreover, one-half of all slave sales involved the separation of children from their parents.[19]

Like their Southern counterparts, Appalachian slaves organized themselves into families headed by two parents. Until events occurred to separate them, 70 percent of the Appalachian slave families had both father and mother present. At southwestern Virginia's Oxford Iron Works in the early 1800s, twenty-three of the thirty slave families had both mother and father present. In one Union Army census, two-thirds of the Montgomery County, Virginia, slave families had two parents. The Freedmen's Bureau marriage registers for two Blue Ridge Virginia counties document stable family structures. About one in four couples had been married between ten and nineteen years, and slightly more than one in five, at least twenty years. Nearly one in ten registrants recorded marriages that had lasted thirty or more years. By comparison with Louisiana families, however, Appalachian slave households were much more often disaggregated. In Louisiana, nearly one-half of the slave households were married couples with children. Only one-fifth of the Appalachian slave households were complete families in which parents and children resided together. Female-headed households occurred nearly four times more often in Appalachia than in Louisiana. Siblings were living alone without parents twice as often in Appalachia as they were in Louisiana, and households were made up of extended kin (other than parents and children) more than twice as often in Appalachia as in Louisiana. Clearly, Appalachian slave families were disrupted much more frequently by forced labor migrations than were Lower South slave families.[20]

Historically, labor migrations – whether forced or voluntary – have caused the emergence of female-headed households and acted as structural constraints against fatherhood. Typically, children have been separated from fathers, triggering the formation of a variety of household forms in which women dominate the families. In the case of enslaved Appalachians, masters structured the absence of fathers from two of every five households. Describing this pattern among Appalachian masters of Loudoun County, Virginia, Stevenson concluded that "the evidence overwhelmingly supports the conclusion that matrifocality was a fundamental characteristic of most slave families, even when fathers lived locally." Legally, offspring were the property of the mother's master. When they were held by different owners than their wives, fathers retained no legitimate right to command visitation privileges nor to maintain linkages with their children. As Fox-Genovese observed, "his claim to the status of father had no basis in law, no confirmation from the society in which he lived." Either master could terminate kinship interaction, so "abroad" fathers must constantly renegotiate this fragile privilege. When they were hired out or assigned to a different work site, fathers maintained contact with their families at the will and whim of their masters. Ben Chambers recalled that his father belonged to another "plantation what ain' fur away." Like other abroad spouses, Chambers' father had to "git a pass eb'ry time he want[ed] to come see" his family. In one other important way, masters structured the absence of fathers from the lives of their children. Mountain slave children were rarely disciplined by their fathers. Appalachian ex-slaves recalled members of the owner's family and overseers as the individuals who administered verbal or physical discipline to them most often.[21]

The legal homes of slave fathers were their assigned *work sites*, while their families lived in the *mothers' cabins*. As one Blue Ridge Virginia father expressed it, "de wife house was often eight or ten miles from de home house, and we would go there Saturday night expectin' to see de wife we had left." The political and economic paradoxes of fatherhood were embodied in this legal and cultural definition of where the center of the family lay. In more than one-half of the Appalachian narratives, ex-slaves defined "family" in terms of the "mother's house." After a slave marriage or after the announced pregnancy of an unwed woman, Appalachian masters "fix[ed] up a house for de wife. He want[ed] to be sho' dere's a nice snug house and yard to take care of all de chillen," that "natural increase" from which surplus laborers could be marketed. Appalachia's abroad wives "faced the challenge of rearing their children and addressing their families' needs without the daily attention or resources of their husbands or the fathers of their children." Moreover, enslaved females who lived on smallholdings much more often grew up and later bore their own children in matrifocal households in which there was no stable male presence on a daily basis. As a result, Mountain South enslavement stripped men of legal and social fatherhood and of their opportunities to participate in the maintenance of family households. According to Fox-Genovese:

the independence and strength of slave women were inscribed in a social system in which slaveholding women had the right to command the obedience and deference of slave men, in which slaveholding men had a right to exploit the bodies of slave women, and in which slave men did not have the right to resist either form of assault, although they often did at the risk of their lives.[22]

To complicate matters, the vast majority of Appalachian slave marriages were never legally registered nor church-sanctioned. Marriage, therefore, did not ensure enslaved husbands any of the legal rights accorded to white fathers. When marriages between abroad spouses caused economic losses, masters intruded to force permanent splits. To maximize his own slave reproduction, Nelson County, Virginia, planter William Massie offered his slave Willis a $20 bribe to induce him to replace his abroad wife and children with one of the women he owned. To separate a wife and children from her barren husband, one Shenandoah Valley master hired the woman in faraway Richmond. When she became pregnant during the extended absence from her husband, the slaveholder rejoiced, "She is now worth $300 more than any one thought her a year ago. . . . I should advocate her being hired in Richmond. Either this or her separation from Old Eunuch Daniel." In Noah Perry's family, the master's elderly father "kept a claim" on mother and children, so he never saw his abroad black father during the six months when his mother served as the elderly man's concubine.[23]

Mothers and children were expected to retain their masters' names, further obscuring the identity of fathers. Very few Appalachian ex-slaves were able to maintain permanent surnames that reflected the identities of their biological fathers. Because "it was the custom for slaves to take the name of the man what owned them," almost all of the mountain ex-slaves had been identified with multiple surnames "from having different masters." As a result, spouses usually did not utilize the same names. For instance, Fannie Tippin's married grandparents had different surnames throughout slavery, even though they were part of an extended family. Joe Wooten was one of the few black Appalachians who was able to have "a long life name." Joe took his father's name, refused to change it when he was sold, and accepted whatever punishment the new master meted out for his disobedience.[24]

Masters structured the absence of males from those households in three ways. First, owners may have removed fathers through sales or gifts to children, and the women had refused to remarry. Second, masters were sometimes reluctant to formalize marriages when intended husbands were owned by someone else. Carl Hall reported that the small plantations in his eastern Kentucky community held too few slaves to permit women to select partners from the populations on their home farms. To avoid acknowledgment of family ties between abroad spouses, "negro men were not allowed to marry at all." Jerry Eubanks "didn't marry" because his master would not approve abroad linkages. That owner thought such commitments were too cumbersome because "dere was a boss over dere and a boss over here" and because visiting privileges lowered laborer output and increased the number of male absences without passes. If an adjacent master "had a woman [Eubanks] wanted, [his] boss would send a note and tell [the other owner]. Den [he'd] visit dat plantation on sich and sich a nights."[25]

Masters structured the absence of fathers in a third way. In several southern states, marriages between slaves and free blacks were illegal, and such family arrangements were almost always forbidden upon by owners. Marriages of free black males to enslaved women were not legally protected. When one Fauquier County, Virginia, master died, he liberated the wife and daughters of a freedman. However, he bequeathed two enslaved sons to his wife with the proviso that she should sell the children to their free father. Instead, the mistress "sold them to the traders," causing the father to have to sell his small farm to pay the $1,800 they demanded for the slave children. When one western Maryland master decided to sell a wife and children away from the free husband, his white neighbor suggested that the owner "hire her out to her husband, who was a free man." Because he feared the liberating influence upon the children, the master refused, convinced that such action would "make all her family worthless." In a southwestern Virginia case, a free husband was not even permitted to leave a small inheritance to his enslaved family. The court ruled that slaves could not own property, thus it was only appropriate to distribute the estate to the woman's owner and to the state. Free black males could never take their residence for granted, and their migration threatened the families they left behind. After Robert Napper purchased his freedom from an Augusta County, Virginia, master, he was accused of "stealing corn from a gentleman of the neighborhood ... whipped at the public whipping post, and ordered to leave the state." Napper migrated to Ohio, leaving behind his enslaved wife and five children. Two years later, the free husband arranged to buy his wife and infant, and the mistress "offer[ed] him another one of his children, a little boy, for $600." The Appalachian slaveholder, however, would, "on no account, sell the eldest three!"[26]

The absence of males was felt severely in those circumstances in which abroad husbands were hired out or assigned to distant labor for long periods. Adult males were so often hired out that Appalachian slave women coined the term "men on the road" to refer to those husbands and fathers who were separated from family by this type of forced labor migration. Fathers were treated like absent shadows who had no rights to demand continued contact with their children. Very few Appalachian slave marriages were publicly acknowledged, and the only record of parentage was maintained as part of masters' written inventories or mental notes. Legally, "de chillen allus b'long to dey mama's marster." If husbands were owned by someone else, their names rarely appeared in such written lists. Instead, children were enumerated alongside the names of their mothers, with no specification of fathers' identities. When mothers died, were sold, or hired out, the wishes of abroad fathers were not considered by owners. It was customary for Appalachian mistresses to take charge of children when their mothers died. Even though Sally Brown's father lived nearby, she was "give away when [she] wuz jest a baby," never to see him again. Mollie Scott was raised by whites after her mother's death. Mollie knew that she "was all the child [her] father had but [her] mother had ten children." Still the young girl lost all contact with her father until he came to find her after emancipation.[27]

After Morris Hillyer's mother died, his father was given to the master's distant son, while the mistress kept the child. When he was born, Steve Connally's mother "took de fever an' couldn't raise" him; he never knew his father because the mistress "kept [him] in a little cot by her bed." After the sale of her parents, Easter Brown "was raised in de house wid de white folkses." She was never told anything about her parents, and she "called Marster 'pa' and Mistress 'ma'" until, at the age of eleven, her father found her after emancipation. Nancy Gardner lost her father through much more traumatic intervention by the master. "I'll never forget when me, my ma and my auntie had to leave my pa and brothers," she lamented. On the Memphis auction block, "dey sold [Nancy] and [her] ma together and dey sold [her] pa and de boys together." Nancy remembered that her mother "grieved to death" about the loss of her husband, and "didn't live long after dat." It was "thirty years before [her] pa knew if [his children] was still living."[28]

Motherhood Lost: Structural Constraints Against Child Rearing

In the South as a whole, children under thirteen accounted for less than 10 percent of all slave sales. In sharp contrast, nearly two-thirds of all Appalachian slave sales separated children from their families – 70 percent of these forced migrations occurring when they were younger than fifteen. Masters had good economic reason to sell children separately. At New Orleans slave auctions, children sold with parents added nothing to the total sales price. However, "the younger the child, the greater the markup in the child's price if purchased separately instead of with the mother." For that reason, some Appalachian speculators specialized in frequent purchases of slave children from neighbors. In Wilkes County, North Carolina, for example, Gwyn and Hickerson regularly bought children aged ten to sixteen and then resold then in distant markets. Dealers, like western Marylander George Kephart, regularly advertised their interest in procuring young Appalachian slaves, particularly those ranging in age from ten to twenty-five. On the auction blocks in small towns, children were often sold away from parents. William Johnson of Albermarle County, Virginia, sums up the ideology of mountain masters when he commented that: "White folks in my part of the country didn't think anything of breaking up a family and selling the children in one section of the South and the parents in some other section."[29]

Experiences like the following cases were common. A western North Carolinian sold away from her enslaved parents a daughter that he "disliked very much." Tillie Duke never knew "nothin' 'bout [her] parents" in Roanoke, Virginia, because she was sold as an infant to a white family who migrated to Kansas. In middle Tennessee, a slaveholder sold to an itinerant trader "Aunt Phoebe's little baby that was just toddling along." One McDowell County, North Carolina, master sold twelve of the sixteen children of one of his slave women "fas' as dey got three years old." Dan Lockhart "was sold at five years of age," never to see his mother again until he was an adult. At the age of seven, Jim Threat's father was exported to Talladega, Alabama, where "he never saw his parents again." At the age of nine, Martha Showvely and two cousins were sold to speculators passing through Franklin County, Virginia, to collect a coffle of slaves for resale by Richmond auction houses. When James Hervey Greenlee settled his father's estate, he retained "4 little negroes," after selling away their parents and extended kin. After being exported from parents, three western North Carolina siblings were sold separately. In addition to permanent separations, one of every ten Appalachian slave children lived with whites, growing up away from both parents. As a result of all these forms of masters' interference, only a minority of Appalachian slave children experienced unbroken bonds and daily interaction with both parents.[30]

Masters' Interference in Child Care

On the one hand, the mothering role of Appalachian slave women was profoundly compromised by the child labor strategies of their owners.

On the other hand, the mothers' own work responsibilities prevented them from prioritizing child rearing. Even though most mountain slave children were part of matrifocal households, their mothers allocated most of their time and energy toward their owners' work. Booker T. Washington recalled that his mother "had little time to give to the training of her children during the day. She snatched a few moments for our care in the early morning before her work began, and at night after the day' work was done." Wash Armstrong and George Kye were kept in plantation nurseries with "a whole lot of children"; they did not live with their mothers in the family cabins because the women "worked all the time." Similarly, Julia Daniels' mother "didn't have much time for anythin' but cookin' all the time" in the master's house. Maugan Sheppard "never saw [his parents] much 'cept upon on a Sunday, cause they went to work before sun-up." Julius Jones had a similar experience, for he "never did see [his] mother or father except on Sunday. [He] stayed in the house they did, but they left in the morning for the fields before [he] was awake, and when they got back [he] was asleep." Jeff Johnson's parents "worked in de fiel', and when dey come in at dark, [the children] be's sleepy and didn' pay 'em no mind." Tom Singleton blamed his lack of family knowledge upon the pressures of work. He did not "'member much 'bout [his] brothers and sisters" even though his parents "had fourteen children." In addition, he did not "ricollect nothin' t'all 'bout [his] grandma and grandpa." During the work day, Tom's family went separate ways. At night, the children "wuz so whupped out from hard wuk [they] just went off to sleep early and never talked much at no time" to their parents. Left without structured care while his mother worked, Perry Madden "would go to the house in slavery time, and there wouldn't be nobody home." So he "would go to the bed and get under it because [he] was scared. When [he] would wake up it would be way in the night and dark."[31]

Appalachian masters also intruded into motherhood through the formation of child care strategies that weakened the bonds between family members and placed young children at increased risk of malnutrition, injury, and inadequate psychological development. At issue here is not whether mothers left their children while they worked. For enslaved mothers and children, the situation was much more complex than that. On the one hand, masters, not mothers, made fundamental decisions about the nature of child care: when, where, by whom, how much or how little? On the other hand, enslaved mothers did not have the option of not reporting to work when their children needed attention. Mothers risked punishment of children if they demanded better child care when the master's arrangements endangered their offspring. If the mother's caregiving conflicted with the master's work, she was required to do her "productive" work, most often in the fields or at nonagricultural sites. We must also be clear about the masters' designs in socializing enslaved children. Appalachian slaveholders received little benefit from strengthening ties between parents and offspring. Instead the master's agenda was to socialize children in such a way as to cement their allegiances to and their obedience of the master and his proxies.

Centralized collective child care may have characterized large plantations in other parts of the world, but less than one-quarter of Appalachian slave children were left in the care of nurseries or elderly caregivers who did nothing else. Only a few of the largest mountain plantations operated centralized nurseries. In fact, the word "nursery" rarely appears in the regional narratives. The typical pattern on mountain plantations was that elderly or infirm slaves were put in charge of loosely structured and informal child care. On a middling plantation, Mollie Kirkland was tended by elderly women in a nursery "for sich what need[ed] care while dere mammies am a-workin'." On Abner Griffin's small plantation, there was "one old man to see after de little chillun" in his cabin. Many large mountain plantations also followed this pattern. Even though it was one of the largest Appalachian plantations, Jefferson's Monticello had no centralized child care; instead, older siblings cared for toddlers. One Franklin County, Virginia, master reported that he had "80 some odd Negroes," sixty of whom were working as full hands. While parents were "working hard," the owner assigned "only one old Negroe" to "mind" his "flock" of nearly twenty children. Whether located on small or large plantations, the primary child care mechanism described by Appalachian ex-slaves was that they were fed and supervised by elderly women and men "who was too old to wok in de fields."[32]

Rawick and other scholars have come to the optimistic conclusion that "the slave community acted like a generalized extended kinship system in which all the adults looked after all children." In our scholarly haste to portray slaves as actors as well as victims, we must be careful not to overstate the degree to which enslaved families controlled their circumstances. If we listen carefully to the voices of Appalachian ex-slaves, what we learn is that unstructured, informal child care amounted to little or no supervision at all during the workday. As a result, more than two-fifths of Appalachian slave children were left with little or no adult supervision during the workdays. Even when centralized child care occurred, the competence of the providers was questioned by nearly one-tenth of the Appalachian ex-slaves. Jim Threat criticized his master's practice of assigning "the old decrepit women" to care for "the babies and small children while the mothers worked." The elderly male at Pierce Cody's farm watched children from "a tall lookout on the roof." To tend children at Sarah Wilson's farm, her "mighty old" grandmother "set on the front porch all the time." Simon Hare and other children on his western North Carolina farm played on their own all day; they would "waller around in de ditch like a old sow; get sleepy, go ter sleep right dare till old lady come rustle [them] up."[33]

Pressured to work away from infants and youngsters, parents developed their own child care strategies within the limited options available to them. More than one-third of the parents took offspring to their work stations. However, nearly one-fifth of Appalachian slave children were left alone during the work day, and another 15 percent were left to play with older siblings (who themselves were ten or younger). Noah Perry was left to his own devices while his mother "run the plow." On Stephen Varner's farm, the children "all stayed under a big oak tree.... While the older ones played they had to watch over the baby brother or sister. The marser would come around to see about them and give them milk." Probably a majority of Appalachian slave children "played around the quarters," until they were old enough to be assigned tasks.[34]

Because of risks and dangers they encountered before the age of ten, many Appalachian ex-slaves recalled the lack of adult supervision vividly. As an infant, Mary Tate was "left alone" in her cradle at the family cabin while her mother was "about tasks on the plantation." The master "became annoyed at [her] crying and as punishment placed [her] in a fence corner. There was snow on the ground." Childhood mischief brought severe punishment from masters. As a motherless child with no supervision except his slightly older sister, Morris Hillyer would "ride de calves, chase de pigs, kill de chickens, break up hen nests, and in fact do most everything [h]e hadn't ought to do." Such property destruction did not go unnoticed or unpunished. While their mother worked in the big house, two middle Tennessee boys "was burning one another with broom sage, and [one] caught fire and went running and hollering." While carrying a piece of bread in the yard, a lone western North Carolina toddler attracted the attention of a boar. When it snatched at the food, the hog "caught the child's hand near the thumb with its tusks. When running off, the hog carried the child with it, dragging it along into the field." However, the greatest "source of evil to slave children" was their masters' offspring. Left without adult care, Ben Chambers' "young marsters cut [his] big toe off wid a hatchet." Because of a prank of her master's teenage son, Sarah Patterson was "crippled all [her] life." The white boy rode his horse into the midst of the slave children, threatening to run them over. To escape, the children "ran and climbed up on the top of a ten rail fence. The fence gave way and broke and fell down." Sarah "caught the load," as all the children fell on top of her, knocking her knee out of place. James

Pennington described "want of parental care" as one of the worst evils of slavery. During his youth, he felt like "a helpless human being thrown upon the world without the benefit of its natural guardians."[35]

Early Work Socialization of Slave Children

Perhaps Appalachian masters paid little attention to centralized child care because of their early work socialization of youngsters. After the age of five or six, the primary child care method was a labor assignment. More than one-third worked under the supervision of their mistress or followed parents around during the work day. Perhaps seeking to acquire better rations of food, shoes, and clothing, nearly 90 percent of mountain slave children began their work assignments well before the age of ten. The youngsters were about evenly divided between chores in the fields and tasks around the master's house. About two-fifths of them were assigned house chores, and about two-fifths of them worked in the fields or tended livestock. Well before the age of ten, one of every eight Appalachian slave children was already employed at an industrial site.[36]

A majority of Appalachian slaves experienced lost childhoods in which they were pressured to grow up fast and to take care of themselves. Mothers attenuated child rearing because their sons and daughters were put to work at an early age. For the vast majority of Appalachian slave children, socialization for their adult work roles began when they were only five or six. One middle Tennessee woman pinpointed the lesson that young slave children were intended to learn from such early separation from parental protection. "I knew I was a slave," she said, "after I got big enough to know that I couldn't do the things that I wanted to do." Lorenzo Ivy was put into the fields just as soon as he "was large enough to use a hoe" to make tobacco hills. When Henry Johnson "was a little bit a fellow," he was assigned "to pack water to twenty-five and thirty men" in the fields. From there he progressed to the use of a short hoe to "dig weeds out of de crop." George Jackson helped his mistress in her garden. He could "remember cryin'" because she would "jump [him] and beat [him]" when he mistook a cabbage for a weed. Hired out before age ten, Fleming Clark "dr[o]ve cows and work[ed] in de 'bacca fields, pickin' worms off de leaves." Henry Williams was "put to work at six years old . . . clearing off new ground" and "thinn[ing] corn" on his knees. Sarah Gudger recalled that very young children were started in the fields, following the instructions of adults. "Effen de chillun wah too small tuh hoe, dey pull weeds." By age nine, Silas Jackson was already at his adult work in the fields. By age ten, Catherine Slim "wuz doin' women's work" in the fields and in the big house. At age five, Sally Brown was taught to hoe, and she was expected to "keep rat up with the others, 'cause they'd tell [her] if [she] got behin that a run-a-way [slave] would git [her] and split open [her] head and git the milk out'a it." Some young children were assigned to dangerous work. By age eight, Israel Jefferson was a trained "postillion" (i.e., he rode the lead horse for a carriage pulled by four horses). A northern Alabama master used John Finnelly as "de gun rest" when he hunted. John would bend over, so his owner could "puts his gun on [his] back for to git de good aim." What the master killed, John "runs and fotches." Hunting "g[a]ve [John] worryment" when he had to retrieve downed ducks from the streams. John "won't go in dat water till massa hit [him] some licks," but he "couldn't never git use to bein' de water dog for de ducks." Exposed to chemicals and fire hazards, Louis Watkins "ran errands in and out of the [gun]powder mill, under the watchful eye of those in charge."[37]

At very young ages, Appalachian slave children were socialized to work at small tasks and errands at the "big house." A small percentage of children worked alongside mothers in the masters' houses, but less than 14 percent of mountain slaves were full-time domestics. Dan Lockhart "was sold at five years of age." Permanently separated from his family, his earliest task "was to clean knives, forks, candlesticks, etc." At age six, William Davis operated a swinging feather to keep flies away from the white folks' table, and he acted as nurse for two younger white children. Lizzie Grant had no happy memories of her childhood. "Our homelife as children was hell, as we never had any play time at all. From the time we could walk Mistress had us carrying in wood and water and we did not know what it was to get out and romp and play." Similarly, Martha Showvely worked in the master's house by age nine, and she "wasn't 'lowed to sit down. She "had to be doing something all day. Whenebber we was in de presence of any of de white folks, we had to stand up." Most young Appalachian slave girls, and some boys, lost their own childhoods to tend their masters' offspring. Tom McAlpin spent his early years "nuss[ing] de chilluns." One boy "walk[ed] alongside de horse to carry [his young master's] books, den go home and fetch him a hot dinner for noon and go back after him at night to carry dem books." Selected girls were socialized from a young age toward a lifetime of white child care. At seven, Millie Simpkins was "hired out ter nuss de white chilluns," and she was cooking by age ten. Because of the abuse she received at the hands of her mistress, Delia Garlic thought "the' wa'nt no good times" in her childhood. When the baby "hurt it lil hand" one day, the mistress "pick' up the hot iron, an run it all down [her] arm an' han', an' took off the flesh as she done it." Exhibiting the normal curiosity of childhood could be costly for young slave children, as Delia discovered when she was caught aping the behavior of her mistress. Delia had "seen her blackin' her eye-brows with smut from the fire-place, an' one day [she] was workin' roun' in there an' [she] thought [she]'d black [her] eye-brows, jus' fo' fun ... an forgot to wipe it off. So [the mistress] come in an' see [Delia] that-a-way, an' she said, 'You black debbil, I'll show you how to mock your betters,' an' she picks up a piece of stove-wood, an' flails it agin [her] head, an' [Delia] didn't know nothin' more till [she] came to lyin' on the floor."[38]

Because family members were often hired out or assigned to work at a distance from one another, labor migrations weakened bonds between mothers and children. Hannah Valentine tended her grandchildren while her daughters were serving their master in the Governor's Mansion. Because the mothers were away during most of the children's early years, they did "not appear to miss" their absent parents very much. Wylie Nealy had almost no contact with his hired mother. Because her mother was hired out, Liza Tanner was kept by an unrelated woman, whom she came to view as her true parent. She saw her mother only sporadically and her father only "a few times" before he died. Mothers lost control over their offspring when masters selected them as house servants or nurses. These children lived with the white family, away from their parents and away from black community bonds. Until he was old enough to work in the fields, Morris Hillyer thought of his mistress as "the only mother [he] ever knew." Little wonder that Morris "didn't know how to act when he was sent out there among strangers." Until age ten, Catherine Slim slept "in a waggoner's bed," a type of bedroll, on the floor at the foot of her mistress' bed. Purchased as an infant, Easter Brown could not " 'member [her] real ma and pa, and [she] called Marster 'pa' an' Mist'ess 'ma' til [she] wuz 'bout 'leven years old." The daughter of a cook, Betty Cofer was selected at infancy to be trained to domestic service. The young mistress "claimed" her when she was born, so she was quickly removed from the mother to grow up alongside the white child who would eventually become her permanent owner. The daughter of the master's son and the cook, Rachel Cruze was kept as a body servant for her grandmother. Even though she saw her mother often, Rachel "looked upon [the mistress] as [her] mother." At twelve, the mistress "felt [she] should get to know [her] mother better," so Rachel was finally sent to live with her own family.[39]

Masters' Interference in Child Discipline

On the one hand, Appalachian masters left slave children at risk without adequate child care. On the other hand, they extended their intrusion into motherhood by breaking the disciplinary link between parents and children. Masters took seriously their ownership of slave youth and often pre-empted parental authority. Not only did slave masters sell and give away young slaves, but they also assigned them tasks when their parents thought they were either too young, ill, or otherwise indisposed to perform them; punished them without parental knowledge or consent; and sometimes offered "favorites" protection from parental disciplinary measures. It was difficult for slave parents to wrestle control from their masters, particularly when owners believed that all slaves, young and old, were psychologically and cognitively like "children."[40]

Nearly three-fifths of the Appalachian ex-slaves identified the white masters, mistress, or children as the individuals who administered verbal or physical punishment to them most often. In this way, slaveholders undermined the authority of slave parents. Jacob Stroyer supplied a family history that pinpoints the lack of parental authority, the inability to prevent white discipline of children, and the attempt to socialize children to behave in ways that would avert punishment. When Jacob was repeatedly switched by an overseer, he ran to his family for rescue.

Father very cooly said to me, "Go back to your work and be a good boy, for I cannot do anything for you." But that did not satisfy me, so on I went to mother with my complaint and she came out to the man who had whipped me. . . . Mother and he began to talk, then he took a whip and started for her, and she ran from him, talking all the time. I ran back and forth between mother and him until he stopped beating her. After the fight, [the overseer] took me back to the stable yard and gave me a severe flogging. And, although mother failed to help me at first, still I had faith that . . . she would come and stop him, but I looked in vain, for she did not come. Then the idea first came to me that I, with my dear father and mother and the rest of my fellow Negroes, were doomed to cruel treatment through life, and was defenseless. . . . [F]ather and mother could not save me from punishment, as they themselves had to submit to the same treatment. . . . [Later] when I went home to father and mother, I said to them, "Mr. Young is whipping me too much now, I shall not stand it, I shall fight him." Father said to me, "You must not do that, because if you do he will say that your mother and I advised you to do it, and it will make it hard for your mother and me, as well as for yourself. You must do as I told you, my son: do your work the best you can, and do not say anything. . . . Father said, "I can do nothing more than to pray to the Lord to hasten the time when these things shall be done away; that is all I can do."[41]

The disciplinary instruction did not end with the complexities of dealing with white adults without parental support or protection. Part of their early work socialization was intended to teach slave children to obey white youth and to prepare the white children to be masters and mistresses. So long as they were very young and playing in the yard together, Lunsford Lane did not perceive the racial hierarchy. At about age ten, however, Lunsford "discovered the difference between [himself] and [his] master's children. They began to order [him] about, and were told to do so by [his] master and mistress." James Pennington recalled the "tyranny of the master's children." James and his brothers were "required to recognize the young sirs as [their] young masters." The white children were taught to feel superior, and "in consequence of this feeling, they sought to treat [black children] with the same air of authority that their father did the older slaves." At the age of seven, Bethany Veney was caught by her young mistress knocking apples from a tree, and her recollection exemplifies the subtleties of the power arrangement into which slave children were being trained. The young mistress called to them "in a loud and threatening tone, demanding what [they] were doing. Without waiting for a reply, she told [them] to follow her; and, as she led the way down to a blackberry pasture not far off, she endeavored, in a very solemn manner, to impress [them] with the importance of always telling the truth." According to the white youngster, "every little child that had told a lie would be cast into a lake of fire and brimstone, and would burn there forever and ever." When young masters broke the rules, the blame was likely to fall upon an enslaved child. When black youngsters "got into a fuss" with their masters' sons, they paid the price for childhood "insolence." Samuel Sutton's master took him and his "Baby Mars" to the fields "to learn to work." Samuel was instructed to "help him and do what he told me to." Soon as the adult left, "Baby Mars' he'd want to eat," and he would send the black child "ovah to the grocery store." When they were caught, both children were disciplined for being "lazy."[42]

Less than one-quarter of mountain slave children were disciplined solely by parents – most often by their mothers, only rarely by their fathers. Noah Perry provides one of the rare descriptions of an Appalachian slave mother who took charge of her child's discipline. He recalled that his mother "never took much foolishness off of any of the hands." When another slave whipped him for an infraction, his mother "drug him out" of the barn and "give him a good thrashing." Even Noah's master left discipline to the mother, and "told her [when] she had to whip" the boy for improprieties. Noah thought of his mother as the person "who always ha[d] taken [his] part." King describes the motivations behind such child discipline.

Parents, often mothers alone, guided youngsters through the muddle of slavery. Their primary objective was to protect their children and others from harm.... Hardworking, decent, courteous children were not likely to offend anyone; nor would they bring retribution upon their mother. Slave parents expected obedience from their children, and it is not surprising that they have been portrayed as harsh disciplinarians.... The underlying motive for their "harshness" was to demand faithfulness, dependability, and family unity.[43]

Because owners structured the absence of adult males, a majority of mountain slave households were headed by women, like this one located on a small plantation on the Tennessee River outside Knoxville. *Source: Scribner's,* May 1874.

The maintenance and reproduction of labor power was a significant function of the Appalachian slave household. By reproduction of labor power, I mean simply that "the task of the family is to maintain the present work force and provide the next generation of workers, fitted with the requisite skills and values necessary for them to be productive members of the work force." Harsh as it sounds, the slave household was expected "to carry out the repressive socialisation of children. The family must raise children who have internalised hierarchical social relations, who will discipline themselves and work efficiently without constant supervision." In Appalachian slave households, mothers were responsible for implementing most of that socialization. There were several reasons for mothers' harsh discipline of children. On the one hand, family and community members might be punished or sold, for the infractions of children and other family members. On the other hand, mothers were convinced that their own discipline could become a shield for their offspring. Obeying rules and a strong work ethic were taught as strategies to prevent punishment or sale by the master. According to one northern Alabama informant, harsh parental instruction toughened children and prepared them to avoid or to bear future brutality. "All mothers were stric'," she said, "that made children stand fear everywhere they went." Mothers also believed that their own punishment would never be as severe as that doled out by masters and overseers. When Jeff Johnson picked up some of the white children's marbles, his mother "tuck [him] back over ter de big house" and spanked him "right there befo' 'em." Stealing was an infraction for which many Appalachian males were punished severely, so there was reason to make sure that the master did not identify her son as a thief. To prevent worse discipline from the whites, William Mead's mother would whip him "for sassing" the master. Alex Montgomery's overseer "neber did whup [him] but [his] mammy wurk'd on [his] back an' sed [he] wus triflin'."[44]

The complexities of discipline were confusing when children found themselves in a tug-of-war between plantation authority and parental influence. Penny Thompson's youthful confusion exemplifies the complex loyalties that young children must demystify. When abolitionists appeared in the slave quarters to help families escape, Penny overheard adults talking and was " 'fraid dat dey am gwine to takes [her] away." Confused about what was happening, she "den goes to de marster's bed a cryin' an' says to him, Ise don' want to go away." Because of her misplaced allegiance, the master foiled the escape to freedom. Sarah Wilson was more perceptive about the disciplinary conflict. Sarah's mistress named her "Annie," after herself. Because her mother "hate[d] Old Mistress," she despised the imposed name. However, Sarah's mother "was afraid to change it until Old Mistress died." Sarah was in a quandary when both women would call her. "If [she] responded when her mistress called 'Annie' [her] mammy would beat [her] for answering to that name, and if [she] didn't go old mistress would beat [her] for that. That made [her] hate both of them, and [she] got the devil in [her] and wouldn't come to either one."[45]

Family Diasporas as Life-Shaping Events

Only about one-quarter to one-third of all Appalachian slave children experienced life in a family in which both parents were present on a daily basis. Two-thirds of all Appalachian slave children were probably raised by families in which forced labor migrations had caused the absence of fathers. In the day-to-day existence of children in disrupted households, mothers were the center of families, while masters kept fathers somewhere else. Even those who "would git to come home every Saturday night" were sometimes seen by their own children as temporary intruders whom they hardly knew. As a result of the structured absences of adult males, one of every five of the Appalachian ex-slaves reported that they were indifferent toward their fathers. A few Appalachian slave children rejected their fathers, defining them as strangers to whom they owed no allegiance. In one instance, the abroad male "jus' come on Saturday night an' us don' see much of 'im. Us call him 'dat man.' Mammy tol' us to be more 'spectful to 'im cause he was us daddy, but us aint care nuthin' 'bout 'im."[46]

Despite the frequent – and often extended – absences of fathers, most Appalachian slave children knew the identities of their fathers and had pride in who and what they were. In addition, most ex-slaves reported positive attitudes toward their fathers, they blamed masters for paternal absences, and they did not demean their fathers when masters punished them. In one-third of the two-parent families, children admired their fathers' work abilities or artisan skills or the esteem in which others held their labor. For instance, Robert Falls remembered his father as "the best waggoner in all that country." John Van Hook recalled that his father "did anything that came to hand; he was a good carpenter and mechanic and helped the [master] to build mills, and he made the shoes for the settlement." Tom Singleton and Sarah Gudger described their fathers as the labor drivers for their masters. Tom thought of his father as "de one in charge," while Sarah remembered that their master " 'pend on [her] pappy t' see aftah ebbathin' faah him."[47]

Another third of the narrators spoke proudly about their fathers' love and loyalty toward their mothers, about their interference to protect their children, or about acts of visible resistance against masters. For example, Laura Bell recalled that her father "comes up an' taken de whuppin'" when the overseer attempted to punish her mother. Another one of every ten ex-slaves remembered with pride their fathers' indomitable spirits. Robert Falls remembered his father as "a fighter" who was sold four times for his resistance. Others focused upon the persistence of their fathers in regular family contacts in spite of difficult circumstances. Jim Threat admired the risks his father took to resist his master's denial of visitation privileges. When the master terminated his regular weekly trips, Threat's father ran away and hid near his family. "He'd slip in to [the family] at night and hide out in the daytime." Jim's "father stayed out for a few days ... then he came back and give himself up and took his whipping." According to Threat, the master tried to demean the punished male before his family. "When they whupped a slave they made him say 'Oh, pray master' to show that he had to be humble."[48]

Narrators reported two different types of reactions when they witnessed the punishment of their fathers, but they never described their fathers as emasculated, as some contemporary scholars claim. When patrollers "burst into their cabin ... made [his father] pull his shirt off" and then "whupped him hard," Alex Montgomery "cried and cried." Perry Madden and Callie Elder reacted differently. Patrollers "tried to git [Madden's] daddy out so that they could whip him, but they couldn't catch him. They shot him – the paterolers did." To emphasize his reaction, Perry added: "But he whipped them. I mean he was a good man." Denied regular family visitations, Callie Elder's father and grandfather ran away frequently. According to Callie,

Evvytime Pappy runned away [to see her mother], Marse Billy sicked dem hounds on his heels and dey was sho' to ketch him and fetch him back. Dey had to keep knives from Pappy or when dem dogs cotch him, he would jus' cut 'em up and dey would die. When dey got him back to de house, dey would buckle him down over a barrel and larrup him wid a plaited whup.

To demean the men who ran away to their families, masters created special devices of punishment. Callie's grandfather "was so bad 'bout runnin' 'way" to visit his wife and grandchildren, that his master "made him wear long old horns." When the master "told him he could take de horns off his head whilst he was in de meetin' house," Callie's grandfather "dropped dem horns and lit like a rag to de woods, and it tuk de dogs days to find him." When a western Maryland master whipped James Pennington's father, the abuse increased family solidarity. "Each member felt the deep insult that had been inflicted upon [their] head; the spirit of the whole family was roused; [they] talked of it in [their] nightly gatherings."[49]

Only one of every eight of the narrators spoke negatively of their fathers. In these instances, both parents were present in the households everyday, but adult males engaged in negative behavior that disrupted family life. Drinking, domestic violence toward mothers, or promiscuity were identified as the three major causes of children's negative perceptions of their fathers. Thomas Cole remembered his father as "a good lookin man" who was unfaithful to his mother. "I was sposed to take my father's name," Cole indicated, "but he was sech a bad, ornery, no-count sech a human, I jes' taken my old massa's name." Liza Tanner recalled that her stepfather "was mean" to her mother "and beat her," causing several miscarriages. "He got drunk whenever he could get to it," she criticized, and "he went off with other women." Alex Montgomery's parents fought frequently because his father "wuz bad 'bout wimen" and "went off to some udder plantation" every Saturday night. In one instance, the entire slave quarter demanded the rejection of one of the male members. The master was forced to sell one father "cause the other slaves said they wuz gonna kill 'im, cause he had a baby by his own daughter."[50]

Due to their masters' forced labor migration strategies and legal restrictions, fathers were permanently or intermittently absent from two-thirds to three-quarters of all Appalachian slave families. Their absence was exacerbated by the political reality that husbands could not establish legally binding marriages or retain legal authority over their own children. Power lay in the hands of the master, and Appalachian slaveholders stripped black families of all the institutional and legal foundations that were guaranteed to Southern white households – to facilitate easy removal of members for forced labor migrations. On the one hand, the high incidence of marriage and family breakups kept these families fragile and dependent, as Fox-Genovese explains.

Afro-American slave women transmitted their condition to their offspring even if the fathers were free. Their "marriages" to black men, slave or free, had no status in law. They could be separated from spouse or children without any recourse except personal pleas. Slave men could not protect their "wives" from the sexual assaults of white men.... "Husbands" did not support their wives, who worked at the will of the master. They did not provide for their children or even fully determine their preparation for adult life.... [Instead], white male heads of slaveholding households provided slave women with food, lodging, clothing, and medical care, assigned them tasks, supervised their work, disciplined them, determined the destiny of their children, and could impose nonnegotiable sexual demands.

On the other hand, most of these oppressed parents were tenacious and resilient in their efforts to keep alive their family ties. In fact, efforts to maintain and to protect family linkages accounted for a greater incidence of everyday resistance by Appalachian slaves than any other factor.[51]

Because of the absence of husbands and children, a majority of adult Appalachian slave women headed partial families, resided in nonnuclear households, or lived alone. Mothers were deeply scarred by the removals of family members, and we should be careful not to anesthetize our research to the long-term impacts of separations upon enslaved women. How could the horror and grief not have been a shaping force in the family lives of mountain slave women, a majority of whom suffered losses of spouses, children, parents, or siblings? Hannah Valentine wrote to her mistress that she "long[ed] for the time to come" when she would see her relocated husband and children at home again. Even after having been sold away from her western South Carolina family more than four years, Vilet Lester sent a painful plea to her former owner.

Dear Mistress, I cannot tell my fealings now how bad I wish to See ... Mother.... [N]ever before did I no what it was to want to See a parent and could not.... [G]ive my manafold love to mother brothers and sister and pleas tell them to Right to me So I may here from them if I cannot See them.... I want to no whether balium [her son] is married or no. I wish to [k]now what has Ever become of my Presus little girl.... I do wish to See her very mutch.

For more than a year, several middle Tennessee children believed their mother had abandoned them because their master had hired her out and "didn't give her a chance to tell them goodbye."[52]

One northern Alabama man felt the pain of losing a mother who was only one county away. When his master died, the mistress moved his mother and siblings to Huntsville, leaving the young boy to work under the supervision of the overseer. "I tole mah mother good bye, dat was de last time I ever seed her, she never did gits ter come back ter see me and I never could goes in ter see her, and I never seed mah brother and sister any more." Such young children were so traumatized by family losses that they must have carried that grief – and the fear of future losses – into the construction of their own households. Sarah Gudger was separated from her mother throughout her formative years, but she never forgot the circumstances in which her mother died.

I 'membahs when mah ole mammy die.... She sick long time.... I went t' de house and say t' Ole Missie: 'Mah mothah she die today. I wants t' see mah mothah afoah dey puts huh away,' but she look at me mean an' say ... 'git back to yo' wok afoah I wallup you good.' So I went back t' mah wok, with the tears streamin' down mah face ... I wanted t' see mah mammy so.... I 'membahs de time when mah mammy wah alive. I wah a small chile, afoah dey tuk huh [to work on another family plantation].[53]

Through their forced labor migrations, their child labor mechanisms, and their prioritizing of work over family needs, Appalachian masters stole many of the opportunities for slave families to construct fully developed collective histories. When masters and mistresses separated youngsters from parents, they stole from the offspring the linkage with family, and they denied mothers the capacity to nurture their children. In the case of Rachel Cruze, for instance, being raised by the mistress from infancy to age twelve implanted in her memory a family heritage that she could never hold as her own. Even as a grown woman, Rachel still thought of herself in terms of her early bonding with her mistress. "I was their baby, and my first recollections are of sleeping in a little bed at the foot of the one occupied by the Major and Miss Nancy." For many enslaved Appalachian families, permanent disruptions and separations were repeated through several generations. Masters and mistresses had a long reach in their destruction of family heritage, as Jim Threat's genealogy shows.

My father, Jim Threat, belonged to Gum Threat, and my mother, Hannah Allen, was owned by Russell Allen. My grandmother's name was Mary Swine. Old man Swine got overstocked with children and sold her along with a passel of kids to Johnnie Bowman. He sold her to Russell Allen. Dan Threat bought my father in Maryland when he was seven and brought him to Alabama. He never saw his parents again. Dan Threat kept him till his son Gum Threat was grown and married and he gave him and three other slaves to Gum for a wedding present.... My father married my mother while he was living with Dan Threat and he would git to come home every Saturday night.

This enslaved man managed to hold onto his empirical past, but he lost forever the combined memory that might have evolved through normal interaction with grandparents and parents. Like many other black Appalachians who were forcibly separated from family, Jim Threat was alienated "from formal, legally enforceable ties of 'blood.'" To replace that constructed family heritage, he had only an orphan's superficial past in which many kin were only shadows, for whom he had no interpersonal memories. Still those missing people were real. Gutman describes the diaspora history construction through which slave families prevented obliteration of their pasts.

The breakup of a marriage had a "geometric" impact upon the slaves involved. It directly affected a particular husband and wife, their children, their parents, and other kin nearby. It was also known to slave neighbors and to those who came to know the partners after the union's dissolution. Such awareness spread over space following sale, but when children were involved, it also moved forward in time.

Mountain slaves kept alive their individual family histories, teaching young children about a past that belonged to them, even if they had never been permitted to experience it. Even though they lived in communities with low black population densities, black Appalachians kept alive their family histories and the pasts of several generations. Diaspora was also preserved as a central theme of songs constructed by Upper South slaves before the Civil War. "See wives and husbands sold apart, their children's screams will break my heart.... There's a better day a coming," lamented a song recalled in one of the slave narratives. Two northern Alabama songs offered historical record of family disruptions. "I'm motherless, fatherless, sister and brotherless, too," began one lyric. Another mourned that, after the loss of family, it was "a mean, mean world to try to live here, try to stay here till we die."[54]

3 Malnutrition, Ecological Risks, and Slave Mortality

> Learned us to steal, that's what they done. Why we would take anything
> we could lay our hands on, when we was hungry. Then they'd whip us
> for lieing when we say we don't know nothing about it. But it was easier
> to stand, when the stomach was full.
>
> – Robert Falls, eastern Tennessee slave

Forced labor migrations were not the only threats to the survival of
Appalachian slave families. Mountain masters structured ecological and
occupational conditions that exposed black households to higher health
risks than those experienced by the region's whites. In the United States,
slaves died at a frequency only slightly higher than that experienced by
whites. Indeed, after the age of twenty-one, whites and slaves died at
about the same frequency. In sharp contrast to national trends, mountain blacks had a much lower life chance than white Appalachians. In
Augusta County, Virginia, for instance, antebellum physician records reveal a slave mortality rate that was 1.6 times higher than that faced by local
whites. Appalachian slaves averaged eleven days lost work time annually
due to illnesses that masters considered serious enough to relieve them
from duties, and they were exposed to one or more epidemics each year.
Respiratory and digestive ailments, both short-term and chronic, were
the most common causes of slave sickness and mortality. Deceased slaves
averaged only twenty-one years of age in 1850, four to five years younger
than the typical white death. One way to assess the extent of health problems is to examine the physical descriptions that were published for runaway slaves. Among 297 western North Carolina and Blue Ridge Virginia
runaways, 95 percent had two or more visible health conditions or physical deformities. Nearly one-third of the runaways stuttered or had speech
impediments. More than one-fifth had broken or decayed teeth. Scars
from burns, knives, and agricultural tools and missing or deformed fingers were visible on the bodies of one of every seven. Judging from this
runaway sample, probably one of every seventeen Appalachian slaves was
missing an arm or hand or had lost toes due to frostbite. Cancerous tu-
mors were evident on one of every fourteen. In addition to natural causes,

one of every seven bore scars from whippings, and one of every ten had
large scars from dogbites.[1]

The Mountain South exhibited higher slave mortality rates than those
regions of the United States characterized by larger plantations.
Appalachian slaves faced a risk of death considerably higher than the
black mortality rate for the entire South. In 1850, an individual mountain slave was 1.4 times more likely to die than other U.S. slaves. Enslaved
Appalachian males faced a risk of death that was nearly 1.7 times greater
than the mortality rate of white Appalachian males. In some Appalachian
counties, slave mortality rates far exceeded national averages. For instance, mountain Georgia slaves were dying at twice the frequency of
other U.S. slaves. A northern Georgia slave enjoyed a probability of
survival that was only about half that of local whites. Surprisingly, a
West Virginia slave experienced a mortality rate that was 1.6 times higher
than the national average. The region's enslaved women suffered even
higher mortality rates than their male peers. Appalachian slave women
labored under the cloud of death rates that were 1.5 times higher than national averages and 1.8 times higher than the risks faced by Appalachian
white women. What, then, are the explanations for these trends? In the
sections that follow, we will examine shortfalls in basic survival needs, environmental hazards, occupational risks, and malnutrition as the factors
that account for these high regional mortality rates.[2]

Shortfalls in Shoes and Clothing

Three-quarters of adult Appalachian slaves were issued two outfits of
clothing annually: one for winter and one for summer. The remaining
quarter of the adults received only one outfit every fall. Until they were old
enough to work, children wore only long shirt-gowns with "just a hole on
each side for the arms and one for the head." Like other U.S. slaves, black
Appalachians dressed in coarse homespun of different weights: "light
cotton clothes in de summer and wool clothes in de wintah." Heavy jeans
and shirts of "linsey-woolsey" (a blend of wool and cotton) were the
typical male attire for cold weather. Women tried to stay warm by adding
extra layers of thin underskirts. Summer clothing was produced from
lightweight cotton, calico, and gingham. "In de summah de women weah
dresses and aprons made ob linen an' men weah pants and shurts ob
linen." The smallest Appalachian plantations issued only "tow clothes,"
coarse hemp "garments like nightshirts," without trousers or underskirts.
In the late fall, the vast majority of Appalachian masters issued to every
adult one pair of "brogans" or "gator shoes." Still one of every eight adults
received no shoe allotment, and children went barefoot year-round until

they were old enough to work in the fields. According to Will Oats, if eastern Kentucky slaves "wore out their winter shoes before the spring weather they had to do without until the fall."[3]

Cliometricians have estimated that U.S. masters issued adequate home-made clothing to more than four-fifths of all U.S. slaves. This optimistic finding is not supported by the narratives of Mountain South slaves. Shortfalls in annual allocations of clothing and shoes were common, especially during the cold months and at industrial sites. Nearly two-thirds of the Appalachian slave narratives include negative assessments of the adequacy of masters' allocations of clothing and shoes. Northern Alabama field hands even noted such shortfalls in a song that began "Lord, I'm standin' here wonderin', will a matchbox hold my clothes?" Their complaints centered around the hardships caused by the failures of their masters to meet their basic needs, to protect them from work injuries and health risks, and to afford them humane privacy. Two-thirds of the Appalachian slaves lamented that their allotted clothing and shoes did not last or were inadequate, so they were forced to subsidize their masters' allotments through personal purchases. Hats, Sunday wear, mittens, coats, and socks were not usually issued by masters. Appalachian slaves also complained that they had so few clothes they could not keep themselves clean. One western North Carolina slave "didn't have but one dress. When it got dirty, [she] went down to de creek and washed it ... but had to put it back on before it got dry."[4]

To exacerbate matters, nearly 15 percent of Appalachian slaves complained that their masters were erratic in their clothing and shoe allotments. When masters were in financial trouble, laborers were short-changed. Jim Threat reported that his struggling master "jest didn't have any regard for his slaves." To cut costs, the northern Alabama owner did not allocate enough clothes for workers to "possibly git along with." Appalachian narratives are particularly critical of the unreliability of masters who owned fewer than ten slaves, for they did not make clothing or shoe allotments on a regular annual basis. One Kanawha County owner provided light wool clothes, but no shoes. As a result, his two slaves "wrapped [their] feet up in cold weather" with "just rags." Reports of shortages occur frequently in the manuscript records for industrial masters. For example, Buffalo Forge workers experienced repeated shortages of clothing and shoes from the 1820s through the 1860s. About 5 percent of the Appalachian slaves described masters who "played favorites" and distributed clothing and shoes unevenly. At one small Pocohontas County, West Virginia, plantation, only "the master's favorites had some kind of footwear." At the Oxford Iron Works, the employer withheld the "good quality" apparel to reward selected artisans. A "coat of blue cloth &

waistcoat of scarlet flannel" were allocated to a few while the majority received only "coats, vests & pantaloons of cotton." When supplies ran out, "watermen" got nothing.[5]

More than one-third of the Appalachian slaves complained about the discomfort of their coarse apparel. Shirts, dresses, and pants were cut from sacklike patterns; so "sometimes it would fit and sometimes it wouldn't." Appalachian slaves frequently "had to wear tore breeches and tore shirts," and they "never did know what a undershirt was in dem days, and no underwear of any kind, summer nor winter." When a British traveler complained about the "miserable manner in which the slaves were clad" at the luxurious White Sulphur Springs, the spa operator retorted that "slaves were among the happiest of human beings" because "they were remarkably able to endure hardships." Shoes did not fit any better because they were issued only once a year. Usually, the shoemaker collected a shoe pattern for each slave, and the forms were rarely adjusted. Constructed of wood soles and roughly tanned leather, slave "brogans" were "hard as rocks." To "keep 'em from rubbin' de skin off [their] foots," they "had to put rags inside 'em." The shoes were "rough and hard," so slaves would "render up de grease or taller" from wild game to try to soften the leather. Some masters passed worn-out boots to male slaves who constructed "clap-down shoes" by affixing the boot legs to their brogans. Mountain slaves personified the discomfort of the wood-soled shoes in this chorus of a song that was popular in West Virginia:

> The Devil he wore hickory shoes.
> And if you don't watch
> he'll slave it on you.
> All my friends, all my friends
> been taken away.[6]

There were noticeable gender differences in the criticisms offered by Appalachian slaves. More than one-third of the males complained that their allotted clothing and shoes did not protect them from work-related injuries. Field workers on the smallest plantations often wore "tow clothes" that were coarse and scratchy, causing inflammations and rashes on sweaty skin. Some field hands were issued shirts only for winter, so they worked in the fields without protection from contact with tools, plants, or work animals. One or two annual issues of clothes and shoes simply were not sufficient to withstand the rigors of field work, construction, or heavy industrial labor. Workers at industrial sites were most endangered by their inadequate apparel, for there was no consideration of safety factors. At the region's iron manufactories, salt wells, railroad construction sites, timbering sites, and coal mines, shoe shortages were common. Iron and coal mines were "so rough they c[ould] not work with out them." When men worked without shoes, they were frequently injured and "layed up." After being short-changed in apparel, Buffalo Forge slaves broke into the company store to steal shoes and clothing.[7]

Appalachian slave women focused on a clothing issue that males did not notice. Clothing and fabric allotments were too skimpy and irregular to meet the physical needs of women during their childbearing years. To manage menstruation during the nineteenth century, white women sewed muslin pads and boiled them for repeated use. One can only speculate about how slave women handled the hygiene problems associated with monthly menses or the childbirth process under conditions in which water was contaminated, weekly laundry was done in the creeks, and fabric and rags were too precious to be discarded. Women's dresses were made during the fall and issued around Christmas. "De dresses had done wore thin 'nough for hot weather by de time winter was gone," so Appalachian slave women "wore dem same clothes straight on through de summer." There were no special considerations for the bodily changes of pubescent or pregnant females, so their once-a-year dresses were painfully tight and "would split" as they gained weight. In order to pick tobacco, women had to tie up their dresses around their necks, but owners did not supply them underwear. Sally Brown complained about having a "sick hard time" because she had no underwear to use during field work. Throughout her pregnancy, Delia Garlic "never had a underskirt," so she felt her privacy invaded every time she worked with the men in the fields. During harvests, pregnant women filled large baskets and had to "move de basket longs" the rows. Skimpy, constraining dresses offered little protection from injury or from gawking eyes. In addition, nursing mothers also experienced health hazards because they had insufficient clothing to keep their breasts clean or comfortable.[8]

More than half the Appalachian slaves complained that their shoes and clothing were inadequate to shield them during the winter months. Most Appalachian masters expected slaves to acquire their own socks, underwear, hats, mittens, and overcoats. Many masters used the same cloth in winter and summer, expecting slaves to stay warm by layering. Others provided thin jackets or coats that were to be added on top of layered clothing. Anderson Furr reported that it was common for northern Georgia masters to issue one yearly outfit that was "made new for winter. By summer dey had done wore thin." When the weather got bitterly cold, Furr's owner "give [them] old coats" that the white family "had done most wore out," so the laborers "warn't none too warm." One Fannin County, Georgia, worker used "homespun jeans pinned around his head," while one western North Carolina slave mother "twist rushes" to make hats for the family. At Monticello, Thomas Jefferson allocated winter blankets only once every three years, and he provided wool "for stockings to those who w[ould] have it spun and knit for themselves."[9]

Overcrowded and Inadequate Housing

Throughout North America and Appalachia, the typical agricultural slave dwelling was a one-room log cabin about twelve feet by fourteen feet in size. Recent archaeological digs have supported the perception of mountain slaves that their "houses wasn't nothin' to brag about." These single-family cabins "consisted of one room with one door and one window. The most part of one end was taken up by a huge fireplace made of mud and sticks." John Finnelly recalled that slaves on his small Jackson County, Alabama, plantation "have de cabins of logs with one room and one door and one window hole and bunks for sleepin'." As travelers observed, slave cabins stood in stark contrast to the dwellings of mountain masters. At Monticello, for instance, a visitor commented that Jefferson's slave cabins were small and "poor," forming "a most unpleasant contrast with the place that rises so near them." Because there was a status hierarchy in Appalachian slave housing, about 10 percent lived in units that had extra amenities like wood or stone floors, extra storage space in the lofts, or adjacent sheds. For instance, Ben Chambers recalled that his northern Alabama owner "had li'l log houses" for most of his laborers, "but dey hab a good frame house for us 'cause my mama was de cook for de white folks." One middle Tennessee slave was convinced that this differentiation had less to do with the slave's occupation than with the desire of the master to "keep from spoiling the looks of the big house."[10]

Appalachian masters who owned twenty or more slaves more often used multifamily dwellings. For example, at Brabson Ferry Plantation in mountainous Sevier County, Tennessee, the owner sheltered forty-nine slaves in only three buildings. About one-fifth of Appalachian slave families lived in multifamily cabins that masters termed "Double Houses." These larger dwellings were constructed with the "chimley in de middle," so "two families [could] live in 'em." One of every seven slave families lived in a room or small space in the master's house or business. Some slept in "one room of the big house," but Jim Threat's mother and children had no home except a "Coosa-filley" bed in the kitchen. Unmarried servants, like Julia Daniels, might live "in the back yard in a little room by the back door," in tiny sheds that were used for other purposes, or in dilapidated cabins. Appalachian slave cabins were crudely furnished, often with no more than "a homemade bed and a chair or two." On the smallest plantations, slaves slept on the ground on mattresses made of

This Page County, Virginia, cabin was typical of the dwellings in which mountain slaves lived. Note the leaning wood chimney chinked with mud, designed to be kicked away from the house when it caught fire. *Source:* Page, *Social Life*, p. 105.

shucks, moss, or grass or on piles of rags. In most dwellings, beds were "lak shelves. Holes wuz bored in de side of de house, two in de wall and de floor," in order to hold the poles that formed the frames. Ropes or wood slats held in place makeshift "ticks" that were stuffed with straw, hay, bark, corn shucks, or grass. In addition to beds, they had "benches and a rough table and a box for to put clo's in. Sometime dey jes' hang em up on pegs on de wall." Slave households "didn't have stoves to cook on, no lamps and not even candles." Martha Cunningham "would take a rag and sop it in lard to make lights."[11]

Industrial slaves lived in worse housing than agricultural slaves; however, such Appalachian housing arrangements were not that different from that supplied to industrial slaves throughout the country. One of every ten mountain slaves lived in dormitories at industrial sites where several might be crowded into single, large rooms. However, the most ecologically dangerous conditions were experienced by one of every eight Appalachian slaves who were assigned to temporary sheds at construction or industrial sites. For instance, living conditions were inhumanly bad in the region's gold mining boom towns. In Auraria, Georgia, slaves were housed in tiny cabins in which they could "scarcely stand upright." At Blue Ridge Virginia and western North Carolina gold mines, slaves were crowded into lean-tos "of a real primitive order," adjacent to the large frame houses of the "respectable gentlemen and master miners." Enslaved gold miners "didn' have no houses, jes kinder shelters dey th'ow together." According to one engineer, "no permanent fixtures [we]re made at the mines for the accommodation of the workers. They all encamp[ed] out of doors, each little company three or four by themselves, sometimes under temporary coverings, made by a few boards, or formed by stretching a few blankets over poles." Similarly, railroad laborers slept and cooked in square pens "made of pine poles, with large cracks," with "no chimney and no floor, no bed clothing and no cooking utensils," in surroundings that were "nothing like as good as the ordinary stable." "Rock was my pillow, cold iron was my bed," sang Talladega, Alabama, slaves who were hired out to work at railroad construction sites. At the Bath Iron Works, two of the seven cabins were "very small & rough, not larger than a common size chicken coop."[12]

Such housing conditions posed a number of ecological threats to family survival, for Appalachian slaves experienced a greater degree of overcrowding than other North American plantations. On average, there were 5.3 persons housed in U.S. slave cabins. In sharp contrast, Mountain South plantations averaged 7.2 slaves per dwelling. Appalachian slaves lived in more crowded conditions than their white or Cherokee masters who averaged only about six persons in much larger dwellings. George

Waters, one of the wealthiest Cherokee slaveholders, provided only seven houses for a hundred slaves. The predominance of one-room cabins for slave housing resulted from planter preconceptions of an Anglo-American cabin tradition that was common among the lower classes. In Blue Ridge Virginia, for instance, poor white landless laborers lived in mud-chinked huts. In eastern Kentucky, the typical slave dwelling was "a structure which was identical with those lived in by many poor whites of that era." While the type of housing and amount of space may have been similar, Appalachian poor whites lived in much less crowded conditions than mountain slaves. Poor white landless farm laborers lived in households that averaged only 5.3 persons.[13]

Appalachian slave narratives provide colorful language to underscore these conditions. Sarah Wilson's family "lived all huddled up in a bunch in a little one-room log cabin." According to John Van Hook, "there was never but one room to a hut, and they warn't particular about how many they put in a room." Another middle Tennessee slave recalled that unrelated families were thrust together "in the same cabin, just as many as could get in, men and women all together." At a West Virginia lumber camp, slaves lived in rude lean-tos "barely wide enough for five or six men to lie in, closely packed side by side." In addition to being crowded inside their dwellings, slaves were also compressed into quarters that were built in rows or in a circle, with only a few feet between cabins. At one of the West Virginia salt company towns, Booker T. Washington's family resided "in the midst of a cluster of cabins crowded closely together." There were a number of health risks associated with overcrowding. To alleviate the summer heat and humidity, some mountain slaves "slept in the barn with the horses and cows," exposing themselves to mold, parasites, livestock-borne diseases, and filthy conditions. Because sick people were not isolated, infectious diseases spread rapidly. Cholera, flux, typhoid, whooping cough, measles, diphtheria, or smallpox quickly assumed epidemic proportions and caused high death tolls. Because she was "puny and sick all de time," Filmore Hancock's mother transmitted tuberculosis to all the children crowded into one room with her. In Fauquier County, Virginia, a streptococcal skin infection killed nine slaves.[14]

Environmental Risks to Family Survival

Because of their lack of sanitation and clean water, North American slave quarters exhibited the same dangerous ecological conditions that characterize urban slums of contemporary poor nations. Even though Appalachian plantations were small by global standards, the environmental risks to families were high. Appalachian masters were less wealthy and more vulnerable to narrow profit margins than Lower South planters. Consequently, they were less willing to expend funds to weatherize slave cabins, to build safe water systems, or to inoculate the entire population. Moreover, they owned fewer laborers who might be shifted from cash-producing work to clean up the grounds. Appalachian masters usually assigned laborers to repair and build slave cabins only during the winter, so routine sanitation was left to the volunteer efforts of overloaded slave families. Human waste was cleared and raked only annually, but most mountain masters did not construct latrines or toilets for their slave quarters. As is evidenced in numerous manuscript collections, the common practice among Appalachian slaveholders was to ignore sanitation problems until they experienced epidemic outbreaks and were instructed by local doctors to clean their grounds.[15]

Since Appalachian slave families lived in more crowded conditions than other North American slaves, sanitation problems were magnified. Only about 15 percent of Southern farms had privies. Instead, males used the woods; and female chamber pots were emptied into creeks, gardens, or stables. Rarely were there privies in the Appalachian slave quarters. Slaves went outdoors, and the "night soil" was used to manure fields, thereby contaminating fruits and vegetables and exposing barefoot slaves to disease. Work in the family garden and the improper disposal of human feces contributed to the high incidence of worms and parasites among slave children. Refuse from the big house was dumped in the yard of the slave quarters where families could engage in garbage picking to retrieve usable household items and food remnants. Slave families usually dumped their own debris immediately behind their cabins. Often livestock were penned behind the slave houses, and hogs and chickens wandered loose. In northern Georgia gold villages, trash and dead animals were left to accumulate in the streets and alleys. Subsequently, the community was scourged with epidemics of measles, smallpox, scarlet fever, typhoid, and cholera. Overcrowding, lack of sanitation, and frequent hog drives kept dysentery, typhus, and influenza virulent throughout the warm months. Because there were no sanitary regulations in West Virginia salt company towns, "the filth about the cabins was often intolerable." In the absence of windows and screens, slave cabins swarmed with flies, mosquitoes, and other disease-bearing insects. Between 1830 and 1850, slaves died in great numbers at the West Virginia salt wells where cholera repeatedly erupted. In 1832, an epidemic of Asiatic cholera killed slaves in greater numbers than whites. In 1833, one-half of West Virginia's salt furnaces stopped production because slaves were dropping "everyday more or less with that fatal Epedimic the Cholera." Over a ten-day period, eighteen slaves died. In one of the longest epidemics to strike the salines, one-third of the deaths were blacks, and one hundred slaves died in three months.[16]

Three-quarters of all Appalachian slaves lived on dirt floors or out-doors on the ground. Even though Thomas Jefferson floored his stables with rock slabs, he housed his slaves in cabins with dirt floors. Living on damp soil caused a higher incidence of tetanus. Bacteria and insects found a breeding ground and were carried on bare feet, and the damp, moldy floor magnified the incidence of respiratory illnesses. Children crawled and played on dirt floors, picking up worms, insect larvae, par-asites, and sometimes engaging in dangerous "dirt eating." Because of the overcrowded conditions, lice proliferated. The "inspection of heads" and the use of cotton cards to comb out nits dropped hundreds of the parasites onto dirt floors. "The young white men liked to visit the quar-ters and have the slaves search their heads. They would stretch full length upon the cabin floors" while slave children combed their lice onto the dirt. Peculiar to Upper South slave cabins were the root cellars that were the only space for hoarding food, seeds, tools, and personal items. Stored vegetables and food were often found to be loaded with "fishing worms" or "sow bugs," no doubt contributing to the high incidence of digestive ailments and dysentery. The root cellars attracted rats and flies into the cabins. In addition to carrying disease, rats frequently bit sleeping chil-dren. Root cellars were also used by slaves to conceal their pilfering, so garbage and rotting food accumulated, becoming a source of disease and the spread of epidemics. One Appalachian master described the ecolog-ical risks associated with such underground storage. On his Blue Ridge Virginia plantation, "typhoid broke out in an old negro cabin, closely underpinned." When the epidemic continued to spread uncontrollably, the physician instructed him "to tear away the underpinning and have all the filth cleaned up." When the sanitation process had begun, he "found an accumulation of foul matter in layers almost denoting the number of years it had been collecting."[17]

Because mountain masters were unwilling to invest funds to dig wells, clean water was often in short supply, even for drinking. Most Appalachian slaves collected rainwater in open cisterns or depended on creeks, springs, nearby rivers, and stagnant ponds for drinking water, for bathing, and for weekly laundry. Alex Montgomery reported that his northern Georgia master dug a second well near the road so that passers-by "could stop an' draw water." However, "down in de quarters dar was no well an' we had to git water out frum a spring." The slaves complained about this inequity, for they were forced to wash themselves and their clothes in the same spring; and the plantation livestock were watered there. Moses Grandy's family experienced the kinds of dirty water that characterizes many contemporary poor countries. When her children needed water during the work day, the mother "sought for it in any hole or puddle formed by falling trees or otherwise: it was often full of tadpoles or insects: she strained it, and gave it round to each of us in the hollow of her hand." In addition to being loaded with parasites and bacteria, these open water sources were polluted by the seepage of human and animal waste and by the improper disposal of garbage. One western North Carolina master constructed slave cabins immediately adjacent to the spring, causing it to be contaminated by all kinds of waste. On another plantation, the owner housed his slaves in cabins above the creek. After runoff swept human and animal waste into the stream, a typhoid epidemic killed fifty slaves and several whites.

Appalachian slaves heavily depended upon natural waterways that were already endangered by 1840. Rapid deforestation of the mountains and hills caused repeated flooding and carried human and animal waste and debris into the springs, creeks, and rivers. The regular movement of livestock drives across the region left behind cholera and cowpox, as sick hogs and cattle transported diseases to the waterways they crossed. Since the Mountain South exported most of its commodities on river craft, the region's largest waterways were engorged with floating debris, dead animals, and human waste. As a result, Appalachian river towns were gripped with annual bouts of dysentery, typhoid, cholera, and other fevers. Because slaves had little or no access to wells, their mortality from contaminated water far exceeded the death toll among whites.[18]

At industrial sites, chemical waste exacerbated the ecological degradation. Appalachian coal mines, salt wells, copper smelts, sawmills, tanneries, iron furnaces, paper mills, textile enterprises, and grain mills poured tons of deadly residues into the air and the water of their laborers. In the region's gold towns, the mercury drainoff contaminated springs, creeks, and rivers. Ore was first ground into a fine powder; then "slaves put a thin layer of mercury" into a wooden trough. Workers caught the runoff and repeated the process several times. "The common mode of working [wa]s ... first, to pick out all the visible grains they can find, and throw the remaining mass into a heap, and afterwards ... to separate the minute particles thoroughly by means of mercury. The amalgam so obtained [wa]s then ... exposed to the action of fire; by which quicksilver [wa]s distilled off in vapour, while the gold remain[ed] behind." The mine runoff carried sulphur, copper, and mercury into streams, killing fish and wildlife and causing "chronic diareah and flux" among people who used those creeks for drinking, bathing, or laundry.[19]

Winter heating posed additional ecological dangers for slave families. Cabins were damp and cold because windows were covered only with

This slave quarter had a well, avoiding the scarcity of safe water that placed so many black Appalachian children at risk. Several depicted sanitation hazards caused high mortality rates among mountain slaves. *Source:* Library of Congress.

loose wood shutters, and cracks between logs "wuz chinked wid clay." "When that dirt would fall off," recalled a Warren County, Tennessee, woman, "you could look out and see the snow falling." Sometimes, the inside "would be full of snow." While constructing a railroad line in western South Carolina, slaves slept on pine boards in "miserable shanties along the line." Because the fireplaces were "clumsily constructed," most of the heat "ascend[ed] the chimney," leaving the cabins "bitterly cold and uncomfortable." Slave cabin chimneys were only "big enough ter take all de knots" that did not generate sufficient heat. Thomas Cole provides the explicit detail we need to comprehend the problem. The masters and overseers "had chimneys made of rocks," and they were "big enuff ter put a stick of cordwood in." Thus, whites consumed only "straight wood with outten any knots" while "all de knots was put off on de slaves."[20]

To exacerbate matters, the chimney was a fire hazard. Above the fireplace, the chimney was built of mud, straw, and sticks. "These chimneys were so easily destroyed by fire that they were often built to lean away from the house and were only held in place by wooden poles." In the event of fire, "a simple kick of the prop would topple a flaming stack away from the wall, saving the house itself from fire." Cabin fires and water scarcity were even blended into a popular Upper South slave song. While they picked cotton, northern Alabama laborers chanted: "House catch on fire, and ain't no water 'round." Sleeping near the fireplace could also cause serious injuries. Since slaves "didn't have much bedclothes," they would often have to sit up at night "to keep good and warm." In open lean-tos, railroad workers slept packed together around a fire that popped out and inflamed the wood shavings upon which they slept. Ann Ladly's mother "got burnt to death" because "she lay down with her back to de fire, and a blazing log fell out and cotched her dress on fire."[21]

Occupational Hazards

Because they were much more often employed in nonagricultural occupations than local whites or other U.S. slaves, black Appalachians were at greater risk of mortality as a result of industrial working conditions. Nonagricultural slaves were exposed to greater occupational hazards than farm laborers. According to Starobin, "the tendency to drive industrial slaves to the utmost, and to feed, clothe, and shelter them at subsistence levels, as well as the inadequate medical knowledge of the time, contributed to a tragic incidence of disease and fatality in virtually all industrial occupations." Permanent disabilities and deaths were so common that insuring industrial slaves was "a very general precaution with owners." Because so many Appalachian slaves were hired outside agriculture, national insurance companies established agencies in those counties that were most industrialized. For example, New York Life and Lynchburg Hose and Fire employed Appalachian agents who were instructed to shield the company against slaves who had been devalued through dangerous occupations. To protect itself from collusion between local doctors and masters, New York Life Insurance kept two physicians on its payroll to assess the risk of potential policyholders. Agents could only "Insure the negroes to an amount equal to three fourths of their value," and this scale was often adjusted to reflect the slave's past work history outside agriculture.[22]

Two contemporary observers described the daily environs facing Appalachian slaves who were hired out to coal mines. "No one has any conception of the apparently perilous attempt in going down these shafts, until he has experienced it," observed a Baptist minister. "The distance and the view descending are truly frightful." Booker T. Washington recalled that "it was fully a mile from the opening of the coal-mine to the face of the coal, and all, of course, was in the blackest darkness." Women, children, and males were segregated into different areas because the mine "was divided into a large number of different rooms." Slave laborers "worked day and night except Sundays – when the water [wa]s drawn [off] . . . to keep the works below from being flooded." Slaves did backbreaking work to drain shafts with one-hundred-gallon buckets. In western Maryland, coal mines often filled with foul air and water, but the only escape route was "one bucket" that carried only a few slaves at a time to safety. Because of the dangers, Appalachian masters were reluctant to hire their slaves for coal production. Miners died in great numbers from pneumonia, respiratory diseases, dysentery, typhoid, and cholera caused by the pollution of air, water, and food. Serious injuries from cave-ins, fires, explosions, and floods were common. Between 1844 and 1846, for example, one West Virginia company recorded six horrible deaths. One slave died within a few hours when his "Arm [was] Broke by Slate and coal falling on him." When the roof caved in a few months later, four slaves suffered massive damage to arms, legs, hands, and fingers. The sixth slave was "suffocated, crushed, and killed" in a collapsing coal bank, a type of accident that also occurred frequently at an eastern Tennessee iron works.[23]

Conditions were equally bad at the region's gold mines and iron furnaces where slaves faced frequent accidents, landslides, flooding, and exposure to deadly chemical residues. Iron works generated sulphur fumes that "ma[d]e the hands faint." At gold mines and coal mines, slaves frequently were required to work in standing water, in all kinds of weather. Some western North Carolina masters were reluctant to hire workers to nearby gold mines because they feared that health risks would permanently impair the value of their slaves. Smoke, chemicals, and long hours characterized the workplaces of slaves who were hired out to tobacco factories. Laborers routinely suffered from skin rashes, eye irritations, and respiratory infections, and many developed tobacosis, a chronic disease similar in symptoms to black lung. At the region's copper smelters and salt wells, smoking boilers, "mournful screaking of the machinery, day and night," and deadly vapors killed vegetation, browned the air with noxious mists, and raised noise to unbearable levels. In southwestern Virginia, one hired slave ran away because the iron furnace manager "wished him to work in the Ore Bank and it was so dangerous that all [the] white hands had quit on that account."[24]

Transportation enterprises proved to be no safer for slaves. Landslides and falls in hilly, mountainous territory claimed workers' lives. After a railroad contractor hired sixty slaves, one eastern Tennessee master complained that the employer "drove them till they could hardly stand, and did not give them half what they ought to eat." Railroad laborers faced weather challenges year-round. One builder noted that "the only chance we have to escape in this climate in such changeable weather is not to expose the hands more than we are obliged to do." Even in the springtime and summer, slaves "suffer[ed] very much from numonia ... or Pleurisy." When they had to clear tracks of snow, slaves developed frostbite and were at greater risk of injury. Although safer than railroad construction, work on rivers and canals jeopardized slaves as well. Drownings and falls were common among slaves who worked for canals or river craft. Slaves who worked on steamboats and smaller vessels could be injured by low-hanging trees and by sudden spring freshets. A western South Carolina slave "got in de way of de pole and it hit him in one of his temples and he fell over in de water dead." River and canal workers "tote[d] all the freight aboard and back to land again on their heads and shoulders, and it [wa]s crushing work." At boat landings along Appalachian waterways, depots, warehouses, or mills were "found on the edge of a rude bank, and the boats r[a]n up close as they c[ould]." Because there was "no staircase, pier, or wharf-boat," slaves "tumbled[d] up and down the bluff." Landslides were common, as the muddy banks "loosen[ed] and crumble[d]," carrying down into the water and onto workers below as much as a ton of soil.

Ecological conditions also took their toll. Steamboat roustabouts were always "grimed with the dust" and chemical residue from the items they loaded and unloaded. "Thousands of tons of debris float[ed] behind, beside, and ahead" of the boats that plied Appalachian rivers. Workers hired out to regional steamboats "complain[ed] very much about their sleeping quarters (being in the hull of the boat) and sa[id] it [wa]s killing them." One Appalachian master feared the health of his hired hands was "in danger from such a life." Damp bunks and bedding kept slaves sick with colds, fevers, and respiratory ailments. Because of the polluted water and the overcrowded housing, epidemics spread rapidly among railroad and river workers. To exacerbate matters, hired workers carried the deadly disease home to their families. Near Christmas, smallpox "broke out on the James River and Kanawha Canal." Since the company was only a

Steamboat roustabouts catching a brief rest on an Ohio River wharf at Charleston, West Virginia. In addition to the dangers of bad food, frequent injuries, and lung infections, such hire-outs exposed Appalachian slaves to frequent epidemics of malaria, smallpox, typhoid, and cholera. *Source: Harper's, 1855.*

few days from the end of its annual contracts, hirelings were returned to their owners, "spreading epidemic through the countryside" due to the "culpable & criminal neglect" of the Canal.[25]

Malnutrition, Disease, and Adult Mortality

Since the early nineteenth century, writers have debated whether slave diets were adequate. In the 1970s, Fogel and Engerman argued that slave diets were substantial calorically and probably exceeded levels of most required nutrients. Height estimates have been utilized to determine that slaves eventually achieved good enough diet to catch up with whites in growth. Critics counter that these approaches ignore (a) whether the diet was sufficient to fuel the required work efforts and (b) whether methods of storage and preservation caused food shortages and contamination.

Therefore, recent revisionist research has directed attention more sharply to nutritional deficiencies. Because of chronic malnutrition, contended Kiple and King, North American slaves experienced a diminished recovery rate from diseases and a lower life expectancy than whites. More than four-fifths of slave calories were derived from corn and pork, with more calories consumed from fat and carbohydrates than from protein sources. Slave diets were probably also low in iron, calcium, niacin, the Vitamin B complex, Vitamin C, and Vitamin D. The slaves' year-round survival staple was corn, a food that presented special nutritional problems. Only about 5 percent of the iron in corn is absorbed by the body, and maize rapidly loses thiamine content in storage. To receive needed minerals and vitamins, slaves could only depend upon erratic seasonal supplements from orange sweet potatoes, a few fruits, molasses, and some green vegetables. Because of several genetic factors, slaves needed diets that supplied higher levels of certain nutrients than did whites. Even if slaves were fed the same diet as white laborers, African-Americans would have exhibited malnutrition to a greater degree. As Kiple and King observed, West Africa endowed people with "marvelous mechanisms of protection for survival in that region. However these same mechanisms contained the potential for provoking severe nutritional difficulties once their possessor was removed from West Africa's specialized environment." Consequently, the most important line of inquiry is not whether the slave diet was adequate in calories but whether the nutrients were appropriate for persons of West African descent. Because of their high incidence of milk intolerance, African-Americans received only about one-third to one-half of the average daily requirement of calcium. Moreover, the slave diet was filled with foods that decreased absorption of the low levels of calcium that were acquired from fruits and vegetables. Sickle cell anemia and the sickling trait increased slave needs for foods that had high levels of iron and folic acid, but slave diets were already low in these nutrients.[26]

According to Fogel's latest research, the daily energy intake of adult slaves was typically 2,500 to 3,000 calories; and slave diets were "substantial by the standards of the day for workers." There is no question, he contended, that the slave diet was sufficient to maintain the slave's body weight and general health. Still, he added, research has shifted to complex health issues that are only now attracting scholarly attention.

That the average diet of U.S. slaves was both high in calories and varied in nutrients does not necessarily imply that it was nutritionally adequate. The nutritional adequacy of a diet does not depend merely on the intake of nutrients but also on the claims made against these nutrients by work, disease, and other environmental conditions. Even if the average quantities of food consumed by U.S. slaves were greater than the quantities consumed by most free working classes at the time, the nutritional status of U.S. slaves could have been far worse than that of most free working classes because of the greater intensity of their work or greater exposure to disease. Moreover, even if the *average* diet was sufficient to meet the varied claims on it and still provide good health by the standards of the time, not all slaves received the average diet or experienced only average claims against their diets.[27]

Recent revisionist research calls attention to three aspects of slave nutrition that are pivotal to an investigation of Appalachian slaves. First, there was a significant difference between the dietary experiences of slaves on small and large plantations. Large plantations offered slaves greater diet variety than small plantations where important supplements, like molasses, were issued only about half as often. In fact, hunger and malnutrition were most extreme on small plantations with one to five slaves. Because most Appalachian masters were small slaveholders, does that suggest that malnutrition was more prevalent among slaves who lived in this region? One way to determine the likelihood of slave hunger is to measure the food outputs of Appalachian masters. According to mountain slave narratives, less than 10 percent of the region's plantations purchased food supplements for black laborers. On the other hand, enumerator manuscripts for the 1860 Census of Agriculture provide evidence that hunger and malnutrition were most likely to occur on Appalachian plantations where masters owned fewer than twenty slaves. Small slaveholders produced corn, wheat, and pork at levels that would not have ensured slaves the same per-capita food consumption enjoyed by laborers on nonslaveholding farms. Masters who owned fewer than ten slaves produced essential food grains and swine at levels that could not have permitted adequate food allowances. Antebellum adults consumed 24.8 corn equivalencies yearly in grains and meat, but small mountain slaveholdings produced these essential foods at levels that would have permitted adult slaves only two-thirds of the annual food requirement. The regional picture is complicated further when we assess the likelihood of hunger on the region's staple-producing plantations. Mountain masters who cultivated tobacco or cotton were simply not producing enough grains and meat to allocate adequate annual rations to their slaves. When they cultivated export staples, not even Appalachian masters who owned more than twenty slaves produced enough grain and meat to prevent malnutrition.[28]

The Appalachian slave narratives support this quantitative evidence about low per-capita food production. Western Maryland slaves documented food inequities in this song:

> We raise de wheat,
> Dey gib us de corn.
> We bake de bread,

Dey gib us de cruss.
We sif de meal,
Dey gib us de huss.
We peal de meat,
Dey gib us de skin.

Indeed, Appalachian ex-slaves reported that their masters supplied them inadequate food more than twice as often as did other U.S. ex-slaves. In addition, Appalachian slaves were more likely to be malnourished because they were employed in nonagricultural occupations three to five times more frequently than their counterparts in the Lower South. On the whole, the diet of U.S. nonagricultural slaves was probably much worse than the food supply received by farm workers. Starobin found that "most industrial slaves lived at a subsistence level; their food, clothing, and shelter were barely adequate to their everyday needs." Since few of them were permitted to hunt or grow gardens, industrial workers rarely received fruits or vegetables to supplement weekly rations of salt pork, cornmeal, and molasses. Clearly, those Appalachian slaves owned by nonagricultural masters fared the worst, for nonfarm sites produced grains and swine at levels that could have met less than half the annual food needs of adult laborers.[29]

Research about the typical U.S. slave diet suggests a second line of inquiry. Appalachian narratives document that corn and fat pork were the staples of regional slave diets, with erratic and limited variations. Were mountain slaves, consequently, more likely to be malnourished? Nearly 60 percent of the Appalachian ex-slaves indicated that their masters provided meat rations of fat pork or pork scraps, which slaves supplemented with wild game and fish. Less than 15 percent of Appalachian slaves received regular weekly rations of mixed fat and lean meats. One-fifth of Appalachian ex-slaves reported that they received almost no meat from their masters except occasional dried fish; these workers were forced to acquire most of their own meat through hunting or fishing. Appalachian industrial masters provided second- and third-grade fat pork and cornmeal, with few additional supplements. Recent archaeological digs indicate that Appalachian slaves probably had a much less diverse meat diet than slaves in other parts of the South. The most abundant meat remains were from the fattest cuts of pork, heads, and feet. Remains of beef, goat, and mutton have rarely been found at Appalachian sites. Indeed the second most abundant meat was rabbit, followed by opossum, raccoon, woodchuck, mole, gray squirrel, turtle, and mourning doves. Fish rarely entered the diet of Appalachian slaves who lived on plantations without large streams. These archaeological digs are supported by slave narratives, for most Appalachian slaves reported that "the colored had

Some mountain plantations processed their own tobacco for export. Dipping and pressing plugs and cigars exposed slaves, including pregnant women and children, to dangerous chemicals that caused lung infections and intestinal ailments. *Source: Harper's,* 1853.

the heads and scraps like that, and then they would have the fat part of the middling, but they would save the lean parts and the shoulders for the white folks." Julia Daniels' master "kilt a beef" near Christmas. This rare annual treat was "jus' pourin' water on [their] wheels 'cause [they] liked best of anythin' the beef." In addition to being an export commodity, beef could not be preserved as easily as pork. Cattle did not pickle or smoke well, and the meat spoiled more easily. Typically, mountain masters did not kill beef until Christmas, but they needed to supply meat to their slaves in October. Silas Jackson recalled that rabbits and opossums were their "choice food" because slaves on his plantation "did not get anything special from the overseer." The larger plantations purchased salted and pickled fish to supplement winter diets.[30]

The vast majority of Appalachian slaves received corn as their only grain; less than 10 percent of Appalachian slaves received wheat flour on a regular basis. "Ash cake" was the primary carbohydrate in the diets of Appalachian slaves. Rolled in cabbage or collard leaves, the corn-bread dough was "placed on the hot rocks close to the fire ... then hot ashes were raked out ... and piled over the ash cakes." Because they received it so infrequently, Appalachian slaves referred to wheat flour as "seldom bread." Despite their rationing patterns, Appalachian masters realized that their "laborers prefer[red] receiving 1 peck of flour to 1 and one-half peck of Indian meal." However, Appalachian masters exported wheat and flour; so they were not willing to use this cash crop to feed slaves. Fundamentally, Appalachian slaves "lived on fat meat and corn bread," supplemented with erratic seasonal rations of molasses, sweet potatoes, fruits, and vegetables, plus wild fish and game. Mountain slaves ate most of their meals in the form of soups and stews that were left simmering while workers were in the fields, so their meats were "mostly boiled." Sally Brown recalled that her family kept food cooking in ovens and pots in the fireplace. "Coals of fire wuz put on top of the oven and under the bottom, too ... there wuz racks fitted in the fireplace to put pots on." In the fall, Appalachian slaves "et collard greens and pork till [they] got skittish of it." In the winter, families kept simmering a "pot full of lye hominy" that "last[ed] several days." Adapting foodways that combined African and Native American customs, mountain slaves used gourds, clay cooking jars, iron pots, and wooden bowls to stretch their food supplies as far as possible. Even though sweet potatoes were only available about one-third of the year, some Appalachian masters recognized the nutritional importance of the tuber for their slaves' diet. After failing in his attempts to produce adequate supplies of sweet potatoes for his labor force of more than one hundred slaves, Dillard Love was convinced that effort was "thrown away to attempt to raise the yam" in the mountains of western North Carolina. So he commissioned botanist Silas McDowell to experiment with hybridizing the plant. McDowell recommended the "negroe killer potato," a hybrid he created by crossing the yellow yam with a Haitian yam.[31]

In addition to their heavy reliance upon corn and salt pork, Appalachian masters utilized a number of other control strategies that exacerbated malnutrition. Despite the availability of summer watermelons, Appalachian slaves did not receive adequate levels of Vitamin C because masters restricted their fruit consumption year-round. On most plantations, slaves could only use the rotting fruit that had fallen from trees, and fruit was available only during late summer and early fall. Only about one-fifth received regular allocations of molasses, and masters punished slaves for stealing the supplement. Moreover, very few Appalachian slaves received regular rations of salt. Monticello rationed one quart of salt per month to adult slaves, as did other large plantations. However, most mountain slaves scrounged for salt. One middle Tennessee slave reported that "the only salt [they] ever got was what drapped down on the ground from the meat that was hanging up." Appalachian slaves "never knowed no other kind" of salt, so they resorted to extreme measures to retrieve the supplement. In one instance, slaves dug up the smokehouse floor, "put dirt in big hoppers and pored water through it"; then the dirty water "was boiled down, till dere was just old brown salt." In another instance, slaves ripped boards from the floor of the smokehouse because they were "soaked with salt and grease. They "took those boards and cooked the salt and fat out of them, cooked the boards right in the bean soup." To complicate matters, many mountain masters regularly rationed alcohol to slaves, at the recommended rate of "6 or 7 gallons to a laboring hand during the year." Some masters provided daily morning rations of alcohol, even though they were providing very little breakfast food. Alcohol consumption diminished the body's absorption of other nutrients and caused slaves to sweat more during their work. The resulting dehydration caused the loss of body salts and minerals that were not replaced in the diet. Alcohol consumption, coupled with the inadequate supply of salt in the Appalachian slave diet, increased the likelihood of heat stroke, dehydration, and heart damage.[32]

Another fundamental explanation for malnutrition among Appalachian slaves lies in the food distribution strategies utilized by regional masters. A tiny percentage of mountain slaveholders refused to engage in malnutrition policies. Andrew Goodman described his master as a man who "give out plenty and said, 'If you need more you can have it, 'cause ain't any going to suffer on my place." Morris Hillyer recalled that his northern Georgia owner "never 'lowanced his [slaves] and dey could always have anything on de place to eat." This master's methods drew criticism in the community, for neighboring slave owners would not permit such privileged slaves "to come among" their workers for fear their master's food policies "would make their slaves discontented." However, the vast majority of Appalachian masters structured rationing systems that required slaves to produce much of their own diet. While more than half of all U.S. slaves received their diet through regular rations, nine-tenths of all Appalachian slaves supplemented their masters' food rations through hunting, fishing, and cultivation of small parcels. Indeed, Appalachian masters were twice as likely as other U.S. slave owners to require slaves to produce much of their own food supply.[33]

Appalachian masters expected most of their slaves to prepare their own meals in their cabins. Consequently, two-thirds of all Appalachian slaves augmented their masters' rations with small vegetable gardens, and Appalachian slaves grew family parcels twice as often as other U.S. slaves. Anderson Hall commented that "slaves had deir own gyardens, and dey better wuk 'em good if dey wanted any gyarden sass to eat." As Thomas Cole put it, Appalachian slaves produced their own variety of vegetables, or they "ha[d] ter do wid out." Typically, slaves grew a greater variety of items in their parcels than masters. Combining African and Native American heritages, Appalachian slaves added to their masters corn/pork diet several nutritious items, including sorghum, okra, cowpeas, onions, peppers, garlic, herbs, spices, eggplant, sesame, watermelon, squash, pumpkin, yams, and black-eyed peas. To fortify their winter diets, slaves strung peppers, onions, peas, okra and herbs and hung them "from the rafters" of their cabins.[34]

To increase their protein intake, 43 percent of Appalachian slaves hunted and fished, and they engaged in these activities 1.4 times more often than other U.S. slaves. Because most slaves were not allowed to have guns or dogs, some Appalachian slaves blended Cherokee and African hunting and fishing methods. One slave recalled that any "wile critters" they "coulden' run down," they "was right smart 'bout ketchin' in traps an' nets." On one Appalachian plantation, slaves made "basket traps that sho' nuff did lay in the fishes." They would set the white oak baskets in the water for several hours, so they could gradually fill with fish. Western Carolina slaves "sot mud baskets fer cat fish; tie[d] grapevines on dem and put dem in de river. [They] cotch some wid hooks," but they also "went seining" and "set nets." The rushing water "come to [their] necks while [they were] seining and [they] git de fish while drifting down stream." Appalachian slaves who were denied parcels, hunting, or fishing and those who were rationed food through centralized meals experienced the least diet diversity and complained most often about hunger. One small West Virginia master did not permit slaves to grow their own parcels; instead "he gave the slaves what he wanted them to have out of his garden, but he never growed anything but greens and a few potatoes." As a result, such slaves did not receive enough vegetables to meet their need for vitamins and minerals. One northern Georgia slave recalled that they "cotch lots of 'possums" but were permitted to eat "mighty few of 'em" because "de white folks et 'em." Centralized meals also left slaves hungry for diversity and quantity. At Betty Cofer's plantation, "the field hands had to hussle to git to the end of the row at eleven o'clock dinner-time." When the cooks brought the midday meal, "they had to stop just where they was and eat ... ash cakes and molasses." One small northern Alabama master centralized food distribution at his "big kitchen." At midday, these workers were fed a meal of boiled meat, greens, peas, or beans, but their breakfast and supper consisted of a large piece of corn bread. This slaveholder "didn't give [his slaves] no way to cook, nor nothin' to cook in [their] cabins."[35]

Because allocated weekly rations of fat pork and cornmeal were nutritionally inadequate, most Appalachian masters required slaves to produce a majority of their own basic survival needs. *Source: Harper's*, 1867.

Mountain slaves received the best diets from midsummer through early winter when there was still a supply of fresh and dried vegetables and pork. However, seasonal shortages were common on Appalachian plantations, especially among masters who owned fewer than twenty slaves. Winter brought malnutrition, as supplies of vegetables and meat dwindled, and slaves were shifted to a diet of hominy and meal. Even large Appalachian plantations ran out of meat by late winter or early spring. Thomas Cole's master was a wealthy northern Alabama planter, but their "meat supply begins ter runs low in de wintah time er early spring." To overcome the shortage, "de overseah would sends some of de slaves ter kill a deer, wild hogs widout any marks er brand on em er jest any kind of game dey could gits." Usually, slaves would be sent out several times to hunt, for they often came home empty-handed. Jim Threat provided a clear example of the dangerous malnutrition that Appalachian slaves faced during the cold months. As winter supplies were depleted, one master resorted to "cotton-seed boiled and thickened with corn meal." "We got along better when spring came," he recalled, "for berries was plentiful and we would go to a pine tree and peel the outside bark off and scrape the body of the tree and eat these scrapings." The manuscript collections of non-agricultural masters show a clear pattern of repeated food shortages and half-rations at industrial sites. For example, one southwestern Virginia iron works reported pork and grain shortages and tainted meat almost twice every year between 1828 and 1860. When food rations ran short at the Bath Iron Works, the manager feared that the slaves would "leave in a body." The owner "must do something to satisfy them," he cautioned, if the furnace "wish[ed] to keep them." At West Virginia's salt wells, slaves received a diet of fatty bacon and corn bread. Because "they labored very hard" and because slaves had to purchase through "over-work" their only supplements of flour, molasses, or vegetables, masters often sued the companies for poor treatment of their laborers. Only a few industrial sites, like the Washington Iron Works, routinely permitted slaves to grow individual vegetable parcels. Appalachian slaves who worked on river craft, at construction sites, at mines, or in timber camps lived in temporary arrangements, so hunting and food parcels were not possible. Consequently, the region's industrial slaves experienced diets that were frequently deficient in iron, protein, thiamine, niacin, and several vitamins and minerals.[36]

Malnutrition was widespread among mountain slaves, but chronic hunger was most prevalent on small slaveholdings. The term *half-strainers* was coined by Appalachian slaves to refer to those masters who operated on such a narrow profit margin that they engaged in severe malnutrition strategies. Olmsted reported that "slaves wanted to avoid sale to masters of scanty means ... because they understood that their own family and community security depended upon their owner's solvency." Appalachian narratives provide anecdotal evidence of malnutrition. Perry Larkey was convinced that slaves were "underfed at most places" in eastern Kentucky, and Estill Countian Peter Bruner "did not often have enough to eat." Wylie Nealy "got hungry lots times" on his small northern Georgia plantation, as did Sarah Gudger who slipped away at night to Buncombe County neighbors to supplement her skimpy diet of "cawn bread an' 'lasses." Jim Threat described his northern Alabama master as "a devil on this earth" who "jest didn't have any regard for his slaves. He made 'em work from daylight to dark and didn't give them any more food" than was barely necessary for them to "git along with." Another Etowah County woman was owned by a master who "neber give his slaves 'nough t'eat," so "sometimes dey actually go hungry." One eastern Tennessee master rationed sweet potatoes so closely that he "would go round about 10 o'clock, searching through their cabins to see if they had stowed any away." Blue Ridge Virginia slave Ben Brown was convinced that nobody got enough food on his plantation, for "de meat house was full of smoked po'k, but [slaves] only got a little now an' den." Josie Jordan described the most visible evidence of chronic hunger. On her White County, Tennessee, plantation, "some of them slaves was so poorly thin they ribs would kinder rustle against each other like corn stalks a-drying in the hot winds."[37]

Shortages and the lack of diversity were exacerbated by the tendency of masters to distribute food inequitably. Industrial managers routinely rewarded high production with greater quantities and variety of food, ignoring the harsh reality that the more demanding effort might be exerted by individuals assigned to tasks that could not exhibit high profits. Appalachian masters also discriminated racially in food allotments. At Buffalo Forge, for instance, slaves received weekly rations of cornmeal and pork, while white diets were supplemented with salt, flour, sugar, and seasonal fruits and vegetables. Masters reserved the leanest cuts of meat and the winter supplies of dried fruits and canned vegetables for their own households. On plantations, white workers received flour, rice, and lean pork, while slaves "wuzn't 'lowed to eat all the different kinds of victuals the white folks et." Blue Sulphur Springs waiters dined on fat pork, cornmeal, and collards while they served to guests elaborate dishes that included nuts, oranges, lemons, and a wide array of fruits, vegetables and meats. Appalachian house servants were much better fed than field workers or industrial laborers, for they "et at de kitchen table jest as good eating as de white folks had." Thomas Cole, for instance, never went hungry like most of the labor force on his plantation. Because his mother was the nurse for the master's household, their family "had lots ter eat dat de other slaves didn't have." In addition, his meals "was allus hot," while field slaves did their cooking "de night before, makin dom eats a cold dinnah." House servants received many more servings of lean meat than field slaves. Such food stratification occurred all over the United States, but Appalachian slaves were particularly hard hit. A much greater percentage of Appalachian slaves worked at hard labor in the fields or at small industrial sites. Because of their concentration into occupational categories that did not get rewarded with such incentives, many fewer Appalachian slaves would have benefited from food stratification.[38]

There is another indication that Appalachian slave diets were inadequate. Mountain slaves reported food stealing three times more often than did other U.S. slaves. Appalachian masters comprehended that their slaves pilfered items because they were hungry. Thomas Jefferson believed that "a man's moral senses must be unusually strong, if slavery does not make him a thief. He who is permitted by law to have no property of his own, can with difficulty conceive that property is founded in anything but force." Morris Hillyer reported that his northern Georgia master "bought every roguish [slave] in the country. He'd take him home and give him the key to everything on de place and say to help himself. Soon as he got all he wanted to eat he'd quit being a rogue. Old Judge said that was what made [slaves] steal – they was hungry." Appalachian slaves also understood the political economy of food shortages, so they expressed their resistance to malnutrition strategies through stealing. Shang Harris of Toccoa, Georgia, rationalized slave behavior this way: "Dey talks a heap 'bout de [slaves] stealin'. Well, you know what was de fust stealin' done? Hit was in Afriky." Another northern Georgia slave expressed the desperation more paradoxically. When masters "didn't provishun" slaves sufficiently, they made it necessary for workers to "slip around" and swipe additional meat. "Some folks mought call that stealin'," he added, but it was justice in his eyes. "When you don't git 'lowanced right, you has to keep right on workin' in the field," and nobody should have to "work with his belly groanin'."[39]

Meat was the item supplied most inadequately by Appalachian masters, so mountain slaves often stole to overcome their protein deficiencies. William Brown remembered his enslavement in Fauquier County, Virginia, as a time when he was always "tired and hungry," and slaves were "obliged to steal." W. P. Jacobs reported that slaves on his Roanoke County, Virginia, plantation "never got any beef unless we stole it." On Julius Jones' small plantation in Coffee County, Tennessee, "the eating" provided by their master "sure warn't nothing to brag on. Most of the time [they] didn't have nothing except meat and bread and the biggest part of the meat was possums, coons, and rabbits." To offset the master's protein shortfall, Jones's father sometimes pilfered pork, and he fed the children "under the bed when he got something he didn't want nobody to know nothing 'bout." On Stephen Varner's plantation, hungry slaves "would break into the smoke house and cut some meat" for a second night-time supper. On one Clay County, Kentucky, plantation, slaves "would slip in the house after the master and mistress wuz sleeping" to cook meat for themselves. Some masters had broad definitions of stealing, so they punished every infraction. Gus Feaster's master "never whipped 'bout nothing much but stealing," and he was even strict on children. "When tracks be seed in de wa'melon patch," the master called up all the slave children. "If de measurements of dere tracks fitted de ones in de wa'melon patch," that child was punished for theft. On another Appalachian plantation, the cook was whipped for baking cookies to "hand them out to the slaves" while the master's family attended church on Sundays.[40]

A diet lacking diversity, inequitable rationing by masters, seasonal shortages, and skimping on several essential foods generated widespread malnutrition among Appalachian slaves. The scanty provision of lean meat and the heavy reliance on corn meant that slave diets were deficient in iron, folic acid, niacin, thiamine, and the Vitamin B complex. Adults need two calories of protein per pound of body weight, but Appalachian slaves did not receive sufficient levels to maintain good health. The typical diet lacked the kinds of high-quality protein that supplies the eight amino acids essential to life. Lactose intolerance and erratic availability of milk caused deficiencies of calcium and Vitamin D. Antebellum doctors warned Appalachian masters that "not nearly enough vegetables [we]re grown and fed to negroes." Lean meats, poultry, eggs, milk, and grains other than corn are the foods required to produce antibodies to fight infections. However, the WPA narratives indicate that Appalachian slaves received such foods sporadically and in small amounts. The erratic supply of molasses would have increased the likelihood of iron deficiencies, and the seasonal shortages of orange yams would have lowered absorption of Vitamin A and calcium.[41]

What, then, would have been the physical outcomes of such nutritional deficiencies? Pellagra is associated with a diet of cornmeal, salt pork, and molasses. Scurvy and beriberi could have accompanied low consumption of fruit. Dirt eating sometimes resulted from a diet low in vitamins and minerals. Shortages of Vitamin A and riboflavin would have caused sight impairment, sore eyes, and cracked lips. Because the diet was low in foods that build antibodies, Appalachian slaves would have been plagued with frequent intestinal disease in the summer and respiratory infections in the winter. Low levels of protein, calcium, and Vitamin D would have caused frequent deformities of joints and rickets. Insufficient iron and folic acid would have led to a high incidence of anemia and susceptibility to disease. In short, the nutrient imbalance that characterized the Appalachian slave diet would have produced chronic hunger, dangerous nutrient deficiencies and malnutrition, thereby causing a substantial number of the region's slaves to be physically impaired or chronically ill. In our investigation of the long-term physical damages from malnutrition, we do not have to rely upon conjecture. Much evidence of chronic malnutrition is available in the newspaper advertisements for runaway Appalachian slaves. Among 297 western North Carolina and Blue Ridge Virginia runaways, the vast majority exhibited health conditions that probably resulted from long-term malnutrition. Appalachian masters used joint deformities and damage from rickets to describe more than one-fifth of the runaways. Running sores were visible on 15 percent of their bodies, and 17 percent were afflicted with scalp diseases or hair falling out. Skin rashes and "breaking out" were equally common, as were various ailments of the eyes, including night blindness, sight impairment, constant weeping, swelling, and discolored eyes. More than one-fifth of the runaways had visible gum or mouth diseases, and terms like "ill looking," lazy, slow, dull, or "lacking energy" were applied to about 12 percent of them. The ex-slave narratives also supply ample evidence of malnutrition. George Briggs "once had 26 biles [boils]." About 15 percent of the narratives describe arms, hands, fingers, or legs that did not develop properly and caused lifetime problems.[42]

4 Reproductive Exploitation and Child Mortality

> I consider the labor of a breeding woman as no object, and that a child raised every 2. years is of more profit than the crop of the best laboring man.
> — Thomas Jefferson, Blue Ridge Virginia planter

> During slavery, it seemed lak yo' chillun b'long to ev'ybody but you.
> — Katie Johnson, enslaved Appalachian mother

In his *Sociology for the South*, George Fitzhugh summarized the power and economic constraints that characterized women's roles in slaveholding households. Southern men did "not set children and women free because they [we]re not capable of taking care of themselves, not equal to the constant struggle of society." Because women were "but grown-up children," independence would be as "fatal to them as it would be to children." Thus, a man was supposed to love his wife and his children "because they [we]re weak, helpless and dependent." In the antebellum literature for Southern elite women, writers idealized three roles for respectable ladies: devoted wife, affectionate mother, and skilled housekeeper. Nineteenth-century courts legalized the subordinate position of women. "The wife must be subject to the husband," admonished one North Carolina judge, for "every man must govern his household." Among Southern elites, women belonged within families and households under the governance of males, while men built the economic and political agendas of their families and households in the outside world. According to Stevenson, articulate experts "took for granted that women should center their lives on addressing men's needs, and that men should provide them with support and protection in return."[1]

The slaveholding woman's home may have been the *feminine sphere*, but it was still part of her husband's *dominion*. Male dominance was not limited to economic spheres, for husbands and fathers presided over all the "webs of production and reproduction" that made up their households. The reproduction process was fraught with moments of contention between men and women, but wives usually conceded much of the decision making to their husbands. Fathers controlled the courting and marriage

114

decisions of adult daughters, and husbands clearly pressured wives into many of their reproductive decisions. New mothers did not even take charge at the moment of arrival, for husbands named new infants. Despite the physical dangers associated with childbearing, Southern white women exhibited higher fertility rates than Northern white women. From a year after marriage until menopause, many elite women bore children about every two to three years. Producing such large families weakened mothers' personal health and increased the incidence of child mortality. For example, one western North Carolina mistress conceived her second child when her first child was not yet one year old. Thus, when the mother was seven months pregnant, she was forced to nurse her eighteen-month-old daughter through a serious illness. As a result of a reproductive history that repeated this pattern several times, this woman experienced several stillborns, premature births, problem pregnancies, and lengthy physical recoveries.[2]

Often over their wives' protests, husbands chose male physicians to care for their pregnant wives and daughters. About half of all elite Southern women relied on male physicians because antebellum medical experts established the stereotype that wealthier women had greater difficulties in childbearing than poor women. Affluent women were believed to suffer more during childbirth due to "overdevelopment of the nervous organization." The procedures used by those male doctors, however, probably endangered mother and fetus more than natural childbirth. The use of dangerous chemicals, unclean instruments, bloodletting, and purges prolonged the natural process and made postpartum recovery more difficult. According to McMillen,

[T]he ambitious approach of the physicians was no safer, no less painful, and no more sensible than the ways of the midwives. Parturient women who used midwives may even have had a better survival rate, because attendants who did not examine their patients and who shrank from intrusions upon the natural process were less likely to expose women to infection.

Death or permanent physical damage resulted from intrusive medical procedures like bloodletting, intestinal enemas, cold water dousings, uterine enemas during pregnancy, use of forceps during delivery, or the insertion of cold water or ice into a hemorrhaging womb. Touted as "quite the most important" of nineteenth-century medicines, calomel was a mercury chloride used to purge the intestines of constipated women. Opiates were another favorite of doctors, and medical guides recommended that husbands keep on hand a box of opium pills to aid their pregnant wives.[3]

Slaveholding women preferred to have female friends and relatives present to assist during the latter months of pregnancy and childbirthing.

However, Appalachian masters resented the presence of in-laws in their households, so they pressured wives to entrust their care to physicians. When they lived too far away to have care or support from mothers or sisters, pregnant mistresses were left to the "judicious nursing" of doctors and husbands who relied heavily on chemicals and bloodletting. When a northern Alabama mistress developed "troublesome headaches" during pregnancy, doctor and husband administered frequent bloodletting and generous laudanum doses. A western North Carolina mistress complimented the "great deal of service" and the "unremitting attentions" rendered by her physician, but she described herself as "an old Boat . . . much shattered" after the delivery. With the help of the husband, one eastern Tennessee physician cut the arms and temporal arteries of a pregnant women having convulsions. When the spasms worsened, he recommended "letting 60 oz. blood and to pierce the jugular vein, if necessary." Heroic medicine left many of these affluent women anemic, physically exhausted, unable to digest foods properly, addicted to opiates, troubled with bleeding gums and ulcers, and generally emaciated. Weakened by numerous medical treatments, Sally Lacy described to her family "how very ill" she had been throughout her pregnancy. As "the time of [her] trial [i.e., delivery] [wa]s drawing near," Sally feared she would not survive the ordeal. Long before the onset of labor pains, Sally had already "suffered as much as [her] constitution was able to bear." After several medical interventions during pregnancy, a western North Carolina mistress wrote to her mother: "this business of having children is an awful thing." During one pregnancy, she was given daily enemas of oak bark and alum, "bled pretty freely," and administered a dose of calomel. Two months after the birth of her child, she was still unable to venture downstairs because she was afflicted with a high fever and headaches. When the infant was four months old, the woman still felt "weak and good-for-nothing."[4]

Over the protests of his mother-in-law that the doctor was overmedicating his wife, one western North Carolina husband permitted a doctor to give the woman a "great quantity of mercury and other strong medicines" while she was pregnant. During a "dreadful fever," the solicitous husband continued to be sure that the physician's chemical concoctions were "pour'd down her." In addition, he pressured his wife to follow the doctor's regimen of intestinal and uterine purges and douches. As a result, the wife remained ill throughout her pregnancy, bedridden and lifeless much of the time. Because of the overdose of calomel during pregnancy, the mistress did not "know what it [wa]s to feel well an hour," and she remained "tired almost to death" three months after the delivery. Continued laudanum doses left her feeling "so stupid" that she "had no sense at all." Even though the woman had to be tended six months by two sisters, she gave birth to another infant one-and-a-half years later.

If mistresses were ensnared in a patriarchal system in which they did not control pregnancy and child-rearing decisions, why should we expect that the enslaved women owned by their husbands had any greater degree of control over their reproductive lives? In fact, mountain slave families were destabilized by three patterns of systematic reproductive exploitation through which owners pressured enslaved women toward early and frequent childbearing:

- Structural control over slave marriages,
- Sexual abuse by white males, and
- Structural interference in pregnancy, breastfeeding, and child rearing.

Structural Interference in Slave Marriages

Encouragement of slave families did not emanate from any unselfish owner benevolence. Organizing slaves into family units offered three economic advantages. First, families were a cost-effective administrative unit for the distribution of food, clothing, and shelter. Second, families were an important vehicle through which masters maintained social control without resorting to force. "By encouraging strong family attachments, slave owners reduced the danger that individual slaves would run away. By permitting families to have de facto ownership of houses, furniture, clothing, garden plots, and small livestock, planters created an economic stake for slaves in the system." Finally, slave "marriages" were the main instrument by which masters hoped to increase their slave populations. In fact, this technique was widely promulgated in the hegemonic ideology as the most efficient approach for "ensuring greater increase."[5]

The primary structural mechanism by which Appalachian slaveholders directly controlled the reproductive process was through their interference into slave marriages. In every instance reported in the Appalachian slave narratives, "the slaves were allowed to marry but were compelled to first obtain permission from the master." One of every eight enjoyed no ceremony at all, like a Jackson County, North Carolina, slave who reported that "when a man wanted a woman, he went and axed the marster for her and took her on. That is about all there was to it." Contrary to Blassingame's claim that the custom was not common, three-quarters of the Appalachian slaves were married "by de marster's word," usually in an informal ceremony in which the master had them step over a broomstick. The actual ceremony varied from one Appalachian zone to another. The broom might be placed flat on the floor or raised between two slaves. In some instances, both stepped or jumped over the broom. In other cases, the bride stood still while the groom jumped toward her over an elevated broom. Most rituals involved forward steps, but Maggie Broyles' parents were married at a Meigs County, Tennessee, cornshucking where "they jumped over the broom back'ards." This ritual was not African in origin but rather had been derived from a pre-Christian practice in western Europe. In their imposition of a custom that held no legitimacy or respect among whites, Appalachian masters demonstrated their unwillingness to acknowledge the right of slaves to form permanent families.[6]

Only about one-tenth of the Appalachian masters permitted their slaves to have religious services. For instance, Anna Lee of Scott County, Tennessee, commented that "[w]e considered if our Maser agreed for us to live together we was lawfully married.... [S]ometimes we would beg our Masers to let us have a preacher to marry us and he would. The slaves they were allowed to ride us on rails dipped in tubs of water no matter how we got married." Even fewer Appalachian slaveholders made any legal record of slave marriages. For example, Thomas George Walton and Hamilton Brown registered the marriages of a select few of their western North Carolina slaves, but not the majority. Even when masters agreed to religious rituals, slave women could not be sure their marriages had been legitimized. Bethany Veney informed her Page County, Virginia, master that she would not marry without a minister. To speed up the process, her owner concurred and located a traveling preacher to conduct the rite. Some time later, Bethany discovered that her new husband had conspired with her master to trick her. The purported minister had been found on the road, peddling his wares from a cart.[7]

Appalachian slaveholders had good reason to avoid church weddings and to keep slave marriages informal. "One of the first issues confronting Southern churches with black members was the impact of the forcible separation of mates upon a slave union. When a slave whose mate had been sold wanted to have a wedding or continue in fellowship with the church after taking a new mate, the clergy had to reconsider the meaning of marriage." Some antebellum Appalachian churches viewed the "double marriage" of a slave as an act in which the master was forcing the partners into an act of polygamy after living mates had been removed against their wishes. In the Broad River Baptist Association of western North Carolina, slaves who remarried after the sale of their spouses were removed from church rolls, and their masters were publicly chastised for forcing their slaves into sin. So long as black unions failed to meet the marriage criteria of white religious and civil authorities, Appalachian masters could dissolve the kinship bonds of their slaves without moral or legal sanction. If masters extended to slave marriages the "sanctity" of the church and the legitimacy of public recording, they would throw into question their racist ideology that blacks did not construct families that were the moral and cultural equivalent of their white owners.[8]

Appalachian slaves were pressured to marry in their teens. Mountain planter James Madison reported in 1834 that one-third of his slaves were children, "every slave girl being expected to be a mother by the time she is fifteen." According to one Appalachian slave, "if a woman didn't breed well, she was put in a gang and sold." Some owners orchestrated the courting process, in an effort to select healthy mates for their slaves. Rachel Cruze described such an eastern Tennessee master.

Saturday afternoons and Sunday nights were the times the young fellows looked about for likely mates. Gainan Macabee, who owned a large farm across the river, had a great number of lively-looking girl slaves, and all the young men in the neighborhood would make it their business to get over there if possible. Gainan he watched his girls closely – used to sit on a chair between his two houses where he could see everything – and if a skinny reedy-sort of [male] made his appearance among the young people Gainan ... would tell him ... "I don't want you comin' over to see my gals. You ain't good stock." ... But when he saw a well-built, tall, husky man in the crowd Gainan would call him and say. ... "You can come over and see my gals anytime you want. You're of good stock."[9]

Slave marriages were economically important to Appalachian masters; so few of them granted their slaves total independence when it came to such a crucial matter. Thus, many Appalachian masters took an active role in marriages that went far beyond granting permission to voluntary spouses. In nearly three-fifths of the cases described in the narratives, slaves were allowed to select their spouses and then marry, after obtaining their masters' permission. However, Appalachian masters strongly influenced about one-third of the spouse selection decisions and unilaterally matched spouses in about one of every thirteen marriages. Coosa, Alabama, slave Penny Thompson remembered that "[m]os' times masters and misses would jus' pick out some man fo' a woman an' say: 'Dis yo' man' an' say to the man 'Dis yo' woman.' Didn't make no difference what they want. Then they read some from the Bible to 'em an' say 'Now you is husban' an' wife.'" When Martha Bennett married without her master's permission, the Loudoun County, Virginia, slaveholder had her stripped naked and "flogged." Katie Johnson described the male dominance over slave marriages. "If a man saw a girl he liked he would ask his master's permission to ask the master of the girl for her. If his master consented and her master consented then they came together. She lived on her plantation and he on his. The woman had no choice in the matter," according to Katie. Kanawha County, West Virginia, slave Lizzie Grant recalled: "I was about 17 years old when I was given to my young Maser, me and the man that I called my husband. So our young Maser put us to live together to raise from just like you would stock today. They never thought anything about it either. They never cared or thought about our feeling in the matter." Her master rationalized such intrusion with the philosophy that "it was cheaper to raise slaves than it was to buy them."[10]

In about one of every twenty-one marriages, the overseers matched up slaves arbitrarily. In the case of Thomas Cole, the overseer "give[d] [him] a log house and furnished [him] a girl." Similarly, a middle Tennessee son reported that the master purchased two slaves, expecting them to marry. His father "was an old man" when he was imported from Maryland while his mother "was young – just fifteen or sixteen years old." Martha Showvely experienced an even more trying situation. At age thirteen, her overseer pressured her to marry an older male she did not even know. "I said yes," she recalled, "den after I got home, I got scared. He came to ax massa for me an' massa ax me did I want to marry him. I said, 'Naw suh.' Den I told de man I didn' know what I was sayin'." Within a few months, however, she relented; and she delivered three children by the time she was twenty.[11]

White Sexual Exploitation of Enslaved Women

The second pattern of structural interference in reproduction was white sexual exploitation of enslaved women. Appalachian masters probably resorted to sexual exploitation of their slave women more often than did their counterparts in the rest of the South. About 5 percent of all the slave narratives in the WPA collection include reports that the slave's father was white. However, sexual exploitation of Appalachian slave women occurred nearly three times more often than that, if we judge by the incidence with which it is reported in regional slave narratives. Escaped slave Bethany Veney recognized the vulnerability of black Appalchian women when she wrote in her autobiography:

My dear white lady, in your pleasant home made joyous by the tender love of husband and children all your own, you can never understand the slave mother's emotions as she clasps her new-born child, and knows that a master's word can at any moment take it from her embrace; and when, as was mine, that child is a girl, and from her own experience she sees its almost certain doom is to minister to the unbridled lust of the slave-owner, and feels that the law holds over her no protecting arm, it is not strange that, rude and uncultured as I was, I felt all this, and would have been glad if we could have died together there and then.[12]

Nearly 15 percent of the Appalachian narratives describe acts of white sexual exploitation of enslaved women, and most of those instances involved acts of male force or physical violence. Moreover, one in ten Appalachian slave families was headed by a woman whose children were the outcome of her sexual exploitation by white males. For instance, John Finnelly knew his father was one of the white males on their plantation, but his mother would never identify him. "I don't know him," John said, " 'cause Mammy never talk[ed] 'bout him 'cept to say 'he am here.' " Even though owners were unable to reduce their slaves to mere chattel, argues Fox-Genovese, "they could still dominate them in innumerable ways, notably their own sexual exploitation of slave women.... [T]he masters' unchecked power over their slave women brought into the center of the household that public violence against which white women were protected." Little wonder, then, that sexual aggression by white males was one of the most frequent reasons given by Appalachian enslaved women for their physical assaults on whites.[13]

Most mountain masters did not force their attentions at random upon women in the quarters. Instead, selected women were brought to the "big house" and set up as cook, maid, or nursemaid in a room or cabin within easy reach of the exploiter. For instance, Loudoun County planter George Carter purchased teenage slave girls for sexual pleasure. About 5 percent of the Appalachian slave narratives describe Appalachian slaveholders who structured more long-term "concubinage" arrangements with enslaved women. When his sons married, one middle Tennessee master would give them "a woman for a cook, and she would have children right in the house by him, and his wife would have children too." Some white parents tolerated their sons' exploitation of house slaves, "if they wanted them"; and, subsequently, they "would heartlessly sell [their] own offspring to some other master." Fearful that their sons would break community moral codes by "ruining the reputations" of the white girls they courted, some Appalachian mistresses selected "good-looking" servants and "closed their eyes" to their sons' sexual exploitation and impregnation of enslaved teenagers. For instance, one master "bring his son" to the cabin of a teenage slave girl. Both males raped her – "the father showing the son what it was all about, and she couldn't do nothing 'bout it." In another instance, the black bride "was her young marster's woman and he let her marry because he could get her anyhow, if he wanted her." One ex-slave explained that enslaved women endured such concubinage because "they had a horror of going to Mississippi and they would do anything to keep from it."[14]

Some Appalachian whites kept slave mistresses throughout their entire lives, like "Aunt Millie" of middle Tennessee, an elderly emancipated woman who lived alone in "a home off from the [master's] house" and who bore one son by the slaveholder. One elderly Chatooga, Georgia, widower kept a wife and husband apart half the time. Noah Perry recalled that the retired master "always kept a claim on mother and us kids. He

Working in the owner's house kept children away from their families most of the time and denied them the parental discipline and support of their fathers. *Source: Harper's,* 1856.

had a little house near the big house and when he was visiting . . . mother kept house for him. He usually stayed about six months and we'd get to live at the little house all that time." When he left, the family would "go back" to the slave quarters. Because she "usually run the plow," the woman "liked to stay with him" because "she didn't have to work so hard there." More importantly, she could prevent the sale of herself and her young children so long as the old master survived.[15]

Among Appalachian masters, Thomas Jefferson engineered one of the most famous of these concubinage relationships. According to a Monticello slave, "Mr. Jefferson promised his wife, on her death bed, that he would not marry again." Instead, he chose as his concubine fourteen-year-old Sally Hemings, rumored to be the slave half-sister of his dead wife. After their two years in France, Sally "refused to return" with her master to Virginia. "To induce her to do so, he promised her extraordinary privileges, and made a solemn pledge that her children should be freed at the age of twenty-one years." Soon after their return, Sally gave birth to Jefferson's baby, but it died quickly; one year later a second infant death occurred. Between 1798 and 1808, Sally Hemings supervised a small staff that accompanied Jefferson to his mountain retreat, Poplar Forest, and she bore four children by him. While he was living, Jefferson never acknowledged his black offspring, and "he was not in the habit of showing partiality or fatherly affection" toward them. Rather than being emotionally linked to the "only children of his by a slavewoman," he directed his attentions toward his fourteen white grandchildren. At his death, however, Jefferson freed only six slaves (Sally's four children, her brother, and an elderly household servant); Sally was freed two years later by Jefferson's daughter.[16]

Masters' Structural Interference to Promote Slave Fertility

Demographic data in the antebellum censuses provide little evidence about structural mechanisms employed to encourage slave fertility. However, it is possible to assess the extent of these practices by examining several indirect measures derived from population trends. First, we would expect that slaveholders who were trying to stimulate reproduction would own more women than men in their slave populations. The effect of this practice was to produce a slave population in which women were disproportionately represented for two reasons. First, a higher ratio of mothers was required if masters were to maximize their reproduction of surplus male field hands and artisans. Second, women outnumbered males because the Upper South exported 7 percent more males than females.[17]

There was slightly less than one female to every male in the entire slave population of the South, reflecting the preference for male field laborers and artisans. In the slave-selling states, however, there was slightly more than one female slave for every bondsman. With 102 women to every 100 males, every sector of Southern Appalachia, except the Virginia counties, exhibited more imbalanced sex ratios than the rest of the slave-selling Upper South. The Appalachian counties of North Carolina, Maryland, and South Carolina ranged from 110 to 120 slave women for every 100 bondsmen, while the slaveholders of the Appalachian counties of Tennessee, Georgia, West Virginia, Alabama, and Kentucky owned 104 to 107 women for every 100 males.[18]

The implication of such a disproportionate share of female slaves becomes clear when we compare Appalachia with the population trends for slaveholding in the eighteenth-century Northeast where slaves were valued primarily as laborers. Slave women with a "record of fecundity" were the least in demand because celibacy and sterility were highly prized. Because childbearing interfered with productivity and since extra children were considered nuisances in white households, masters got rid of slave women at the first sign of pregnancy. Newspapers carried frequent advertisements like that for one woman being sold "for no other fault but that she breeds fast." A cook was unwanted "because she breeds too fast for her owner to put up with such inconvenience," and a husband and wife were "sold for no fault, save getting of children." Because they were a costly "botheration," surplus slave children were given away by their masters. Because childbearing was devalued, there evolved a marked disproportion between the sexes in the North's black population that was just the reverse of the trends typical of Southern Appalachia. Because slaveholders prized labor productivity over any potential sales that might be derived from natural increase, Northern male slaves significantly outnumbered females. Had Southern Appalachians not been seeking to accumulate profits from the natural increase, it is unlikely that they would have been retaining greater numbers of women than men.[19]

We can arrive at another crude index of slave fertility by calculating the ratio of infants younger than one to the number of women of childbearing age. Interregional comparisons of these averages provide support for the notion that the slave-selling states were maximizing the reproduction of slaves in order to market surplus laborers. The slave-buying states were characterized by 153 infants for every 1,000 women of childbearing age. By comparison, the slave-selling states produced nearly 1.2 live births for every infant in the Lower South. Yet the averages for Southern Appalachia were even more extreme. Averaging 189 infants per 1,000 potential mothers, mountain counties were reproducing slaves at a rate that was 1.06 times greater than that in the rest of the Upper South. West Virginia and western Maryland fell behind Upper South fertility rates, but the rest of the Appalachian counties far exceeded averages for the slave-selling states. Surprisingly, the highest fertility rate occurred in eastern Kentucky where slaveholders were procreating infant slaves at a rate that was 1.2 times that of the Upper South. Similarly, the Appalachian counties of Georgia, North Carolina, South Carolina, Tennessee, and Virginia exhibited a fertility ratio that was 1.1 times that typical of the rest of the slave-selling states. These fertility estimates are conservative, for the census only counted children alive at the time of the enumeration, and census enumerators tended to underreport infants younger than one.[20]

A third indirect measure of slave fertility is the degree to which children too young for labor were disproportionately represented in the population. Where agricultural laborers were in greatest demand, plantations reproduced less than one slave child for every adult. On the other hand, the slave-selling states were characterized by nearly 1.2 children for every adult. Except in western Maryland and West Virginia, Appalachian slaveholders owned 1.3 to 1.4 times more children than adults, a ratio that exceeded the practices of their Upper South counterparts. Butlin argued that such disproportionately high slave birth rates could not have been achieved without the structural interference of masters.[21]

Structural Pressures Toward Early Childbearing

On average, U.S. slave women probably reached menarche at age fifteen, but they postponed pregnancy another five to six years. If slave owners had successfully manipulated the fertility of slave women by pressuring them to reproduce as soon as possible, Trussell and Steckel argued, the observed mean age at first birth would have been closer to eighteen years. In sharp contrast to national trends, mountain slave women averaged only 17.2 years when they delivered their first baby, evidencing the structural interference of owners in the reproductive process. Three-quarters of the black Appalachian mothers endured their first pregnancy before the age of nineteen. For example, Delia Garlic had "one baby in her arms, another in [her] pocket," before she was twenty-one. To complicate matters, Appalachia's enslaved women averaged fewer than two years between their pregnancies.[22]

Appalachian reproduction strategies are startling when compared with fertility averages for other populations. For the U.S. South as a whole, the average age of enslaved women at the birth of their first child was about twenty-one, and these mothers were spacing more than two years between pregnancies. Promiscuity and loose morals do not account for these differences. Frank Menefee recalled that black Appalachian parents in his community set teenage abstinence as the standard for appropriate behavior. "Iffen a gal went wrong, [parents] beat her nearly to death." Moreover, emancipation signaled a dramatic change in the reproduction patterns of the region's African-American women. After black Appalachian women were emancipated, they made very different reproduction choices. Among those women who delivered their first baby between 1865 and 1870, more than half of the women were nineteen or older. The most startling change was that fewer than 2 percent of the postbellum births occurred to mothers who were younger than seventeen – a pattern that was in sharp contrast to childbearing trends during slavery.[23]

Structural Pressures Toward Higher Lifetime Fertility

It is a bit more difficult to estimate the average number of children reproduced by slave women. In a region characterized by a high incidence of family disruptions, plantation lists, census manuscripts, and slave narratives obscure the identity of infertile women and underreport children who are not present in the mother's current household. In addition, we cannot establish a reliable estimate of pregnancies that ended in miscarriages, stillborns, or infant mortalities. Appalachian ex-slaves offered four explanations for their lack of knowledge about their mothers' reproductive histories. At young ages, nearly one-fifth of the ex-slaves were separated from their mothers through sales or forced labor migrations. For example, Easter Brown recalled only six of her mother's offspring, adding that she did not "riccolec' de others" because "dey wuz sold off." More than 8 percent of the ex-slaves were not certain how many of their siblings had died or been sold away. For instance, Jordon Smith told the interviewer that he "had seven brothers and sisters live to be grown." More than 10 percent of the ex-slaves were aware that their mothers had children who were absent from the households. Anna Lee's mother was sold before she "was old enough to remember," so she never knew anything about distant family. In the White household, only five offspring lived with the mother, but Sallah did not know what had happened to the others. Mollie Scott's mother "had ten children [she] knowed of," plus others that were removed from the household before her birth. Ben Chambers reported that "dey was seben children what [his] mam kep' wid her," but he knew nothing about the missing siblings. Ex-slaves were also unsure how many children their mothers bore by males other than their fathers. Alex Montgomery's mother "had six chilluns by [his] pappy," but he was not acquainted with offspring she bore in previous households. Robert Falls mother "was sold three times before [he] was born," so he lacked information about children born in those previous households.[24]

About one-third of the Appalachian ex-slaves could not provide accurate recollections of their mothers' live births. Consequently, these incomplete counts cause a downward bias. After we isolate the inaccurate reports, however, we can discern two extreme patterns in the reproductive histories of Appalachian slave women. The ex-slaves provide three explanations for the low fertility of some women. The mother of one of every ten ex-slaves died in childbirth, shortly after delivery, or before the respondent reached age ten. More than 5 percent of the ex-slaves recalled that their mothers were in such poor health that they could not carry pregnancies to term. Although the narrators did not report them, these women probably experienced a high incidence of miscarriages, stillborns, and infant mortalities. Another 2 percent of the ex-slaves described mothers who refused to remarry or have more children after their husbands died. Thus, nearly one-fifth of the mothers of ex-slaves averaged only two to four children – a fertility rate well below the national average. No doubt, most of these women experienced the worst degrees of malnutrition, ecological risk, and overwork that characterized the region's plantations.[25]

Because of malnutrition and higher mortality risks, more than 15 percent of the mothers died young or were too ill to reproduce successfully. At the other extreme, nearly one-half the ex-slaves were raised by their own mothers, and the women in those households averaged 13.2 offspring. When we factor these two reproductive histories together, we discover that the mothers of Appalachian ex-slaves averaged 10.4 live births. Nationally, U.S. slave women averaged about 9.2 live births over the span of their childbearing years. More than half of all Appalachian slave women endured more pregnancies and bore more children than other U.S. slave women. Among those households in which ex-slaves were raised by their own mothers, more than one-third of the women bore fifteen or more children, 3 percent of them reproducing several sets of twins and triplets. Another one-quarter of these mothers experienced ten to fourteen live births while nearly 16 percent reproduced at a level that matched the national average. When we examine only the reports of ex-slaves who are able to provide complete counts of their siblings, we can see that nearly 60 percent of the mothers produced more live births than was typical of the reproductive history of U.S. slave women.[26]

Plantation Characteristics and Slave Fertility

How, then, do we explain these fertility trends? Why were Appalachia's slave women beginning to bear children five years earlier than other U.S. slave populations? Small plantations, like those that typified the Mountain South, were characterized by higher fertility rates. In comparison to larger slaveholdings, slave women on small plantations usually married younger, were less likely to remain childless, bore their first children at younger ages, and had longer childbearing periods. In contrast to Lower South cotton or sugar producers, slave women on tobacco and wheat plantations (like those of the Mountain South) married earlier and continued childbearing to a later age. Moreover, the probability of having a white father was much greater on small plantations. In fact, whites fathered slave children seven times more often on small slaveholdings engaged in mixed farming in the Upper South. In addition, the size of the owner's labor force had a direct impact upon slave household structure. Smaller slaveholdings had a higher incidence of one-parent households and of children separated from parents. Even though less than half the U.S. slave population lived on plantations with fewer than twenty slaves, these small holdings accounted for nearly two-thirds of all slaves living in divided residences and for over 60 percent of the slaves in one-parent residences.

In short, small slaveholders destabilized families much more frequently than large plantations.[27]

There is also a nutritional explanation for the higher fertility of mountain slave women. Malnutrition does not necessarily delay the onset of menarche or impregnation. Numerous studies have shown that young girls fed a protein-deficient diet still reached menarche by age fifteen or earlier. In the 1970s, researchers demonstrated that a minimum fatness of the female body is a necessary prerequisite to menstruation. Moreover, high-fat diets have been linked to earlier onset of menarche. As we have seen, Appalachian slaves consumed a diet that was high in fat pork and lard. If researchers are correct, that high-fat diet probably caused mountain slave women to reach menarche at an earlier age than slave women on larger plantations where there was more adequate intake of protein.[28]

There was a close relationship between the economic goals of slaveholders, slave fertility, and slave family structure. Like their Upper South counterparts, Appalachian masters thought it sound agricultural practice to be concerned about the procreation of their slaves and to emphasize strategies for maximizing reproduction. For instance, one Blue Ridge master instructed his overseer: "I wish particular attention may be paid to rearing young negroes ... that the number may be increased as much as possible." Likewise, the president of the Albermarle, Virginia, Agricultural Society counseled Upper South slaveholders: "Your negroes will breed much faster when well clothed, fed and housed." Thomas Jefferson believed that there was "no error more consuming to an estate than that of stocking farms with men almost exclusively." The annual crop production of male laborers was consumed for the maintenance of the farm. However, the reproduced offspring of the slave women were "an addition to the capital." For that reason, women and children should be managed as investment commodities, not as field workers. Jefferson admonished his estate manager: "the loss of 5. little ones in 4 years induces me to fear that the overseers do not permit the women to devote as much time as is necessary to the care of their children.... [W]ith respect therefore to our women & their children I must pray you to inculcate upon the overseers that it is not their labor, but their increase which is the first consideration with us."[29]

Appalachian slaves offer few anecdotal descriptions of masters who openly engaged in systematic forced matings. However, Appalachian owners routinely judged the suitability of women slaves in terms of their likelihood to reproduce. Describing the mindset of eastern Kentucky masters, Mandy Gibson was convinced that "young slave girls brought high prices because the more slave children that were born on one's plantation the richer he would be in the future." Similarly, a Warren County,

Tennessee, mistress frequently bragged to visitors that she "wouldn't take $2000" for one of her healthiest young slaves. "That's my little breeder," she causally chuckled to her neighbors. Lula Walker's mother was rated "a good breedin' woman" by her master because she delivered thirty children "in two's and three's." Infertile females were sold, usually by age twenty-five, indicating the expectation that they would begin reproduction young. Sarah Wilson's teenage sister "was sold off ... because she wouldn't have a baby."[30]

Structural Interference in Pregnancy

Antebellum planter manuals advised owners that pregnant women "must be treated with great tenderness, worked near home & lightly. Pregnant women should not plough or lift, but must be kept at moderate work," and they should not be worked after 9 P.M. in the summer or 8 P.M. in the winter. Appalachian masters like Jefferson may have espoused a "lighter" workload for pregnant women, but their schedule of *moderate* work and shortened work hours was still too arduous. Such labor decisions were grounded in the medical myths of the times. Antebellum physicians were convinced that poor women were physically and psychologically tougher than affluent mothers. One physician claimed:

In spite of the unfavorable conditions of her bringing up, poor food, privations, and hard work, the impoverished, working female comes to maturity a strong healthy woman. . . . The working woman goes through her pregnancy with little or no trouble . . . she ordinarily comes to labor in good physical condition to endure the strain, and goes through perhaps a hard labor without reacting unduly either to the pain or the muscular effort which she undergoes.

In the United States and England, poor white women worked in the mills until shortly before childbirth. Because of widespread acceptance of medical stereotypes associated with the race and class of the pregnant woman, Southern slaveholders structured work regimens that kept pregnant women at work right up until delivery. On average, a pregnant slave was removed from field work only about twenty days throughout her entire pregnancy. In contrast, Southern doctors recommended that affluent pregnant women limit their physical exertion to activities no more strenuous than those conducted "in carriage," and elite women took regular afternoon naps.[31]

Throughout the U.S. South, there were few instances in which pregnant women were released from regular tasks for extended periods. There was probably no letup during the first two trimesters and very little relief in the third trimester. Pregnant slave women continued at about three-quarters of their normal work load. In fact, most pregnant slaves did physical labor until the week of delivery. In northern Alabama, pregnant women continued to fill cotton baskets that weighed seventy-five to one hundred pounds. The pickers had to "move de basket longs" the rows until it was filled. Hard work severely restricted the amount of weight gained by pregnant women because masters provided few nutritional supplements to compensate for physical labor. Masters may not have worked field hands to death, but they were guilty of so overworking pregnant women that infant death rates were pushed to extraordinary levels. According to Fogel:

The heavy pace of work diverted nutrients from the development of the fetuses to sustaining the energy output and health of the mother. Under these conditions slave mothers produced underweight babies which, even if they were not neurologically impaired, were highly vulnerable to infections that sturdier infants could have survived. As a consequence slave death rates in infancy were about 30 percent and another 20 percent of the survivors died between ages one and five.

There is no evidence in slave narratives or in plantation records that Appalachian masters treated mothers any better than other Southern slaveholders. One Appalachian physician considered anything more than four days a month lost work time extravagant on the part of pregnant slave women. Robert Falls's mother "kept on working" during pregnancy because her western North Carolina mistress "was meaner than old Marster." During childbirth, the woman began to have convulsions, and she continued "having fits" the rest of her life.[32]

To entrench themselves in the lives of elites, antebellum physicians promulgated the false perception that mistresses had more difficult deliveries and required closer care than slave women or poor whites. Medical experts claimed that affluent white women were in labor twice as long as enslaved females. Doctors perpetuated the racist myth that stillbirths occurred five times more frequently among white women than among slaves. Masters showed their disdain for the vulnerabilities of slave women through two major fiscal management strategies. First, Appalachian masters maximized profits by keeping pregnant women at work as long as possible. Jordon Smith recalled that his northern Georgia master made pregnant women "stack hay in the fiel" after harvest. "Sometime one of them got sick and wanted to go to the house, but he made them lay down on a straw-pile in the fiel'. Lots of chil'ren was born on a straw-pile in the fiel'. After the chile was bo'n he sent them to the house." One middle Tennessee cotton planter kept pregnant women working so late in their pregnancies that they often had a "miscarriage right there in the field." George Jackson was born in "de weavin' room" because his mother was required to finish her nightly quota of textiles production. Second, Appalachian masters maximized profits by limiting the use of paid physicians in slave pregnancies. Believing that they were protecting their wives, affluent Southern males provided physicians to wives in about half of all childbirths. In contrast, less than 3 percent of Appalachian slave women were treated by doctors during pregnancy or delivery. Slave midwives tended the vast majority of pregnant mountain slave women, and an enslaved Appalachian infant was nearly twice as likely to be delivered by a midwife as one of the master's offspring. Some slave midwives attended slave, free black, and poor white women. Surprisingly, mountain mistresses delivered slave babies nearly four times more often than physicians. In fact, Appalachian slave women rarely saw a doctor until their health had deteriorated to a crisis point that could not be handled by mistress or midwife.[33]

Because their masters denied to them the quality of prenatal care that they made available to the adult white women in their own households, Appalachian slave women developed their own oral tradition of alternative medicine. One mountain midwife admonished her charges "to drink plenty of water, but it got to be spring water, fresh an' strained so dey won't no spring lizzard nor crawfish eggs in it." While this midwife did not mention bacteria or parasites, she comprehended that water was often contaminated. She told women with "mawnin' sickness" to boil their drinking water everyday. She advised an expectant mother to "eat a plenty of anything she want," and she particularly recommended large quantities of cold milk "fixed wid de egg and nutmeg" and watermelon – dietary supplements that would have increased intakes of protein, iron, and several essential nutrients that contemporary experts recommend for pregnant women. The midwife also recognized the dangers associated with a pregnant woman standing at work for long periods during the day, so she insisted that she "mus' soak her feets in strong salt water every night." What made the midwife's regimen problematic was the scarcity of the recommended supplements on most Appalachian plantations. Watermelon was seasonal, and salt was a precious commodity not rationed to slaves. Even if milk were available, a high percentage of African-American women would have been lactose intolerant. Appalachian slaves did raise their own chickens, however, so eggs were probably in greater supply than the other recommended supplements. Still nearly one-third of the Appalachian slave narratives describe women or mothers who exhibited symptoms of weakness and tiredness that might have been caused by iron deficiencies and chronic anemia. Given the widespread hunger and malnutrition on the region's plantations, it is likely that half or more of the pregnant Appalachian slaves were malnourished.[34]

A pregnant woman who continues to engage in physical exertion needs 3,135 calories daily, including fifty-one grams of protein and higher levels of iron, Vitamin A, Vitamin C, thiamin, riboflavin, niacin, and calcium. The primary cause of infant mortality is low birth weight of the baby, and that low weight results from maternal dietary deficiencies. Maternal malnutrition does the greatest damage to fetal development during the first half of pregnancy. However, it was that period during which slave women were worked hardest and were most likely to receive fewer nutrients than needed. The Appalachian slave diet was probably best from midsummer to early winter when garden vegetables, fruits, fish, and pork were available in greatest quantities. However, reproductive cycles were linked to the masters' production cycles, so one-third or more of all conceptions occurred after the fall harvests. Consequently, most mountain slave women delivered their infants between March and June when nutrients were in short supply, but spring planting put added demands on a pregnant woman's health. To complicate matters, more than one-third of black males suffered from syphilis and gonorrhea, increasing the likelihood that their sexual partners would have miscarriages and their offspring would be born with defects. Black children had rickets fourteen times more often than white children. Rickets caused distortion of the pelvic canal in adult females, and fetuses were often trapped in the deformed pelvis, increasing the incidence of stillborns and maternal mortality. Young women were also more susceptible to tuberculosis, and the disease developed most rapidly when they were pregnant. On one western North Carolina plantation, two pregnant slave women suffered with "consumption" throughout their pregnancies. The master described their illness as "a mortification [that] took place in [the woman's] throat and breast . . . something like the influenzy." One mother died five weeks after delivering a tiny infant; the other followed three months later.[35]

Antebellum medical guides recommended four to eight days of postpartum bed rest for affluent women, and they were admonished not to walk for two weeks and to wait three to four weeks before venturing outdoors. Appalachian mistresses customarily spent four to six weeks recovering from childbirth. In the Caribbean, laws ensured enslaved women five weeks work release after delivery. In contrast, Sally Brown described a regimen on Appalachian plantations that paralleled the work routines of poor white mill women. By the fifth day, northern Georgia slave women were walking outdoors. Within two to three weeks, Appalachian slave women returned to their work schedules, spending less than half as much time in their "lay-in" as their mistresses enjoyed. Solicitous toward their own wives, Appalachian masters described postpartum slave women as malingerers. At the Oxford Iron Works, women were viewed as "lazy" if they did not quickly return to their production duties. A Blue Ridge Virginia master told Frederick Olmsted that the slave women on his plantation would "hardly earn their salt" after childbirth.

They don't come to the field, and you go to quarters and ask the old nurse what's the matter, and she says . . . 'she's not fit to work'; and what can you do? You have to take her word for it that something or other is the matter with her, and you dare not set her to work; and so she lays up till she feels like taking the air again, and plays the lady at your expense.

In addition to their early return to work, postpartum Appalachian slave women were endangered by extended malnutrition. Already anemic and undernourished from pregnancy, probably one-half of all recent mothers did not receive the additional 500 to 1,000 calories needed daily to support lactation.[36]

In regions dominated by large plantations, enslaved women were generally healthier than their male counterparts. In the U.S. South, enslaved males experienced a slightly higher mortality rate than their female counterparts. Moreover, only 2 percent of all U.S. slave mothers died in childbirth or shortly after. Conditions on Appalachian plantations stand out as a sharp contrast to these national trends. Mountain slave women labored under the cloud of death rates that were 1.5 times higher than national averages and 1.8 times higher than the risks faced by local white women. Northern Georgia's white females were 2.7 times more likely to survive than local slave women. Similarly in the Appalachian counties of South Carolina and West Virginia, slave women were more than twice as likely to die as local white females. Black Appalachian women also died 1.8 times more frequently than the white males who so frequently exploited them sexually. In sharp contrast to national trends, the region's enslaved women even suffered higher mortality rates than their male peers. In the Appalachian counties of South Carolina and Tennessee, enslaved women died at about the same rates as black males. In the rest of the Mountain South, 107 slave women died to every 100 male slaves. In West Virginia, an adult enslaved woman was twice as likely to die as a white male and 1.3 times more likely to die than her black male peers.

Only black children younger than ten died more frequently than did Appalachia's childbearing slave women. The masters' strategies of malnutrition, high fertility, and inadequate work release during pregnancy and childbirth were the major causes, for mountain females died disproportionately during their childbearing years. Prior to their teens, enslaved females survived at higher rates than boys, but the situation reversed itself for Appalachian female slaves after they reached menarche. Malnutrition, pressures toward early and frequent childbearing, and overwork during pregnancy and after delivery increased the incidence of maternal mortality. However, higher mortality rates are also associated with pregnancy intervals of two years or less, the trend that typified the reproductive careers of mountain slave women. As a result of these forms of structural interference during pregnancy, 7.5 percent of the mothers of the Appalachian ex-slaves died during delivery or from physical complications caused by childbirth, a maternal mortality rate that was nearly four times higher than the national average. Even when they survived pregnancy and childbirth, slave women were seriously weakened by their dual roles as workers and reproducers. After giving birth to a four-pound baby, one sixteen-year-old slave mother "heard the doctor say [she] could not survive till morning." After several weeks, the woman finally "was able to leave [her] bed," but she "was a mere wreck of [her] former self. For a year there was scarcely a day when [she] was free from chills and fever," and her infant stayed weak and "sickly." Such descriptions of weakened young mothers are common in the Appalachian slave narratives.[37]

Structural Interference in Breastfeeding

Modern medical research documents the powerful biological linkage between breastfeeding and child survival. Infants who are breastfed longer than one year have the highest survival rates, more consistent growth rates, and greater natural immunization against infections, allergies, and a number of diseases. In fact, modern pediatricians recognize that no other food supplies all the chemicals and nutrients that are present in human milk. The longer the duration of breastfeeding, the more health benefits are accrued by both mother and infant. If humans weaned their offspring according to infant development needs without regard to cultural or economic pressures, most children would be weaned somewhere between 2.5 and seven years of age. Worldwide, the average of complete cessation of breastfeeding is 4.2 years.[38]

Appalachian elites may not have had scientific evidence, but mistresses comprehended that their infants were healthier and less likely to die when they breastfed their own infants well past their first birthdays. In the guides and periodicals written for elite women, male experts recommended weaning of babies over a one- to two-week period when they were eight to twelve months old. Despite the high child mortality and the recorded fears of elite mothers about risks associated with wet nursing, slaveholding women were pressured by husbands to return to their sexual duties, their social schedules, and their household management as soon as possible after delivery. In the male view, breastfeeding interfered with the "normal" operation of his household. Despite male pressures, there is little archival evidence that upper-class Southern women engaged in early weaning that was as extreme as those practices imposed upon slave women. On average, elite mothers weaned infants a few weeks after their first birthdays. After about the sixth month, affluent mothers combined personal breastfeeding with bottled breast milk or supplements from a wet nurse. In their diaries and letters, elite mothers recognized that early weaning endangered infant health. They probably also favored longer breastfeeding because lactation delayed conception. Elite mothers were advised that their duty was to "nurture the infant," even to the exclusion of husband and older children. Most experts advised upper-class women not to establish a rigid feeding schedule, but instead to leave it up to the baby to establish its own routine as to time and frequency of nursing. Judging from archival sources, Appalachia's slaveholding women continued breastfeeding well beyond the weaning age recommended by doctors. Already walking when weaned, one white Appalachian male reported that his mother "allowed [him] to use her breast very late." When her one-year-old daughter "shewd symptoms of disgust whenever she took nourishment" from the wet nurse, the mistress began breastfeeding her again without substitutes. With respect to another child, this mother wrote: "I have not weaned a boy that is large enough to talk of horse-racing, can make a fire, and feed calves."[39]

Infants need to be fed on demand ten or more times daily in the first nine months, and they should be fed nothing but breast milk during the first six months. At nine months, two solid meals should be supplemented by breastfeedings. In the nineteenth century, middle- and upper-class European and American mothers suckled infants on demand for at least the first year. To maximize their own profits and to capture the labor of women, Appalachian slaveholders "rationalized" breastfeeding in ways that interfered with all these natural processes and rhythms. First, Appalachian masters structured a regimented feeding schedule for slave infants. Women returned to their work schedules within the first three weeks of birth, placing their infants on a limited feeding schedule. In contrast to child-initiated breastfeeding, nearly one-half the Appalachian slave women were called from the fields two to three times daily to nurse their infants. The first feeding was completed in the morning. Women with newborns were allowed to report later to the fields. As soon as the women "takes care of de babies, dey comes ter work." After that, the slave mother was "not allowed to see her baby except ... at certain times a day." In sharp contrast to the breastfeeding customs of mistresses, plantation manuals recommended three daily feedings for enslaved infants. According to the *Southern Cultivator*, nursing mothers should "visit their children morning, noon and evening until they [we]re eight months old, and twice a day from thence until they [we]re twelve months old." According to Andrew Goodman, "the mammies wuz give time off from the fields to come back to the nursin' home to suck the babies." On one middle Tennessee plantation, "they had a horn and every woman could tell when it was time to come and nurse her baby by the way they would blow the horn." Without scientific evidence, masters developed nursing methods that have been supported by contemporary pediatricians. After strenuous exercise, contemporary mothers are advised to wait ninety minutes before nursing a baby. Physical exertion releases increased lactic acid, causing the infant to be colicky for four to six hours. Plantation manuals instructed slave mothers "to be cool before commencing to suckle – to wait fifteen minutes, at least, in summer.... It [wa]s the duty of the nurse to see that none [we]re heated when nursing as well as of the Overseer & his Wife." To encourage infants to sleep between two widely spaced daily feedings, the caretakers for the offspring of poor white mill women dosed them with opiates and herbal mixes. Early weaning combined with the introduction of such dangerous chemicals deterred growth and muscular development and led to high infant mortality rates. Appalachian plantations followed similar regimented feedings. Alex Montgomery remembered that "sometimes you'd hear as many as five or six cryin' at one time. Granny wud give dem some kind uf tea to make dem shut up."[40]

Two-fifths of the women carried their infants with them to work, feeding them at prescribed intervals between their tasks. On a Coosa County, Alabama, plantation, "the mother was forced to return to the field as soon as she was able and leave her children." Some of these women left babies in the care of older siblings at row ends, stopping periodically to nurse. A middle Tennessee woman recalled that mothers with infants "were allowed to take their babies to the field and put them under trees until nursing time. A woman had better not stop to suckle her baby until she was told to do it else she would be beat." More than 8 percent of the slave mothers did not nurse their own infants during the workday. Instead, one slave wet nurse tended all babies until the evening hours. The wet nurses for slave infants were women who had recently born babies, but who were still unable to return to their own normal duties. Instances of slave resistance against regimented breastfeeding can be found in regional manuscripts. Mollie Moss described an eastern Tennessee mother who hit her master in the head with a shovel " 'cause she was nussing a sick baby an' he tell her she got to git out in dat field an' hoe." At one Blue Ridge Virginia plantation, nursing mothers left the fields as a group to feed their infants five times daily. The owner ordered his overseer to whip the women, and he reduced the nursing schedule to "half an hour before they went to work, half an hour before their breakfast; and half an hour

Elderly slaves, like this Rockbridge County, Virginia, woman, tended children while mothers worked. Due to attenuated breastfeeding, malnutrition, and inadequate child care, more than one-half of all Appalachian slave children died before age ten. *Source: Harper's*, 1856.

before they go in at night." After women left the harvest fields five years later, the master resigned himself to tolerate their more liberal feeding schedule. "Our wenches have all taken it into their head," he wrote, "to cry out at this busy time."[41]

Weaning is rarely child-initiated until age four, but nineteenth-century middle- and upper-class American mothers weaned their babies when they were two to three years old. More affluent women correctly intuited that the safest weaning procedure was one that gradually replaced one feeding at a time with solids. To maximize women's productive labor in the fields or at hired locations, Appalachian masters denied to enslaved women the breastfeeding regimen that was customary among the women in their own households. Supplementary foods were introduced to black babies by the sixth month, earlier than the digestive tracts and tongues of most infants are developed enough to handle such intake. After the 1830s, elite women could use bottles and nipples to continue to supplement weaned infants with their own breast milk. This was not an option available to slave women, so they were forced to rely on food supplements when infants were younger than six months. To complicate matters, slave weaning was usually abrupt, leading to loss of appetite and malnutrition in infants and to postpartum depression and breast infections in mothers. When slave infants began cutting teeth, mothers were expected to diminish breastfeeding considerably, if not entirely.[42]

Appalachian masters also accrued profits by maximizing the reproductive capacity of slave women. Because it postpones the return of the menstrual cycle and fertility for more than a year, breastfeeding is the most important determinant of the length of the interval between one pregnancy and the next. Appalachian slave women were aware of this biological fact, for late weaning was an African cultural derivative. West African women nursed children two to three years and abstained from sexual intercourse until the child was weaned. This custom produced an interval of three to four years between pregnancies, much longer than that usually found among European women in the eighteenth and nineteenth centuries. If widely practiced, extended breastfeeding would have severely depressed the birth rate among black Appalachian women. To spur higher fertility, masters required mothers to return to work within a few weeks of childbirth and to wean their babies by the end of the ninth month. Appalachian masters offered rewards for weaning children because they were aware that the fertility of slave women dropped while they were nursing infants. As market demand for slaves increased, Appalachian masters expanded their interference into slave childbearing and breastfeeding. Between 1750 and 1850, Appalachian plantation records document a steady decline over time in the age at which female slaves experienced their first pregnancies and a steady decline in the time interval between pregnancies. To accomplish that increased fertility, masters regimented feeding schedules and pressured slave women to engage in weaning practices that were dangerous to both child and mother.[43]

Appalachian masters engaged in a third form of structural interference in slave women's breastfeeding. While masters required early weaning of slave children, they employed black mothers to serve as wet nurses and caregivers for white offspring, who were typically breast-fed for nearly two years. At the same time that mountain slave women were weaning their own infants early, one-fifth of them worked as wet nurses for white infants. One western North Carolina mistress attributed her child's robust health to the slave wet nurse. This "fine, healthy, careful Negro woman" was still in her master's household nine years later. The wet nurse "has plenty of milk for her child and mine," claimed the mistress. When one Appalachian family lost the services of their favorite wet nurse, an uncle wrote to the husband humorously: "Does it not make you weep to think that you have forever lost the services of Lucy & her 'Catnip.' As she has always been a necessary institution in your Domestic affairs, I see no other channel for you in the future, than to 'shut up shop' and discontinue the Business" of reproducing children.[44]

Motherhood lay at the core of the personal identities of Appalachia's slaveholding women. One northern Alabama mistress affirmed that family and child rearing "engross[ed her] mind to the exclusion" of everything else, whether "religious or social." Even though white mistresses attached deep emotional significance to kin and family, they intruded routinely in the mothering roles of enslaved women. On the one hand, the placement of wet nurses represented an active segment of mountain slave hiring. John Van Hook's grandmother was removed from her own children so her owner could hire her out to wet nurse "the little orphan baby" of an adjacent slaveholder. Caroline Foster was purchased away from her own family to "nurse de chillun" of a new owner. On the other hand, enslaved mountain women were more likely to serve as wet nurses in the homes of their own masters. Georgia Flourney was a "nu' maid" throughout her reproductive years, and she breast-fed every "las' baby" of her mistress. Chaney Mack experienced two generations of ill effects from wet nursing. Although she was "a seven-months baby," her mother put her "on a terbacco pipe." In order to sustain her duties as wet nurse in the master's family, the mother introduced her infant early to solid foods. When Chaney's later mistress died in childbirth, the young slave mother and her new baby were moved into the master's house so she could wet-nurse the orphan.[45]

On the one hand, wet nursing claimed the benefits of breastfeeding for the offspring of white masters while denying or limiting those health advantages to slave infants. On the other hand, wet nursing required slave mothers to transfer to white offspring the nurturing and affection they should have been able to allocate to their own children. The mothers of Fannie Tippin and Sarah Allen wet-nursed their masters' children, leaving their own youngsters in the care of elderly slaves. Even though she was a field laborer, Anna Lee wet-nursed the babies of her eastern Tennessee mistress. While she cooked meals for her own children, she would have the white baby "in one arm." When he was nine years old, Thomas Cole's northern Alabama mistress announced to him:

What a big fine strong boy you is, you ought ter be big enuff ter do mos any kine of work now, you aint a baby any more.... I bought a nice place up dar [in town], so I'se goin ter take your ma wid me as she has allus been our nurse, but I'se goin ter leave you out here on de plantation. I'm sure [the overseer] will take good care of you, and besides you will be grown in a few more years. Purty soon [his] mother comes out and tells [him] ter be a good boy and do all dat [the overseer] tells [him] to do and ter stay up wid de rest of de slaves and dat she would comes ter see [him] de first chance she gits and fer [him] ter do de same thing.... [D]at was de last time [he] ever seed her, she never gits ter come back ter see [him] and [he] never could goes in ter see her, and [he] never seed [his] brother and sister any more.

Wet nursing often broke the health of slave women. Andrew Goodman's "maw wus a puny little woman" as a result of repeated, long-term wet nursing. While her own babies were "comin' 'long fast," another wet nurse tended her master's ten children. As an elderly woman, she lamented that she "don't do nothin' all [her] days but nuss, nuss, nuss." She served as wet nurse to "so many chillen it done went and stunted [her] growth," causing her to become "nothin' but bones."[46]

Only about 20 percent of all affluent women relied on wet nurses to breast-feed their infants, but almost all mistresses employed slave women to be the nurses and babysitters for their offspring. At some point during their enslavement, two-thirds of the mountain slave women were employed as caregivers to white children. Prior to their adult assignment to field labor, most young Appalachian slave girls were trained into the nursing roles that would characterize their reproductive years. From "a wee bitty baby," one western North Carolina girl was taught "to serve" the master's children. Sallah White slept in a "trunnel" bed, in order to serve her young mistress during the night. Catherine Slim "wuz doin' women's work" at ten, losing her own childhood to tend the master's toddlers. Appalachian masters could recoup part of their investment and expenses by hiring girls "till 10 years old to serve as nurses."

Before she was big enough to work in the fields, Millie Simpkins "wuz hired as nuss girl at seven y'ars ole." While she was still a child herself, Melinda Ruffin was auctioned from the "sellin' block" of Augusta County, Virginia, to work as a nurse to white children. McMillen has observed that the black caregiver "performed most of the labor that the mistress fancied she had done herself." Similarly, Fox-Genovese contended that enslaved women "did whatever their mistresses needed or wanted done, and rarely, if ever, did those mistresses acknowledge their efforts as work, much less as skill or craft." While Maggie Broyles's mother tended the master's offspring, her mistress would "ride off when she got ready," leaving the slave mother to go "right on wid the work" for which the master's wife took credit. Martha Zeigler never had any children of her own; she was so busy nursing the mistress' children that she "didn't have no time to think 'bout such things" as marriage and family. When Anna Washington's free husband attempted to purchase her freedom, the owner refused, commenting that he had been instructed by the mistress "never to sell Nellie and to keep her to raise his white children." Sarah Patterson watched all her own children die except one while she nurtured the master's children. When asked why she did this, she responded perceptively: "I was a woman. I wasn't no man."[47]

Slave Child Mortality in the Mountain South

In the United States in 1850, 51 percent of all black deaths were children younger than nine. Until age fourteen, the mortality rate of slave children was twice that of the white population. A slave infant was 2.2 times more likely to die than a white baby, and white children between five and fourteen survived 1.9 times more often than did slave children of the same ages. Recent research has isolated five risk factors that increased the likelihood of infant mortality. The pregnant mother's dietary deficiencies often caused premature labor and low birth weights. Malnutrition at conception or near delivery caused a high incidence of stillborn babies. In fact, a majority of slave newborns probably weighed less than 5.5 pounds, and 10 to 15 percent of all births were stillborn. Malnutrition of the fetus also increased the incidence of sudden infant death syndrome (SIDS), which occurred much more frequently among slave infants than among infants in white families. Maternal and fetal infections were higher in situations characterized by malnutrition and poor sanitation. Infant deaths were 56 percent higher among antebellum mothers younger than twenty. Work during pregnancy, especially effort that required extended standing, dramatically increased the incidence of infant mortality. Attenuated breastfeeding added another risk factor for infants and developing children. Little work time was lost after the second month following delivery, and enslaved women began to return to near-normal work loads within four weeks after giving birth. While white mistresses breast-fed their own babies more than a year, slaveholders required enslaved women to terminate breastfeeding when their infants were nine months old. Without doubt, then, the malnutrition strategies of masters were a major cause of the high rates of infant and child mortality among American slaves.[48]

In 1850, mountain white children were dying at levels slightly below the national average. However, the mortality risk of Appalachian slave children was above the national average. At least three of every ten Appalachian slave infants and 2.7 of every ten youngsters aged one to ten died. Nearly 60 percent of Appalachian slave children died before the age of ten, a rate that was 1.25 times the national trend. Appalachian slave children were at greater risk of mortality because of nine profit-maximizing strategies structured by their owners. As we saw earlier, malnutrition and chronic hunger occurred more often on small plantations, like those that characterized Appalachia. Thus, nutritional inadequacies were a common experience among the region's enslaved pregnant women, thereby increasing the incidence of premature births, low birth weights, infections, stillborns, and SIDS. In seven Blue Ridge Virginia counties, physicians reported SIDS three times more often among slave infants than among white babies, and more than half those deaths occurred before the fourth month of the infant's life. Because of malnutrition strategies and ecological risks, Appalachian slave mothers died more frequently than did slave women in other parts of the United States, leaving infants and young children without their crucial support. To maximize the number of laborers available for export through the interregional slave trade, masters pressured teenage slaves to begin childbearing at an earlier age than was typical for the rest of the United States. More than half of Appalachia's enslaved mothers began childbearing at a younger age than other U.S. slave women, vastly increasing the incidence of infant mortality, stillborns, and SIDS. Because Appalachian slaves were more often sold or hired out, there was a greater likelihood that mothers would be separated from infants.[49]

In response to structural interference from their masters, Appalachian slave mothers ended breastfeeding too early to ensure the future health of their offspring. As evidenced by the regional slave narratives, it was the common practice of their masters to require the early weaning of infants to a diet high in carbohydrates, but low in proteins and milk. Foods other than breast milk introduced pathogens and allergens to infants, and

A majority of Appalachian slave women worked as caregivers to young or elderly whites at some point during their work lives. In those adult roles, they would be forced to wean their own offspring too young and leave them without adequate child care. *Source: Harper's,* 1856.

African-American babies were genetically inclined to be lactose intolerant. Fogel has noted that

Weaning to gruels and porridges could have prevented catch-up growth and promoted high death rates in two different ways. If the gruel was prepared mainly with water, then it was likely to have been *protein deficient*. If the gruel was prepared with raw cow's milk, infants and young children may have been exposed to increased risks of contracting tuberculosis, undulant fever, and salmonellosis, all of which may be transmitted by raw cow's milk. These diseases would have prevented catch-up growth by inducing loss of appetite (thereby reducing the nutrient intake of infants and children) or by promoting diarrhea (thereby preventing the body from utilizing the nutrients that were ingested).

Nationwide, the highest infant mortality rates occurred after food supplements were begun. More than 30 percent of all slave children died before age one. Moreover, black children died four times more often than white children from convulsions, teething, tetanus, lockjaw, SIDS, and worms, and all six of these diseases were linked to early weaning.[50]

In addition to the risks they imposed upon infants, Appalachian masters maximized profits by structuring shortfalls in the minimal survival provisions of older children. As we have seen previously, Appalachian masters kept operating costs low by housing slaves in overcrowded, inadequate cabins; by minimizing their construction of wells and privies in the slave quarters; and by skimping on food rations to families. Moreover, mountain masters supplied little or no professional medical care to pregnant mothers, infants, or youngsters. Thus, children struggled to survive in households that were already strapped for the necessities of life. Crowded into small cabins with several other people, children often slept on dirt floors, and they frequently incurred serious burns while lying near open fireplaces. Gip Minton "slept in an outhouse that was too rickety for a family," while Hannah Moore slept in the tannery. Hannah's "bed of straw and old rags" was put every night in the big "tan trough" which held the chemicals to cure leather. Sarah Gudger "nebbah sleep on a bedstead till aftah freedom." Instead, she slept on "jes' an ole pile o' rags in de conah" of the master's kitchen, with "ha'dly 'nuf t' keep us from freezin'."[51]

Moreover, a higher proportion of Appalachian slave children were exposed to the dangers of nonagricultural environments. On the one hand, mountain slave children were more often born to parents employed in industrial occupations. On the other hand, Appalachian masters frequently hired out slave children to mines, to river craft, and to manufactories, thereby increasing their exposure to ecological risks and to physical dangers. Children who worked at tobacco manufactories suffered debilitating respiratory ailments during the developmental stages of their lungs. On the canal boat between Cumberland and Harper's Ferry, "the black boy who drove the horses ... fell into the lock in which the Boat lay and was drowned." Working late at night in gold mines, young boys quite often stumbled to their deaths or suffered permanent disabilities. Antebellum coal mining exposed workers to very dangerous working conditions and stunted the healthy development of child laborers, as Booker T. Washington reported about a Kanawha County mine. "The work was not only hard," he wrote, but "there was always the danger of being blown to pieces by a premature explosion of powder, or of being crushed by falling slate." Boys who "were compelled ... to spend a large part of their lives in these coal-mines" were often left "physically and mentally dwarfed."[52]

Appalachian slave children were especially endangered by the efforts of masters to lower clothing costs. Most black Appalachian children "didn't have nothing to wear no how but shirts," and "there wasn't no difference in the cloth they used in the winter and the summer." At Easter Brown's plantation, children "wore no clothes in summer" and only cotton clothes "in de winter." Typically, slave children wore lighter weight fabrics than adults, and they had no underwear, hats, or coats. Uniformly, Appalachian slave children went barefoot the year round, exposing them to the dangers of cold weather, injuries, worms, parasites, cholera, typhoid, and other infectious bacteria that proliferated in the unsanitary quarters. Typically, Appalachian slaves "never knowed what it was to have a pair of shoes" until they were "grown up" enough to work productively. Baily Cunningham "never had a hat or shoes until [he] was twenty." Isom Starnes "tote[d] water on [his] head and a bucket in each hand." As he climbed the hill, "he stumped [his] toe on the rocks till they would bleed." As a child, Sarah Gudger was "always cold n' hungry, and she had to "walk barefoot in de snow" of the western North Carolina mountains. Similarly, Fountain Hughes remembered a grim childhood in which he was always "barefooted an' col.'" Still his pain "didn' make no difference" cause he "wasn't no more than a dog" to his master. Children scrounged carpets, rags, and natural materials to wrap their feet in cold weather, but their "foots cracked open 'til dey looked lak goose foots." When George Jackson had to work "fore daylight" his feet "would 'most freeze." Easter Brown suffered through northern Georgia winters with her "foots popped open from de cold." One middle Tennessee slave complained that her "feet were so frost-bitten that you could track [her] everywhere [she] went through the snow."[53]

Malnutrition and Slave Child Mortality

However, the most pervasive profit-maximizing strategy of Appalachian masters was the structured malnutrition experienced by slave children. Even though widespread among adult Appalachian slaves, chronic hunger did greater damage to the region's enslaved children. Three-quarters of Appalachian slave children were fed a corn bread–buttermilk mush; the rest received corn bread blended with "pot liquor" from boiled meats. Less than 17 percent received regular fruit or green vegetables, and fewer than 16 percent received any regular ration of meats. Only about one-fifth were supplied molasses on a regular basis, and less than 10 percent reported eating sweet potatoes, peanuts, wild game, or stolen fruit. The vast majority of Appalachian slave children were fed in centralized containers, away from their families. Using a custom adapted from seventeenth-century England, Appalachian masters served food to slave children in "trenchers," wooden trays from which people ate communally. Callie Elder recalled that once a day "dey sot a big old wooden bowl full of cornbread crumbs out in de yard and poured in buttermilk or pot liquor. . . . Den dey let de chillun gather 'round it and eat 'til de bowl was empty." When they were lucky, the women added rabbit or opossum to the mush. Callie "never seed no fried meat 'til [she] was a big strappin' gal." Tom Neal was fed "milk or pot-liquor out in a big pewter bowl on a stump." Similarly, Alex Montgomery reported that

ebery day two wimmen brung big pots uf pot licker and corn bread down in de quarters an' poured it in big troughs an' we all wuz handed a spoon an' told to eat it. Sometimes Granny roasted [sweet] tater in de fire place an' give us one an' sometimes she parched goobers an' let us eat dem – we had thick black lasses an' sometimes we got a piece uf bread an' dug a hole inside uf it an' den filled dat hole wid lasses.

Bad nutrition was not the only hazard associated with such feeding methods. One Kentucky ex-slave described the lack of sanitation that existed in his daily eating arrangements. Sometimes, he said, "dat trough would be a sight, 'cause us never stopped to wash our hands, and before us had been eatin' more dan a minute or two what was in de trough would look like real mud what had come off our hands." Contamination of food and the spread of infectious diseases would have been common among the children who ate with their hands twice a day.[54]

On most Appalachian slaveholdings, "children would just have mush, but the grown folks would have meat." One middle Tennessee girl would "see grown folks eating the best things" that were denied to children, and youngsters "dasen't to look at it." During lean times on small plantations, children were fed items like ash cake and persimmon beer, squash or cabbage soup, or hoe cakes and molasses. On one Blue Ridge Virginia plantation, children were fed cabbage soup at midday, then they "were allowed to go to the table where the white folks ate and get the crumbs from the table." It is doubtful that children who worked in their masters' houses escaped malnutrition. One western North Carolina girl grabbed her bites of food while working in the dining room. Her young mistress would "fix [her] a piece of somethin' from her plate an' hand it back over her shoulder." The girl would "take it an' run outside to eat it ... an' go back to stand behind [the young mistress] again to wait for another bite." Similarly, Jerry Eubanks was a dining room servant at the age of twelve. "When de boss and Misses got up from de table," his meal consisted of "what was left in de plate."[55]

Children on Ben Brown's farm were supervised by a "boss mammy" who "looked aftah de eatins" to ensure that "nobuddy got too much." As a result of such feeding arrangements, Appalachian slave children were chronically hungry, not only for protein, but for diversity in their diets. Jane Holloway reported that she and the other children "wus always hungry." Wylie Nealy "got hungry lots times," and another western South Carolina slave "went hungry many days" and would "have to pick up discarded corn on the cob, wipe the dirt off and eat it." Henry Williams "got scraps" from the white table, so he "wasn't starved out till [he] was about grown." Sarah Gudger was so underfed on her diet of corn bread and molasses that she would run away to the neighbors at night to beg food. One northern Alabama girl was employed in the fields at an early age, but her master did not supplement her diet. Corn bread "to eat on the way to the fiel' was all [she] had fo' breakfas', an' fo' supper, the same." At midday, she was given boiled greens, peas, or other vegetables. When she dropped her bread one morning, she was frantic with hunger. Late to the fields and risking punishment, she "started back to fin' it" in the dark, and snatched it from a growling dog. One western North Carolina boy was so malnourished that neighboring slaves would hide baskets of baked sweet potatoes in the fields for him to consume at night. Like adults, Appalachian slave children resorted to stealing to battle their malnutrition. One young middle Tennessee girl pulled the barrel over on her when she tried to steal molasses. In her view, she "wouldn't have to steal it if [they] had give them enough." Because she pilfered molasses and sugar, Harriet Miller's mistress "turned [her] dress back and whipped [her] so [she] couldn't hardly set down." A hungry preteen would pilfer "roas'n ears" and milk from neighbors. Appalachian slave children rarely received desserts or treats, even when they served such items to their master's families. After she took part of a pie, Ann Ladly was given a dose of ipecac and "put out in de field to work." Another northern Georgia boy would "slip 'roun on de bakin day" to grab bread or cake crumbs. For Sally Brown, the weekly waffles consumed by the whites "was a picture," so she "jest couldn't keep from takin' one." Booker T. Washington had such a restricted diet that he had never seen cake or dessert. When he saw the young mistresses eating ginger cakes, they seemed to him "to be absolutely the most tempting and desirable things [he] had ever seen."[56]

Appalachian slave children were malnourished in patterns that parallel conditions in contemporary poor nations. Since such feeding strategies led to protein-calorie malnutrition and deficiencies of several vitamins and minerals, *kwashiorkor* must have been prevalent among underweight Appalachian slave children between infancy and age five. Evidenced by general emaciation and growth retardation, *marasmus* would have been pervasive among children aged five to fourteen. Such malnutrition causes extraordinary stunting of growth so that the height of the typical slave child would trigger alarm in a modern pediatrician's office. A vegetarian diet lacking in protein leads to deficiencies in most vitamins and essential amino acids, and children who consume large amounts of maize are at high risk of multiple nutrient deficiencies. The type of mush fed to Appalachian children was characterized by high dietary fiber content, but it was low in energy density, protein, fat, nitrogen, iron, zinc, magnesium, and copper. Even when Appalachian children received adequate calories, sickle cell, dark pigmentation, and lactose intolerance would have increased their requirements for many of the very nutrients that were never available to them, especially iron-rich foods. Black Appalachians who were malnourished before the age of three would have experienced retarded growth and decelerated metabolism and body chemistry for years after the malnutrition was ended. Moreover, chronic nutritional deprivation would have stunted the mental development of Appalachian slave children so that they would have been apathetic, emotionally withdrawn, and less assertive. Malnourished Appalachian slave children would have suffered lowered levels of psychomotor, problem-solving, and language skills. In addition, they would have experienced lowered visual ability, causing them to have an incapacity to separate visual figures or to learn to read.[57]

Regional slave narratives offer us powerful insights into the physical effects of long-term malnutrition among Appalachian slave children. Simon Hare did not comprehend the unhealthy signs of nutrient deficiencies, but he recorded the evidence of kwashiorkor among the young slave children on a small western North Carolina farm. They were fed a protein-iron-deficient diet of "peas an' bread an' taters" which "kep' [them] fat." In 1838, an enslaved Abingdon grandmother wrote to her distant daughters about the health of the children they had been forced to leave behind. The two abandoned children were showing signs of kwashiorkor and marasmus. Described as being "not very large, but quite plump," one girl was underweight, but showing the distended belly that accompanies early childhood malnutrition. The second daughter was a little older and had begun "eating dirt," an ailment resulting from longer-term deficiencies of several vitamins and minerals. Weaned early and separated from her hired mother, another Blue Ridge Virginia girl suffered such nutritional deficiencies that she began to eat dirt. Long before the age of ten and well before she was assigned any heavy labor, Liza Tanner "was so tired" all the time that she was always dropping off to sleep in the daytime. Probably suffering several nutrient deficiencies or sickle cell anemia, Liza would risk punishment to "slip off and go up in the loft and soon be asleep." Chaney Mack was "a 'seven-months' baby, and wuz a sickly chile" whose growth and development were stunted. To try to stimulate her growth, her Cherokee mother had her smoke herbs in "a terbacco pipe" and fed her chicken and turkey scraps. As an infant and young child, Oliver Bell spent his days under an oak tree near the fields where his mother plowed. Weaned early and fed only when his mother stopped at midday, Oliver was very slow to "lern to walk," indicating deficiencies of nutrients necessary for the formation of bones and muscle. After long-term malnutrition, Thomas Cole experienced psychomotor damage and visual impairment, so he was very "slow" at learning to read because he "was too thick headed to larn anything." One White County, Tennessee, boy was still being fed corn bread and buttermilk, even after he had been assigned to plowing. At fourteen, he was still "quite a small boy," reflecting the lack of protein and diversity in his diet. One middle Tennessee slave child "was so long getting grown," she swore that if she "ever had any chillen, [she] wouldn't treat them like [she] was treated."[58]

5   Slave Household Subsistence and Women's Work

> From the time I got up until bed-time I didn't have no time to eat idle
> bread. I had some hard times. To stop to look at a book or anything else
> was almost death. I was beaten so much that I don't see how I kept my
> right senses.   – Anonymous middle Tennessee slave

Super-exploitation is that circumstance in which productive workers contribute labor twice to their employers: once to produce market commodities and again to engage in *self-provisioning*. Production by the laborers
of their own subsistence allows the employer's investment to be less than
the actual cost of the maintenance and reproduction of the labor power
utilized. The low and sporadic food and clothing rations provided by
Appalachian slaveholders were insufficient to cover the living costs of an
enslaved household. By engaging in "direct robbery from the labourer's
necessary consumption fund," mountain masters extracted greater surplus value and maximized their accumulation of wealth. In an antebellum
economic treatise, Upper South slaveholder Nathaniel Ware summarized
the extent of this super-exploitation.

The slaves live without beds or houses worth so calling, or family cares, or luxuries,
or parade, or show; ... instead of sun to sun in their hours, are worked from
daylight to nine o'clock at night. Where the free man or laborer would require
one hundred dollars a year for food and clothing alone, the slave can be supported
for twenty dollars a year, and often is. This makes the wages of the one forty cents a
day, of the other six cents only. ... A slave consumes in meat two hundred pounds
of bacon or pork, costing in Kentucky, ... Tennessee, and Western Virginia, $8;
thirteen bushels of Indian corn, costing $2; this makes up his food. Now for salt
and medicines add $1, and it runs thus: a year's food is $11. Their clothing is
of cottons – fifteen yards of Lowell, $1.50; ten yards linsey, $4; one blanket, $2;
one pair of shoes, $1 – making $7.50. Now this sum of $18.50, say $20, divided
among the working days, is six cents. This is not fancy, but every day's practice.
So the wages of a slave is one-sixth part of the wages of free laborers.

By structuring an indirect transfer of surplus value to the slaveholder, such
survival shortfalls provided mountain masters with a higher profit than
would otherwise have been possible. Because mountain masters supplied

150

inadequate allocations of food, clothing, and medical care, slave households developed *resource pooling strategies* by which they could accumulate and distribute basic survival needs to their members.[1]

Household Subsistence Production

Most of the time of a black Appalachian was absorbed by two forms of unending labor. While doing "the masters' work," the slaves produced commodities for local and distant markets, but they also generated the surpluses that afforded their owners a lifestyle that was much more affluent than that of most white Appalachians. When engaged in "work for the family," the slave subsidized the master's inadequate survival rations. Black Appalachians reported that their masters supplied them inadequate food more than twice as often as other U.S. ex-slaves. Consequently, two-thirds of all mountain slaves augmented their masters' rations through a number of pooling strategies. Such household subsistence activity was necessary because Appalachian slaveholdings produced grains and meats at levels that would have permitted adult slaves only two-thirds of their annual food requirements. In addition, most mountain masters expected slaves to prepare their own meals. Some masters even offered small monetary Christmas rewards to spur increased food cultivation by their slaves. Mountain slaves often raised chickens and hogs, and they gathered nuts and berries from adjacent woods. To increase their protein intake, more than two-fifths of the Appalachian slaves hunted and fished, and they engaged in these activities 1.4 times more often than other U.S. slaves. However, their most significant food production strategy was the household garden, and black Appalachians grew family parcels twice as often as other U.S. slaves. On some plantations, the slaves constructed a platform above the parcels. "Dey put dirt on dat and buil' a fire upon it so dey hab light to wuk dey own li'l plot and garden at night." Even some industrial slaves supplemented food rations by planting gardens and raising swine or poultry. Black Appalachians also pooled resources from another source; they stole food three times more often than did other U.S. slaves. Slaves produced these additional food resources on weekends and at night, after they had completed the master's full regimen of work.[2]

John Finnely described the extent of subsistence production by enslaved households on his northern Alabama plantation. "We'uns make shoes, and leather and clothes and cloth and grinds de meal. And we'uns cures de meat, preserves de fruit and make 'lasses and brown sugar." In addition to food subsidies, Appalachian slaves built and maintained their own cabins, cut their own firewood, manufactured their own furniture and household items, and crafted their own clothing, bedding, and shoes. On the one hand, mountain plantations permitted slaves to develop a greater variety of skills than larger-scale enterprises in other parts of the South. On the other hand, those opportunities to acquire skills came at a dramatic cost to the laborers. In sharp contrast to the rest of the United States, few Appalachian owners assigned slaves full time to any of the elite occupations, to domestic duties, or to artisan production. The vast majority of the region's slaves worked regularly in the fields, or they interspersed other duties with fieldwork. To maximize profits, most mountain masters required slaves to supplement their primary occupations with artisan production. Only about one-third of the region's slaves worked full time in a single occupation, without being required to utilize evening hours to manufacture items needed on their plantations. Those slaves who were fortunate enough to be assigned to one occupation were among the four categories of slave elites who worked with least supervision and received differential rewards for their labor: drivers, full-time domestics, industrial artisans, and commercial laborers. However, most Appalachian slaves were forced to augment their primary daytime duties with evening manufacture of commodities consumed or sold by their masters or of items that were essential to survival of the laborers themselves. In addition to their regular fifty-eight hours of field work each week, more than half the mountain slaves were assigned to craft production after sunset. Another 16 percent were required to complete evening handicrafts, after daily work in their masters' houses. The smaller the plantation, the greater the responsibility of slaves to generate much of their own subsistence. In the face of short rations from their masters, Appalachian slaves fell back on "self-exploitation" in the production of craft commodities necessary to operate their households. Appalachian slaves were ten times more likely than other U.S. slaves to be semiskilled artisans, such as tanners or basketmakers. The difference with respect to textiles production is even more striking. Appalachian slaves were assigned to produce cloth eleven times more frequently than slaves in the rest of the United States.[3]

In addition to pooling material resources, Appalachian slaves shared indigenous health care knowledge within and among households. Self-treatment was the primary medical strategy of the vast majority of mountain slaves, for only a few Appalachian owners relied on paid physicians for anything except the most serious cases. As Tom Neal observed, "there wasn't any doctors seeing after colored folks." Mothers tended their own families until the illness grew too complicated, then they called on one of the community's black healers. Most slave babies were delivered by black midwives, and experienced "grannies" provided prenatal advice and tended postpartum mothers. Elderly "root doctors" or "herb healers" handled community health care, and "some old woman too old for field work" often cared for the sick. On many mountain plantations, "old negro mammies" used their accumulated medical wisdom to treat everyone in the quarters, and sometimes on adjacent farms. The most expert slave healers were *conjurers* who were able to diagnose and treat complex conditions with herbal concoctions, charms, diets, and physical regimens. Combining African and Native American knowledge about indigenous plants, these healers used a variety of teas, poultices, and ointments derived from plants gathered from the woods or cultivated in garden parcels. Many of the herbal remedies documented in the slave narratives have been identified in modern scientific studies as effective medicinal plants that grow wild in the Appalachian Mountains.[4]

Cash Earning by Mountain Slaves

Even though the vast majority of mountain slaves engaged in garden cultivation and household production, less than 12 percent of the Appalachian ex-slaves reported that their households ever earned cash or participated in monetary transactions during their enslavement. In most instances, slaves sold their surplus produce, food items, and crafted items to their own masters. "Each family had a chicken house," and they routinely sold poultry and eggs to masters. Archaeological digs indicate that mountain slaves rarely consumed the chickens they raised, so they must have sold or traded most of them. Sometimes, a household raised surplus swine. During the winter, men and boys would hunt or trap and cure the hides and furs for sale to their masters. Appalachian slaves also marketed items to the stores owned by their masters or employers. At Traveler's Rest in northern Georgia, for example, slaves exchanged garden produce and poultry for store items. One West Virginia "vegetable man" left his surplus produce on consignment at his master's grocery store. At industrial sites, slaves traded food and craft items to the company stores. At Etna Furnace, for instance, slaves regularly traded sweet potatoes, corn, poultry, pork, bacon, brooms, calves, pottery, and herbs at the commissary.[5]

However, a few disposed of their items in nearby towns. One Amherst County, Virginia, mistress allowed her slave households to raise pigs or poultry and to cultivate garden parcels. She permitted them "to dispose of their wares as they saw fit," so they sold brooms, nails, fruits, vegetables, yarn, woolen cloth, rag carpets, quilts, pigs, chickens, and eggs at the Saturday town markets. Betty Spence hawked two kinds of ginger cakes on weekends. Occasionally, a slave operated a "trading cart," and some males caught and dressed small animals or birds. Despite the tendency of towns to drive out itinerant nonwhites, black Appalachians engaged in illegal street and door-to-door vending of their wares. Still others aggressively used "street cries" to call attention to their commodities. Common throughout Southern towns, black street cries combined the sales pitch for the commodity with religious verbiage and with language intended to evoke sympathy from whites. At Jonesboro, Tennessee, an elderly female slave "carrie[d] about a basket of vegetables to people's houses, and solicit[ed] their custom in a tone of distress." In the 1840s, an enslaved woman advertised her garden produce in Staunton, Virginia, with a ditty that played on the sympathies of whites and reassured them of her religious decency. "I live fore miles out of town," she boomed. "My strawberries are sweet and soun'. I am gwine to glory. I fotch 'em fore miles on my head. My chile is sick, an' husban' dead. I am gwine to glory. Now's de time to get em cheap. Eat 'em wid yer bread and meat. I am gwine to glory."[6]

A few mountain masters permitted slave households to cultivate cash crops. When slave households raised cotton or tobacco, the master marketed it with his own exports, and then credited the family at the end of the year. Some larger farm owners engaged in antebellum forms of sharecropping with their black laborers. One Coffee County owner allowed his slaves to cultivate corn and hay on shares. Another western North Carolina master permitted slaves to raise corn on shares. One Franklin County, Tennessee, master advanced seed and work stock in exchange for a share of the crops produced. The owner "gave each family an acre to work as they would, and he'd loan them the seed for whatever they wanted to raise." While most "raised what they needed for a better table," a few households "planted their entire acre tracts in some kind of money crop. Some raised nothing but cotton, and sold it with [the owner's] crop each year."[7]

Mountain slave households also manufactured a wide variety of homemade items. For a share of their earnings, mountain masters sometimes permitted shoemakers, blacksmiths, wheelwrights, and coopers to produce shoes, barrels, and metal items for neighbors. John Day's father "could make axes, mattocks, hoes, plow shares, knives and even jew's harps." When he had done "de day's work for [his] master," the owner "would let him work in de shop and keep de money he made working for other folks." In the fall, neighbors would bring their leather to a middle Tennessee shoemaker. For a fee that he split with his master, the artisan "made fine shoes and coarse ones." Another artisan did "fine tin work by hand" and divided his earnings with his owner. Female artisans produced knitted items, fabrics, clothing, and quilts. At night and on weekends, entire households creatively refashioned scraps into cornshuck horse collars, brooms, and straw hats. Blending traditions from their African and

Cherokee heritages, men and women wove baskets from reed, willow, pine needles, split oak, and other natural vines; they produced baskets that were used for all kinds of household purposes, for fishing and hunting, and for gathering cotton and tobacco.[8]

Mountain slaves also earned cash by charging fees for unusual services. One middle Tennessee fiddler "learned how to play on a long gourd with horsehair strings on it"; then he earned extra money by playing for local white gatherings. Similarly, Moses Stepney's father "used to sneak out at night and play for house dances." Like many other black Appalachian women, Isom Starnes's mother "made money washing and ironing" for local whites. A western Maryland slave woman earned fees for preparing the bodies for white funerals. To earn extra money, Catherine Slim's father "made caskets for de dead people." A few slaves sold cordwood to town families. Between ages eight and twelve, Lindsey Moore was so skillful at marble shooting that his "master began taking him into town to compete with the little slaves of other owners." Masters gambled, and Lindsey got to keep "pennies that some of the spectators tossed him." A few slaves engaged in illegal trafficking of stolen items or whiskey, particularly to nearby poor whites. Hired slaves sometimes managed to steal small gold nuggets from the mines where they worked in northern Georgia.[9]

Households could also accumulate cash when members marketed their labor time. Slaves who were hired to railroads, mines, iron furnaces, salt wells, or other industrial or commercial sites routinely engaged in *overwork*. Slaves accrued credits at the company stores for all time worked above the contracted amount due to their owners. Some mine operators permitted slaves to prospect for gold on shares. However, self-hiring was, by far, the most frequent method through which mountain slaves earned wages for their labor time. Male agricultural laborers and artisans frequently hired their time to neighbors at night or on weekends. While most slaves worked short-term and remained under their masters' control, a few effected independent hires. In such arrangements, the slaves kept everything they earned above the contracted fee due to their masters. Indeed, available records reveal that owners often received more from slaves hiring themselves out than they did by leasing them through annual contracts. In Appalachian towns, surplus slaves were generally allowed to "hire their own time," by giving "their master a certain sum per month; and all that they ma[d]e over that amount they retain[ed]." For example, Cyrus McCormick granted his "faithful servant, Joseph," permission "to work as he pleased." William Walker allowed his western North Carolina slave Elyos to hire himself out to several employers across the state line in eastern Tennessee. The Waltons permitted their livestock artisans to

Only about 12 percent of all mountain slaves, like this West Virginia fiddler, earned cash during enslavement. *Source: Harper's,* 1855.

drive herds to Charleston every fall for area farms. For fifteen years, one western North Carolina owner permitted three male slave artisans to operate independent shops, so long as they paid him annual contractual fees for their time. Some Blue Ridge Virginia slaves hired themselves to operate small artisan shops, while a few West Virginia slaves worked on steamboats, sometimes earning $100 yearly after paying their masters.[10]

Only a few women were permitted to hire themselves out. One western North Carolina owner permitted a female to hire herself out "during her life at 50$ pr year." Bethany Veney effected an unusual arrangement with her owner. Her master agreed "that if [she] should bring him one dollar and a half every Saturday night, he would be satisfied." She rented a cabin on her own so she could take in washings, clean houses, and work in the fields, "getting a job wherever [she] could find it." After several months, her master agreed to let her pay him $30 per year, and "whatever [she] earned above that should be [her] own." A western Maryland slaveholder gave one woman permission "to work for herself provided she gave him one half." As a sideline to her job as cook in the village tavern, she prepared and sold pies and pastries. Her business increased to the point that "it became necessary that she should buy a horse and wagon to convey her goods." Later, she began "running a second hand clothing store on a small scale and made quite a respectable living."[11]

Was Subsistence Production Liberating?

Other U.S. slaves earned cash nearly three times more frequently than mountain slaves. Why did so few mountain slaves participate in cash earning? The answer does not lie in owner prohibition, for less than 4 percent of the Appalachian ex-slaves indicated that their owners banned such activities. One explanation lies in the area's geography, for most mountain slaves worked on small plantations or at isolated industrial sites far from towns. Second, Appalachia was inhabited by a sizeable majority of nonslaveholding farmers, and more than half the region's white households were poor landless laborers. Thus, mountain slaves had to compete for customers with a large poor white population. More importantly, however, it is clear in the WPA narratives that mountain slaves recognized that such activities were an extension of their masters' exploitation and control over their households and their communities. Cultivation of garden parcels, self-hire, handicraft production, and overwork were self-exploitation by desperate people to survive the cost-cutting strategies of inhumane owners. Despite the advantages, mountain slaves were aware that their subsistence production profited their owners, perhaps more than it benefited them. Thus, some slaves refused to engage in self-exploitation because of the extra work involved and because masters reduced rations to the extent slaves could feed themselves. Some mountain slaves also understood that cash earning could have a divisive effect upon their community by unleashing a variety of petty property conflicts among slaves. The focus by mountain slaves on the blinding drudgery that characterized their daily lives provides another loud clue. No matter how hard they labored, household production and cash earning did not guarantee them a better life. On the one hand, few mountain slaves ever accumulated any surplus toward future independence, for they were required to apply most of what they produced or earned to subsidize the owner's shortfalls of food, clothing, and shoes. Indeed, ensuring the welfare of the family was the central purpose of slave household production. On the other hand, such activities certainly did not make them healthier. It is clear from the WPA narratives that mountain slaves worked longer hours and pushed themselves to their physical limits in order to engage in household production and cash earning. In this region where slaves produced more of their own food than was characteristic of the rest of North America, malnutrition was prevalent, and slaves experienced higher mortality rates.[12]

Free blacks and slaves often relied on whites to market their commodities, frequently paying commissions on the transactions. Appalachian masters customarily sold the home manufactures produced by their slave artisans, quite often tolling them a share of the proceeds. For example, shoemakers were often permitted to sell coarse footwear or to make shoes from the leather brought to them. A northern Georgia master even marketed the knitted articles made by one of his slave women. White mistresses often arranged to sell the garden produce, chickens, and eggs of their slave women. For instance, a Charleston, West Virginia, house servant "gether[ed] de turkey eggs an' guinea eggs" from the fence rows, and her mistress marketed them for her. A Jackson County, Alabama, mistress "allus help[ed] all de slave women wid their buyin' and sold all der chickens and eggs." By relying on the cooperation of whites, Greenup County, Kentucky, slave children picked up apples and "put 'em in big sacks ... and put 'em by the side of the road. Some one on the plantation would be going to town and would pick them up and sell them." By acting as their intermediaries, masters limited the independent access of mountain slaves to markets and to business enterprises. In this way, masters could set prices for slave commodities below their market value, once again maximizing their own profits. In addition, masters could keep slaves under control on their own plantations, and they could restrict how slaves spent their earnings. Most importantly, masters kept themselves in the economic loop, thereby absorbing back into their own coffers as much as possible of the slave household production.[13]

Cash-earning activities also remained dependent on the goodwill of whites because slaves were rarely paid in money. On the one hand, the vast majority of mountain slaves were illiterate, and that illiteracy extended to their incapacity to count, to recognize denominations of money, or to make change. To Ben Brown, for instance, "all money coins wuz a cent, big copper cents, dey wuz all alike." Mountain ex-slaves reported that the white community treated them with suspicion if they learned to "know paper money or gold in denominations greater than $1.00." Thus, mountain slave households were forced to rely on the honesty of masters and mistresses, for most of them "couldn't count money good." On the other hand, mountain slaves rarely saw cash for any of their economic transactions. On their home plantations, masters credited wages for overwork and sales of produce, livestock, crafts, or staple crops against additional allocations of food, clothing, or shoes to the slave family. Except for a very few instances, not even self-hires generated cash for the slave households. Most Appalachian ex-slaves reported that neighbors settled their wages with their owners. Masters, in turn, usually recorded such receipts in their journals, permitting the family to acquire extra food or clothing items against those credits. In other instances, employers paid hired slaves with store goods. For example, one Nelson County, Virginia, merchant kept running accounts for slaves who worked for local farmers. The laborer carried a paper chit to the store and charged goods against the amount that was to be paid by the white employer. The slave never handled any real cash, had no choice about the business to be used or the prices paid, and lost part of the wage in store surcharges for credit. Similarly, overwork at industrial sites rarely brought cash to slave households. Instead, overtime was credited to the laborer's account at the company store, and the slave charged goods against the accumulated earnings.[14]

Clearly, household production, cash earning, and trade did not liberate mountain slaves from the ownership of their masters or from the constraints imposed by the legal system. It simply was not possible for enslaved households to construct or to operate an economy that was independent of the numerous laws and ordinances enacted to narrow the slave's margin of autonomy, choice, and mobility. Every Southern state prohibited ownership or inheritance of property by slaves. A northern Alabama court case declared "the house of the slave is the house of his owner." The Cherokee Nation prohibited slave possession of "property in horses, cattle, or hogs," and their livestock was to be confiscated and sold "for the benefit of the Cherokee Nation." Strict public regulation of the movement of Appalachian blacks prevented their open participation in structured trade mechanisms. Even though many mountain slaves engaged in the practice, it was illegal for slaves to hire themselves out. Public assemblages of more than five blacks were prohibited and closely sanctioned, and black Appalachians could be whipped for violating town evening curfews. In addition to such negative social controls, there were economic constraints. On the one hand, tolls for stall space or for inspections put the town market-house out of the economic reach of slaves. On the other hand, slaves could neither apply for nor afford the required peddlers' licenses and business taxes. In Virginia, for example, peddlers were required to pay an annual fee of $15 to the state, plus an additional 25 cents to the clerk of every county in which they did business. It was contrary to public policy for any master to grant a slave "general permission to go at large and trade." In all eight Southern states where Appalachian counties were located, towns placed legal restrictions on sales by slaves in public markets. Appalachian communities routinely criminalized black peddling and often jailed violators. It was illegal for a free person to buy any article from a slave without written consent from the master. To be legal in many towns, exchanges with slaves had to be executed in the presence of their masters. Towns and states also regulated the types of articles that slaves and free blacks could buy and sell. Slaves could not legally trade medicines, drugs, or alcohol, and they were prohibited from purchasing knives, guns, ammunition, books, and newspapers. Though such transactions were not prohibited, merchants frowned upon black acquisition of attire usually worn by whites. In all circumstances, masters retained the legal right to set the terms of sales and the prices of commodities marketed by slaves. Most towns even prohibited the presence of blacks near public buildings, so they could not take full advantage of the trading that occurred during monthly court days.[15]

To complicate matters, common credit systems were closed to blacks. On the one hand, slaves had "no power to make a contract" and no legal right to collect debts. Black Appalachians had no legal recourse if purchasers cheated them or stole their wares, for neither slaves nor free blacks could bring civil suits. The only time that Anderson Furr, a northern Georgia slave, "ever got in de gyardhouse" involved an incident when he tried to collect a debt from a poor white man. When he asked the white for his money, "he got mad and knocked [Furr] down." Anderson "got right up and knocked him out, and right den and dar [he] was sont to de gyardhouse." On the other hand, merchants could not take legal action to recover debts, so they did not extend credit accounts to mountain slaves, except in those situations where employers charged purchases against wages or overwork at their company stores. Unless their masters or employers guaranteed their accounts, mountain slaves had no means of trading directly with local merchants who would credit their produce and home manufactures toward future purchases, the typical manner in which whites made store transactions.[16]

Far from being economically independent, nonwhite families were often forced into the underbelly of the market; they engaged in a variety of illegal, nonwage activities that brought them very low economic returns. Nearly half the free blacks living in Appalachian towns were unemployed three months or more each year. Another 11 percent relied totally on income from activities in the informal sector. Unstably employed males earned income from irregular day labor, from fishing, or from chopping wood. For example, the Ferry Hill Plantation irregularly provided day wages to "free negroes cutting wood." James Hickey was an impoverished peddler in Knoxville. Perhaps the most vulnerable of this category were the households headed by women who worked overwhelmingly as wash-women, prostitutes, or seamstresses. For example, washwomen headed more than half the free black households in the tiny town of Kingsport, Tennessee. In 1860 Botetourt County, thirty of the forty-eight free black households were headed by women who supported their families through poorly remunerated economic activities at the fringe of town life. In 1851 Winchester, Virginia, eight washwomen, three spinners, and one seam-stress worked out of their homes. In the major towns of western North Carolina, there were twenty-eight free black washwomen, weavers, or seamstresses. Twenty-seven-year-old Mathilda Lyon washed and ironed clothes while her seventeen-year-old sister worked as a "Fancy woman." In violation of legal restrictions against medical sales, a few free black women worked as herb doctors who prescribed health remedies, rendered cupping and leeching services, and delivered babies.[17]

In reality, a majority of the commercial activities of slaves and free blacks occurred in the informal economy. Appalachian slaves "done different things to make a little money," and the informal sector provided the only mechanism by which "a slave had of getting any money" outside the publicly regulated system. There were several significant disadvantages to this pattern. First, black Appalachians traded in the informal economy only at the mercy of local authorities. Sheriffs and patrollers intensified surveillance when there was community anxiety about possible slave rebellions, a common exaggerated fear among white Appalachians. Second, slaves were dependent upon the honesty of masters and other whites to sell their wares. Third, blacks probably received lower-than-market value for most of the commodities they traded. Fourth, blacks had to compete with poor, nonslaveholding whites who did not face the same legal restrictions or credit limitations. Finally, slaves and free blacks could not make legal contracts, so they had to depend upon whites to front for them in transactions.[18]

There was an even more significant way in which the household production of mountain slaves was not part of an independent economy, for Appalachian slaves were part of the worldwide commodity chain of cotton production. Household subsistence production by mountain slaves

Since mountain plantations provided little medical care to their laborers, black herb doctors, like western Maryland's John Cupid, administered most of the health care received by Appalachian slaves. *Source: Harper's,* 1855.

made it possible for Appalachian masters to export to the Lower South surplus edibles and laborers. On the one hand, Appalachian slave households reproduced, fed, and clothed the surplus laborers exported by their owners. Those surplus slaves provided direct labor to produce the cotton that was exported to the world economy. On the other hand, household production made available for export crops and livestock that should have been part of the rationed diet of black Appalachians. By externalizing to slave households the costs of their own reproduction and maintenance, mountain masters expanded the supply of foodstuffs they could export. Those large quantities of cornmeal, lard, flour, pork, vegetables, and fruits provisioned the labor force that produced Southern cotton. While Appalachian slaves experienced widespread malnutrition and pressures from masters to produce much of their own food, Lower South slaves were better fed. Through their household hardships and their higher fertility, mountain slaves subsidized the production of Lower South cotton.

Gender and Slave Occupations

Clearly, mountain slave households were units of production and resource pooling. That is not to imply, however, that members shared equally in the workload, for the slave occupational structure was bifurcated by gender. By 1820, staple crop production had generated "a marked increase in sexual division of labor" so that male slaves were assigned a "greater variety of tasks." Females were increasingly assigned to unskilled manual field labor, and the work of slave women "was less varied than that of men." No matter the staple crop or the scale of operation throughout the New World, females were disproportionately assigned to field labor, freeing males to work at more profitable occupations. Thus, females experienced fewer alternatives to field labor than male slaves. Almost universally, skilled labor was men's work, and slave women's work was limited to the house and the field. The upper echelon of the occupational hierarchy (about 20 percent of the slave labor force) was heavily dominated by male slaves who were drivers, blacksmiths, carpenters, millwrights, wheelwrights, mechanics, coopers, tanners, shoemakers, and skilled livestock experts.[19]

In the Mountain South, males were employed as drivers, skilled artisans, and manufacturing or commercial laborers fourteen times more often than females. Surprisingly, mountain slave women were overrepresented at field labor, but they were underrepresented in nondomestic crafts and in nonagricultural occupations. Only about one-quarter of all female mountain slaves worked full time in nonfield labor, and most of those women were employed as domestics in their masters' households or at hired locations. On his home plantation, an enslaved Appalachian male was twelve times more likely than his female counterpart to be assigned to full-time duties other than field labor or domestic service. Even when women were employed in industry or commerce, they were fifty times more likely to be utilized as unskilled laborers. While mountain slave women were most often hired near home as domestic servants, hotel maids, or field laborers, males were more likely to be hired out to distant industrial or commercial employers.[20]

On Appalachian plantations, slave women worked alongside men at most productive economic tasks, including field work, meat production, tobacco manufacturing, milling, cotton ginning, and leather tanning. Despite this gender blurring with respect to unskilled, nonmanagerial labor, women did the dirtiest, least-skilled, most back-breaking tasks. Even when slave women assisted with skilled crafts, their contributions remained hidden or unacknowledged. To support the male-dominated shoemaking process, for instance, women did most of the labor to gather tanning bark, to keep fires fueled, and to prepare and cure the hides. At one western North Carolina farm, women gathered the bark from the woods while a male operated a "bark mill" to grind the wood into the powder that would be used to produce tannic acid. Women cleaned, stretched, and dried the hides; in the evenings they also kneaded and rolled them to make them more pliable and soft. Women also made small animal skins into shoe strings and prepared a mixture of tallow and beeswax to soften and waterproof shoes. Women carried wood and maintained fires under the vats while a male stirred hides in the tannic acid solution. When males were needed elsewhere, women also stirred the vats, investing as much as a year to tan a hide. Once the hides were tanned, women stretched, dried, and softened them again. In fact, women probably contributed several weeks labor in the tanning process to every hour that males spent finishing the leather into shoes. Still, it was the male shoemaker who was rewarded with the release time, the cash-earning opportunities, and the diminished white supervision that went along with the higher work status.[21]

Slave women clothed the entire labor force, and sometimes the owner's household, thereby minimizing the cash outlay of their masters for manufactured goods. Why, then, were textile artisans less rewarded than male shoemakers or blacksmiths? Clearly, the explanation does not lie in the complexity or the physical demands of the gender-segregated tasks. First, it is inaccurate to presume that most male elite jobs required greater strength or skill than women's crafts. In reality, masters utilized height and skin color as much more important criteria for selecting elite male artisans than brute strength or intellectual prowess. If women were assigned less often to crafts because they were not as physically strong as men, why were there fewer enslaved males than females working the fields? Moreover, women worked longer hours than males each day; they utilized textiles equipment that required dexterity, stamina, and physical strength; they endangered their eyes and backs. In many ways, textiles production required much more accumulated knowledge, manual dexterity, and persistence than any of the elite male crafts.[22]

The work of male artisans was not ranked at the top of the occupational hierarchy because it required greater skill or stamina. Neither were

Appalachian slave women were disproportionately represented among field laborers, so they rarely were able to earn cash, as did this West Virginia blacksmith. *Source: Scribner's*, December 1874.

males at the top of the occupational hierarchy because slaveholders were reluctant to assign females to work under male overseers. Men supervised most of the field tasks done by mountain slave women, but most male artisans worked without close supervision. Rather elite occupations were linked directly to the profit-making enterprises of the master and generated significant cash returns. The economic value of "women's work" was unrecognized and hidden because it was more clearly tied to the subsistence needs of the master's household and the quarters. Even in the assignment of slave laborers, the dominant gender conventions of mountain slaveholders reflected the values, aspirations, and anxieties of the dominant Southern class. Outside the kitchen, masters rarely placed women in command of men, and they assigned women to the least profitable enterprises. Appalachian slave women were experiencing the cultural and economic redefinition of their labor as "nonwork" that had less value than the labor of male peers. Wallerstein contended that historical capitalism brought with it "a steady devaluation of the work of women ... and a corresponding emphasis on the value of the adult male's work," the transformation that occurred to the work of mountain slave women. To relieve men for hire-outs at higher profit rates, mountain masters assigned more women to field and domestic tasks that produced the lowest cash return. Thus, there were definite economic rewards for training males to be occupational specialists. Males were more often assigned to elite occupations for two reasons. On the one hand, a skilled male artisan was priced 150 percent higher in value than an unskilled male of the same age, but craft skills rarely increased the sales value of female slaves. On the other hand, the market demand was greater for skilled male artisans and nonagricultural workers, while women were valued in the Lower South for their greater productivity in field labor, especially cotton picking.[23]

Women's Inequitable Workload in Household Production

On the one hand, mountain slave women received an inequitable share of their masters' workload because male slaves were more often assigned to elite occupations. In addition to being less physically demanding and less time-consuming, elite occupations provided males with release time from field labor, enabled them to work without white scrutiny, and afforded them skills and travel opportunities through which they were able to earn cash and to resist their masters' control. On the other hand, females bore an inequitable share of the family's work, for women did most of the subsistence production in mountain slave households. Masters may have blurred gender lines when it came to using women at less-skilled men's work, but male slaves did not assume more women's work in any sphere. Consequently, there was a "polarization of reward" in the master's occupational structure and within the slave household. Mountain slave women were not only overrepresented in the most onerous tasks needed by masters to produce export commodities but also more likely than males to be engaged in household subsistence production. First, masters structured the absence of husbands from nearly three-quarters of the mountain slave households. Because they headed families in which adult males were more often visitors than day-to-day participants, mountain slave women bore the burden of creating additional resources to subsidize ration shortfalls. Moreover, males were given the privileges to travel to visit abroad spouses, while women remained bound to their home plantations. For that reason, males had many more opportunities to earn cash, to venture into towns to trade, and to avoid much of the work associated with household maintenance.[24]

Second, mountain slave women provided the bulk of the labor necessary to transform raw materials into items that the family could consume. The hallmark of poor rural women the world over has always been their capacity to weave together a creative tapestry of household and external outputs in order to accumulate "a consumption fund adequate for sustaining and replenishing" the labor force. Tending garden parcels and raising poultry were overwhelmingly done by women, with the regular aid of children and extended kin and with only the transient help of husbands who were erratic visitors. Household crafts were also the domain of women. After they had completed their daily work assignment for their masters, more than three-quarters of the mountain slave women engaged in subsistence craft production. As part of their elite occupations, male artisans produced shoes, metal items, spinning wheels, flax wheels, looms, and candle molds for their households. However, less than 10 percent of the males produced evening handicrafts for household consumption after they had completed another daily assignment. Thus, women produced most of the family's clothing, household utensils, and medicines. As men were assigned to elite occupations or removed from households, mountain slave women even came to dominate household crafts that had historically been male specialties. Basketmaking, fiber weaving, woodworking, and iron work were traditional male crafts in West African households, and men continued to dominate these crafts in other parts of the New World. In the eighteenth century, Appalachian male slaves commonly did the more complex weaving, while women did the less-skilled spinning. By the late 1700s, however, mountain owners were shifting male slaves away from their traditional African crafts. At Monticello, for example, Jefferson ordered young girls to be trained at spinning and weaving, while young boys were to be sent to the nailery. In other sections of the United States, "basketmaker" was an occupation claimed only by male ex-slaves, but men and women alike engaged in this craft throughout Southern Appalachia. By the late antebellum period, mountain slave women were making baskets thirteen times more often than men, and they were doing almost all the weaving without male assistance other than young boys. Part of the explanation for this gender shift lay in the Cherokee influence upon slave households. Among indigenous Appalachians, baskets, weaving, and pottery were "women's work." Thus, black Appalachians acquired these skills through their ethnically mixed families, from Cherokee slaves on their plantations, or from Indian neighbors.[25]

In addition to taking on more and more subsistence chores, mountain slave women worked longer hours than men. Masters allowed male artisans release time from primary tasks to make shoes, furniture, wheels, shingles, buckets, or metal utensils for slave household consumption, but women's household crafts were completed in the evenings and on weekends. Shoemakers, blacksmiths, and furniture artisans either produced items for household consumption as part of their primary work assignment, or they were permitted to leave the fields to do these tasks. On a western North Carolina plantation, for instance, a male artisan was sent from the fields to begin "bottoming chairs" for the slave quarter, while women continued to thresh oats and flax. Women threshed and cut straw, and males did shoemaking and coopering. In the evenings after that field work, those women were responsible for cloth production. One middle Tennessee field hand "hardly ever done any work in the fall of the year, but make shoes ... plumb up to Christmas." In sharp contrast, mountain slave women were 3.5 times more likely than men to be required by the master to combine an evening craft with their primary daily work. In fact, the overwhelming majority of adult slave women returned from their work in the fields to spend the remainder of the daylight hours and much of the night for their second set of tasks. When men finished their primary occupations, "der day's work was done," and women "was de onliest ones dat had to ever work atter dark."[26]

In addition to their handicrafts, women did most of the tasks necessary to manage a household, including meal preparation, cabin cleaning, food preservation, and caregiving to the young, the sick, the pregnant, and the dying. The typical mountain slave woman "nebbah knowed whut it wah t' rest." They had to "do ebbathin' dey wah t' do," so they "jes wok all de time f'om mawnin' till late at night." On Lizzie Grant's West Virginia farm, women "would work every day just long as [they] could see." Lula Walker "hadda work powerful hard" plowing, ditching, splitting rails, and everything else that men did; then, at night, she worked for her own family and produced textiles. Weekends did not bring an end to the work. After half a day's work for their masters on Saturdays, women usually washed and repaired clothes and tended gardens. The family "washing for de next week" was backbreaking. To prepare for weekly laundry, the women produced their own detergent from scraps of "ole meat and grease" and "strong lye" they collected by "pour[ing] water over wood ashes which was kept in a rack-like thing." Since there were rarely wells in the quarters, most mountain slave women did their family laundry in creeks, rivers, or ponds. "Ebery Sat'day de black wimen tote deir clothes to de spring an' dar dey washed but dey toted deir wet clothes back to de house to hang out." Maggie Pinkard's mother was not released from the master's tasks on Saturday afternoons, so she added the family laundry to her evening labor. While one of her children held a grease lamp, she carried clothes "down to the creek at night." Maggie remembered that "washing wasn't so easy." Similarly, Elizabeth Sparks's mother would "be washin' clothes way up 'round midnight." Working along the bank, the women pounded the heavy garments and wrung them by hand. Since the women had no washboards for scrubbing, they spread the clothes on a flat board or a log, after they had soaked and soaped them. "The clothes was taken out of the water an' put on the block and beat with a battlin' stick, which was made like a paddle. On such days you could hear them battlin' sticks poundin' every which-away." As one mountain slave woman observed, "That was work!" The women in Easter Brown's quarters "wuz so wore out" by the week's cumulative workload for master and family that "dey wuz glad to stay home and rest up" on Sundays.[27]

Most Appalachian ex-slaves expressed sharp memories of the long days of mothers who seemed to work all the time. During the early evening hours between the master's work and dark, groups of women made baskets, candles, soap, horse collars, hats, mats, and kitchen utensils. The pottery of Appalachian slave women had a noticeable cultural impact upon regional crafts, especially the African face jugs that were popular in northern Georgia, northern Alabama, western North Carolina, and southeastern Tennessee. Everyday household pottery contained both African and Cherokee traditions. However, textiles production demanded a greater variety of skills and consumed more of women's time than any other subsistence activity. Through this craft, mountain slave women contributed dramatically to their masters' households and to their own. In the United States, only 5.8 percent of all slave women worked regularly at cloth production; however, more than half of the mountain slave women produced textiles year round. In the Lower South, textiles production was limited on smaller plantations to the cutting and sewing of garments from purchased fabrics, but most larger plantations purchased slave clothing. By the 1850s, explained Fox-Genovese, "women above the rank of the smallest slaveholders did not dress in homespun and did not commonly work at spinning wheels or looms, although many of their slaves did. As a rule, slave women paid much more attention to basic household textile production than their mistresses did." On mountain slaveholdings, however, textiles production was highly organized and developed into an art form that required women to specialize in several different stages of the production process. All female slaves participated in some segment of cloth manufacturing. The least-skilled young girls prepared the raw materials and gathered wild plants and barks for dyeing. Most women prepared raw materials, treated the thread, completed a daily quota of spinning, knitted socks, and quilted. The more skilled women operated the looms and finished the fabrics into garments. Mary Tate recalled how labor groups manufactured textiles on her eastern Tennessee plantation. Children "helped pick and seed cotton." Teenagers and less-skilled women "carded and spun, then reeled and spooled" the cotton into thread. One woman "slayed and warped" the thread before three skilled craftswomen put it on the shuttles of the loom to begin weaving. In the final phase, the seamstress designed, cut, and sewed the garments. Still another older woman did nothing but knit stockings. On the largest plantations, a seamstress produced women's clothing, while a tailor specialized in men's pants, jackets, and coats; special cabins were set aside for equipment storage and work space. This hierarchy of textiles specialization was replicated on most mountain plantations so that several small gangs of women usually were supervised by a "boss mammy" who was considered to be the most experienced at many different tasks. If the farm had few slaves, women accomplished the tasks by pooling their labor with neighbors at seasonal work parties. Except to supervise, very few mountain mistresses participated in textile manufacturing for slave households.[28]

Using pine torches, candles, or lamps that burned rags, mountain slave women worked late into the nights to effect their artistry and skill into a wide variety of textiles that were consumed by slaves and masters or sold for cash. The smaller the plantation, the more likely it was to depend almost exclusively on slave production of fabrics, bedding, and clothing. Mountain slave women took great pride in their abilities to "take the wool offen the sheep's back an' kerry it through ter clawth. Wash it, card it, spin it, weave it, sew it inter clothes." Using flax, hemp, cotton, and wool, mountain slave women produced textiles that ranged from everyday slave clothing to more elaborate items that were displayed in the master's home or sold commercially. Mountain slaves wore two qualities of everyday clothing, depending on the economic status of their owners. Because flax and hemp were less valuable as market commodities, rough homespun and tow cloth were commonly processed into heavy duck or denim to be used for pants, jackets, and work aprons. For winter clothing, mountain slave women most often wove heavy yarns or linsey-woolsey, a fabric in which strands of wool and flax or cotton were alternated. On the larger plantations, cotton was more often used to produce clothing, especially lighter-weight shirts, dresses, skirts, underskirts, and "waisties." In addition to clothing, mountain slave women wove flax into coarse ducking that was used for slave mattress covers and for the bags to export cotton, flour, meal, and other commodities. Cloth for the master's household had a "finer texture" and greater artistic detail than most of the clothing that was distributed to slaves. Clearly, however, mountain slave women mixed colors and varied materials to create unique garments for the slaves themselves. After one Blue Ridge Virginia weaver and spinner ran away, her master alerted the countryside that Polly could be recognized by her artistic clothing, which included "a striped country cloth coat and jacket," a white cambric skirt, and a yellow striped shirt. Mountain slave women also produced different qualities of bedding, ranging from the rough blankets and quilts used by slaves to elaborate, multicolored coverlets and counterpanes displayed on the mistresses' beds. For the masters' households, Appalachian slave women also produced colored rugs and "articles of table linen and bedding of the best quality." Some mountain slave women were so expert at textiles production that their plantations specialized in the production of slave clothing or cloth bags for export by their masters.[29]

By combining their varied skills, mountain slave women completed a manufacturing process that required significant labor input every day, all year-round. In the first stage, women spent many hours preparing the raw materials. After a small eastern Tennessee plantation gathered the seed to produce oil, women cut down the flax and "left it to dry where it fell. When the sun had dried it, the outside skin would crack, and then they'd scutch it." The fiber "would fly out like feathers," and the women would "wind it on a big ball," ready for spinning on the flax wheel. On a large middle Tennessee plantation, slave women used a "flax house" and more equipment. They spread the flax plants on logs to dry. After the stems rotted, they ginned it to "get the stems out." Flax bark was then used to produce the stout cords for slave beds, and the fiber was used to weave fabric. Large plantations sent their wool to nearby mills for carding into yarn, but most mountain slaves completed the entire process by hand. On small plantations, wool preparation was a time-consuming process that began with washing and cleaning. Mountain slave women used two sets of metal cards, one to separate fibers and one to comb wool into rolls for spinning. On small mountain farms, owners either grew "a patch" of cotton, "just enuf fo de women to make cloes," or they did not use cotton at all. After ginning, raw cotton needed to be cleaned of stems, seeds, and debris before it could be carded. According to George Fleming, children "picked de seeds out of de cotton, den put de cotton in piles." Women then carded the cotton by "brushing it over and over on de cards till it was in lil' rolls."[30]

In the second stage, women spent many hours spinning the raw fibers into threads or yarns. The vast majority of Appalachian slave women were assigned daily quotas of spinning that was to be done "after the slaves would do their day's work." The women "had to work in the field and spin four cuts before they went to bed," each cut consisting of 300 yards. The "head spinner" organized the night's work and production goals. She had to "portion out" the cotton, wool, or flax "dey was gonna spin an' see dat each got a fair share." As the crew worked, the supervisor sang a song to challenge them to finish their work before sundown. "Keep yo' eye on de sun, see how she run. Don't let her catch you with your work undone. I'm a trouble, I'm a trouble. Trouble don' las' always." The women wanted to finish their evening work before dark " 'cause it mighty hard handlin' dat thread by fire-light." Robert Falls's mother worked until ten o'clock every night "because her part was to spin so many cuts a day." After a day's work in the field and the master's house, Sarah Gudger "had t' ceard an' spin till ten o'clock." With such an extended work schedule, Sarah "nebbah git much rest" because she "had t' git up at foah de nex' mawnin' an' sta't agin." While some women did the spinning, others "wrapped so many cuts of thread in hands for de loom." According to Sally Brown, "the thread wus made into big broaches, four broaches made four cuts, or one hank." To produce a "broach," Rachel Cruze added, the women wound the thread "on a reel" to "make a great hank of thread." Robert Falls recalled that his western North Carolina mistress "would sit by the spinning wheel and count the turns the slave women made. And they couldn't fool her none neither." According to one western North Carolina slave, spinning was organized into a hierarchy of specialties and tasks, causing some women to have to work later into the night than others.

Dem spinning wheels sho did go on de fly. Dey connected up wid de spindle and it go lots faster dan de wheel. Dey hold one end of de cotton roll wid de hand and 'tach de other to de spindle. It keep drawing and twisting de roll till it make a small thread. Sometimes dey would run de thread frum de spindle to a cornshuck or anything dat would serve de purpose. Dat was called de broach. Some of dem didn't go any further dan dat, dey had to make sech and sech broaches a day.

Dis was deir task. Dat's de reason some of dem had to work atter dark, dat is, if dey didn't git de task done befo' dat. Dey run de thread off de broach on to reels, and some of it was dyed on de reels. . . . Atter while, de thread was put back on de spinning wheel and wound on lil' old cane quills. It was then ready for de looms.[31]

In the third stage of textile production, threads or yarns were treated to prevent shrinkage, to whiten them, or to add colors. Women "would first size the thread by dipping it in some solution." Then they might boil it until it was bleached white. To create an array of browns, reds, blues, yellows, and blacks for vast quantities of thread, "dye stuffs would be gotten from the barks and roots of different trees." The least experienced women gathered barks, leaves, roots, and berries from walnut, hazelnut, sumac, oak, hickory, and poke root, prepared the dye barrels, and boiled the threads. To generate large amounts of dark brown dye for the men's pants on her farm, Anna Peek put walnut hulls "in a big hogshead and pounded with a heavy club." Once the juice was extracted, she added water and boiled the thread hanks, water being added to make the different shades of brown." To create blues, she used the small patches of indigo that women had grown in their family parcels.[32]

At the top of the hierarchy of artisans were the weavers who specialized in the fourth and most-complex stage of textiles production. On small mountain farms, "weaving was a thing the women prided in doing," and the loom "was kept going all the year." Clara Allen was an "extry fine weaver" who learned intricate African designs from a male slave. On her West Virginia plantation, the women at first "set [their] own warp," a process that Clara described as a "hard thing to do." Clara's early handicrafts were "jus' plain, didn't have no fancy figgers." Eventually, she interacted with a neighboring slave who taught her how to weave fancy patterns by setting the warp and woof precisely. Typically, loomers "didn't do nothing but weave," after other women had prepared the thread. Before weaving could begin, however, the woman spent eight to ten hours filling the loom with threads. The typical daily quota for a weaver was six to seven yards of cloth. The mountain loomist would

work the broaches and make a shuttle, then the broach would lay down in there so as not to ruin the thread and scotch it. There was little fine places like broom-straws, and they would run the shuttle through them. Then they'd use something that they'd run up there to beat the thread through, and that would make the actual cloth.

As a young child, Betty Cofer heard the weaving noises late into the night.

De looms- boom! boom! sho could travel. Dey put de quills, atter de thread was wound on dem, in de shettle and knocked it back and forth twixt de long threads

Most mountain slave women were assigned nightly quotas of textiles production, and black Appalachians were four times more likely than other U.S. slaves to produce their own clothing. *Source: Harper's,* 1854.

what was on de beams. Can't see de thread fly out of dat shettle it come so fast.
Dey sho could sheckle it through dar. Dey peddled dem looms, zip! zap! making
de thread rise and drap while de shettle zoom twixt it.

In addition to fabric and rough bedding for the slaves, women "wove
the cotton and linen for sheets an' pillow slips an' table covers" for the
master's household.[33]

In the final stage, seamstresses and tailors collected patterns from all
the slaves and then cut and sewed garments. Although not as respected by
slave women as the weaver, the seamstress or tailor was also highly skilled.
Except on the smallest slaveholdings, only a few women transformed the
fabric into the final items of clothing. On small mountain plantations,
the mistress sometimes "cut out all the clothes" and supervised sewing
by slave women. "They'd be sewin' for weeks and months." Almost all
the women "learned to knit and made stockings" for slave use. On one
western North Carolina farm, "one woman knitted all the stockin's for
the white folks an' colored folks too." As a result, "she had one finger all
twisted an' stiff from holdin' her knittin' needles." After the woven item
was removed from the loom, the weaver collected the "thrums." Those
ends of thread left on the loom were collected by slave women as their
household supplies of thread for daily repairs and for embroidery. Candle wicks were woven from thread scraps, and fabric remnants provided
the materials for patching and for quilts. Individually at night, women
cut scraps from old clothing to piece quilt tops in front of the fireplace.
Later, they quilted in groups after returning from their day's labor. There
were not enough slaves on many mountain plantations to complete all
the needed textiles specialties, so women organized communal work parties. The neighborhood's most respected textiles artisan supervised the
work, assigned tasks, and set quotas, whether it was spinning, dyeing,
weaving, rugmaking, or sewing. If they were quilting during the winter,
they would "just go from one house to another" in the community until everyone's bedding was completed. "It warn't nothin' for 'omans to
quilt three quilts in one night." While women did textiles production in
groups, neighborhood men might shell corn at a cornhusking. When the
gender-segregated groups had finished their quotas, they came together
again for food, music, and dancing.[34]

As children, most Appalachian ex-slaves spent their evenings on the
floor at the feet of women who gathered in groups to work late into
the night at spinning, weaving, sewing, or quilting. Mothers cared for
youngsters by involving them in the least-skilled aspects of the production
process. When Robert Falls was "a little shaver," he would "sit on the floor
with the other little fellows" while their mothers worked. Quite often, the

toddlers "slept right there on the floor." Children of both sexes teased and carded wool, picked up the loom shuttles, and knitted. Jim Threat's mother had all her children "help her spin and weave." Youngsters of both sexes assisted their mothers with errands and unskilled tasks around the looms. For example, Lindsey Moore "skillfully assist[ed]" the women weavers by "cleaning rods, clearing the looms, and other operations." As youngsters, Abner Griffin and John Boyd assisted the women with nighttime sewing. By the time they were ten or so, however, mountain slave boys were shifted to men's work outside the household production that consumed so much of their mothers' time. At about eight, Robert Falls was shifted from women's work in the weaving cabin to join the adult men who were shelling the master's corn at night. In contrast, females began textile production when they were very young, and they continued this craft all their lives. One young slave girl and her siblings assisted their mother late into the night. The children took turns holding a pine strip, "the only light" they ever had for nighttime work. The girl marveled at how her "mammy stand such hard work," for her mother "work in the field all day and piece and quilt all night." The slave woman had "to spin enough to make four cuts for the white folks every night," or she had to piece quilts. Sometimes the children "never go to bed" at all because they would "have to hold the light for her to see by."[35]

Inequities in Household Resource Distribution

Frequently disrupted by masters though they were, mountain slave households were significant units of production and sustenance pooling. That is not to imply, however, that members shared equally in the maintenance of households or in the distribution of resources. Even when they resided with their families permanently, males contributed much less work than women to the subsistence production required for household survival. Masters structured the absence of adult males in more than two-thirds of all mountain slave households. When visiting their families, abroad males consumed household resources that women and children had produced. Because their visits were short, however, abroad males did not contribute equitably to the production of what they consumed or to the production of resources to feed their offspring. Even those males who earned cash did not necessarily utilize those extra resources for the common good of the household. The women, children, and men who lived together at the same residence used cash primarily to purchase clothing, food, and shoes for family members. Abroad husbands, on the other hand, spent most of their cash earnings for tobacco, whiskey, or clothing purchases for themselves. A few absent husbands saved their earnings for annual contributions toward family needs, but hired males consumed most of their accumulated overwork earnings throughout the work year, contributing little toward household needs. In addition, many industrial employers charged "time off" fees of fifty cents per day from laborers who visited their families during the year.[36]

Because of their harder work and their inequitable share of resources (especially during pregnancy and breastfeeding), mountain slave women faced a higher mortality risk than their male peers. Even in comparison to women, however, children received the most inequitable treatment within mountain slave households. Even though they began to contribute to household subsistence production at an early age, children received an inequitable share of the family's food and clothing until they were old enough to work at the master's tasks. In households in which there was not enough food or clothing, allocations were made first to those who worked hardest. According to Booker T. Washington who spent his childhood in Blue Ridge Virginia and West Virginia, children got food in a haphazard fashion. "It was a piece of bread here and a scrap of meat there. It was a cup of milk at one time and some potatoes at another." As a result, the mortality risk of Appalachian slave children was much higher than the death rate among adult mountain slaves. Mothers recognized that their children were not being given enough meat, and their only solutions were to short-ration themselves or to steal. One of Washington's "earliest recollections [wa]s that of [his] mother cooking a chicken late at night, and awakening her children for the purpose of feeding them." Such incidents were captured in a song that was popular among mountain slaves. "Yo daddy ploughs ole massa's corn. Yo mammy does the cooking. She'll give dinner to her hungry chile when nobody is a lookin." Adult supervision and caregiving were also family resources of which mountain slave children were often deprived, especially in the daytime. Child care was highly problematic because fathers were usually absent and mothers had daytime and evening labor quotas. Women's work extended from early morning through late night. Consequently, child care had to be combined with night work, or children were left to fend for themselves. After the day's field work on John Van Hook's farm, women "finished up the chores for the day"; then they worked in their own behalf. After preparing meals, women still had to carry water and prepare food and clothing for the next day. On moonlit nights, they "would work in their [garden] patches." Jim Threat remembered his mother as always working and tired. Her "daily task was to milk seven cows twice a day, cook all the meals for the [white] family and weave seven yards of cloth at night." Under such circumstances, women were stretched beyond their physical limits, and there was an increased risk of child neglect and abuse. One northern Georgia woman "worked all the time," in the fields, at textiles production, at weekly housekeeping for the family, and in the family's vegetable parcel. "If she had to walk from the cabin to the house she would always knit." Tired and exhausted from all that work, Sara would sometimes "whip [her children] for nothing."[37]

I fought to free my mammy and her little children all through Nashville
and Franklin and Columbia, Tennessee, and all down through Alabama
and Augusta, Georgia.   – nineteen-year-old Chattanooga slave

The Mountain South may have been harder hit by the Civil War than
any other section of the country. On the one hand, Appalachian counties
were deeply split politically over secession, and local populations divided
their loyalties between the Union and the Confederacy. On the other
hand, this region lay geographically at the heart of the Civil War. By the
end of the war, eighty Appalachian counties had been devastated by major battles or campaigns or had been overwhelmed by the establishment
of military facilities (see Map 4). The "official" battles between the two
armies probably brought less devastation and destruction to most mountain counties than did the frequent and continuing raids and assaults
by guerillas, partisans, and robber bands. As the map shows, a majority of Appalachian counties experienced ongoing guerilla activity. Every
major Appalachian town (especially Knoxville, Chattanooga, Staunton,
Winchester, and Rome) was caught in the grips of continuing warfare;
and the disruption of trade connections caused shortages and prevented
the export of regional commodities.[1]

Civil War Conditions Faced by Mountain Slaves

In the best of times, most Appalachian slaves were underfed and malnourished, and their diets lacked many of the nutrients essential to good
health. As the food supplies of their owners were depleted by foraging
raids, hunger and uncertainty magnified for slaves. Thomas Cole recalled the impact on his small northern Georgia plantation. "Corn was
hauled off [by soldiers and guerillas] ... hogs and cattle was rounded up
and hauled off, and things begin lookin bad. Instead eatin corn bread
made outen corn meal, we eats corn bread made outten kaffir corn
(ground corn cobs)." By winter 1867, many mountain slaves received

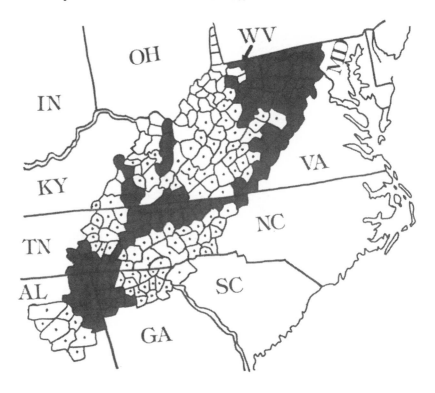

■ Major battles, army campaigns, or permanent military facilities

[•] Frequent guerilla warfare between Unionists and Confederate and/or foraging and
pillaging by soldiers and guerillas

[ ] Minimal military or guerilla disruption

Map 4. The Civil War in the Mountain South. *Sources: Encyclopedia of
American History*, pp. 278–79; O'Brien, *Mountain Partisans*; McKinney,
Southern Mountain, pp. 12–29; Noe and Wilson, *Civil War*; Bouwman,
Traveler's Rest, pp. 178–99; Patton, *Sketches*, pp. 41–46; Wayland,
Twenty-Five Chapters, pp. 355–402; Kimzey, *Early Records*, pp. 503–
06; Raulston and Livingood, *Sequatchie*, pp. 136–40; Wright, *Racial
Violence*, p. 26; *Appalachian Slave Narratives*.

only one-third of their usual pork allotments. Even though much of the
meat supply of mountain slaves derived from wild game, home guards
collected firearms and large knives from slaves, making hunting difficult. Appalachian narratives are filled with comments about the loss

of chickens and eggs, the most numerous protein sources produced by slaves. At Marshall Mack's plantation, guerillas "killed chickens and picked dem on horseback." At age ten on a small eastern Tennessee plantation, Mollie Moss watched the devastation of her family's cabin, furniture, hog, and poultry. The partisan "see a chicken go under de house, he plop down and shoot, and den call me to crawl under de house and fetch it." After ransacking the house and barns of Mollie Tillman's master, soldiers "got all de chickens an' eggs dey could fin'." At Maggie Pinkard's farm, soldiers "killed the chickens running in the yard." Only halfway into the war, slaves on Jim Threat's northern Alabama plantation had no provisions but "cottonseed boiled and thickened with corn meal." Adults were so hungry that they abandoned field work to scrape the inside of pine bark or to look for berries and nuts in the nearby woods. Destitute elderly slaves were the most endangered. When food supplies ran low, mountain masters stopped feeding or expelled those who could not work.[2]

Those slaves who lived in areas where there were long-term encampments or major campaigns experienced the most extensive foraging. Union soldiers destroyed or removed all food supplies from Wylie Nealy's northern Georgia plantation, "so de slaves had to scatter out and leave." Mountain slaves did not view Union soldiers as benevolent rescuers, for the foraging raids left them much more destitute than their owners. At Fountain Hughes's Blue Ridge Virginia plantation, the soldiers did not stop at destruction and confiscation of the slaveholder's property. "They took all the good horses an' throwed all the meat an' flour an' sugar an' stuff out in the river an' let it go down the river." Fountain deeply resented this act because the soldiers distributed no part of the food to slaves when "they knowed the people wouldn't have nothing to live on." Sometimes soldiers "be passing by all night long." When such troop movements occurred, slave cabins were repeatedly invaded. "If you was cookin anything to eat in there for yourself," Fountain recalled, "they would go an' eat it all up, and we didn' get nothing. To hide her only coin, Callie Elder's grandmother "dropped it in de churn," but it did not protect her property. After they ransacked the master's house and barns, their search turned to the slave cabins where they "poured dat buttermilk out ... got grandma's money," then "tuk what dey wanted" from the chickens, hogs, and belongings of the slaves. In northern Alabama, Jackson Daniels's slave community was raided by both sides. First, the Confederates took "all the meal and meat." Later, Yankee soldiers "come and drove the hogs right off." Despite the plea of an old man that "the cow and bull belonged to the black people," the foragers took the livestock anyway.[3]

Many Appalachian ex-slaves clearly recognized the difference between soldiers and local partisans or deserters. Rachel Cruze described guerillas as "bands of robbers who followed both armies, stealing anything they could get." Samuel Sutton's eastern Kentucky master "harbor[ed] rebels" who would "come and want horses once in a while." His activities attracted the revenge of pro-Union guerillas who were "a-spying and a-raring, riding around dere." At Lula Walker's northern Alabama plantation, partisans "burnt up their cotton dat wuz stored and dey taken lots of cawn and things. Dey eben run dere horses through de house." In addition to organized raids, mountain plantations were depleted by itinerant deserters from both sides. Andrew Goodman recalled that small groups "come by carrying they little budgets and if any was walking they would look in the stables for a horse or a mule and they just took what they wanted of corn or livestock." Mountain slaves viewed the guerillas on both sides with greater contempt than Confederate or Union soldiers. Partisans were also more physically brutal toward blacks than soldiers, and military records document the rape of black females by foragers on both sides. Guerillas always ransacked the slave cabins just as thoroughly as the master's house and barns. Andrew Goodman recalled that Confederate deserters targeted the slave cabins for plundering, but they rarely ransacked his master's house or barn. According to Marshall Mack, Bedford County guerillas and deserters "took Negroes' and all de white people's food." In mountainous Campbell County, Tennessee, Mollie Moss "see'd de blue and ... de gray" guerillas, and she never forgot the hunger after they "came foragin. Dey got all dey wanted." On Gip Minton's farm, guerillas on both sides "took everything they could find. Looked like starvation was upon de land." After guerilla raids in northern Georgia, Mollie Tillman recalled that "eatin' was kind o' slack wid us atter dey lef'." In Jefferson County, Tennessee, guerillas were active throughout the war, so Mary Tate's family was repeatedly raided. "Every day spies were making their rounds," she recalled. After scouting the area, guerillas "both Yankee and Rebel" would invade their cabin "taking what they could find, bacon, molasses, meal, anything they wanted." Like other mountain slaves, Mary's family hid provisions and belongings in a root cellar "under some boards of [thei]r cabin." Still the raiders searched "until they found" the household's limited supplies.[4]

Slaves were often at greater risk from soldiers and guerillas than whites. On Frank Menefee's farm, "marsa shot at some" of the Unionist guerillas. To retaliate, the guerillas physically abused the slaves, and then stole the slaves' "cabin wagons." During raids, owners often assigned slaves to hide livestock, provisions, and valuables, placing them at risk of being shot or whipped. When owners "refugeed away" ahead of the Union army, slaves were typically left to manage the plantations. One middle Tennessee slave recalled that "the hands usually stayed on the place" while their owner's family escaped to safety. Quite often, the master did not even warn the slaves of the approach of soldiers, leaving them unnecessarily vulnerable. To try to prevent escapes, mountain masters maintained a coercive code of secrecy. Although he was twenty-two when the war began, Andrew Goodman still "didn't know what the war was 'bout." According to Pierce Cody, "knowledge of the war was kept from the slaves until long after its beginning. Most of them had no idea what 'war' meant." On Cody's plantation, the slaves first heard about the war from itinerant peddlers. "When the master discovered this information was being given out," he solicited the aid of the home guard to ensure that peddlers would not "go near the quarters." The ex-slave's recollection is confirmed by regional newspapers, which often carried news and bounty notices about dangerous itinerant whites. For instance in May 1861, the Rockbridge County Home Guard offered a $50 reward for the capture of an Irish peddler who had been "tampering" with slaves and "instigating their insurrection" by giving them details about the war. At Julius Jones's middle Tennessee plantation, the slaves "couldn't get much news 'bout what was going on" because "the white folks ... didn't let no information out." Robert Falls and Sarah Gudger thought "dat wah" was an "awful time" in western North Carolina because the slaves "didn't know nothing about what was going on." When Sarah's family heard rumors about raiding forces, that news most often came from other slaves. If they were forewarned, they would "take [thei]r food and stock an' hide it till we sho' dey's gone." Although their owners had left days earlier to avoid the soldiers, Ruben Woods's quarters was not alerted. When they saw guerillas "comin on der horses," they "was runnin and a squattin like pahtridges a hidin. Dem guns was a fiahin (firing) ... spoilin fields and killin hogs." Because "dey made it mighty ha'hd (hard) for [them] awhile," Ruben's family and neighbors "stay[ed] hid erbout a week" in a nearby cave. After their owners left, Maggie Pinkard's quarters were even less prepared, so they lay "hiding in the oatfield, scared to death" while the Yankees ransacked the plantation.[5]

In addition to greater austerity and dangers from foraging raids, slave families experienced three other increased risks:

- Intensified community surveillance and greater restrictions on family visitations;
- Increased workload;
- Greater probability of family separations due to sales, migrations, and military impressment.

Guerilla raids were worse threats to slaves than to white owners, who "refugeed away." Such raids depleted food supplies, damaged cabins, and put black Appalachians at physical risk. *Source:* Library of Congress.

Because of the absence of white males, fears of slave assaults increased, and communities tightened their legal constraints over blacks. Prosecession elites in western Carolina posted circulars that warned whites to support the Confederacy or face "the terrible calamity of having three hundred thousand idle vagabond free negroes turned loose on [them] with all the privileges of white men." The remarks of a middle Tennessee planter typify white panic about uncontrolled blacks. He claimed that "the Negro population" of McMinnville was "giving much trouble" because they would "leave their homes and stroll over the country, uncontrolled." Despite that exaggeration, he was not overstating when he added that "their insolence and threats greatly alarm and intimidate white families." Western Carolina slaveholder William Vance Brown wrote to distant family that he feared Unionists in his area would "do awful damage & destruction by & through [thei]r slaves. Once arouse them to insurrection & they will carry murder, Rape & arson into the midst of our firesides." To prevent runaways and rebellions, Appalachian communities expanded patrols into larger home guards. Vigilantes acted on rumors to search out and punish suspects. During the early months of the war, the Christiansburg, Virginia, Home Guard "detected a Scoundrel ... attempting to incite the Negroes ... to Robbing and murdering the Whites." In reality, a white named Williams had informed slaves that the coming war would free them. For that "insurrection," the vigilantes put him "secure in jail." The diary of a western Carolina master provides a glimpse into the operation of these local patrols. In May 1861, forty-five Wilkes County slaveholders "[f]ormed a committee of Vigilantes," immediately tried three black males "for burning the woods," and sentenced them "to 39 lashes on their bare backs, half the head shaved & ... jail." He ended his entry with the comment that he was "Sorry to hear that some men who ought to do better ... condemn the action of our Committee."[6]

In addition to increased surveillance, the war meant a more demanding work routine for mountain slaves, especially women and children. After adult males were impressed into service by the Confederate army, young children, house servants, and elderly women "had to go to the field and work and chop." Masters were expected to contribute provisions to the Confederate war effort, and that increased output required higher slave productivity. According to Robert Falls, the "half-grown" slaves had to work his western North Carolina plantation because all the farmers had to give "a tenth of their crops to help feed the soldiers." Thirteen-year-old Jim Heiskell was one of those youngsters from whom the work of an adult male was demanded. "He put so much work on me, I could not do it; chopping & hauling wood and lumber logs." Because he was not productive enough, his overseer "whipped [him] three or four times a week." At most small mountain plantations, laborers "begin goin ter de fiel earlier and stayin a little later each day den we did de year befo."[7]

The war also increased the probability that Appalachian slaves would be separated from their families. One of the most painful impacts of the war on Appalachian slaves derived from restrictions on travel by abroad kin. According to Thomas Cole, "the colored men that had wives at other places, they wouldn't let them go to visit them at all; they said they'd get to talking, and they threatened to shoot any who tried to go." One Knoxville master took drastic steps when one of his slaves ran away to find his brother. The owner amputated the man's feet "to terrify and intimidate the colored people." Forced removals of slaves through interstate sales or westward migration of owners never lessened during the war. In fact, sales continued at an increasing pace as the war progressed. After the Emancipation Proclamation, the wife of a Blue Ridge Virginia minister made a diary entry that typified the cocky mood of many mountain slaveholders. "The first year [of the war] has come & gone, & Lincoln's proclamation has brought no desolation.... The whole agitation about slavery wh[ich] has prevailed at the N these years, is the most monstrous humbug ever got up since the flood. I am, if possible, a thousand times better satisfied at the propriety of slavery than I was before the war." The demand for slaves never declined during the war, and regional slave traders continued their auctions, annual hire-outs, and exports. As their need for cash increased, owners expanded their sales of unhealthy, older, or unruly slaves, runaways, and laborers they feared might escape to the Yankees. Desperate to prevent military conscription of their slaves, masters sent them South or westward. In 1864, a Staunton master ordered a male "taken South where he will have but little chance to get to the Yankees." Trying to avoid loss of slaves to the approaching Union army, Maggie Pinkard's owner "took a bunch of the field hands down in Louisiana somewheres." When the Confederate army recaptured slaves that had been impressed by the Union forces, their owners typically ordered them sold. One mistress noted in her diary that the household "had such a scene with poor Eliza who had heard that her husband Jim was among the contrabands taken at Harper's Ferry and that Dr. D. his master intended selling him."[8]

Military Forced Labor Migrations

Between 1820 and 1860, Appalachian slaves had experienced several generations of forced labor migrations and family disruptions at the hands of their owners. However, families were threatened by an even higher probability of permanent separations during the war. On the one hand, masters continued to remove slaves through hire-outs, sales, and migrations, disrupting a higher percentage of black families than they had during the late 1850s. On the other hand, military impressment caused the disruption of more kinship networks than would have been severed by five years of pre-war slave trading. In the wake of army movements, mountain slaves were confronted with a new type of forced labor migration, and those removals once again placed black families at risk. More than half the slaves described in Appalachian narratives were impressed into service by one or both of the armies, were removed great distances from home, were unable to contact spouses for much of the war, and were faced with a higher risk of death or starvation in army camps than on plantations. For example, Delia Garlic lost two husbands to army impressment. The Confederate army conscripted her first husband "to build breas' works, an' dig trenches, and [she] never see him any more." After her remarriage, the Union army conscripted her second husband to work on an Alabama railroad.[9]

The Confederate army requisitioned from mountain counties thousands of general laborers, teamsters, miners, carpenters, coopers, millers, cooks, sawmill operators, munitions workers, hospital aides, laundresses, musicians, burying crews, and builders of roads, bridges, boats, and railroads. County courts set quotas of black males aged eighteen to forty-five to be acquired from local owners; then local sheriffs collected and transported the workers to military authorities. Women were impressed to work as cooks, laundresses, officer's servants, and hospital workers. For their services, owners were paid $16 monthly. By late 1864, more than one-third of the slaves impressed into Confederate labor in Virginia came from Appalachian counties. For example, 340 slaves were requisitioned from nine mountain counties to maintain salt production in southwestern Virginia. In middle Tennessee, so many adult males had been conscripted that "little ones of any size" had to assume their duties in the fields and barns. In western North Carolina, Henry Williams made a ten-mile circuit daily "hauling for the Rebel soldiers." William Irving and his father were conscripted to make shoes and boots "for de rebel soljers." When the town's blacksmith was conscripted, Brownsburg citizens petitioned for his exemption because the town would be "subject to great inconvenience should they be deprived of his labour."[10]

By surrender, 43 percent of Appalachia's male slaves and 20 percent of the females had been impressed into labor by one of the armies, and thousands of others had escaped to work at Union contraband camps. Eastern Tennessean Rachel Cruze reported that "when war came all the men left the plantation but one colored man," most of them conscripted to labor for one of the armies. For every soldier, the federal forces impressed

As "contraband of war," 43 percent of mountain male slaves and 20 percent of women were impressed as Union military laborers, removed to
contraband camps, and separated from their families. In this scene, the
officer is informing slaves that the elderly, women, and children will not
be permitted to accompany impressed male laborers to military sites.
Source: Illustrated London News, 16 September 1863.

two to nine slaves as laborers; the Confederate army conscripted slave
laborers throughout the War. By the end of 1862, more than 200,000
Upper South blacks lived and worked under federal auspices. If we take
into account the mountain slave women who escaped to follow their impressed husbands, the females in Union contraband camps far exceeded
the number of males. Indeed, by the middle of 1863, there were nearly
four women, children, and elderly persons to every soldier or male laborer
in the contraband camps.[11]

Slaves in the Appalachian counties of Alabama and Tennessee were
disproportionately represented among the laborers who were conscripted
by federal forces. At Chattanooga, the Union army needed thousands of
teamsters, drovers, dockhands, railroad workers, and common laborers.

After his escape from a northern Alabama plantation, sixteen-year-old Thomas Cole was sent to Chattanooga "wid a company of men ter guard de supplies and de captured rebels and take care of the wounded soldiers." According to Cole, "Chattanooga was a important distributing center for de Union forces, dat is why dey keeps so many men and supplies dar all de time." The Quartermaster "would gits a order in dar ter send supplies ter some other General and it was [Cole's] job ter helps load de wagons er box cars.... Dar would be a train of wagons leave sometimes. [They] got all out supplies in Chattanooga mostly by boat and sent dem out different ways ter other parts of de country." At major Appalachian rivers, slaves maintained bridges and erected pontoons. Slaves from eastern Tennessee, northern Georgia, northern Alabama, east Kentucky, and southwest Virginia repaired roads and built railroads over which the Union army transported food, livestock, and materiel. Thomas Cole remarked that the "culured soldiers was all used ter clear roads and help build dese temporary bridges." Any time the army fell short of workers, "dey took lots mo [slaves] from somewhere else."[12]

In fall 1863, the Union army ordered the impressment of six thousand slaves to build and repair military roads and another eight thousand to build a railroad to connect Lebanon, Kentucky, and Danville, Virginia, to eastern Tennessee. After their conscription, the army contracted the laborers to the Louisville and Nashville Railroad Company. The policy of the army was to pay $10 a month to owners and two dollars to the workers. By 1862 in Appalachian Tennessee and Alabama, "all officers commanding troops in the field" were authorized to "conscript and employ" as many slaves as possible, including "taking the servants of loyal people" when necessary. Because the need for them was particularly great by 1863, officers were instructed that "every cook or teamster shall be properly enrolled and mustered into service . . . without delay." As a result, the Union forces composed "invalid regiments" of slaves unfit for field service but capable of fatigue labor and garrison duty. When they were unable in 1863 to obtain enough teamsters to move supplies to Knoxville, the Union army enlisted three thousand slave teamsters from eastern Kentucky, southwestern Virginia, and eastern Tennessee by paying $300 bounty to each of their owners. When he recruited teamsters in the Big South Fork bordering eastern Kentucky and eastern Tennessee, one Union officer complained that the only available whites were "a very worthless class, who marauded and neglected every duty." His prejudice was only a form of ideological camouflage, for the officer was much more interested in paying the lowest wages possible. He notified the District Commander that he "was compelled to impress a few free negroes and some few slaves.... I ordered the impressment of more, and I am fully

Slaves from the Appalachian counties of Tennessee and Alabama, like this teamster, were overrepresented among Union military laborers and soldiers. *Source: Harper's,* 1864.

satisfied that the negroes are the best teamsters.... I believe it will be great saving to the government to have negro teamsters."[13]

Not all military laborers were conscripted; many fled to the Union lines. After he successfully escaped from his Blue Ridge Virginia owner, John Boston joyously wrote home to his wife: "this day I can Address you thank god as a free man. I had a little truble in giting away.... I am free from al the Slavers Lash."[14]

White northern resistance to the draft fueled the formation of Union policy to conscript as many slaves as possible. White northerners younger than twenty were exempt, and many married men were excused on the grounds of family hardship. Such humanitarian concerns were not reflected in Union conscription of black Appalachians. Marshall Mack reported that Union forces "took every slave that could carry a gun." Consequently, the army did not restrict its impressment to adult slaves, and it ignored family circumstances. Three of Larkin Payne's western North Carolina teen and preteen brothers were conscripted laborers, one for the Confederates, two for the federals. In early 1862, John Finnelly joined a group of ten northern Alabama runaways. "De Yanks put [them] on de freight train and [they] goes to Stevenson, in Alabama. Dere [they were] put to work buildin' breastworks." After a few days, however, twelve-year-old John "gits sent to de headquarters at Nashville" where he worked as "water boy" and stretcher bearer during battles. Even as an elderly interviewee, John recalled the horror he experienced as a young boy.

Dere am dead mens all over de ground and lots of wounded and some cussin' and some prayin'. Some am moanin', and dis and dat one cry for de water and, God A-Mighty, I don't want any sich 'gain. Dere am mens carryin de dead off de field, but dey can't keep up with de cannons. I helps bury de dead and den I gits sent to Murphysboro and dere it am jus' de same.

A White County, Tennessee, ex-slave reported the manner in which he joined the Union army. "After [the] colored regiment come there, they took us to town.... They come right in my house, I walked right out with them." Mary Tate recalled that a regiment took her brother away, and they "never heard from him for several years after the close of the war." By the time Yankee troops came though his area, Julius was sixteen, so he enlisted and fought more than two years. At age seventeen, a White County slave joined and fought twenty-two months. John Young was the sixteen-year-old "kittle drummer" who "marched right in the center" of the line of battle of the fifty-seventh Colored Infantry. At age twelve, Wylie Nealy was impressed as a military laborer; however, the boy was sent to Chattanooga where he "was in a colored regiment" that accompanied "Sherman's army till it went past Atlanta."[15]

Military Service by Mountain Slaves

After 1863, nearly 179,000 African-American males joined the Union army, representing 10 percent of the federal soldiers. Surprisingly, black

Appalachians were disproportionately represented among those slave-soldiers. Even though less than 7 percent of the country's enslaved population resided in this region, the Mountain South provided more than 30,000 recruits, nearly one-fifth of the Union's black soldiers. In the country as a whole, about 14 percent of male slaves aged sixteen to forty-five enlisted. However, black Appalachians were four times more likely to enlist than slaves in other regions. In the mountain counties of Alabama, Kentucky, and Tennessee, more than two-thirds of the available male slaves enlisted. One-third to one-half of the available male slaves in the mountain counties of Georgia, Maryland, South Carolina, Virginia, and West Virginia were mustered into Union ranks. There was less army presence in western Maryland than in any other section of Southern Appalachia. According to Berlin and Rowland:

Aside from small bodies of troops along the Baltimore and Ohio Railroad and the Potomac River, the rural sections of northern Maryland escaped sustained military occupation. The corps of observation along the river offered little to would-be fugitive slaves, thanks to commanders like General Charles P. Stone, who instructed subordinates to return runaways to their owners.... Spurned by the troops nearest home, some slaves crossed the Potomac and found employment as teamsters with the federal armies in Virginia. Others joined the labor crews that constructed and reconstructed fortifications and pontoon bridges at Harper's Ferry.... Although military circumstances in Maryland occasioned little sustained employment of black laborers by the Union army, both federal officials and local authorities were quick to commandeer black men whenever the enemy threatened. Every invasion by Confederate forces engendered massive mobilization, with impressment as likely as the muster of volunteers. As Robert E. Lee's army advanced into western Maryland in June 1863 ... some 4,000 free-black and slave men were hastily assembled.

Because they were closer to Union forces in northern Virginia or West Virginia, blacks in western counties were more likely than other Maryland slaves to enlist. Even in western North Carolina where only one-quarter of the available black males enlisted, that region's slaves were twice as likely to see combat as other U.S. bondsmen.[16]

When they were interviewed by WPA workers in the 1930s, more than half of the male Appalachian ex-slaves who had been older than sixteen during the Civil War reported that they had seen service in the federal forces. We cannot explain these high rates of Appalachian enlistment simply by claiming a higher spirit of voluntarism among mountain slaves. There were four explanations other than voluntarism for high Appalachian enlistment. First, Union forces occupied several areas of the Mountain South early and throughout the war (see Map 4), increasing the likelihood of escapes and impressments. A second causative factor was the presence of a greater percentage of pro-Union Appalachian slaveholders than within the South as a whole. Because of these "loyal" slaveholders, Congress exempted numerous mountain counties from the Emancipation Proclamation, including those in Tennessee, all those counties that became West Virginia, and several counties in northern Virginia. Since Kentucky and Maryland did not secede, the Appalachian counties of those states were also not covered by the edict. Since Appalachia's pro-Union masters benefited financially from military employment of their slaves, many of these slaveholders hired out their laborers to the army. After 1863, they were paid a high bounty for every bondsman who enlisted. Third, there was a higher incidence of army foraging and guerilla activity in Appalachian counties, and coercive recruitment of slave-soldiers occurred during those raids. Fourth, most of the mountain slaves who enlisted had already been conscripted as military laborers and were being held at contraband camps. Enlistment was not far removed from the duties many of these laborers had already been assigned. Even though they were supposed to be noncombatants, all male laborers were "organized and mustered into service by detachments or companies, as Infantry." Most of them were armed, they often guarded prisoners or supply depots, and they were left as holding forces when white soldiers were moved elsewhere. As Thomas Cole observed, they marched like everyone else, "wadin water up ter [thei]r chins and holdin [thei]r guns and ammunitions up above [thei]r heads." In addition to the coercive aspects, enlistment was sweetened by two carrots. On the one hand, families of black soldiers were immediately emancipated under congressional regulations. On the other hand, the army promised to protect and to provision their families at camps, thereby alleviating the food shortages and owner abuse that their kin were enduring.[17]

After 1863, the Union army recruited nearly 12,000 black soldiers in the mountain counties of Tennessee and Alabama, indicating that two-thirds of the adult male slaves in those areas enlisted. Due to the combined effect of slave voluntarism and coercive enlistment tactics, recruitment in eastern Tennessee and in northern Alabama was highly successful. In fact, so many military laborers enlisted that the Knoxville post commander worried that there were "not negroes enough ... to drive the teams and to work about the city." At age twenty-two, J. O. Johnson escaped his Jackson County, Alabama, owner to join the army. He was injured twice "by missels" at the battles of Murfreesboro and Shelby. By war's end, he was ill and seriously weakened by battles and "expo[sur]es to camp life." When Thomas Cole "first goes into de war dar wasn't many colored men in de service but long de last year of the de war dar was lots of dem." At age twenty-three, William I. Johnson joined one of the black regiments that was made up of western Virginia slaves; these troops fought at Petersburg, Danville, Manassas, and Richmond. As a member of one of those regiments, Ruphus Wright alerted his wife that he had survived his first major battle of "five hours" in which they "whipp[ed] the rebels out ... killed $200 & captured many Prisener." Though they had lost thirteen men and the leadership of their sergeant, the regiment "expect[ed] an Attack every hour."[18]

The recruitment of black Appalachians was especially coercive, particularly during the last year of the war. James Ayers traveled throughout the rural areas and small towns of northern Alabama and southeastern and middle Tennessee pressuring blacks to enlist. Appalachian slaves resisted Ayers's flowery recruitment pitch because they feared permanent separation from kin and white abuse of their families in their absence. Moreover, mountain slaves had historical reason to be suspicious of whites proposing their long-distance removal. Early in his assignment, he wrote in his diary that he had spent the day "Looking after Darkies" among the laborers who were unloading boats. "None seemed willing to inlist" because they would rather continue to work as they were "than be soldiers" far away from wives and children. After repeated failures at verbal persuasion, he began to utilize force to impress unwilling enlistees. On one trip into Jackson County, he "had ten Colored troops with [him] armed," so he successfully "Brought in five Recruits." Some of his enlistees escaped the camp and headed into the mountains to hide. On this trip, he captured two of those deserters, "but they Boath made there Escape through the Carelessness of the gards." Rachel Cruze recalled the element of threat and force. "When you were asked to join up a bayonet was shoved into your back and it stayed there until you were safe" in the army camp. Press gangs like those managed by Ayers sometimes resorted to kidnapping. A McMinnville Unionist complained that "officers in command of Colored troops [we]re in constant habit of pressing all able bodied slaves into the Military service of the U.S."[19]

Not all black mountain soldiers served in the Union army. In Virginia, Lee's recruiting officers solicited and organized black regiments from the Appalachian Counties of Wythe, Patrick, and Franklin. In western Maryland, a Union officer reported the capture of black Appalachians among the defeated Rebel troops. "Most of the Negroes ... were manifestly an integral part of the Southern Confederacy Army," for they bore rifles; rode on horses, mules, or caissons; and were led by blacks playing bugles, drums, and fifes. Levi Miller escorted his Rockbridge County owner to war, "regularly enlisted in the Confederate Army," and saw combat in Virginia, Tennessee, Georgia, Maryland, and Pennsylvania. The WPA narratives describe twelve mountain slaves who served in the Confederate army and another three males who first served with Confederate forces and then escaped to the Union army. For example, Jim Threat recalled that his owner "went to the war and as he was so used to having somebody to wait on him he took my mother's brother with him to be his special servant. Uncle took smallpox and died and was buried at the camp." Tom Singleton "wuz in de War 'bout two years" with his master. The slave "waited on him, cooked for him, an' went on de scout march wid him, for to tote his gun, an' see after his needs."[20]

George Kye served as a military substitute for his master. "I went off to serve because old master was too old to go, but he had to send somebody anyways." For two years, he served in the Confederate army, under his master's name. According to George, "they was eleven negro boys served in my regiment for their masters." One Blue Ridge Virginia slaveholder routinely sent twelve-year-old Ben Brown "with the young recruits goin' to de army headquartahs at Charlottesville to take care of de horses an show de way." Tom McAlpin recalled that

Jeff Davis' officers would go th'ough de streets, an' grab up de white mens an' put ropes 'roun' dere wrists lak dey was takin' 'em off to jail.... Dey made all de white mens go. It was called de 'scription. Some [slaves] went too. Dem [slaves] fought raght side of dere masters. Some went as body guards an' some went as soldiers.

At age nineteen, McAlpin himself was conscripted as part of a black regiment that was sent "to Richmond to bring some of the wounded Federates." Some mountain slaves served on both sides of the conflict. William I. Johnson's master

carried him to war as servant and horseman.... Whenever they were fighting, [the] Negroes had the camp to look after and when the shooting was over [they] had to bring in the wounded. In between battles [they] had to keep [thei]r masters' boots polished, the horses and harness cleaned and the rifles and swords spic and span. Sometimes, too, [they] were all put to digging trenches or throwing up breastworks.

Johnson admitted that during this period he "didn't know what the war was all about nor why they were fighting." After his master's regiment "captured a gang of Yankee soldiers," the Union prisoners convinced five of them to run away to the Union lines. Such escaped laborers carried valuable reconnaissance to Union forces. For example, Jim Taylor, Dick Williams, and Henry Strange identified the camps, concentrations, and movements of Confederate forces around the towns of Leesburg, Winchester, and Charlestown. Coffee County free black Frederick Starkey "brought [a Unionist] across the Tenn. River when the rebels were after him." West Virginia slave Thomas Laws acted as a spy for

Sheridan prior to the Union invasion of Winchester. Bradley County slave Richard Traynor "was pressed into service & compelled to help throw up entrenchments dig & shovel" at Nashville. From his vantage point as a Confederate teamster, Traynor "aid[ed] and assist[ed] certain Union men in going across the mountains into the federal lines."[21]

Army Treatment of Black Union Soldiers

Black soldiers and regiments were quite often treated with racial contempt by their white peers. One eastern Tennessean remembered that "sometimes they wouldn't let [him] fight at all." One middle Tennessee regiment was utilized as a guerilla holding force." They would "go and clean up the place and hold the places that had been taken" by the white Union regiments. Made up mostly of inexperienced recruits from eastern Kentucky and western Virginia, the Fifth Colored Cavalry regiment was loudly ridiculed by white soldiers, as they marched into battle at the saltworks in southwestern Virginia. A Union colonel reported the events prior to and during the battle of Saltville.

On the march the Colored Soldiers as well as their white Officers were made the subject of much ridicule and many insulting remarks by the White Troops and in some instances petty outrages such as the pulling off the Caps of Colored Soldiers, stealing their horses etc was practiced by the White Soldiers. These insults as well as the jeers and taunts that they would not fight were borne by the Colored Soldiers patiently.... The point to be attacked was the side of a high mountain, the rebels being posted about half way up behind rifle pits made of logs and stones.... The Rebels opened upon them a terrific fire but the line pressed steadily forward up the steep side of the mountain until they found themselves within fifty yards of the Enemy.... Out of the four hundred engaged, one hundred and fourteen men and four officers fell killed or wounded.... At dusk the Colored Troops were withdrawn from the enemies works, which they had held for over two hours, with scarcely a round of ammunition in their Cartridge Boxes.[22]

Five months after this bloody siege, a member of the Fifth Colored Cavalry wrote a letter to the War Department complaining about the conditions endured by the black soldiers. According to the eastern Kentucky recruit, white officers

are laying here and learning us nothing[.] instead of them learning us Something they are Robing us out of our money[.] i think it is mighty hard for us to Stand that after just coming from under bondage[.] there are men that has never had the chance to learn anything[.] they will give them change for a one dollar for a fifty dollars in Stead of teaching them better[.] that is the way they treat them.... we have payed nine hundred dollars for the rasing of our brass ban[.] now they want to claim the instruments off of us[.] its now more than what [our] masters would have done[.] the los[s] of this fifth regiment is over thirteen hundred dollars by these officers. . . . they will not let us tra[d]e out side of the Sutlers[.] if we do they want to punish us[.] things that the Sutler has got that is oneley worth a dollar they charge us Seven or eight dollars.

While the most common complaint of black soldiers was that they did not receive their pay, there were even worse problems. Even when they received letters about family crises or abuse of wives by slaveholders, black soldiers rarely were granted leaves. A Fifth Colored Cavalryman reported that they had not been permitted "[s]ix days furlough to See [thei]r wives" even though they had "been in the army fourteen months." To acquire such a pass from a corrupt white officer, the black soldier was required to "pay thirty dollars for a ten days pass." When their wives managed somehow to travel to the camp, "they [we]re not allowed to come in camp and [the soldiers] [we]re not allowed to go See them." Instead, the women were "drumed of[f] and the officers Says go you damed bitches." Typically, there were no "regimental Surgeons with the Colored Regiments to treat and arrest disease in its early stages." Consequently, black soldiers were usually "past recovery before being sent to Genl. Hospitals." In addition to those forms of discriminatory treatment, black soldiers were disproportionately represented among those men who were executed by the military. While they represented less than 10 percent of the Union army, more than one-fifth of all executed federal troops were black soldiers. Rape of white women was the most frequent crime of which they were convicted. The executions were not always legal, as was the case when a black soldier was lynched for rape at Saltville, Virginia, after he stared at a white female.[23]

Slaveholder Treatment of Union Soldier Families

Men and women experienced the war very differently, as Berlin, Reidy, and Rowland have observed.

Because black men served as soldiers and black women did not, military service created important differences in the way they experienced war and emancipation. Army life exposed black men to the rigors of the march and the perils of battle, but it also incorporated them into an institution whose power and sovereignty dramatically superseded that of the slaveowners. When black women met the slaveholding enemy, they only occasionally did so under direct military auspices. . . . If armed service, in all its various aspects, helped liberate black men from the narrow confines of bondage and second-class citizenship, black women enjoyed no comparable experience.[24]

Owners increased their daily surveillance and physical punishment of soldiers' wives and sometimes even resorted to "keeping children

Hostage" in the Big House. When "the Union soldiers took [her] father to work on the fortifications" at Chattanooga, her "mother also went," out of fear of bad treatment if she and her children were left alone. After her husband's enlistment and subsequent death in the Battle of Saltville, Patsey Leach's owner, a "Rebel Sympathizer," began a pattern of continuing abuse.

He treated me more cruelly than ever, whipping me frequently without any cause and insulting me on every occupation. About three weeks after my husband enlisted, a Company of Colored Soldiers passed our house and I . . . looked at them. . . . My master followed me and knocked me to the floor senseless. . . . When I recovered my senses he beat me with a cowhide. When my husband died my master whipped me severely saying my husband had gone into the army to fight against white folks and he my master would let me know that I was foolish to let my husband go he would "take it out of my back," he would "Kill me piecemeal." . . . The last whipping he gave me he took me into the Kitchen tied my hands tore all my clothes off until I was entirely naked, bent me down, placed my head between his Knees, then whipped me most unmercifully until my back was lacerated all over.

Shortly after, Patsey and her infant ran away to Union lines, but she was forced to leave her other five children behind.[25]

In Greenup County, Kentucky, Jane Coward was desperate to have her enlisted husband "come to [thei]r relieaf at home." Her owner had threatened to "kill every woman that he knows that has got a husband in the army." After she had been beaten "nearly to death," Jane knew that she and her family would "have to leave [the area] on the account off the rebels." She complained to a union officer: "If a man ever leaves his wife and children at home by thar selves thay are abused by some one of them. . . . I have two children in the union army and we have two children that was killed in the union army and i think that [I] aught to have some peace." From a southwestern Virginia camp, a Union officer described the pressures on eastern Kentucky soldiers.

A large number of them have families still remaining in servitude, who are most shamefully and inhumanly treated by their masters in consequence of their husbands having enlisted in the union army. . . . Unable to read and write they are entirely dependent upon their masters for any information they receive from husbands and friends who are in the service. In a great many instances, letters have been returned with some miserable, contemptible expression. . . . Under such circumstances, it would be extremely unsafe to forward money to their families, for the reason that it will fall into the hands of [the owners of the soldiers' families].[26]

Army records and slave narratives report the mistreatment of the elderly after masters lost most of their productive laborers to the war effort.

Jim Threat remembered the panic when his abusive master and overseer decided to eliminate costly elderly slaves.

As the war come on food and clothes got powerful scarce. Gum [his master] and Alex [the overseer] decided they would kill off their old [slaves] so they wouldn't have to take care of them any longer.... They was all on their way to the woods where they had planned to do the killing when Alex Jordan's gun went off and blowed the top of Gum's head off. This broke up the killing game.

Threat's extreme story is supported by army records and by other slave narratives. When "the Feds were coming through" Mary Myhand's middle Tennessee county, they would "take all the boys with them." As the able-bodied males were impressed, the families began to worry that owners in the area would "kill all the old." After the Yankee troops had passed through Washington County, Virginia, young Katie Johnson overheard "white folks at the big house making up a plot to clear the [slaves] out of the Quarters." After a warning from the child, "next morning there wasn't a hand on the place." As the war progressed and provisions dwindled, masters in southeastern Tennessee and northern Alabama became more ruthless. In the fall, after "their crops [were] made & winter coming on [slaveholders began] *driving* their negro's away in order to save taking care of them during winter." In western Maryland, Union and Rebel owners evicted the families of soldiers who had "gone away and left their dependent relatives behind." One Union officer encountered more than six hundred "in a destitute condition ... almost without any Clothing" because so many slaveholders had "turned off the old women, the Mothers with their helpless Children."[27]

Family Life in Union Contraband Camps

The Union army treated the wives and children of black soldiers even worse than the enlisted slaves. Field commanders were ordered to furnish each black soldier "with a certificate of subsistence for his family, as soon as he [wa]s mustered." The family of any black soldier who should "die in the service by disease, wound, or battle" was entitled to six months of continued provisions from the army. Despite those promises, a Fifth Colored Cavalryman in southwestern Virginia lamented that their "wives and children [we]re laying out doers and we have no chance to get a home for them." Indeed, the families of these fighters waited in dangerous conditions at Cumberland Gap, Kentucky. Their families had been evicted from Camp Nelson and "turned back at all points." More than four hundred women and children were "sitting by the roadside and wandering about the fields"; some had died, and "all [we]re in a starving condition." Most of the families of eastern Kentucky and southwestern Virginia recruits had been sent to Lexington's Camp Nelson where families constructed makeshift huts, hired themselves out, and received no formal provisions from military authorities. The camp commander was a slaveholding Kentuckian who periodically expelled the refugees to try to force them to return to their owners. Thus, the soldiers' families went through several cycles of eviction and resettlement. In July 1864, one of those evictions was initiated in order to put the families "beyond the camp that they may proceed to their respective homes where their masters under the laws of Kentucky are bound to support them." The commander notified masters that "all women and children w[ould] be delivered up to their owners upon application." When officers tried to distribute passes to their masters' homes, "there [wa]s not one among two hundred (200) that want[ed] to go." Most of them preferred to "go outside the Lines" where they would "shift for themselves" because they feared they would "be Killed by their masters if they return[ed]."[28]

A few days later, the commander ordered "that all negro women and children, old and infirm, negro men unfit for any military duty ... be at once sent beyond the lines with instructions not to return." The families of Fifth Colored Cavalrymen who were stranded at Cumberland Gap were among those who were evicted. According to a camp missionary:

it was a bitter cold day the wind was blowing quite hard [when] many of the women and children were driven from the Camp. I counted six or eight wagon loads of these women & children being driven away.... When they were expelled their huts were destroyed.... [At Nicholasville] I found that one hundred or more had taken shelter in the woods ... [and were] entirely destitute of shelter or food.... [At Lexington] I found fourteen in an old shed doorless & floorless sitting around a stick of burning wood with no food or bedding. One woman was apparently overcome by exposure, and another had given birth to a child in that place.... In another building I found about half a dozen sick without even the necessaries of life.... [O]ne woman had been so pressed with hunger as to offer her child for sale in the city.

Another woman "wandered from place to place until driven by starvation to her former master [where she was] so cruelly beaten that she died." When eastern newspapers publicized the inhumane events, the Union army countermanded the evictions, only to expose black families to worsened conditions. Within a week of the new order, more than four hundred women and children had returned. "Owing to the fact that their former humble homes were ruthlessly destroyed by the military authorities," they were housed in a single barracks. Within two weeks, the number had risen to more than a thousand, with "hundreds crowded together in one room ... some ragged, all dirty, filthy."[29]

While Camp Nelson may have been the most scandalous of the Union contraband camps, Union refugee settlements were no better in other areas. The families of western Carolina and northern Georgia soldiers were most often sent to the camp at New Bern, North Carolina. According to an 1863 post report, the Quarter Master issued "*sixteen* times more" provisions to whites than to slaves. In fact, the New Bern camp issued four times more meal, sixteen times more flour, and thirty-two times more meat per capita to whites than to blacks. The Thirty-Sixth Colored Regiment complained about the inequitable treatment of their families.

We have served in the US Army faithfully and don our duty to our country ... but at the same time our family's are suffering. ... When we were enlisted in the service we were prommised that our wifes and family's should receive rations from government. The rations for our wifes and family's have been (and are now cut down) to one half the regular ration. Consequently three or four days out of every ten days, they have nothing to eat. [A]t the same time our ration's are stolen by [the Assistant Superintendent] and sold while our family's are suffering. ... [T]he cause of much suffering is that Capt James has not paid the Colored people for their work for near a year and at the same time cuts the ration's off to one half so the people have neither provisions or money to buy it with. There are men ... that were wounded in the service of the US Army ... that Cannot get any rations and are not able to work, some soldiers are sick in Hospitals that have never been paid a cent and their familys are suffering.[30]

The families of soldiers from the Appalachian counties of Tennessee and Alabama were most often sent to camps at Tunnel Hill, Nashville, Chattanooga, and Knoxville. The largest Tennessee camp was located at Nashville, an "aggregate of wretchedness and misery" caused by corrupt and incompetent officers. An officer from the district command found conditions at the Nashville camp "wretched in the extreme, using terms like "culpable neglect." Because the dead were left unburied, the corpses and the adjacent barracks were "lined with vermin." One investigator reported:

The stench arising from the excrement & urine in and around their quarters was intolerable even in the coldest weather, and ... was the cause of many deaths among them. ... [T]heir surgeon used scarcely any exertions sanitary or medicinal in their behalf. ... I have seen them dying in the alleys & houses and on the steps of their quarters, with no one rendering them assistance.

A month later, the white officer of a Chattanooga regiment pleaded to the district commander for relief of the soldiers' families who were interred in these conditions. He reported that "the suffering from hungar & cold is so great that those wretched people are dying by scores – that sometimes thirty per day die & are carried out by wagon loads, without coffins, & thrown promiscuously, like brutes, into a trench." After his wife's death at

The women and children among these fugitive slaves coming into Union lines near Chattanooga were relocated to the contraband camp at Nashville, where living conditions were horrific and officers defrauded workers of their wages. *Source: Harper's,* 1864.

the camp, one soldier's six children were returned to the Chattanooga regiment. "They [we]re nearly starved, their limbs [we]re frozen, – one of them [wa]s likely to loose both feet." Families of a Knoxville regiment were facing starvation and homelessness. Despite extensive recruitment in the area, no "adequate provision ha[d] either been made or authorized" for the destitute families of the slave enlistees. No camp was ever established at Knoxville, so most of the soldiers' families were "yet in the Country" where small plantations were "almost entirely destitute of Subsistence." Whether they stayed with owners or relocated to distant camps, the families of recruits from the Appalachian counties of Virginia, Maryland, and West Virginia faced similar desperate conditions.[31]

Union Treatment of Military Laborers

When Union forces impressed laborers, black Appalachians were quite often "brought away without shoes & some without coats, many without any change [of clothing] whatever." When the Confederates recaptured Winchester in 1862, a local woman reported in her diary:

on the approach of Jackson the negroes, who had many of them left their homes and were living in town [under protection of the Union troops], began a flight that was only equalled in speed and madness by the Yankees themselves.... They had been told by the Yankees that Jackson's men would have no mercy on them but that they would be put to the most cruel death.

Because he had worked as a federal teamster, one male slave "had hidden in a field under a haystack, and remained there ... sleeping in the wet hay," until he developed "a violent fever." The man's wife followed the troops toward Harper's Ferry, but soon returned to her mistress, reporting that "the Federals had induced them to fly, but could not succor them in their distress." The slave woman "with her baby in her arms and [her young son] following her, the picture of famine and grief," recounted how she had seen other black mothers "drop by the roadside with their babies to die."[32]

The Union army designed the camps as collection points only for impressed male laborers and the registered families of active black soldiers. As increasing numbers of slaves escaped to the Union lines and families joined impressed workers, the camps and adjacent temporary slums expanded chaotically. Military laborers impressed in western Carolina or northern Georgia were most often sent to New Bern, a "stationary camp" on the seaboard. Mary Barbour recounted the escape of her family to the New Bern Camp. Her father was owned by an Avery County, North Carolina, master while her mother and children were held in McDowell

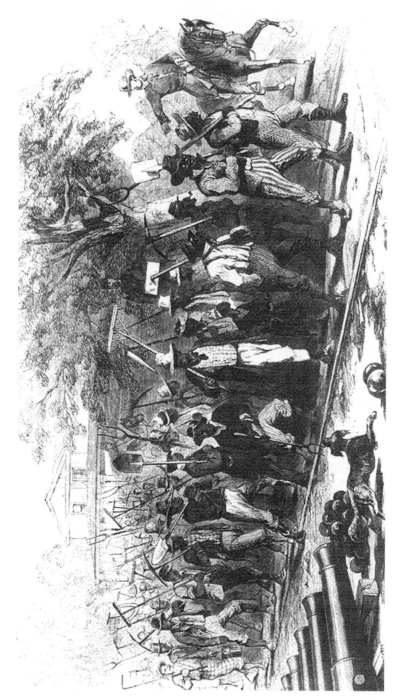

The Union Army impressed hundreds of slaves from the Appalachian counties of Kentucky, Tennessee, Alabama, and Virginia to build and repair railroads. *Source:* Library of Congress.

County. After a Union raid, Mary's father stole a wagon and mules and drove more than fifty miles to collect his family. At about age nine, Mary lay in the back of the wagon eavesdropping on her parents' subdued night voices.

As we rides 'long I lis'ens ter pappy an' mammy talk. Pappy wuz tellin' mammy 'bout de Yankees comin' ter de plantation, burnin' de co'n cribs, de smokehouses an' 'stroyin' eber'thing. He says right low dat dey done took [his master] ter de Rip Raps down nigh Norfolk, an' dat he stol' de mules an' wagin an' 'scaped. . . . Pappy says dat we is goin' ter jine de Yankees. We trabels all night an' hid in de woods all day fer a long time.

After a treacherous journey of more than three hundred miles across the entire state, they finally arrived at the Union camp on the coast. Shortly before the arrival of the Barbours, the camp superintendent had written regional headquarters that "there is at present *not a team nor an animal* for the whole colony. Our greatest want at present lies in this direction." Consequently, "de Yankees takes de mules an' wagin" from the Barbours. Because the army required that "all colored persons able to work must engage themselves at some steady labor," they immediately put the husband to "mak[ing] Yankee boots." Without such employment, the family would have faced starvation because the government was supplying rations to less than one-quarter of the destitute escapees.[33]

Fundamentally, the fugitives were treated as if they were still enslaved, for the Union army defined slaves as captured property, *contraband of war*. In the words of one black laborer, they were "Liven . . . just as much Slave" in the contraband camps "as the[y] was . . . before the war broke out." In a pattern that aped their experience on the plantations, blacks "[we]re not allowed to go away" unless they requested and were provided a written pass. At New Bern, there was "[a] great distinction made between the white and col.d" with respect to medical care. When blacks were "taken with the small pox," they did not receive "half [the] medical attendanc" provided to whites, and the dead were buried in mass graves. Railroad and bridge workers probably faced the worst living conditions. Along the railroad between Chattanooga and Nashville, a Union officer reported that "there [we]re not far from 1,000 [military laborers] scattered along the RR Line for more than ninety miles." The men lived "mostly in the woods." In both southeastern Tennessee and eastern Kentucky, impressed railroad workers were "in a filthy condition and destitute of clothing, so much so, that they [we]re in a suffering condition." In January, an officer reported that "it [wa]s hard to see men working out doors all day, such weather as this, when I know that there are great holes in their shoes, and they have no drawers, under-shirts or mittens; and then to see them lie down in front of the fire to sleep."[34]

Food shortages, horrible ecological conditions, confiscation of property, and inequitable provisions were not the only problems faced by black
military workers. Like slaveholders, the Union army recognized the fiscal advantages of labor coercion. It was the Union policy to pay higher
monthly wages to whites, but blacks were more cost-effective. Poor whites
were discharged when they complained or when the army could acquire
blacks for "about one-third of the wages paid white laborers." Not only
were blacks cheaper, but they also were more easily controlled. One officer
observed in 1863 that "a gang of Irishmen ... are crabbed and will work
only so many hours a day; but these [black] men are afraid and ... they
will work nights or any time and do any thing you want done." Through
its employment policies, the Union army triggered white harassment of
blacks. New Bern refugees complained that whites would "steal [thei]r
chickens rob [thei]r gardens and if any one defend[ed] their-Selves against
them they [we]re taken to the gard house for it." Laborers impressed from
the Appalachian counties of Virginia encountered similar perils at contraband camps in that state. Early in the war, black laborers repeatedly
complained that whites were "[S]tripping them of whatever [wa]s found
in their possession." A camp officer acknowledged that most of the acts
were "Carried on out of hatred to the Col^d people."[35]

In addition to inequitable wages and to racial tensions with unemployed whites, fugitives were compelled to accept work contracts with
slaveholders or to work on government farms. At war's end, one Union
inspector publicly descried policies at the contraband camps, claiming
that "avarice imp[el]led men to make wholesale conscription of the negro" in order to profit by hiring them out. As Union troops stabilized their
occupation of Appalachian counties, they instituted an employment policy that would ensure that freed slaves became "self-sustaining, and not a
burthen upon the Government." Some black Appalachians were assigned
to government farms in middle Tennessee and parts of Virginia. Established on abandoned or confiscated plantations, these farms instituted
a sharecropping system that kept the blacks just as economically dependent as they would be under a similar system after the war. By early 1863,
Union occupancy forces in Virginia had "commenced taking farms and
placing the negroes upon them," most of the workers being women and
children. It was the policy to "promise them one half what they raised."
Like postbellum landholders, the army "supported them until [they] got
the crops" and "furnished everything – Seeds, ploughs, &c." In 1863,
such Virginia farms had "three thousand acres of land in cultivation –
mostly in grain." The government farms there were "going into cotton
to some extent, tobacco more largely." In addition to agricultural output,
they were also operating two grist mills, a saw mill, and a large cordwood

yard. To manage these farms, the army employed overseers "who were accustomed to work [blacks] as slaves." In an accounting method that foreshadowed postbellum sharecropping, the overseer kept an account of each worker's daily production. "Every Saturday night the amount of work they ha[d] done during the week [wa]s made known to them." After crops were harvested and sold, each laborer was assigned a share of the crop that equaled their labor input, then subsistence costs were deducted from that share.[36]

For the majority who could not be assigned to government farms, the army mandated that "all coloured persons male or female able to work steadily, contract for labor, by the month, season, or year." A "loyal responsible citizen" was appointed "Superintendent of Labor." Those seeking to employ "field or house servants" made application to the Superintendent. By early 1864, only a small percentage of the blacks at Union posts in or near Appalachian counties were either working for the army or farming on government-controlled lands. Instead, the majority labored under contracts with local farmers and private employers, most of whom were slaveholders. In Tennessee, the military camps allowed "civilians of known loyalty, having possession of plantations, farms, wood-yards, or otherwise engaged" to hire laborers from the commandants of the contraband camps. In effect, a slaveholder could take the loyalty oath and contract with the army to retain his own slaves. Monthly wages were set at $7 for males, $5 for females, and $3 for children. The employer was supposed to supply medicines, but laborers were now to be charged for food, clothing, and housing. Greedy officers also illegally hired out black soldiers to work for adjacent whites. While based in southwestern Virginia, a Fifth Colored Cavalryman reported that

the major makes his Brages that he will keep these dam [blacks] in until he makes a fortune[.] they have us cleaning up farms and cutting up Stumps for these citizens and they pay the officers for it and they are allowing these citizens to run over us[.] if we Say anything to them we are put in jail and two or three months pay docked from us.[37]

Black Appalachians who worked for the Union army had problems of their own. When conscripted, most of them had been employed under agreements that paid an initial bounty to their owners and promised them monthly wages. From the first, impressed laborers were not paid on a regular basis. On the one hand, Union officers often acquiesced to owners who demanded the monthly wages of slaves. The Quartermaster at Chattanooga found that honoring the laborer's wage contract was "a delicate case." He wrote to Washington for a policy decision when he received letters from thirty eastern Tennessee and eastern Kentucky masters "claiming the pay due said slaves, and giving references in regard to their loyalty. What am I to do," he queried. "Shall I continue to pay the Slaves, or if the masters are loyal – am I to pay the masters." Because black Appalachians in Tennessee were exempted from the Emancipation Proclamation, the Chattanooga officer was instructed "if a contract was made with their masters, they are entitled to the wages." In November 1863, another Chattanooga officer complained "there is a large amount of money due negroes for work on the fortifications ... and I am informed ... that there is money in hand to pay them. Many families are suffering for want of money earned from six to twelve months since." Indeed, six months earlier, the district commander had released $30,000 to be distributed for the work of those impressed laborers. While the workers scrambled for food and shelter, the bureaucracy waited for the War Department to "decide whether the slaves should be paid, or their masters." When concerned supervisors made inquiry in behalf of the destitute blacks, the Cumberland Headquarters responded that "the negros employed ... were collected from all quarters," therefore, it was "extremely difficult & in most cases impossible to ascertain to whom they belong[ed] or whether their owners [we]re loyal or disloyal." Consequently, "no disbursing officer [wa]s willing to pay [the laborers] when their owners may hereafter appear and claim the wages." After workers had waited more than half a year for their wages, the Chattanooga Headquarters recommended that this situation be used as leverage to encourage black males to enlist. As enlisted soldiers, they were legally freedmen, so the Quartermasters would be obliged "to pay them." The problems were not all political, for corrupt Quartermasters embezzled the funds due to black workers. In 1863, one camp superintendent testified that impressed laborers could have supported their own families if they "had been in the regular receipt of their pay by the Government." He reported that the typical impressed laborer actually received only about 16 cents per month of the contracted wages of $5 to $8. It was common practice for these officers to withhold most of the wages, only providing small partial payments. "Instead of paying them for ten, twelve, or fifteen months [the officer would] pays them for only one month and lets the rest run, and perhaps in three or four months he will pay them for another month and keep the other back."[38]

Women, children, and the elderly fared worst at Union camps. Periodic evictions were designed to rid the army of the cost of supporting large dependent populations. As early as 1862, the Union army experimented with the policy of turning families out of the camps to force their return to their Confederate masters. Many high-ranking officers of the Army of the Cumberland advised the policy of "segregate rather than congregate negroes." The rationale was that "if the women and children compel their owners to subsist them the cup of rebellion which they drink will be more bitter." Army records document that this policy was widespread throughout all the southern states where contraband camps emerged. Kentucky's Camp Nelson undertook so many purges of this kind that its inhumanity excited the attention of northern newspapers. After the camp commander had ordered the forced removal of hundreds of people in the dead of winter, the post physician justified that decision by claiming that the evictees were only "negro women, children and old men . . . very destitute, a burden to themselves as well as others." What was more they had caused "pestilence and famine in camp." The doctor reasoned that the owners of these fugitives would "care for & provide for the women and children" and "should be allowed to do so." Furthermore, he advised, the army could avoid any future "evil" at Camp Nelson "by peremtorily forbidding any more [escaped slaves to] enter." In an attempt to depopulate a small northern Alabama camp of women, children, and elderly dependents, the commander "sent by rail" about one hundred people and had them "dumped at the Chattanooga depot" where they were "left for hours between the tracks," without water, food, shelter, or any plan for their final disposition. North Carolina camps reduced or cut off rations to the families of soldiers "to induce them to find employment" away from the camps, for it was "the design of the Government to return these families to their former masters to be supported." One army chaplain warned that

the sweeping reduction of the rations brings hundreds suddenly face to face with starvation. There are numerous cases of orphan children . . . who are now cast off because they have nothing to eat. There are many more who are sick and disabled whose ration has been cut off. . . . It is a daily occurrence to see scores of women and children crying for bread, whose husbands, Sons and fathers are in the army today.[39]

To recruit slave soldiers, Union forces promised to protect and support their families, but camp officials required them to support themselves. A few of the women were reassigned to government farms; even more were hired out to area slaveholders. When they worked for the army, women fared just as badly as other laborers. At Chattanooga, officers received numerous complaints from black females who had been cheated of their wages by corrupt whites. Anna Irwin and three others were impressed in northern Georgia to work in field hospitals. Over a two-year period, the women were relocated by the army to nine different locations in Georgia, Tennessee, and Alabama. Promised "four dollars pr week," the women went unpaid because white officers "took the money and made away."

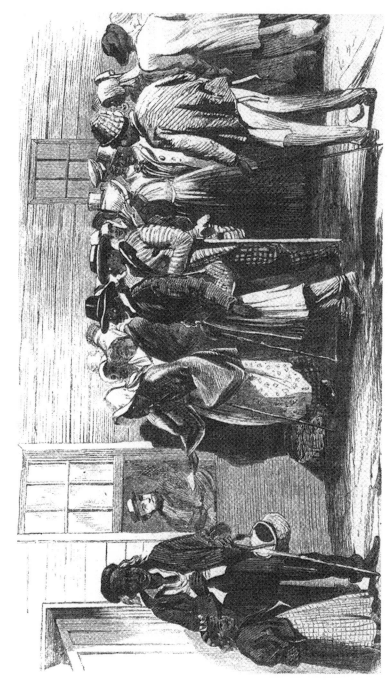

Union officers allocated most of the camp provisions to whites, defrauded impressed slaves of their wages, and repeatedly evicted the families of black soldiers. *Source:* Library of Congress.

210

Sexual exploitation by whites was another danger. Contraband camps replicated the kinds of abuse black females had known at the hands of slaveholders. Many of the officers and soldiers "selected mulatto women with whom they were in the habit of sleeping." Eastern Kentucky and southwestern Virginia husbands frequently complained about white male assaults on their families in the camps. Their "familys ha[d] no protection" against white soldiers who "br[oke] into [thei]r houses [and] act[ed] as they please[d]." As a result, many of the women were pregnant, "half or more labouring under venerial diseases," contracted from rapes and abuses by white soldiers.[40]

7 The Risks of Emancipation for Black Families

> And so freedom come, and so it come with a proclamation, with a
> jubilation, with a shout and a juba, and then folks went on back to the
> quarters and commenced to go back to work, 'cause what else could
> they do?   – Linda Brown, African-American novelist

"We didn't never have no experience with the soldiers, 'cause we was all
freed when de war was about half over," Julia Gurdner told the WPA interviewer in 1937. Owned by a loyalist eastern Tennessee physician, this
woman was the only Appalachian ex-slave who reported being freed by
an owner after the Emancipation Proclamation was enacted in January
1863. Even though there were so many Unionist slaveholders in the region and even though federal forces were present in several parts of the
Mountain South between 1861 and 1865, very few of the Appalachian
ex-slaves were emancipated voluntarily by their owners during or after the
war. Indeed, few mountain masters were influenced by the Emancipation
Proclamation to free the blacks they controlled. The Appalachian counties of Kentucky, Maryland, Tennessee, northern Virginia, and West
Virginia were legally excluded from the provisions of the order. Thus,
slaveholders in those counties continued to exploit black laborers in their
agricultural, industrial, and commercial enterprises; and they actually intensified their slave selling and hiring. Once Union forces occupied other
mountain counties, federal policies exempted slaveholding Unionists
(including Confederate sympathizers who took the oath of allegiance)
and issued instructions to field officers "to safeguard the property rights"
of those who supplied the army with skilled military laborers. Consequently, most mountain masters benefited directly from hiring slaves to
the Union army and continued to control black laborers with little Union
interference.

Emancipation Through the Eyes of Mountain Masters

From the perspective of Appalachian slaveholders, emancipation must
be carefully orchestrated, if their communities were to preserve safety

212

and cultivate food supplies for whites. Even before they had liberated their own slaves, many mountain masters were growing increasingly concerned at the numbers of blacks who were in motion on local roads. At war's end, 40 percent of the region's male ex-slaves and 20 percent of the females were returning from army service, from military sites where they had worked as laborers, or from contraband camps to which they had been relocated. In addition, growing numbers of blacks were searching for family members, pestering slaveholders to release their spouses and children. Some owners evicted slaves rather than accept them as wage earners, so a small number of blacks were seeking employment. James Gwyn's July 1865 diary entry typifies the anxiety of mountain masters.

The worst disturbance ... now is from the negroes Who are all said to be free & many of them have left their homes & are prowling about, disturbing others who would remain at home till fall or winter if let alone. poor deluded Creatures, its a death blow to them; in a few years they will be perishing and down and in twenty years the race will almost be extinct.

About the same time, a Pickens County, South Carolina, mistress commented in her diary: "The negroes being freed, almost everyone is turning them away by hundreds to starve, plunder, & do worse. The times ahead a fearful.... An insurrection is much dreaded." Mountain masters did not worry only about the security problem, they feared loss of their workers just as harvests were near. At Charlottesville, there was a "meeting of Masters" to strategize how they would prevent neighbors from recruiting one another's freed slaves. At Traveler's Rest in northern Georgia, the slaveholder waited until after crops were harvested to emancipate blacks. Throughout the spring and summer, the slaves had talked of "the coming of emancipation," and they "had made inquiries" to their owner. Not until late fall did he inform them that he "could no longer employ them, and that they must find homes for themselves." The whole company very soon scattered, without assistance or provisions from the slaveholder. To avoid feeding them through the winter of 1866, small plantations in western Maryland "turned off the old women, the Mothers with their helpless Children."[2]

Fear of uncontrolled blacks was an ideological justification for deterring emancipation as long as possible. At war's end, Appalachian plantations were slower to liberate slaves than large plantations in counties with more sizeable black populations. However, that deterred emancipation was caused less by local attitudes (which were no different from racism in other parts of the South) than by federal policy decisions. Union occupational forces were reluctant to alienate loyalist owners, so they did

Like most Appalachian masters, this owner emancipated slaves in the middle of winter, after crops had been cultivated and stored. After such announcements, a majority of Appalachian ex-slaves remained with former owners two years or longer. *Source: Harper's New Monthly,* 1885.

not police them as closely as they scrutinized Confederate sympathizers. Because the state was the last to abolish slavery, eastern Kentucky slaves were not emancipated until 1866. Mountain plantations which were located in counties that did not have large Union occupational forces at war's end were able to defy the emancipation order longer. Because the U.S. War Department prioritized large plantations and counties with massive black populations, the army and the Freedmen's Bureau were slow to initiate operations in counties with low black population densities. In Appalachian counties with small occupational forces, slaveholders were left undisturbed as long as eighteen months after surrender. After Johnson's Reconstruction Proclamation in May 1865, western North Carolina master James Hervee Greenlee

[t]old those [he] had controlled that they were free. They appeared astonished, told them it was so & they could go when they pleased or if they wanted to stay would deal fairly with them & give them what was right of what was made. They said it was poor freedom to starve they had nothing to live on or to work on.

Without the required federal authorization to do so, Greenlee told them he "would make a firm bargain if they would do what was right and make a crop they should have a due proportion." A week later, he reported "Hands replanting corn." Six weeks later, he traveled to Charlotte to take the oath of allegiance and to receive clearance to make contracts with his ex-slaves. Union troops did not appear in his county to enforce the emancipation order until October.[3]

It was obvious to James Gwyn by February 1865 that "hard times" lay ahead because slaveholders "must submit to the authority of U.S. with the Constitution as amended which abolish[es] slavery." Unlike Greenlee, Gwyn waited six months after surrender to free his slaves. Because there was no federal detachment in his community, Gwyn kept his slaves hard at work throughout the spring and into the fall. After the crops were cultivated and harvested, livestock gathered from the mountains, hogs slaughtered and stored, and his family's provisions ensured, Gwyn went down to the quarters in late November "to dismiss the Negroes & let them look out for homes." After he evicted them, there were only two male laborers left, for Gwyn had decided temporarily to produce nothing but his family's subsistence needs and "only work 3 or 4 hands." Throughout this period, no Union forces ever appeared on Gwyn's plantation to enforce the emancipation order or to police his treatment of blacks. Emancipation occurred much sooner in those Appalachian counties that had a greater number of large plantations and more sizeable black populations. Change came much faster, for example, in Pickens County, South Carolina. While Gwyn and Greenlee were working their ex-slaves illegally in western North Carolina, Union soldiers had already scoured the countryside of northern South Carolina. One mistress noted that, by July 1865, "all negroes have now asserted their freedom," and the federals were confiscating abandoned lands "to be divided . . . among the negroes."[4]

Emancipation Through the Eyes of Mountain Slaves

The WPA narratives provide a great deal of detail about the process of emancipation and the early adjustment of freedpeople to the chaos that characterized that period. Less than 7 percent of black Appalachians were emancipated voluntarily by their masters during or after the war. Most of the owners who voluntarily emancipated slaves did so after they had taken the loyalty oath, like Andrew Goodman's owner, and had received permission from the Freedmen's Bureau to negotiate labor contracts with their ex-slaves. Frank Menefee's family was luckier than most mountain ex-slaves. Their master "called [them] all up an' told [them that they] was jes' free as him. He give [them] a suit of clo'es, some money, a mule, a cow, a hog, and li'l corn to start off on." Others voluntarily liberated slaves because they wanted to rid themselves of the expense of maintaining them. Penny Thompson's master "gave [them] lots ob confidence money (confederate)," told them "dat [they] was free," and that they should "go an' make a home" for themselves elsewhere.[5]

Three-quarters of the Appalachian slaves were emancipated by Union soldiers during the war or by the Freedmen's Bureau after the war. Nearly one-half the mountain slaves were told they were free by Union soldiers during the war. That emancipation was hazy, however, for most of these "liberated" slaves joined the ranks of impressed military laborers, enlisted soldiers, or refugees in army contraband camps. Owners continued to receive bounties and wages for those laborers and soldiers, and the movements of these individuals were just as restricted as they would have been under their masters' surveillance. Even after the war had ended, the army was slow to release the black populations housed at contraband camps. One-third of the mountain slaves were not freed until the Freedmen's Bureau forced their owners to emancipate them, a full year or more after the Confederate surrender. The slaves at John Payne's northern Georgia plantation "didn't know it was freedom for a long time. They worked on till that crop was made and gathered." The Freedmen's Bureau "sent word to the master ... he better turn them slaves loose. Some of the slaves heard the message. That was the first they knowed it was freedom." Elizabeth Sparks's master "tried to fool the slaves 'bout freedom an' wanted to keep 'em on a-workin' but the Yankees told 'em they wuz free." Teenager Ben Chambers learned how costly it was to alert other slaves to their emancipation before their owners were ready. Ben drove his master into town and heard a Union official instruct him to liberate his slaves. According to Ben, his owner had not "let none [of them] free yet," even though the army had "done establish[ed] a buro (bureau) ... so dey could go out and see iffen de [blacks] was tu'n free." When Ben arrived home, he was "mos' too excite' to onhitch de hosses. [He] run down and tell all de [slaves] de Yankee man ... say us all free." Ben's master heard the jubilation "and come down and whipped [him]. He say [Ben] tryin' to free his [slaves]." Once word had been leaked prematurely, "de nex' day dey swore him [loyalty oath]," gave him permission to negotiate labor contracts with the ex-slaves, and then he told them they were free. When the soldiers arrived to force Jim Threat's Talladega County owner to liberate the slaves, the owner immediately evicted them. "Git away from here jest as quick as you can," he told them. Mountain masters refused to release family members when spouses or parents came to claim them. For example, a Fauquier County slaveholder refused to release a family to the husband. The master "told

Very few mountain masters voluntarily freed their slaves, and Union policies slowed emancipation in Appalachian counties. Thus, many mountain slaves were not liberated until eighteen months or longer after the war had ended. *Source: Harper's*, 1864.

him that the war was not over yet – that the [slaves] were not free ... that nobody should take them away, and that if anybody come into the yard he would shoot them." John Berry filed a complaint with the Freedmen's Bureau in August 1865, but his wife and six children had still not been released in December 1866.[6]

After months of rumor and speculation, emancipation was a bittersweet, often stunning moment in history for mountain slaves. Fifteen when she was freed, Catherine Slim recalled that "eberybdoy cum to life then. It wuz a hot time in de ole place when dey sezs freedom." When slaves on Fleming Clark's small plantation were freed by Union soldiers, "dey were all shoutin'." According to Booker T. Washington, "most of the ex-slaves left the plantation for a few days at least, so as to get the 'hang' of the new life, and to be sure that they were free." When Betty Jones' grandmother was emancipated by the Freedmen's Bureau, "she dropped her hoe an' run ... to ole Missus an' looked at her real hard. Den she yelled, 'I'se freed! Yes, I'se free! Ain't got to work f' you no mo'. You can't put me in yo' pocket [sell me] now.'" Slaves on a small

Blue Ridge Virginia plantation were stunned by the news, until one of the elderly women started a traditional ring shout of jubilation. Charlotte Brown remembered that

[w]e was all sittin' roun' restin' an' tryin' to think what freedom meant. . . . All at once ole Sister Carrie who was near 'bout a hundred started in to talkin':

> Tain't no mo sellin' today,
> Tain't no mo' hirin' today,
> Tain't no pullin' off shirts today,
> It's stomp down freedom today.
> Stomp it down!

An' when she says, "Stomp it down," all de slaves commence to shoutin' wid her. . . . Wasn't no mo' peace dat Sunday. Ev'vybody started in to sing an' shout once mo'. Fust thing you know dey done made music to Sister Carrie's stomp song an' sang an' shouted dat song all de res' de day. Chile, dat was one glorious time![7]

If we focus only on such jubilation, however, we do not measure accurately the reaction of most mountain slaves to the realities of liberation. Overwhelmingly, black Appalachians were cynical and frightened about their new freedom. Poverty, the need to provide for children and elderly, and local white violence were tangible, measurable truths, while their freedom was like "a great big empty place in the sky, and no way of knowin' what to put in there." For most mountain slaves, this was a bitter freedom that did not bring the kinds of economic resources or structural supports they needed to survive the hardships of the communities into which they were being discharged. We cannot discount the cynicism of mountain slaves as interviewer bias. When narratives are grouped and compared according to ethnicity of interviewers, no difference is evident between the reactions of ex-slaves who were interviewed by whites and those questioned by blacks. They were illiterate and without the financial resources to migrate or to feed their families. Many had been evicted and were without shelter or employment. Others were reluctant to leave owners because they feared losing contact with kin who might be working their way back to them. Most Appalachian ex-slaves felt celebration give way to a sense of desperation and danger.[8]

One western North Carolina ex-slave remembered how the reality sank into them.

It was de awfulest feeling dat everybody in dem quarters laid down wid dat night, de new feeling dat dey was free and never had no more marster to tell them what to do. You felt jes' like you had done strayed off a-fishing and got lost. It sho won't no fun to be free, kaise we never had nothing.

Mary Tate, member of a small black population in Grainger County, Tennessee, recalled their ambivalence. "When emancipation was declared some rejoiced, while others seemed to think that they could not depend on themselves [and] refus[ed] to leave the plantations, while others were driven away." Fifteen at war's end, Ann Ladly described the heavy weight of freedom. "I'se hear dat in some places de colored folks shouted and carried on a heap, but ... it was dat quiet – jes' most like a funeral. Dey wasn't no one said nothing.... [D]e colored folks start for de quarters and most of 'em was crying." Andrew Goodman was twenty-six years old when he was emancipated, and he was in despair about the future for his family "cause they don't know where to go." Older slaves had a difficult time comprehending the structural meaning of their new freedom. At Goodman's small plantation, some of them "can't hardly git used to the idea. When they wants a pass to leave the place, they still go up to the big house for a pass. They just can't understand 'bout the freedom."[9]

On such small plantations in counties with few blacks, emancipation existed in name only. They had not been liberated from poverty, land-lessness, or hunger, and many feared that their circumstances were about to get worse. Sixteen at war's end, Anna Lee described conditions on a small plantation in mountainous Scott County, Tennessee, where there were few slaves and no black community support mechanisms.

We begin to wonder what we was going to do for we did not have no job and nothing to eat, and we did not know what we was going to do. We begin to beg Maser to keep us there with him but he told us he did not know if he could or not, that about all he had was wiped out during the war.... There were some negroes that they just turned a loose, no place to go or no way to make a living, they just had to roam the country and beg what they could for a living.

According to Ruben Woods, emancipation brought no change in white racism; "You changed yo clo[th]es, but you hadn't changed yo voice." Another mountain slave put it even more bluntly. Because of their poverty, illiteracy, and white control over land, emancipation meant that they were "Liven ... just as much a Slave as the[y] was ... before the war broke out."[10]

Emancipation and Immobility

Less than one-third of the emancipated Appalachian slaves left their own-ers' plantations within the first year of their freedom. About one-fifth departed immediately to seek other opportunities, but the vast majority remained with their former masters two years or longer. One-third of them remained longer than five years, and more than 10 percent stayed

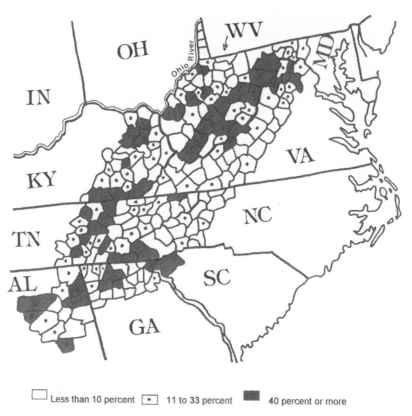

Less than 10 percent   11 to 33 percent   40 percent or more

Map 5. Out-migration of blacks from the Mountain South, 1860–70.
Source: Analysis of Censuses of Population, 1860 and 1870 (NA).

a decade or longer. Indeed, the Appalachian ex-slaves represented in the WPA narratives averaged a postbellum stay of nearly five years with the whites who had owned them. Only 15 percent of those ex-slaves migrated by 1870 from the counties in which they were enslaved.[11]

These findings from the slave narratives are supported by analysis of regional census data and by trends for the rest of the South. Very few ex-slaves migrated out of the South during Reconstruction. Like other parts of the South, Appalachia's black population declined by less than 6 percent between 1860 and 1870. Within the region, however, there was a great deal of diversity. In ninety-six counties, the black population declined less than 10 percent between 1860 and 1870 (see Map 5). Another sixty-nine counties lost 11 to 33 percent of their ex-slaves, and fifty counties lost 40 percent or more of their black citizens over the decade.

The greatest population declines occurred in Appalachian counties that had the smallest numbers of blacks. Those mountain counties that lost 50 percent or more of their ex-slaves averaged black populations of about four hundred in 1860. In contrast, those counties that exhibited population declines of less than one-third of their ex-slaves averaged fifteen hundred to three thousand slaves in 1860. Clearly, black Appalachians were more likely to migrate when they lived in areas where they did not have "protection in numbers." Even when they did migrate, however, most of them moved only into adjacent counties or into the region's towns, as evidenced by the low population decline for the entire region. We must, however, put these statistics into their proper perspective. Regional population change between 1860 and 1870 was caused by three factors other than the postbellum out-migration of black Appalachians. First, mountain masters continued throughout the Civil War to export slaves through interstate sales and to remove great numbers through interregional migrations of owners. Second, the 1870 census undercounted black Americans by about 10 percent, especially in rural counties. Third, 5 to 7 percent of black Appalachians would have died as soldiers. Probably one-sixth of black Appalachian males aged sixteen to forty-five died during their Union enlistment, a mortality rate that exceeded the national average. Though this region would experience a massive out-migration of blacks after 1880, that loss of population had not begun by 1870. Ex-slave Henry Freeman summarized the situation accurately when he told the WPA interviewer that "for [a] good many years mos' of dem stayed wid dere ole Marsters."[12]

When compared with census data, it is clear that the regional slave narratives provide an accurate view of the immobility of emancipated black Appalachians. In White County, Tennessee, "it was a long time after the War" before Josie Jordan's family "left old master Lowery. Stayed right there ... working in the fields, living in the same old cabin, just like before the War." Tom Windham's northern Georgia parents "stayed right there till they died." At Andrew Goodman's plantation, "three families went to get farms for theyselves, but the rest just stay on for hands on the old place." Evelyn Williams's grandfather remained all his life "about three miles from where he was held a slave." Andrew Goodman was twenty-six when the war ended, but he "got married and lived on the old place till [he] was in [his] late fifties." One ex-slave told a Fisk University interviewer: "I live right in the house now that I lived in when I was a slave.... [M]e and my wife bought the place from mistress.... I stayed right in the house with them until a little over a year before I married." According to Ann Ladly, "dey wasn't a single one of Marse Tom's colored folks what left right away. Course, later, some get 'em a piece of ground and goes to raising a crop, but some stayed with Marse Tom for a long time." James Day's family "stayed with the old master eighteen years, den [his] father bought a place."[13]

After emancipation, why did so many black Appalachians stay in their prewar circumstances? On the one hand, the Freedmen's Bureau was less active and had a lower visibility in most mountain counties. On the other hand, the Freedmen's Bureau did little to facilitate the movement of ex-slaves from their local communities or their former owners. Military regulations put pressure on black Appalachians to find employment quickly and permitted former owners a lot of latitude in developing labor contracts with their former slaves. The bureau's philosophy was that "the most essential condition of a state of freedom [was] a visible means of support." In the view of Union officials, freedpeople had to be disciplined to know that "they must work for their support now, the same as before they were free." In response to white fears of wandering blacks and landowner demands for workers, the bureau prioritized the allocation of black laborers to farming. "The good of all classes require that the lands should be refenced and cultivated," wrote a bureau agent at one Appalachian county office. "But it is impossible for the farmer to pursue his work successfully" without laborers who would "remain with him to the end of their engagements." In effect, then, the bureau deterred and punished black mobility. According to Berlin and his associates,

federal regulations often undermined the ability of former slaves to support themselves. Many military officials saw unemployed or irregularly employed black people as a threat to good order. Accordingly, they adopted pass systems and vagrancy regulations to 'clean out' former slaves who lacked 'steady' employment or independent means, thereby treating as criminals those who were self-employed or who earned a living by 'chance work.'

In most Appalachian counties between 1865 and 1870, local and state laws criminalized unemployment and made it nearly impossible for freedpeople to search competitively for new positions. Ex-slaves without stable positions were placed to work without pay under military guards, until they accepted a farm labor contract. Enticement laws declared it a crime for an employer to hire away a black laborer who was under contract to someone else. Under vagrancy laws, sheriffs could arrest anyone who did not have a labor contract and then hire them out as part of a convict lease system. In mountainous Scott County, Tennessee, where there was a small black population, Anna Lee thought that ex-slaves "done just about what [they] could after the war." Whites in her area "would not let [them] get out and hunt other places to stay and work, as they were use to making us do just what they wanted."[14]

In addition to that legal coercion, the ex-slaves provide several graphic explanations for their inertia. Judging by the frequency with which ex-slaves mentioned their destitution, immobility was probably caused more by lack of survival resources than any other factor. After emancipation, Ellen Miller's eastern Kentucky owner "gave the ex-slaves just barely enough for them to keep body and soul together, very little food and no clothing, this of course was done to keep them from running away." Anna Lee recalled: "we did not get nothing except we were turned loose like [a] bunch of wild hogs to make it the best we could." In her view, ex-slaves were "forced to stay on as servants" because they "most had to stay and to do what [their former owners] told [them] so'es [they] could get something to eat." Women who headed households, like the mothers of Sallah White, Josie Jordan, and Mary Myhand, almost always remained with former owners longer than married couples or single men. It was much harder for women with children to find new positions. Landholders wanted to avoid the expense of feeding children too young to work, and they feared that child care would keep women from field work. Unable to find anything else, Lula Walker "stayed on de plantation eight years atter de war." Then in the 1870s, she scrambled from work "in de field" to coke loading "in de mines," only to end up "in de poor house" where "dey didn't gib [her] much to eat." Perhaps Simon Hare sums it up best: "Some was glad ter be free, some was sorry because dey was wuss [worse] off, work a whole year an' git nothin'.... Had a bad time! We stayed right there.... I stayed on till I got grown." A Nelson County, Virginia, slaveholder commented that emancipated blacks "expect[ed] to be provided with homes & land by the Yankees." Henry Banner was one of those who believed the Freedmen's Bureau promise to resettle blacks on confiscated slaveholder lands. When "it got out that they were going to give [ex-slaves] forty acres and a mule," Henry "went to town" to register for his new property and discovered that there was none. "Before the war you belonged to somebody," he lamented cynically. "After the war you were nothin' but a nigger. The laws of the country were made for the white man." Simon Hare succinctly outlined the hardships facing most mountain freedpeople. "Come de Surrender, colored folks had a bad time.... Didn' have nothin,' not even a hat.... Marster jes said, Yawl is free! an' he didn' do nothin' mo' fer us."[15]

Fountain Hughes's family faced economic circumstances that were typical of many mountain ex-slaves. His father was dead, and his mother had four children. They "didn't have no property," and they "didn't have no home." If the household were to survive, "she had to put them all to work." Fleming Clark's father found no work except "makin' charcoal," so the Botetourt County household "lived very light de first year after de war." Those who could not find positions were faced with starvation or indenturement by the poorhouse. Others resorted to scavenging and stealing. In Warren County, Tennessee, Ann Mathews's father, a single parent, "went back in de woods en built [his children] a saplin house en dobbed hit wid mud." Then he struck out to search for work. The children "staid in dat house in de woods" and "didn't see a bit ob bre'd." After two weeks, Ann wandered to a house several miles away and begged for food. Because abandoned black children were being indentured into long-term labor by the Freedmen's Bureau, the youngsters were afraid "bein' dere 'lone." Ann would "set up wile [her] br[oth]ers slep', den [she]'d sleep in de daytime." After several weeks of near starvation and fear of violence, Ann's father reappeared. He still had not found work, but he had managed to steal "two sacks ob food." Some died of starvation or exposure from living outdoors without adequate food or water. One small town reported two such deaths between February and July 1867: a freedman "was found in a dying condition" on the main street and a woman died "from the effects of sun-stroke."[16]

Appalachian counties had a surplus of laborers because half or more of the white populations were poor and landless, so there were few job opportunities other than farm labor for blacks. Mountain South plantations evicted great numbers of elderly blacks, mothers with young children, the sick, and pregnant women. Most of those removals occurred in December and January, so those who were evicted by former owners had the hardest time. Millie Simpkins's family "didn't git nothin' " at emancipation. They were "jes druv 'way widout nothin' ter do wid." They "got in a waggin en druv ter nuther man's plantashun," and her husband "made a crap dere." When Eli Davison's West Virginia owner was forced to emancipate his slaves, he first "made [them] work one whole week so'es [they] could keep the clothes [they] had on." After that, according to Eli, "he called us to his door one evening late and told us as soon as we finished eating that he wanted us to get along. We had no money, no clothes except what we had on, and nothing to eat. He said if he got up the next morning and found a negro on his place that he would horse whip him.... [H]e just turned us out like a stray bunch of cattle to graze or starve to death." During the first eighteen months after emancipation, Jim Threat's family was hired and then expelled from three farms after they rebuilt damaged buildings and fences for the owners. When Threat's owner evicted them, his father

was stumped for he didn't know what on earth he was going to do with that big family. Old man Ramsey told father that he had an old house down in the field that needed a floor and chimney that he could have if he would fix it up. Pappy and the older boys set in and built a chimney and we moved in on the dirt floor. We stayed there about a month when Ramsey said he needed the house so we had to move out. Our old doctor moved . . . and he let us have his house . . . for three weeks. Old lady Drummonds let us build a house on her place and we lived there [awhile]. We would work for folks and take our pay in meat scraps, cornmeal, shorts, and anything they was a mind to give us.

Henry Banner pinpoints the lack of employment options. Sixteen at war's end in Russell County, Virginia, Henry "went to town and rambled all around but there wasn't nothin' for [him]." Since he "couldn't get nothin' to do," he "jus' stayed on and made a crop" for his former owner. Since they knew they "still had to look to the white man" for employment, ex-slaves quite often found it easier to deal with those with whom they had past ties. Those black soldiers who returned to home counties typically had pro-Union masters, so they relied on their former owners for protection and employment. When the war was over, all the black soldiers who had enlisted from Rachel Cruze's plantation returned and were employed by their former master. Anna Peek lived with her owner's family until the 1930s because they aided her husband after his release from military service. Even though he ran away to enlist, "he returned to his white folks and they gave him a home as long as he lived."[17]

If these reasons caused most ex-slaves to stay with former owners, what propelled some to leave? Black Appalachians left their owners primarily for four reasons. Loss of property to creditors and the deaths of former owners forced the relocation of ex-slaves, like the families of Penny Thompson, John Brown, and Georgia Flourney. Some black Appalachians who were living in contraband camps or military labor sites stayed near those locations after the war. Third, some migrated into towns or areas where they could work at nonagricultural occupations. More than any other reason, however, ex-slaves migrated outside their home counties to try to locate and to reunite with family who had been forcibly removed by owners. According to Delia Garlic, "When we knowed we's free, everybody wanted ter get out. The rule was, if you stayed in your cabin, it was still yours, but if you left it, you couldn't come back." At emancipation, Delia's husband was still working as a conscripted military laborer for an Alabama railroad company. For a long time, Delia's husband "slipped in an' out" to visit her, and he kept warning her not to leave because of the chaotic conditions. "He said folks was gettin out ever'where. Babies was bein born in fence corners, anywhere." When Delia became pregnant again, she was determined to rebuild their family and to end the kind of abroad relationship they had endured during slavery. So she "jus' made up [her] min'" to join her husband at the railroad construction site. With "one baby in [her] arms, another in [her] pocket, an [her] bundle on [her] back," Delia walked more than 300 miles to reunite with her husband in northern Alabama.[18]

Emancipation Deferred for Soldiers and Their Families

Freedom was even more illusive for many black Appalachian soldiers and their families. At war's end, black mountain soldiers learned that the Union Army would not keep its promise to protect their families from slaveholders. Before surrender, Union contraband camps enacted policies that aided masters to keep many of their laborers and made it difficult for ex-slaves to leave their former owners. Throughout the nine states in which Appalachian counties were located, the Union army used its military authority to protect the interests of former masters. "In all cases where the owners of slaves shall declare in writings to their slaves that they will in all things regard them as hired servants and ... pay them wages for their labor, the arrangements will be protected ... by military authority.... Colored soldiers are advised to enter into the agreements contemplated in this order." To complicate the economic crises faced by their families, many black soldiers were retained by the Union army long after whites had been mustered out. Berlin and Rowland report that:

As white soldiers were discharged, black regiments made up a growing proportion of Union troops in the defeated Confederacy; the postwar army of occupation was blacker than the army that fought the war. Federal officials worried about the effect of black soldiers on the expectation of former slaves, and white southerners insisted that the presence of black soldiers undermined efforts to maintain order. Such concerns resulted in the removal of many black regiments to distant parts of the South, far from the centers of black population. Thousands of black soldiers were sent to the Texas border to guard against the threat of French imperialism in Mexico.[19]

The black soldier's view was that they "never was freed yet Run Right out of Slavery in to Soldiery & [they] hadent nothing at all." One black regiment complained "Wee are said to be US Soldiers and behold wee are US Slaves." As part of that campaign, West Virginian Gus Wells died in Brownsville, Texas. His distraught mother pleaded with the army to confirm his death. "Let me know if I can get him," she pleaded, "please let me know the distance to Texas and what it would cost." The mother received the terse reply that her son "had died at Post Hospl. of Chronic Diarrhoea." Even though he had been injured and spent time "in one of those war hospitals," Julius Jones was ordered to Texas, so he "wasn't turned loose till 1866" when his regiment was "mustared out in Baton Rouge, La." A Chattanooga regiment was notified at war's end that they were to be reassigned to the Rio Grande, and they "d[id]nt want to go

there whilce [thei]r Familys [wa]s in a Sufference condishion." The ex-
slaves had been apart from their families since enlistment, and "there
Wives [wa]s Scatered about the world." While the regiment spent most
of its time "Poleasing [policing] Ground, some of [them] ha[d] not heard
from [thei]r Wivies for 2 & a half [years]." After "their Masters Run them
off," some families had moved into ramshackle shacks outside the camp,
and they were "Threadless, Shoeless without food & no home." While the
soldiers were facing westward transport, their families were "suffering for
the want of Husband Care." The regiment stated that they had enlisted
for a three-year term, but "the war is over," and they were prepared to
"Stack their Arms," a Civil War reference to collective refusal to perform
duties.[20]

Postwar Conditions in the Mountain South

Warfare and guerilla activity devastated much of the land area of Southern
Appalachia, particularly the Tennessee Valley, the valleys of Virginia, and
northwestern West Virginia. For example, Sheridan's 1864 campaign destroyed two thousand farms and seventy mills in the upper Shenandoah
Valley. "The country everywhere had been laid waste by the soldiers of
both armies," according to Page County ex-slave Bethany Veney. War had
completely altered the once prosperous Harper's Ferry, according to this
1865 account.

Freshets tear down the centre of the streets, and dreary hill-sides present only
ragged growths of weeds. The town itself lies half in ruins. . . . Of the bridge across
the Shenandoah only the ruined piers are left; still less remains of the old bridge
across the Potomac. All about the town are rubbish, filth and stench.

Throughout the Mountain South, returning soldiers and local guerillas
continued their retaliatory raids, magnifying the devastation of the war.
In the western Carolinas, three diaries provide glimpses of the guerilla pillaging and violence in the early months after war's end. James Greenlee's
farm and home were ransacked by pro-Union neighbors. James Gwyn
provides a clue of the disorder in his diary: "I hope the people are getting quiet & civil. I hear of no violence or outbreaks." A Pickens County,
South Carolina, slaveholder's wife wrote that the freedpeople were "pretty
quiet," but the county was being plagued by the "casual disturbance and
murders" committed by newly formed white regulators. "This country is
getting very unsafe," she added, "people are constantly called from their
houses at night and shot."[21]

All Southern slaveholders felt economic losses from the war, but
Appalachian plantations were economically marginalized to a much

greater extent than Lower South planters. On the one hand, the higher incidence of military campaigns, soldier encampments, foraging raids, and ongoing guerilla activity devastated agricultural output and drained away the profits once accumulated from the export of grains, tobacco, cotton, and livestock. For instance, an eastern Tennessean wrote to his western North Carolina kinsman: "you have all been very much blessed in North Carolina.... [E]verybody's ruined in Tennessee; we have had the armys on us all the time for the last 4 years.... [W]e have lost so much since the war; we have lost everything but our land." Loss of slaves was not his only economic dilemma. "The armys ha[d] taken everything [they] made for the last 4 Years, and paid us nothing, not a dollar for nothing." As a journalist rode the train through Amherst and Nelson Counties, she observed a countryside that had been sprinkled with prosperous small plantations before the war. Five years after surrender, "little but rough craggy hills and bare fields c[ould] be seen." Periodically she would spot a large farm house that was "now deserted and in ruins." Near each of them were "the mud-daubed, wood chimnied, windowless cabins, once occupied by the slaves."[22]

On the other hand, the war broke trade linkages between the Mountain South and the Northeast, ended the antebellum boom in extractive industries, milling, and light manufacturing, and closed the 134 mineral spas that had attracted tourists from all over the world. Because they were the wealthiest elites in their home counties, Appalachian slaveholders did not just operate plantations; they also controlled many of the commercial and industrial enterprises. For example, western Carolina and northern Georgia slaveholders invested in gold mining and were still accumulating small profits from them in 1860. At war's end, one Pickens County, South Carolina, slaveholder hoped that he could recognize quick cash, if he drove "to Dahlonega ... to see about [his] gold mine there." In Cherokee County, Alabama, the war had damaged every economic investment of slaveholders. "Have lost everything on earth we had but the home we now occupy, and the Coal Stock, and the Yanks almost ruined that," one of them wrote in early 1866. Not only had the capitalist lost all his slaves, but military raids had also torn up the railroad and "injur[ed] the mines so much that it w[ould] take a great sum of money to put them in working opperation." To exacerbate his economic difficulties, the slaveholder feared that he had also lost his political influence because "they [we]re now putting the Negroes in office." Before the war, one small western South Carolina plantation had derived profits from agriculture, slave trading and hiring, railroad investments, gold mining, milling, timbering, and tobacco manufacturing. A few months after the war, the mistress began to board summer travelers. "We are compelled to

do something for a support," she apologized to her wealthier kin. To add
to their economic crises, Mountain South plantations were faced with
county and federal taxes. In May 1865, James Gwyn reported in his diary that "Tax oppressors & collectors [were] moving" in western North
Carolina. "How we are all to pay the taxes I cant tell – Money is scarcer
than I ever knew it in this Country before. Great cry for corn in some
parts." A few months later, another western North Carolina slaveholder
"returned [his] United States tax" and prayed for divine relief "from
ruin & ungodly men." In the Shenandoah Valley, many plantations were
"broken up into small holdings" when owners could not pay taxes or
afford the necessary labor. W. E. Hobbes summed up the predicament of
most Appalachian plantations at war's end. The middle Tennessean had
lost all his slaves, the soldiers had confiscated most of his valuable property and provisions, and his only remaining wealth was his land. "The
main reason we had such a hard time was because we couldn't get any
price for our stuff we raised. Then, taxes took a good part of our money.
Another thing, labor [costs] got pretty high ... because the Government
made the growers pay a good wage for the help they had been getting for
nothing. . . . Then to top it all off, crooked politics put the [Negroes] in a
better position than the white man for awhile."[23]

The ex-slaves recognized that their own poverty was closely tied to
the loss of economic assets by Appalachian plantations. John Van Hook
commented that western North Carolina ex-slaves were "in a sad and
woeful want after the war." Once John asked his father why they were
all "so hungry and ragged." His parent replied: "How can we help it?
Why, even the white folks don't have enough to eat and wear now." When
Henry Williams's owner returned from the war, "he had nothing but the
land," so he could only pay them "in corn and a little money." Ellis Ken
Kannon expressed a similar sentiment about middle Tennessee. The ex-
slaves " 'spected ter git 40 akers of land en a mule but nobody eber got hit
as fur as I know. We didn't git nuthin. Our white people wuzzent able ter
gib us anything. Eve'ythin' dey had wuz tuk durin' de wah." In northern
Alabama, small cotton plantations "didnt has nuthin ter pays anyone ter
work fer dem," so they "couldnt work as many as dey did befo de war."
In Russell County, Virginia, hungry owners of small plantations stood in
lines at the army commissary to be fed the same "hard tacks" that were
being distributed to destitute blacks.[24]

> Slavery had not ended, no we just went from slaves to peons.... They
> did free them in one sense of the word, but put them in a whole lot worse
> shape as they turned them loose to make their own way with nothing
> to make it with.... [W]e mostly had to stay with our [former owners] if
> we got anything.... [W]e were forced to stay on as servants, yes, if we
> expected to live.... [T]hey still made us do just like they wanted to after
> the war.
> — Lizzie Grant, West Virginia ex-slave

The farm journal of a northern Georgia slaveholder provides us unique
insight into the structural constraints upon black Appalachian families
during Reconstruction. Before the war, John Horry Dent had operated
a thriving small plantation, but he reported only land worth $7,500 and
personal wealth of $1,500 to the 1870 census enumerator. By Fall 1866,
Dent had hired thirty ex-slaves, "prime men to be paid $10 a month,
women $6, Boys and girls $4." The hands were "to find themselves rations," meaning that Dent would charge food against their wages. By the
following spring, he was beginning to see "the first symptoms of insub-
ordination" because the black laborers "commenced to walking off and
leaving their work under the most frivolous pretexts." Dent was alarmed
at the degree of change he was seeing in the freedpeople. On the one
hand, ex-slaves could no longer be completely controlled by their employers. On the other hand, former slaveholders now had to compete for
the labor of blacks in a way they had never experienced under slavery.
Dent was convinced that "there [wa]s but little dependence to be placed
in the freedman as a farm laborer" because he carried in his head "Two
Promises." His first aspiration was "to work in Cities ... and the next
[wa]s to rent or purchase a piece of ground and labor for himself." Like
other mountain masters, Dent resisted the demand of ex-slaves for opportunities to rent and farm their own land. "The best policy is to hire the
laborer for monthly wages by the year paying him quarterly half what is
due reserving the other half as insurance on his contract." To increase his
degree of control over them, Dent charged 20 percent interest on "cash
advances" against the wages of freedmen, and he defined an advance as

any funds from those reserves he was holding from wages already earned. "When we had our Slaves as laborers," he reflected, "they were trained to our system of labor hence we could carry on our work systematically." As his neighbors succumbed to sharecropping contracts by late 1867, Dent grew increasingly angry about the bargaining of black laborers.

In July 1868, he was still insisting that "[c]ropping on shares with Negroes wont do. They are part owners in the crop and as such they exercise an independence which renders their proper management impossible, especially in working the crop.... It is best to contract them by the month or year for money wages and have a white foreman over them and keep them steadily employed all the time." Because he found it difficult to acquire malleable workers, Dent was outraged that "there [we]re Negroes swarming over the Country," and he "hoped that the Bureau w[ould] make all such go to work." By the end of 1869, Dent was convinced that the sharecropping policies implemented by his neighbors were exacerbating his own labor shortages.

From some cause the negroes are more stubborn this year than last, that is, they are harder to hire and show more Independence. It seems that they are influenced by a few leading spirits who drill them to do as they tell them. This Independence and indifference is no doubt the results of the Whites renting them lands, of course such a policy makes them feel independent of the whites and they are proud in showing it and using [it] to their advantage. The evil has to run its course until a more intelligent class of farmers come into the country and rule this matter. For my own part, I would like to see the Negro master such whites that let selfish needs overcome all principles of honor and succumb to a race [of] their enemies and inferiors.

The relations of production had changed, and Dent was growing desperate enough to think that he would have "to procure White Labor" in order to raise his profit margins. "In short, the relations are changed," he added at year's end in 1868, "instead of the Laborer being the humble Servant and dependant on the Capitalist, Capital has become the Servant and dependent on the laborer.... I am an advocate for intelligent white labor that will bring the ignorant Landlords to their senses."

On New Year's Day in 1870, Dent reflected back over the previous five years of black emancipation, applying principles he had adapted from reading the work of Adam Smith.

The Farmers and Planters throughout the whole country became alarmed about the chances of procuring laborers and they placed themselves completely in the power of the Negroes, by yielding to their terms – Capital yielding to Labor which of course reversed the Natural Order of things – hence our present conditions. It is the only instance known where the landed estate and capital of the country has been turned over to an irresponsible and utterly unreliable class of laborers.

By 1870, one-quarter of the mountain ex-slaves were concentrated in towns, like Staunton, Knoxville, or Rome. However, few of them were employed in the kinds of nonagricultural jobs for which they had been hired or owned during enslavement. *Source: Frank Leslie's Illustrated Newspaper*, 30 September 1869.

Economic independence for ex-slaves was a threat to land owners in another way. "When poverty strikes," he was convinced, the freedman "is polite, kind and obligeing and will work well for you. But so soon as you get him up and [he] begins to be prospered, he becomes impudent, independent and unmanageable and feels big and free." By June 1870, Dent was even expressing ire at the demands of ex-slaves for the continuation of the kinds of work parties that mountain masters had utilized before the war to maximize production. Even though such harvest meals were customary throughout the Southern Mountains well into the 1940s, Dent was feeling the financial pinch of every extra that he provided to black laborers. He drew a large pointing finger in the left margin of his journal to draw attention to this comment:

AFRICA EXCELSIOR AMERICA AT ZERO
The Negroes engaged at Harvesting demand $1.50 cash per
day Chicken pies and Hot Coffee and cream Etc.
"The bottom Rail away on top"
"Shoe Fly don't bodder me."
Another year Champaign and Sherry will be required and the
"White Trash" to serve them at table.

Other small plantation owners, like Louisa Minor, agreed that ex-slaves "seem[ed] to be having all the fun and goodies."[1]

Recapturing Agricultural Laborers

Even though Dent felt as though he had lost control, former slaveholders were still the wealthiest families in Appalachian counties, and their political clout was reflected in the local and state regulations designed to keep ex-slaves in debt peonage. In 1870, three-quarters of black Appalachians either reported agriculture as their only household occupation, or they combined farming with some earnings from nonagricultural jobs. By 1870, only about half of them were sharecroppers, the rest were farm laborers. None of the sampled black agricultural households were identified as tenants or tenant farmers, an occupational category reserved for whites. In addition to the census manuscripts, white oral histories and regional slave narratives document the tendency of Appalachian plantations to reserve tenant farming for whites only – a mechanism, no doubt, for creating the illusion that these poor whites still had a higher racial status than the ex-slaves. Sharecropping and tenant farming were not new to the Mountain South. Before the Civil War, more than one-quarter of the region's farms were operated by poor whites identified in census manuscripts as croppers, tenants, or farm managers. Throughout the antebellum period, it was common for slaves, free blacks, and poor whites to work fields together, often in racially integrated crews. James Hervey Greenlee initiated his first share-renting contracts with ex-slaves between October 1866 and February 1867. He subdivided his land into his own fields, upland parcels for white tenants, and several black sharecropping parcels. White tenants farmed for half share of the crop, while croppers contracted for one-third share. It is clear from Greenlee's diary that he continued to work ex-slaves in crews and that they worked their cropper parcels after completing assigned tasks in the owner's fields, the same patterns that prevailed during slavery. When the croppers needed to use his mules or wagons, they had to contract to do extra work. According to Greenlee's records, for example, two cropper families gathered ten acres of corn in exchange "for the use of a wagon & team & 2 bus of Corn a day." In another instance, he indicates that several farm laborers were cutting his winter supply of cordwood "to pay for use of horses." When Greenlee needed winter clothing for his children, he contracted with a cropper's wife by paying her in "wool & a bunch of yarn."[2]

Cottage tenancy, a labor arrangement in which the household worked in exchange for housing and rations, was also common. After emancipation, most black Appalachians worked one or two years in this type of labor arrangement. In addition to white tenants and black sharecroppers, Greenlee hired black day laborers who lived in the slave cabins. Noah Perry remained in his former slave cabin and was paid "$10 a month," from which the owner deducted his food and lodging. James Gwyn paid some ex-slaves in food and shelter by the day; others he employed on annual contracts. In December 1867, he settled the annual employment contract with Payton, by paying the ex-slave "balance for his last year's work $1.12," the rest having been advanced as housing and food for the household. Callie Elder recalled that this type of farm laborer had no more economic independence than her family had known as slaves. For "sev'ral years atter de war," Elder's former northern Georgia owner paid them "10 a month," against which "he 'lowanced out de rations." For a month's work, her household received twelve pounds of fat meat, four pecks of meal, four pecks of flour, one pound of sugar, and one pound of coffee. Sixteen-year-old Henry Banner "worked for two bits a day" while teenager Georgia Jackson did field work for which their former owner provided his mother his food and clothes. William Davis's father contracted to work for "$120 de year," minus their provisions. On an even smaller plantation, Anne Lee's family worked for monthly wages of two dollars each, plus rations of meal and fat meat and the right to continue the kind of garden parcels they had cultivated as slaves. Typically, ex-slaves worked for wages (really their subsistence) for several years, hoping eventually to rent their own parcel. For example, Tom Singleton "stayed on wid [his former owner], and wukked for wages for six years, an' den farmed on halves wid him." Perry Madden's family gradually renegotiated their labor contract. At emancipation, the Maddens "didn't have no stock nor nothin'. They made a crop just for the third of it. When they quit the third, they started givin' them two-fifths.... Then they moved up from that and give them half.... If you furnish yourself [i.e., supply one's own food and work animals], they give you two-thirds and take one-third."[3]

However independent John Horry Dent and other landowners thought ex-slaves were becoming, black Appalachians saw no improvement in their daily living conditions. Five years after emancipation, nearly 96 percent of black Appalachian households were landless, and three-quarters of the adults were still illiterate. Little wonder that 70 percent of them reported zero wealth to the 1870 census enumerators. Among those ex-slaves who reported any accumulated assets (about 30 percent), the average household wealth was only $65.41. Many black Appalachians dreamed that sharecropping would bring them a certain degree of economic independence, but it certainly did not. For most, enslavement was replaced by the bondage of a legally protected debt peonage system. Gip Minton was typical of black Appalachians; he "never owned no farm, no livestock, no home. The only thing [he] ever owned was a horse one time." According to Jim Threat, "nobody had much to eat or wear and it was nearly out of the question to ever git any money." Anna Lee thought that "the reconstruction period was hard on the old slaves.... It was hard going to live as our wages were so low that we could hardly feed ourself, much less our children.... We got from 15 to 30 cents a day for our work, and sometimes they never paid us that." Most of the farm laborers and sharecroppers still resided in the same cabins in which enslaved households had lived before the war. In McDowell, North Carolina, one sharecropping household "had a rough time." Once they had paid the landowner's share, they barely had enough corn left to feed their few cattle and a mule. They generated their only few dollars by collecting pulpwood and bark to sell to the tannery. In West Virginia, Eli Davison "made a crop on the halves." The employer provided him a cabin, team and tools, and the household "stood good for all the groceries" the family consumed. When the crop was gathered and accounts were settled, "it took all [Eli] made that year to pay [his] debts." Oliver Bell remembered the close accounting. At harvest, the landowner:

measure de corn out ter all uv um whut wus sheer [share] han's. He'd take er bushel en give dem er bushel. When he mos' th'ough he'd th'ow er year er corn to dis one, en give hisself er year, den he break ey year in two en he take part en give dem part. Dat wuz close measurin', I tell you.[4]

The Freedmen's Bureau received "daily complaints" of employer fraud. Mollie Scott of Bartow County, Georgia, described the vicious cycle of dependency and racism.

> They run us from one year till the next and at the end of the year they say we owe it bout all. If we did have a good crop we never could get ahead. We couldn't get ahead nuff not to have to be furnished the next year. We did work but we never could get ahead. If an [ex-slave] sass a white land owner he would be whooped bout his account or bout anything else.... [Freedpeople] have to take what the white folks leave to em and be glad we's livin.

Freedmen's Bureau records bear out her assessment. In Shenandoah County, Virginia, a freedman was beaten because he "complain[ed] of unfairness" when the owner divided the corn crop. The bureau filed charges, but the Grand Jury returned a "No Bill" since "the negroe had no right to be impudent to a white man." Sharecroppers in Ben Chambers's community "go up to de sto' for dey clo's and food on credick 'till de crop was sol'." Andrew Goodman's family knew they were being cheated but risked job loss and white violence if they overtly resisted. Andrew's father was "running the farm" of his former owner "on halfance." During the first year's contract, the household "raised lots of grain and other things and 57 bales of cotton." Even though "cotton was 52 cents a pound," the owner paid them only "a box of candy and a sack of store tobacco and a sack of sugar," claiming that "the 'signment done got lost." As Wiley Nealy saw it, "there wasn't no difference" between slavery and the debt peonage that followed sharecropping " 'cept they couldnt' sell us." Mountain plantation records document not only the debt peonage of Appalachian ex-slaves but also the family immobility structured by the system. In 1880, James Hervey Greenlee was still reporting work assignments and provisions for ex-slaves who began with him as croppers in 1867. Moreover, few of the ex-slaves migrated from Appalachian counties until well into the 1880s, and the vast majority of them continued in agriculture, never owning land.[5]

Nonagricultural Employment of Ex-slaves

In 1870, John Horry Dent was growing increasingly alarmed about labor scarcity. However, he was residing in a county that had lost only about 12 percent of its ex-slaves, and more than half the population were poor white landless laborers. Even though there was no empirical labor scarcity, his farm was located near Rome and Chattanooga, which had become

More than two-fifths of Appalachia's emancipated black households were headed by women. In towns, washwomen were common sights because there were few nonagricultural opportunities for these females. *Source*: King, *Southern States*, vol. 2.

magnets for emancipated blacks. Because he did not offer direct wages between 1865 and 1870, Dent reported loss of laborers to the railroad, to town jobs, to mines, to three Chattanooga iron works, and to the Rome Brick Yard. Another Floyd County plantation attempted to recruit ex-slaves through the same aggressive strategy that railroad recruiters used. Desperate for workers to harvest his crops, Jerry Eubanks's former owner organized a barbecue to which he invited all the community's ex-slaves. "Den he made a speech to about 300 negroes from different plantations. He says, 'I'll give you 3rd and 4th and feed you to close this crop. All who are willing raise your hands.'" Between 1865 and 1870, most of those black Appalachians who migrated resettled in the region's towns, sought jobs with extractive industries that reopened after the war, or worked for the railroads. Due to the relocation of blacks into towns, thirty-five Appalachian counties experienced black population increases that exceeded the national average (see Map 6). By 1870, nearly one-quarter

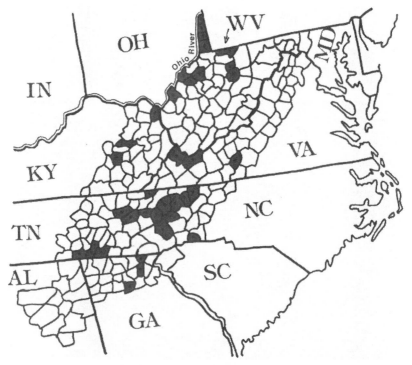

Map 6. Mountain South counties in which black population increased more than the national average, 1860–70. *Source:* Analysis of Censuses of Population, 1860 and 1870 (NA).

of black Appalachians had relocated into towns; thus, the region's ex-slaves were much more urbanized than resident whites. That trend had already begun before the war; in 1860, slaves and free blacks made up one-quarter to one-third of the population of Appalachian towns.[6]

Despite that urban migration, less than one-third of black Appalachian households included persons in nonagricultural occupations in 1870. Indeed, there were fewer mountain blacks in nonagricultural occupations in 1870 than there had been in 1860. More than one-third of Appalachian slaves had been skilled artisans, labor drivers, or managers of their owners' commercial facilities. While they were enslaved, two-fifths of them were employed by manufactories, extractive industries, commercial enterprises, or transportation companies. Clearly, opportunities for black employment outside agriculture declined after emancipation. For several economic reasons, ex-slaves were leaving agriculture faster than poor whites. Nonfarm blacks reported greater wealth accumulation than agricultural households. Moreover, nonagricultural households were much more likely to own some small town-based enterprise (such as a blacksmith shop, a livery, a restaurant) than agricultural households were to own farm land. Nonagricultural occupations did help to establish a small minority of prosperous entrepreneurs, but two-thirds of the ex-slaves in such occupations were frequently unemployed.[7]

All kinds of work in towns made up the major category of nonagricultural employment between 1865 and 1870, and most of these jobs were low-paying and short-term. Towns offered employment for porters, day laborers, hotel and restaurant workers, street cleaners, and artisans. Most female heads of household listed their occupations as washwoman, laundress, or servant. Though stably employed, most domestic servants worked for their subsistence. Clara Allen peddled her crocheted mats and counterpanes and her handwoven fabric and clothing. Zek Brown's family fared better economically than the vast majority of black Appalachians, so they were able to sever ties with their former owner quickly. His "fo'ks stayed one yeah an' den [they] moved to a place dat him buy." Zek's mother was hired by the Freedmen's Bureau to teach school, so her income provided them cash that most ex-slaves did not have. Though 7 percent of mountain slaves had been employed in extractive industries before the war, such opportunities disappeared after emancipation. In 1870, not even 0.1 percent of the ex-slaves reported income from extractive industries. Once dependent on slave labor, iron manufacturing in the Appalachian counties of Virginia and Kentucky hired only a few emancipated blacks. Similarly, iron production boomed in Chattanooga and Knoxville, but these companies reserved for whites those skilled positions that slaves had once occupied. Beginning in the late 1880s,

Some emancipated slaves, like Booker T. Washington's father, continued to work in West Virginia's salt industry. However, black Appalachians were employed in industrial jobs during slavery much more frequently than they were hired for such jobs between 1865 and 1870. *Source: Scribner's,* 1874.

Appalachian counties in Alabama, Kentucky, Maryland, Tennessee, and West Virginia would undergo in-migrations of small concentrations of blacks to coal mines, iron manufactories, and other extractive industries. However, such jobs were not open to ex-slaves during the first two decades of emancipation.[8]

Every Appalachian town with a railroad terminal attracted ex-slaves. Larger towns like Knoxville, Chattanooga, and Wheeling experienced the greatest population growth. Even small communities like Corbin, Kentucky, and Keyser, Parkersburg, and Fairmont in West Virginia developed larger postbellum black populations. Railroad depots were filled with ex-slaves hawking produce, meats, prepared foods, crafts, and clothing. "Little black ragamuffins, dirty and hungry-looking" worked the passengers, trying to "do anything for five cents." Ben Brown was one of those homeless orphans trying to eke out a living alone. He "got some clothes and a few cents an' travelers give [him] small coins foh tending dere horse an' [he] done odd jobs here an dere." Seven of the male ex-slaves reported to WPA interviewers that they secured railroad jobs soon after emancipation. Labor agents recruited in western Carolina, telling the ex-slaves "about folks getting rich working on the railroads in Tennessee." John Van Hook's brother took a job on an eastern Tennessee railroad and "never came back." By May 1867, a Freedman's Bureau agent reported that "railroads in Kentucky and Tennessee [we]re taking away the best class of hands" from Nelson County, Virginia. Positions as porters, linemen, and brakemen provided ex-slaves higher, more-stable earnings than they could hope to acquire from any other occupation. However, the vast majority of Appalachian ex-slaves were recruited for construction crews, positions that did not afford the same economic mobility as the railroads' town-based jobs. Competition over black laborers was sometimes contentious, judging from newspaper accounts of the period. In one instance, a labor recruiter for Mississippi plantations made the mistake of trying to entice away construction workers. "Words ensued," and the railroad agent killed the recruiter.[9]

Between 1868 and 1871, N. J. Bell supervised crews of construction workers building lines in northern Alabama, southeastern Tennessee, and western North Carolina. Soon after emancipation, the company "had men in east Tennessee and Virginia getting up hands." In addition to ex-slaves, the company recruited recent immigrants, including "a gang of Irishmen from New York." The company also had transported twenty-two hundred workers from China. All these men were worked and housed in ethnically segregated crews; "each gang had a boss and interpreter." Working conditions were dangerous and health-threatening, and employers defrauded workers in ways that paralleled treatment of sharecroppers. Construction crews were rarely paid on time, and they often went months without receiving wages. Employers deducted housing, food, clothing, boots, and broken tools from wages, and a worker could not leave the company's employ until all transportation costs to the job site had been repaid. Bell carried a hickory stick, a pistol, and a knife, and he often used them. In one instance, he disciplined an ex-slave with a heavy shovel. When ex-slaves "quit work ... on account of not being paid off for months," the supervisor hired a squad of whites to ride through their camp shooting. In western North Carolina and northern Alabama, a large number of ex-slaves "worked till the last grading was done. They had left their homes ... and had to return home penniless and ragged." None of them collected all their wages, and most of them were defrauded when their savings were stolen. A representative of the Freedmen's Savings Bank "would follow the men who paid the men along the line, and get money from a great many of the negroes and some white men." By the time their employment ended, a bank official had absconded with all their savings.[10]

In an 1869 pamphlet assessing postwar labor mechanisms, Virginia's planter-sociologist George Fitzhugh correctly pinpointed the ephemeral freedom experienced by black Appalachians, whether employed in agriculture or in nonagricultural occupations. "Our negroes will be more profitable to their employers than were slaves to their masters," he predicted. That greater profit would derive, he thought, because former slaveholders had "adopted the high-pressure system of free competitive society." Rather than using the physical coercion of "hickories," those landholders were now using "hunger" to compel obedience and productivity. Though she stated the situation differently, West Virginia ex-slave Lizzie Grant agreed with Fitzhugh about the circumstances of agricultural laborers. At emancipation, Lizzie was a twenty-one-year-old mother of three owned by a Kanawha County plantation that held seven slaves. Her master had died in the war, leaving the mistress nearly destitute. Lizzie pinpointed the precarious economic conditions facing black Appalachians. Just after the war, her former owner paid them "$2.00 a month to stay there and work.... [W]e were forced to stay on as servants if we expected to live.... [W]ages were low and then we never got half what we did make. There was no way of making them pay either, no sir, we just had to take what they would give us."[11]

Nonagricultural jobs did offer ex-slaves some degree of independence and mobility. Lorenzo Ivy described the positive transition his family made from agricultural debt peonage to town employment. After emancipation, the family stayed to work on shares with their former owner.

I never worked harder in my life, for I thought the more we made, the more we would get.... We raised a large crop of corn and wheat and tobacco, and finished one month before Christmas. Then we went to our master for our part ... but he said he wasn't going to give us anything, and he stopped giving us anything to eat, and said we couldn't live any longer on his land. Father went to an officer of the Freedmen's Bureau.... He said our master said we wasn't worth anything, and he couldn't get anything for us.... We made out to live that winter – I don't know how. In April, 1866, father moved to town where he could work at his trade. He hired all of us boys that were large enough to work in a brick-yard from three to six dollars a month. That was the first time I tasted the sweet cup of freedom. I worked all day, and went to night-school two terms and a half, and three months to day school.

The family moved to eastern Tennessee in 1868. By 1874, the family was doing well enough to spare Lorenzo and three of his siblings to attend school at Hampton Institute.[12]

Postwar Racial Violence in Appalachian Communities

During Reconstruction, eastern Tennessee capitalists were anxious to reinstate their trade linkages with the Northeast and to attract mineral investments from outside speculators. As postwar violence escalated throughout the South, Knoxville's merchants sought to distinguish themselves as Union sympathizers. Toward that end, they published one-page advertisements in Northern newspapers and circulated a trade pamphlet to prewar business connections in Pittsburgh, Philadelphia, New York, and Cincinnati. Assaults on blacks, Ku Klux Klan activity, and destruction of freedmen's schools almost daily made the newspapers in Northern cities, but the Knoxville Industrial Association claimed:

The people of East Tennessee are at peace. The outrages of which strangers may read are in Middle and West Tennessee. There are no Ku Klux Klan outrages here. During the late Civil War a very large majority of our people sympathized with the National Government. Those who took the opposite side in East Tennessee are totally law abiding and peaceful citizens quietly engaged in legitimate business.... Let not East Tennessee be confounded with other divisions of this state or with other parts of the South. We are a distinct and peculiar people.

Knoxville's entrepreneurs did generate some increased trade and investment, but their claim to nonviolent peculiarity was false propaganda. Eastern Tennessee had been a hotbed of partisan conflict during the war, and those rivalries continued well after emancipation. Indeed, the entire Mountain South was a cauldron of retaliatory violence, and Civil War alignments bifurcated local politics.[13]

As late as 1878, one journalist would write of eastern Kentucky: "the war, diversified and perverted, perhaps, but the war, still, has never ceased in this country." Indeed, eastern Kentucky was the scene of continuing partisan violence throughout the Reconstruction period. Outlaws and vigilante bands were active in almost every county, and they were particularly virulent in Breathitt, Carter, Harlan, Perry, and Leslie Counties where mines and iron producers recruited small numbers of ex-slaves. Not all the violence was connected to long-term political rivalries, for white outlaw bands also emerged during Reconstruction. At war's end, thousands of poor white Appalachians were homeless and facing starvation. In northern Alabama, there were nearly fifty-three thousand whites entirely destitute, and many of them lived in the woods or took over abandoned properties. "Organized bands of thieves" roamed the countryside, stealing cotton and livestock. According to one ex-slave, postwar vigilantes in western Carolina were local men "who had fought in the war and came back home to find all they had was gone, and they just had to live some way." Disguised as Union veterans, two bands of marauders plundered Cherokee County, Alabama, houses and robbed citizens on the roads. No part of the Mountain South was left untouched by these postwar rivalries; sometimes the army sent forces to intervene. In St. Clair County, Alabama, "they had a great deal of trouble" because "they had not gotten over the war feelings." At one point, Union soldiers acted as a peacekeeping force. However, most Appalachian counties did not have a local garrison, and about one-third did not have a local office of the Freedmen's Bureau. Because military forces were stationed in the counties with the largest black populations and because bureau agents were responsible for two or three counties, white partisan conflict went virtually unchecked.[14]

Like the eastern Tennessee trade pamphlet, far too many scholars have treated the Mountain South as an exceptional part of the South. Because of the Union leanings of about half of white Appalachians, some writers have claimed that the region was less racist and less violent toward blacks. Even early twentieth-century black scholar Carter Woodson ignored the empirical experiences of ex-slaves to paint a rosy picture of positive race relations in Appalachia. Such romantic images are, however, no more than fiction. Against the backdrop of white political animosities, the violence against emancipated slaves escalated. Contrary to idealized images of this region, black Appalachians faced a higher probability of day-to-day violence than freedpeople in other parts of the South, and this trend continued well into the 1930s. In 1870, less than 9 percent of the black population of the states of Alabama, Georgia, Kentucky, North and South Carolina, Tennessee, and Virginia resided in Appalachian counties. However, those mountain counties accounted for nearly one-fifth of the violent incidents against ex-slaves between 1866 and 1868. When we examine the incidence of racial violence per capita, we discover that ex-slaves in mountain counties were nearly twice as likely as non-Appalachian Southern blacks to be assaulted, raped, murdered, or lynched by whites. In comparison to black residents of other counties, ex-slaves in the mountain counties of Alabama, Georgia, and South Carolina were twice as likely to be attacked or killed. Black Appalachians in Tennessee faced a probability of racial violence that was 1.6 times greater than the incidence of violence visited upon their peers outside the mountains. Surprisingly, the danger of racial violence was actually highest in those counties with the smallest black populations. An ex-slave in eastern Kentucky or western North Carolina was five times more likely to be assaulted than an ex-slave who resided in other parts of those two states. In comparison, Virginia had the largest black populations within the Southern Mountains, but that zone exhibited the lowest probability of racial violence (only 1.3 times greater than the Tidewater incidence). In fact, the risk of white violence was five times greater for an eastern Kentucky ex-slave than for a black Appalachian in Virginia.[15]

By 1868, the Ku Klux Klan was organized and active in every Appalachian county. Despite the visible presence of the Klan in Appalachian counties, that organization was implicated or suspected in only about 15 percent of the hate crimes investigated by the Freedmen's Bureau in Appalachian counties. In more than half the incidents, individuals or fewer than three whites committed the acts. However, one-third of the murders, rapes, and lynchings were carried out by white mobs of ordinary citizens. It is clear, then, that racial violence was fairly widespread, and that hate crimes were not just perpetrated by that tiny minority who belonged to the Klan. Ex-slaves in rural areas experienced the greatest incidence of violence even though they were scattered in small pockets. Black veterans of the Union army were more often assaulted by white mobs and small groups than other Appalachian ex-slaves. Without protection and support from respected local whites, soldiers' wives faced rapes and beatings, and the men were refused employment, beaten, and sometimes killed. When Thomas Cole was mustered out of the Union army at Chattanooga, he could not return to family and kin in northern Alabama.

After de war was ovah and we was all turned loose we jest scatters out, no whar to go and nothin' ter do, nobody ter goes to fer help. I couldn't go back to [Jackson County, Alabama] whar I had run off from ter looks fer work, fer ... dey calls us traitors ... and dey would kills us iffen dey knew we had runs off ter de north to help dem fight.

Cole was wise not to return to the county where he had been enslaved. In Montgomery County, Virginia, "there [wa]s a decided hatred ... to colored men who ha[d] been Soldiers in the United States Army." In July 1866, a group of twenty white males surrounded a black soldier and beat him to death "in an unmerciful manner [by] inflicting Seven Severe Wounds on the Head, fracturing the skull and exposing the Brain."[16]

A northern Georgia newspaper bragged in 1866 that "the race will die out – in 50 years a black face will be as rare as an Indian is now." Perhaps the newspaper was reflecting the level of Klan activity in the region, for the secret organization was more violent in northern Georgia than in those counties that had been characterized by large plantations. Three mob lynchings occurred in two counties in 1866. One ex-slave was killed for living with a common-law white wife, another was lynched for a rape even though five whites testified he was out of the county during the crime. As a result of Klan violence in Chattooga County, two hundred blacks fled to Rome. Anderson Furr recalled the appearance of a Klansman at their Hall County cabin soon after emancipation. "One of dem Kluxers come to our house and set down and talked to us 'bout how us ought to act, and how us goin' to have to do, if us 'spected to live and do well. Us allus thought it was our own old Marster, all dressed up in dem white robes." The coercion may have had the desired effect, for Anderson followed that statement with the comment: "None of Marster's [ex-slaves] left him for 'bout two or three years." William Mead described the Bartow County Klan that "would come at night fifty or sixty or more, and take [an ex-slave] and whip him unmerciful. Some time they would kill whoever they were whipping."[17]

Pickens County, South Carolina, exhibited a higher incidence of racial violence than most counties further south in the state. "Right atter de war de Ku Klux started," one black Appalachian recalled. To create a fearsome presence, "dey would march up and down the road." Drowning was a favorite tactic in the mountain counties of South Carolina. According to a white Klansman from this area, the local klaven "made a boat 25 feet long to carry the negroes down the river." They tied wood rods around the necks of their victims and threw them into the water. Two such mysterious drownings were reported in one month of 1867. The Klan kidnapped the father of one ex-slave, and the family "nebber did see pa no mo'." One ex-slave had a vivid childhood memory of "de Ku Klux riding." Her mother "heard de hosses a-trotting" and quickly buried the children "in de fodder out in the barn" while both parents "hid in de edge of de woods." For Millie Bates's family, "de worsest time" was the Klan lynching of one of their neighbors. "Dey took Dab Black and hung him to a simmon tree. Dey would not let his folks take him down either. He jus stayed dar till he fell to pieces." Some Pickens County blacks formed their own armed "negro militia" for self-protection. One blacksmith in the area developed a strategy for identifying the night riders. He "marked de horse shoes" and kept a log of all the designs. "Then atter a raid, he could go out in the road to see if a certain horse had been rode.... As soon as de Ku Klux found out dey was being give away ... dey killed him."[18]

Between 1865 and 1869, county klavens administered forty-four shootings, murders, and lynchings in seven northern Alabama counties – accounting for one-fifth of all the Klan violence in the state. Two ex-slaves recalled the role of the Klan in coercing laborers to work for certain landholders at lower wages. Thomas Cole claimed that Jackson County, Alabama, blacks knew that the Klansmen "was jest a bunch of farmers and business men, mostly all plantation owners dressed up in a white robe and der horses covered up wid a white cloth too and eyes cut fer dem and de horses." According to Cole, a refusal to work for a land-holder might bring quick retaliation. "De Klan comes roun at night and knocks on your do an tells you ter go and work fer Mr. Brown ter morrer. Iffen dey tells you ter go and work fer Mr. Brown fer a bushel of taters you bettah go and works fer de taters er you gits whipped by the KKK tomerrer night." Ex-slaves suspected of stealing also attracted Klan at-tention. One of Cole's neighbors was kidnapped "right outten de bed." Klansmen "makes him own up ter all he steals and makes him promise ter gits a job and go ter work and never steals any more, den dey whips dis [man] till he couldnt hardly stand up." Oliver Bell recalled that mas-ters competed for laborers by increasing the crop share they offered to ex-slaves. Oliver's extended family "wuz workin' on halvens," but the ad-jacent landholder paid only one-third crop share. "One day de Ku Klux come ridin' by," led by the neighbor. Croppers who "rented um lan' " for a half-share "wuz makin' money" and raising the expectations of other ex-slaves. When their threatening visit did not work, the Klansmen killed two of Oliver's uncles on the road. Group strikes or sit-downs also drew retaliation from Klansmen. When ex-slaves struck because they had not been paid in months, the northern Alabama railroad supervisor hired a squad of men to "make them go to work the next morning." When that threat failed, the supervisor sent for help from his white friends who were "anxious for the sport" and had told him "they could raise a hundred men in thirty minutes."[19]

The Klan was also organized and active in those parts of the region with the smallest black populations. By 1868, county klavens had emerged in the northern panhandle of West Virginia, including the town of Blacksville. Lizzie Grant pinpointed two major forms of coercion that the Kanawha County organization directed against the ex-slaves. They used violence, threats, and economic constraints to maintain a ready supply of cheap labor for farms and for the salt industry. "There was them KKK's to say that we must do just like our white man tell us, if we did not, they would take the poor helpless negro and beat him up good." In 1868, a Freedmen's Bureau teacher reported that "[a]rmed and masked bands of men exercise[d] unlimited sway" over ex-slaves in eastern Kentucky. Between 1866 and 1870, eastern Kentucky blacks ac-counted for only about 3 percent of the state's population, but nearly one-fifth of the state's mob lynchings of ex-slaves occurred there. White Union veterans and Republican Party supporters also were harassed. Over a four-month period in 1868, the Klan murdered nineteen men in Magoffin, Perry, Breathitt, and Wolfe Counties. Slight increases in the influx of black laborers spurred white racism and Klan activity. Be-ginning in 1870, nearly four hundred skilled blacks migrated into Estill

County to work for the Red River Iron Works Company. The Klan began a series of raids that halted mining, and company officials allowed the ex-slaves to be driven off. Similar removals of black industrial laborers occurred in Bell and Carter Counties. In western North Carolina, "ever'body knowed about de Kloo Kluxes," according to Simon Hare. "Git you off an' whup you so you be sca'ed ter show yo' face an' not go messin' wid white folks's' bus'ness." The Klan was particularly active in Polk and Rutherford Counties, but there were incidents throughout the area between 1866 and 1870.[20]

Every Appalachian county in Tennessee and Virginia also had its local klaven of the secret organization. The Freedmen's Bureau reported that civil authorities in the counties of western Virginia were "aware of the organization but t[ook] no measures to stop it." At Roanoke, a freedman was "abused and shot at by the K.K.K.'s." The ex-slave was fined $300 for breach of the peace "while the men who fired the shot were fined $1.00 for unlawful shooting." In Washington County, Emory and Henry College students formed their own Klan chapter. Dressed in hoods and sheets, the group "visited [a freedman's] house and called him out telling him they had come after him. When rushing upon [the freedman] to seize him, he fired," severely wounding a student. Since the black male had shot to defend himself, the Freedmen's Bureau decided to "do nothin further in the matter, it being generally believed that the students had no malicious intentions but only desired to amuse themselves." In May 1868, one of Coffee County's former slaveholders wrote his western North Carolina kinsman that the area was filled with "many strong rebels" and that there was "a good deal of excitement in regard to the 'Ku Klux'!" The white landholder went on to say that, in his rural area, the group was "a regularly organized band, though there [wa]s such profound secrecy observed in regards to their movements and regulations that no one professe[d] to be acquainted with their tactics." According to the letter, "the good people" of his community thought "it a great institution" that had "been a great protection to the Country. They [we]re a great terror to the Radicals and the Negroes, ha[d] dispatched a good many of both classes in rather an unceremonious manner." Ex-slave Millie Simpkins confirmed those comments. The Klan was so "red hot" in their Coffee County neighborhood that Millie Simpkins's family "wuz skeered ter op'n [their] do'er atter dark." When Anna Lee's eastern Tennessee mistress sent a Cambell County male for a doctor, the Klan "caught that poor negro and hung him to a tree limb." After Sidney Graham accidentally spilled hot water on a white worker at an Ooltewah powder mill, he was warned that the Klan would see him that night. Graham "barricaded his dwelling" and "prepared to make a resistance." When "the sheeted forms" appeared and tried to burn him out, he "instantly killed" one man, and escaped the county permanently.[21]

White Attacks on Black Organizations

Assaults against black community activities account for more than one-third of the incidents of racial violence investigated by the Freedmen's Bureau in Appalachian counties. Indeed, this ratio would be higher if the Bureau had more carefully documented that victims were political activists, voters, teachers, or ministers. Attempts by ex-slaves to hold political meetings, to run for office, or to vote attracted white violence in one of every ten of the hate crimes. In Kanawha County, West Virginia, Lizzie Grant's husband "never did vote" because the Klan was always "there to say we could not vote, and they said none of us was able to read or write and therefore did not know anything about voting." When the Klan wanted a particular candidate elected, however, Kanawha County ex-slaves were threatened with violence and job loss, unless they obeyed when "[thei]r white man made [them] vote." During 1868 elections in Asheville, one ex-slave was killed and eighteen others were wounded when black males went to the polls to vote. The Freedmen's Bureau documented thirty-three instances in which the Klan or white mobs raided political meetings of black Appalachians. In Franklin County, Virginia, and in Colliers (Hancock County), West Virginia, for example, white mobs twice broke up black political meetings. At the Colliers meeting, whites "followed and surrounded" the participants in order to identify them for later Klan disciplining.[22]

Such coercion, however, did not completely disenfranchise ex-slaves. In Appalachian counties in Alabama, Georgia, the Carolinas, Tennessee, and Virginia, blacks held twenty-eight offices during Reconstruction. In fact, black Appalachians were overrepresented among the elected black officials of Alabama, Georgia, and Tennessee. The vast majority of these elected officials were literate town dwellers, and more than half of them had accumulated more than $100 in wealth. Only about one-fifth of them were farmers or agricultural laborers. The Union League, a secret racially mixed Republican organization, centralized its activities in the region's small towns and cities. Therefore, black Appalachians who were more concentrated in rural areas (as in the Appalachian counties of Virginia and the Carolinas) did not acquire their equitable share of public offices. Mountain ex-slaves made up more than one-fifth of Virginia's population, but they accounted for only about 1 percent of the state's black officials. More than 3 percent of the citizens of the Carolinas resided in the mountain region, but they held only about 1 percent of the public offices. In contrast, one-fifth of Tennessee's black officials were Appalachian ex-slaves, like Chattanooga's cooper, Andrew Flowers. After being elected a justice of the peace, Flowers was whipped by the Klan because he "had the impudence to run against a white man for office and beat him."[23]

Despite their impoverishment and despite the likelihood of white retaliatory violence, black Appalachians built and maintained community institutions. Churches were recognized by whites to be the most strategic organization that was empowering ex-slaves. One of every fourteen "outrages against freedmen" was aimed at terminating the religious independence of black Appalachians. Church burnings, assaults on ministers, disruption of religious services, and night visits to threaten church members were common occurrences in Appalachian counties. In White County, Tennessee, the Klan broke up the Sunday night service. According to ex-slave Josie Jordan, the riders "was all masked up." All the church-goers "crawled under the benches when they shouted: "We'll make you damn niggers wish you wasn't free!" The raiders "whipped the women just like the men," but "the preacher got the worst whipping." Betty Cofer recalled that ex-slaves "buried out around [thei]r little churches" after emancipation in Wilkes County, North Carolina. However, many of the tiny churches operated on tenant farms or on the lands of friendly whites, so the "colored folks didn't get no deeds to 'em." After churches were burned, the cemeteries were "plowed under an' turned into pasture." A northern South Carolina ex-slave recounted a battle between the Klan and ex-slaves. "De Ku Klux and de [ex-slaves] fit at New Hope Church," and blacks "killed some of de Ku Klux." Later, the Klan trapped the church ringleader, tortured and shot him, leaving "him lying in de middle of de road" as a warning to the community. Black ministers were closely watched by whites, and they were overrepresented as the victims of violent incidents documented by the Freedmen's Bureau. When the Klan lynched one ex-slave, the black minister "prayed and preached over the body." In retaliation, riders "came to kill" the preacher "for doing this." Jim Alexander had been a slave preacher, so he continued prayer meetings after emancipation. His mistress called him "Praying Jim Jesus" because he led singing and prayers in the fields, a work disruption that "disturbed her." After the woman complained to the Klan about "the noise" that the nighttime meetings caused, riders invaded a service in Jim's cabin. When they "pulled him out the room, the crowd run off." However, the whites beat the black preacher "till they thought he was dead and throwed him in a fence corner. He was beat nearly to death, just cut all to pieces."[24]

In addition to those forms of violence, nearly one-fifth of the acts of white violence against black Appalachians were aimed at schools and the individuals who operated and supported them. Black schools were destroyed, ransacked, or pillaged nearly three times more often than churches and eighteen times more frequently than the small businesses of ex-slaves. School burnings, mob raids on classes, and property destruction were common throughout the mountain counties. Quite often, the damage occurred within a few weeks after ex-slaves had constructed a new building or initiated classes. Shortly after Chattooga County sharecroppers built a small school, the Klan rode through, destroyed the edifice, and whipped the black teacher. When the families moved classes into their new church, the Klan burned that building and continued their violence and threats for more than a decade. Noah Perry recalled the difficulty of the Freedmen's Association when they started a new Chattooga County school. Noah was taught briefly by "a white teacher that come down from the north . . . but the Ku Kluxers made him quit teaching so he went back home." A missionary in another northern Georgia county observed that "the people accuse us of partiality to the colored & say we do not care what becomes of the poor white children." In his view, poor whites "look[ed] on with jealousy at the instruction of the negro." In northern Alabama, white groups burned seventeen schools and killed one teacher. At Harper's Ferry, West Virginia, whites stoned the school, disrupted classes, and assaulted teachers.[25]

In eastern Kentucky, Berea College and its normal school were repeatedly attacked between 1867 and 1871. The lives of school officials were in danger, so armed pickets patrolled the grounds to prevent burning or ransacking of buildings. When one employee attempted to recruit black students, he was ambushed by a mob and almost killed. In eastern Tennessee, Maryville College had been a hotbed of abolitionism before the war, so its interracial pedagogy attracted white violence after emancipation. At one point, whites engaged for months in violent "negro on the brain" marauding of the school, teachers, and students. At Knoxville, whites burned a school, warning "they w[ould] have none of that." The Klan threatened publicly to burn a black-owned tavern "if they g[o]t up a school in it." After a Union colonel organized a freedmen's school at that site, "the citizens look[ed] for the tavern to be burnt every night." The white teacher of a freedmen's school at Charlestown, West Virginia, was "obliged to board with a colored family, as there [wa]s no white family in town willing to endure the 'disgrace' of boarding a teacher of a nigger school." At Frostburg, Maryland, the black male teacher was "frequently threatened with violence. Various notes [were] received ordering him to leave town but another part of whites encourage[d] him to stay."[26]

Postbellum Education of Black Appalachians

There were structural explanations for white violence toward black schools. In 1860, white Appalachian adults were 2.2 times more likely than other Americans and 1.5 times more likely than other Southerners to be illiterate. With the exception of western Maryland, which provided widespread schooling for the poor, none of the Appalachian states provided free public education. In their resistance to higher taxation, the planter-controlled legislatures repeatedly voted down bills to create funding for public schools. Since elites employed tutors or paid for their children to be educated at private academies, they refused to be taxed to benefit those great numbers who made up the lower classes. Little wonder, then, that there was so much white antagonism toward the education of freed slaves. The Ku Klux Klan openly defied the use of public funds for black schools, and they frequently threatened county officials who attempted to implement such policies. To establish a freedmen's school, the local community of ex-slaves had to raise funds and locate sites. In most Appalachian counties, ex-slaves recalled that "white folks wouldn't let Negroes build schools on their land," a community sentiment that is confirmed over and over by Freedmen's Bureau records. John Horry Dent, a northern Georgia slaveholder-turned-farmer, typified the animosity of most white Appalachians of all classes and political leanings. In reaction to Freedmen's Bureau calls for black schools in his rural area, he stated publicly and wrote in his journal:

One great error is endeavoring to enlighten the negro, for in so doing, you merely arouse his suspicions, confuse his ideas, and results in making him more persistent in believing in and doing what you have tried to make him not believe or do. They can never amalgamate with the white race by education or by social contact. Nature has made them too different in all respects for such, hence it is all folly and waste of time to try and enlighten them.... [T]hey are a blight upon all things they come in contact with. No country can prosper with them as laborers or Citizens."[27]

Throughout the Mountain South, "the opposition to freedmen's schools was generally bitter," and that white animosity probably accounted for the scarcity of black schools in the region. As Map 7 demonstrates, black Appalachians were provided formal schools in only forty-six counties. Consequently, only about one-third of the region's freedpeople were in geographic proximity of the few facilities that emerged. Spurred by Berea College, Madison County hosted the only school for ex-slaves in eastern Kentucky. Only seven counties in northern Alabama, northern Georgia, and the western Carolinas developed schools, serving far less

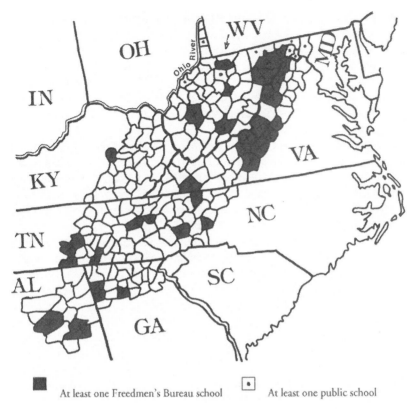

At least one Freedmen's Bureau school   **At least one public school**

Map 7. Black primary schools in the Mountain South, 1866–70. *Sources:* NA, Records of the Education Division, Freedmen's Bureau, Monthly Reports; *Appalachian Slave Narratives.*

than one-third of the black population of those areas. The twenty schools in the Appalachian counties of Tennessee and Virginia were accessible to far less than two-fifths of the ex-slaves in those areas. In West Virginia, eighteen of the state's twenty-two schools were concentrated in five counties of the northern panhandle. The presence of a freedmen's school certainly did not mean that all a county's blacks were served, for the bureau prioritized the establishment of Appalachian schools near the largest black population densities, such as towns or industrial sites. Thus, the vast majority of rural black Appalachians were neglected. Typically, these small facilities served specific communities and enrolled only about thirty students. Educational personnel were usually responsible for a multi-county area, so teachers operated short-term schools by riding a circuit of geographically scattered schools. Even though a majority of black Appalachians lacked access to primary schools, several normal schools and colleges were founded. By 1867, Berea College (Kentucky) and Maryville College (Tennessee) were accepting ex-slaves. Normal schools opened in the counties of Blount, Hamilton, and Knox in Tennessee, and Montgomery County, Virginia. Between 1868 and 1875, black colleges were founded in Harper's Ferry, West Virginia; Knoxville, Tennessee; and Talladega, Alabama.[28]

Since the states of West Virginia and Maryland operated public schools for whites, the Freedmen's Bureau hoped that those areas would make great progress in black education. In 1867, however, the Freedmen's Bureau reported that the new "State School Law" in West Virginia was bringing "some advance ... in establishing schools for the Whites," but "nothing had been done for the Colored." Three years after emancipation, West Virginia counties were still slow to fund schools for black populations. In 1868, the district educational superintendent of the Freedmen's Bureau reported that "the school officers of West Virginia need to be visited often and urged to the performance of their duties. In some places, they are timid, in others they are negligent." In many circumstances, the Klan made public warnings to officials. The bureau encountered much less resistance in western Maryland where there had been antebellum schools for poor whites. The postwar school law in Maryland "provide[d] that the school tax paid by the colored people w[ould] be expended for the education of colored children." In an 1867 letter, the district superintendent reported that "the feeling of the white people is generally passive toward us, they will not oppose neither do they help." In contrast to the delays in West Virginia and the Appalachian counties of Virginia, western Maryland school boards "acted very fairly with the colored schools." Not far away in the northern panhandle of West Virginia, bureau agents were reporting that "some of the bitterest rebels lived" in Hardy and Hampshire Counties. Their "rebellious spirit [wa]s yet very manifest." Former masters were openly hostile, saying "it [wa]s hard that they ha[d] not only to loose their slaves, but also be taxed for their education." Consequently, ex-slaves found the new state school law "very obnoxious" because they paid annual taxes that supported new white schools while no facilities were opening for them.[29]

White violence dampened educational efforts, for the vast majority of the destroyed or damaged schools were funded and built by local blacks without subsidy from the Freedmen's Bureau or philanthropic associations. After working months or years to accumulate the funds and the land needed for their schools, rural ex-slaves watched their dreams go up quickly in flames. In addition, a majority of the teachers who were assaulted or killed were not northern whites or employees of Freedmen's Associations. In the Southern Mountains, the vast majority of those teachers were local blacks. Given the unwillingness of counties to allocate public funds and the frequency of white violence and Klan political activism, it is no surprise that one-half the Appalachian ex-slaves interviewed in the 1930s were still illiterate. Indeed, three-quarters of black Appalachian adults were illiterate in 1870, showing that few of them were educated between 1865 and 1870. Two-thirds of these black Appalachians never attended a freedmen's school or a public school during Reconstruction.[30]

It is miraculous, therefore, that half of the Appalachian ex-slaves learned to read and write, for most of them had averaged far less than one year's schooling. Moreover, the vast majority of black Appalachians received their only schooling from other ex-slaves or they participated in informal field schools or sabbath schools in black and white churches. John Van Hook "started teaching in old field schools with no education but just what [his] white folks had taught [him]." John voluntarily taught his western North Carolina peers during breaks in the fields, at night, and during slack periods. Jeff Johnson irregularly attended such a northern Georgia school. When he did not have to work in the fields, he walked three miles to Finley's Quarters where he and others were instructed by a "colored man school teacher." Another White County ex-slave held classes at the "colored church." One Warren County, Tennessee, ex-slave freedwoman taught ex-slaves "their a, b, c's out of old fashion spelling books." Albermarle Countian Ben Brown "wanted some learnin but dere wuz no way to git it until a white man cleared a place in de woods." Fleming Clark was a youngster on a small plantation in Botetourt County where one freedmen's school operated. Still "dey wuz no school for Negroes" that he could attend. George Jackson went to school "bout three months" when he was twenty years old. According to Kate McDonald, "they would go to school about four months in the year, and the blue back speller, figuring and writing was the large course of study, the white folks believed that was enough for the negroes to know." For four years, Mary Tate attended a freedmen's school at rural Mossy Creek. Taught by a northern white woman and a black male Knoxvillian, "six weeks to 3 months was the limit of the session." Most children could not participate fully because it was a "part time pay school and part time free school." Leonidas Star was luckier than most rural black Appalachians. Since he lived at Knoxville, he attended a year-round freedmen's school operated at the First Presbyterian Church where he was instructed by "white folks from the North."[31]

White violence was not the only explanation for the limited education available to black Appalachians. Before a federally subsidized school could be established in a community, local blacks were required to raise funds, locate white supporters, find land, and then apply formally to the Freedmen's Bureau. If the bureau approved the request, contacts were typically made with one of several religious philanthropic organizations. In most Appalachian counties, the U.S. government funded no more than the materials to construct a building; church associations and local black church congregations provided teachers, books, and much of the operating expenses. Quite often, the location of schools had more to do with the presence of specific church groups in a community than with the demand from a large population. Obviously, church politics, the extreme poverty of ex-slaves, and local violence slowed the emergence of schools in most of rural Appalachia. In addition to those factors, many black Appalachians were needed in the fields or at paid jobs if their families were to survive. Fountain Hughes recalled that most of his young life there "wasn' no schools. An' when they started a little school ... there couldn' many of them go to school" because children were needed in the fields. The necessity to work probably determined who attended schools, even when they were accessible.[32]

Among those Appalachian ex-slaves interviewed in the 1930s, age at emancipation determined whether they received an education. More than three-quarters of the ex-slaves who were sixteen or older when freed remained illiterate, reflecting the economic pressures on productive teenagers and young adults. For instance, Senya Singfield was unable to attend school. At emancipation, her "mother was a widow and [she] had to start out and make a living." Even though there was a freedmen's school nearby, Rachel Cruze rarely attended, and her comments point to other reasons for poor attendance.

I was about thirteen years old before I went to school. That was about a year after the war ended, and the Freedman's Bureau ... sent two colored teachers down to the new box-like affair they built on [a neighboring plantation]. One of those teachers was meaner than the other. They treated the colored students more as if they were dogs than humans.... [One teacher] was finally given a good whipping by the boy students, and the community sent both of them packing, and brought other [black] teachers from Knoxville. I was lucky if I got to school two days a week.... I dropped corn, hoed corn, thinned corn, and in the fall I pulled corn.

The vast majority of the ex-slaves who could read and write in the 1930s had been younger than fifteen at emancipation. Since they were too young to be needed in the fields or at paid jobs, more than two-thirds of those who were younger than nine when freed were literate.[33]

Family Reconstruction and Disorganization

At emancipation, two-thirds of the families of Appalachian ex-slaves were in disarray. More than half had been permanently disrupted by inter-regional slave sales or by the long-distance migrations of their owners. Another 16 percent of them lived in households in which members were "abroad" because their owners had hired them out or assigned them to work sites away from families. Probably more than one-third of all black males aged sixteen to forty-five had enlisted as Union soldiers. More than one-third of those enlistees died in action; some veterans did not return to families because of white violence in their home counties; still others were absent because the army extended their terms and shipped them to Texas. To complicate matters, probably two-fifths of black Appalachians had been uprooted during the war, and they were situated in contraband camps away from kin. Union officers based in mountain counties were overwhelmed by ex-slaves who were on the roads, desperate to find kin they had not seen in years. In Blue Ridge Virginia, Freedmen's Bureau agents frequently filed reports in 1866 and 1867 saying that "there are still large numbers of Freedmen & women traveling around the country in search of husbands, wifes, mothers & other relatives who have been seper-ated for years." A Freedmen's Bureau agent in western North Carolina made a similar assessment of the status of ex-slaves in that area. Bureau agents were also swamped by hundreds of letters in which distant kin were searching for relatives, but could offer only meager clues about their whereabouts.[34]

Forced labor migrations, abroad marital arrangements, and the war took their toll on the families of emancipated black Appalachians. Less than 10 percent of the mountain ex-slaves who reported broken families saw their kin reunited successfully after emancipation. Nearly three-quarters of the spouses who had been forcibly separated never saw one another again. Before the war, about 16 percent of the mountain slave households involved abroad relationships in which spouses had different owners or worked at different sites. Not even all those spouses reunited after emancipation, for only about 12 percent of separated spouses rebuilt their families at war's end. Two-thirds of the ex-slaves had been sepa-rated from their parents during childhood, so four of every five of them never saw their parents again. Only about 9 percent of removed children were able to reunite with their families after emancipation. None of the ex-slaves who had been separated from siblings ever reunited with their missing brothers and sisters, even though about half of them successfully located the whereabouts of their relatives. Over all, three-quarters of those black Appalachians who were forcibly removed lost contact with their families forever. Moreover, a majority of those who reunited were able to do so because they were situated within fifty to sixty miles of one another.[35]

A little more than one of every ten knew the whereabouts of their kin but could not reunite after the war. Sold away from her Blue Ridge Virginia parents as a child, Juda Wright was living in desperate poverty in Georgia because she had "never got any pay for [her] work" during the three years she had been liberated. It is doubtful that this letter she sent to the Farmville office of the Freedmen's Bureau ever reached her family.

Dear father, pray that the lord may open the way that I may see you before I die.... I have been gone 21 years and never expect to see home.... My heart is often filed with joy [to] think that we [may] every meet again [and] never part no more. [F]ather there is no more selling.

After Rosanna Kelly's family was freed, her mother "always wanted to go back to her home at Bedford [County], Virginia, but she had no way to go back except to walk." Chaney Mack's sister was left behind in southeastern Tennessee when her Cherokee owner was removed west in 1838. Long after the war, they received information about her from the Freedmen's Bureau. "My mother lived to be 112, and den she jest drap dead from joy when dey tole her dat Rachel, my sister what we hadn't seen in a long time, was still alive." Appalachian slaves who had been liberated and relocated to Liberia by the American Colonization Society were unsuccessful at locating and retrieving children they had been forced to leave behind. Sold away at age seven, one Tullahoma, Tennessee, slave searched for parents and siblings until 1890. After he learned that his father had died as a Union soldier, he continued his search for his mother. He "was gone from her 33 years before [he] knew anything about her. [He] wrote letters of inquiry until [he] found her." The reunion was not a happy one, however. "I went to get her, and she wanted to come, but she belonged to the Catholic Church, and they wouldn't let me have her. She was 73 years old and earning wages. They drove me out of there when they found I was a Protestant."[36]

Only about 44 percent of the ex-slaves reported that their families were stable and never disrupted by forced labor migrations. If we optimistically presume that most of those unbroken families were not destabilized by the war or by return of spouses to earlier marriages and if we add to their number those that reunited, less than 60 percent of the Appalachian ex-slaves could have resided in complete families after emancipation. These findings from slave narratives are borne out by the census manuscripts. In 1870:

- More than two-fifths of all black Appalachian family units were headed by one parent, in a majority of instances the mother.
- More than two-fifths of the households contained two or more families and were complex combinations of kin and nonkin, the children from several marriages, women who merged their own offspring with orphans and elderly, sometimes even multiple spouses.
- More than one-quarter of the family units still resided as laborers in white households.
- More than one-quarter of black Appalachian children lived away from their families to work as laborers in white households, just as a high percentage of youngsters had done during enslavement.

In one of every five of the family units, there were two or more surnames, reflecting the past ownership by multiple masters. About two of every five black Appalachian households lived next door to another black family with the same last name, indicating proximity to kin and to ex-slaves who had been owned by the same master. It is phenomenal that the kinship networks of about three of every five black Appalachian families persisted. Marriage registers demonstrate that ex-slaves did not consider their familial arrangements to be loose sexual alliances. When the Virginia Freedmen's Bureau ordered Nelson and Rockbridge County, Virginia, officials to record the marriages of emancipated slaves, 460 black households registered marriages that had occurred ten years or more earlier during slavery. Of those ex-slaves who registered their marriages in those two Appalachian counties, more than three-quarters of those older than forty legalized their bonds to spouses to whom they had been connected longer than twenty years.[37]

What is even more spectacular is the extent to which some Appalachian slaves were able to rebuild their separated families after emancipation. Locating relatives often took years of persistent search and the reuniting of members scattered in numerous locations in several states. For example, Dan Lockhart "was sold at five years of age, and when [he] first saw [his] mother to know [her], [he] had a wife and child." Somehow a Sevier County couple managed to retrieve their son from Texas. Bethany Veney returned from the north to find her daughter was "grown to womanhood, married, and had one child."[38] Family reunions were not always easy, and they were not without psychological trauma. At emancipation, Henry Johnson was seventeen, but he "never saw [his] mother and father until [he] was in [his] twenty's." Henry was reunited with his family, only after his father kidnapped him away from his white employer.

A colored man kept watching me so much I got plum scared. Dis was after de war was over. . . . Den he said I am your father and I am goin' to take you to your mother and sisters and brothers down in Greenhill, Virginia. When he got me dere, I found two sisters and four brothers. Dey was all so glad to see me dey shouted and cried and carried on so I was so scared I tried to run away, cause I didn't know nothin' 'bout none of them. And I thought dat white man [his employer] what brought me down here ought to have saved me from all dis. I just thought a white man was my God, I didn't know no better.

Former owners sometimes intervened to try to prevent family reunions. John Horry Dent recorded his reactions to two instances of family rebuilding. In January 1867, he reported:

there is a Negro here in the neighborhood that is persuading our hands to leave and return with him to Tennessee. Understand that our cook Oney who is his sister-in-law is going to go with him. Also Buck. We are helpless as the Freedman Bureau backs them in such conduct and allows them to violate their contracts as they please.

When a daughter and granddaughter moved in with a female sharecropper, Dent intervened more aggressively. He reported that he "ordered her off twice and she won't leave. If she does not leave by tomorrow, will have her ejected by the law." Still thinking of this young mother as he would an enslaved female, he added, "This is a prime young woman that will not work!"[39]

Two of every five independent black households were complex combinations of kin and nonkin, the children from several marriages, women who merged their own offspring with orphans and elderly, sometimes even multiple spouses. Most of these households contained two or more families, reflecting the tendency of ex-slaves to incorporate adult siblings with children, aunts or uncles, and elders from their previous plantations. Freedmen's Bureau agents reported with disdain the constructive efforts of ex-slaves to protect and embrace their own. When a western North Carolina washwoman "benevolently t[ook] in and was nursing a sick woman of her own race," the agent called her act "thoughtless charity." Many of the bureau officials thought "the industrious were too much given to supporting the thriftless" because "receiving another poverty-stricken creature" was "characteristic of the freedmen." Family rebuilding created new stresses when offspring were blended from several marriages. After the death of their mother, Morris Hillyer and his two sisters spent most of their childhood without contact with their abroad father. Although they were reunited with him, "he was so mean to [Morris] dat [he] run away" three years later. Rachel Cruze found it very difficult to live with a stepfather who knew that she was the child of her mother and the master's son. Gertrude Vogler had a similar experience with a violent stepfather. Gertrude's mother and children were removed from the husband to eastern Kentucky. After the war, the stepfather became physically abusive because he "did not want them." When he "threatened to kill" them, the mother "fixed [the children] a little bundle of what few clothes [they] had and started [them] out to go back" to their father in Virginia.[40]

The legacy of multiple spouses was particularly problematic. Freedmen's Bureau agents devised a tactic for resolving conflicts. "Whenever a negro appears before me with 2 or 3 wives who have equal claim upon him," one agent reported, "I marry him to the woman who has the greatest number of helpless children who otherwise would become a charge on the Bureau." Typically, the woman selected was younger, following the assumption that middle-aged females had children old enough to support them. Some households did not undergo legal ceremonies because wives decided to live with the husband in combined families. Emanuel Elmore's parents were separated through three interstate sales that transported them from Staunton, Virginia, to Alabama and South Carolina, leaving some of the children with the father. After emancipation, Emanuel's mother "was months making her way" from Alabama to her family in South Carolina. She arrived "lanky, ragged and poor," to find that her husband had remarried. The first wife decided that the second wife "had cared so well for her children while she was off, that she liked her." So the women agreed to "live in the same house" with Emanuel's father, and the family remained this way until the first wife died. Ex-slave Richmond Randolph observed that "hundreds ... returned to their former homes" to find that spouses had remarried.[41]

About 8 percent of the ex-slaves reported that multiple marriages made successful family reunions impossible. In 4 percent of the cases, wives had remarried by the time husbands returned. About 4 percent of the men abandoned one wife and set of children to stay with another. After four years of searching, Laura Spicer located her removed husband, but he sent a painful reply that advised her:

I would come and see you, but I know you could not bear it. . . . I love you just as well as I did the last day I saw you. . . . [I]f you and I meets it would make a very dissatisfied family. . . . [Y]ou know it never was our wishes to be separated from each other, and it never was our fault. . . . I had rather anything to have happened to me most than ever have been parted from you and the children. . . . The woman is not born that feels as near to me as you do. . . . I thinks of you and the children every day of my life. . . . My love to you never have failed, Laura, truly, I have go[t] another wife, and I am very sorry, that I am. You feels and seems to me as much like my dear loving wife, as you ever did.

The husband only had two requests of his former wife: "please git married" and "send me some of the children's hair." Perhaps the existence of multiple families explains the reluctance of black Appalachians to remarry as state laws and Freedmen's Bureau policies required. A middle Tennessee ex-slave recalled that his parents were remarried before the magistrate, "but some slaves wouldn't do it." Indeed, Freedmen's Bureau records show that Appalachian ex-slaves registered their marriages less frequently than those from other parts of the South. In Virginia, for example, two-thirds of Tidewater ex-slaves remarried, while only about one-third to one-half of the spouses in Appalachian counties completed the civil ceremony to formalize their marriages.[42]

In 1870, three-quarters of Appalachian ex-slaves were residing in independent households. However, economic constraints and the structural interference of former slaveholders were working against family stability. Playing upon desperate poverty and racial violence, former slaveholders targeted women and children as the most controllable, most submissive laborers, and they attempted to weaken spousal and parental ties by requiring separate labor contracts for men, women, and offspring. In short, former slaveholders sought to maintain the same degree of control over black households that they had enjoyed during enslavement. Female-headed households were the most vulnerable. Five years after emancipation, one-quarter of the black family units were still residing as laborers in white households, and the vast majority of them were women and their offspring. However, women in independent households with adult males were also targeted for labor coercion from former owners. Some scholars have accepted the biased assessment of the Freedmen's Bureau that emancipated slave women stopped working in the fields or were leaving the labor force entirely. Former slaveholders repeatedly filed written complaints with the bureau that their former slave women were refusing to enter into labor contracts separate from those of their husbands. One such landholder urged the bureau to use the vagrancy act to compel women to accept field labor contracts.

Most of the Freedwomen who have husbands are not at work – never having made any contract at all – Their husbands are at work, while they are as nearly idle as it is possible to be.... Now these women have always been used to working out & it would be far better for them to go to work for reasonable wages & their rations.... Now is a very important time in the crop.... I think it would be a good thing to put the women to work and all that is necessary to do this in most cases is an order from you directing the agents to require the women to make contracts for the balance of the year.... Are they not in some sort vagrants as they are living without employment – and mainly without any visible means of support – and if so are they not amenable to [the] vagrant act?

I AM
COMMITTEE

1st. No man shall squat negroes on his place unless they are all under his employ male and female.

2d. Negro women shall be employed by white persons

3d. All children shall be hired out for something.

4th. Negroes found in cabins to themselves shall suffer the penalty.

5th. Negroes shall not be allowed to hire negroes.

6th. Idle men, women or children, shall suffer the penalty.

7th. All white men found with negroes in secret places shall be dealt with and those that hire negroes must pay promptly and act with good faith to the negro. I will make the negro do his part, and the white must too.

8th. For the first offence is one hundred lashes—the second is looking up a sap lin.

9th. This I do for the benefit of all young or old, high and tall, black and white. Any one that may not like these rules can try their luck, and see whether or not I will be found doing my duty.

10th. Negroes found stealing from any one or taking from their employers to other negroes, death is the first penalty.

11th. Running about late of nights shall be strictly dealt with.

12th. White man and negro, I am everywhere. I have friends in every place, do your duty and I will have but little to do.

This poster appeared in the West Virginia Panhandle in 1867. The Ku Klux Klan was responsible for about 15 percent of the violent assaults against Appalachian ex-slaves during Reconstruction. *Source:* Library of Congress.

Numerous complaints from landholders about the "evil of female loaferism" appear in bureau records and in the manuscripts of owners of mountain plantations. For instance, northern Georgia's John Horry Dent claimed that "the women are for indoor occupation."[43]

However, scholars should be very skeptical about Reconstruction claims that freedwomen had left field labor entirely. About the issue of black women's work, bureau and slaveholder documents are unreliable. House-bound domesticity characterized only elite and upper-middle-class Southern females, for poor white women could not afford the luxury of leaving work outside the home to males. Why, then, should writers assume that such a strategy was possible for recently emancipated black families? Indeed, bureau documents are a direct reflection of slaveholder ideologies and of the paramilitary enforcement strategies of the Ku Klux Klan. As this 1867 broadside shows, the Klan threatened "idle men, women, or children" with "the penalty." Women and children were warned that they must be employed by whites, and "Negroes found in cabins to themselves" could expect retaliation.[44]

In sharp contrast to those racist documents, slave narratives and the 1870 census manuscripts indicate that women were still hard at labor on the farms. Even when there was a husband in the household, Appalachian ex-slaves reported that women continued to work in the fields and at other forms of employment. In Kate McDonald's household, for instance, "the girls did the major portion of the field work" that was needed to raise cotton and corn on shares. All the women who headed households were employed outside their homes, the vast majority of them employed at agricultural labor. In 1870, most black Appalachian female heads of household were illiterate, and they were concentrated into two kinds of labor: agricultural work or domestic service in white households. Both occupations kept the women in debt peonage and bound their offspring to labor contracts that were only a shade different from enslavement. With young children to feed and no financial assets, female heads of household sharecropped or did farm labor, just like the men. For example, a woman named Caroline contracted herself and three children to do field work for a western North Carolina farm, in exchange for "food and raiment and $50 a year." Alex Montgomery's household was typical. After emancipation, the husband abandoned the wife and children. According to Alex, his mother plowed, harvested, and worked in the fields. Alex marvelled that his mother sharecropped "till we chaps wus grown" because they "never made nuff to leave dar." Obviously, emancipated women were not staying home, like the wives of their white employers. What they resisted, when they could afford to do so, were those situations that replicated the vulnerabilities of bondage. On the one hand, they refused work arrangements that threatened or denied their ties to husbands, sons, and other adult black males. On the other hand, they feared work that made them vulnerable to a continuation of the white sexual exploitation they had endured as slaves. For example, one mother went "into the field ... and made her leave" when she discovered where the overseer had assigned her daughter. She became "very violent and threatening" toward the owner because the youngster had been put to work alongside white males who might molest her.[45]

The second indicator that economic constraints were working against the stability of black families was that nearly one-quarter of the children lived away from their families to work in white households, just as a high percentage of youngsters had done during enslavement. The average age of these child laborers was 12.2 years, and very few of them had attended school during the previous year. Appalachian slaveholders used long-term indenturement of youngsters as a mechanism to maintain control over laborers. After emancipation in western Maryland, whites were "laying hold, by violence, of Coloured peoples Children, carrying them to the Orphans Court and having them bound to themselves in Spite of all remonstrance upon the part of Parents. They [we]re taking Boys and Girls as old as Sixteen years." To speed removal of large populations from federal support, the Freedmen's Bureau aided and abetted the indenturement process. The Amherst County Freedmen's Bureau refused to intervene when Nelson Tinsley complained that the county court had illegally bound his children to a Georgia slaveholder. In Franklin County, a black father was arrested for abducting his own child, a youngster who had been bound by the county court to an employer who was planning to migrate.[46]

The experiences of ex-slaves provide graphic details of an emancipation they never celebrated. Robert Falls master "fooled [them] to believe [they] was duty-bound to stay with him till [they] was all 21." Zek Brown was kidnapped by a neighbor and removed to Texas. Thirteen-year-old Sally Brown "didn't know 'bout surrender and that [she] was free 'till after [her mistress] died several years after the war." Tillie Duke's former owner took her to Kansas after the war, causing her to lose all contact with her family. Ruben Woods and Fleming Clark were bound to their former owners, so they "earned no money ... just food and clothes" until age twenty-one. Similarly, Ann Ladly "stayed and took care of de [owner's] children till [she] gets growed." When the war was over, Ben Brown's "missie nevah tell [him] dat [he] wuz free," so he "kep' on workin' same as befoah." Betty Farrow "don' 'member bein' tol' [she was] free," and she "stayed right dere on de farm." After securing labor contracts from the bureau, one northern Alabama small planter "hitched [the two boys]

The Union Army initiated the notion of chain gang labor. Ex-slaves who refused to sign agricultural labor contracts were jailed and put to work at public service under the control of soldiers. *Source: Harper's,* 1869.

to a double plow and turned all his ground and planted cotton.... He made four bales of cotton and sold it for a dollar a pound. All the boys got was what they et and a suit of clothes." At age ten, Gip Minton was removed to Arkansas by his former owner. "I don't know nothin about that freedom," Gip told the WPA interviewer. "I reckon I was freed, but I was raised by the white folks and I stayed right on wid em. Dat freedom ain't never bothered me."[47]

Theoretical Reprise

> Any broad theory of master-slave relationships in antebellum America must either take careful account of family separations or rest upon treacherous foundations.
> — Michael Tadman, historian

It is not coincidental that the current dominant paradigm on the African-American slave family emerged after the publication of the Moynihan Report. Deriving from Frazier, DuBois, and Stampp the notion that slavery and Reconstruction had broken families, Moynihan argued that "three centuries of injustice have brought about deep-seated structural distortions in the life of the Negro American." Gutman sought to counter the report by proving that Moynihan had begun with incorrect assumptions about the state of the black family at the end of the Civil War. In his capstone work, Fogel offered a summation of the political and intellectual backdrop against which current notions about the slave family emerged.

Discontent with the reigning paradigm ... surfaced during the late 1960s. From 1968 through 1972 Herbert Gutman ... began to argue that the black family emerged from bondage with a high degree of stability. John Blassingame ... wrote that however "frequently the family was broken, it was primarily responsible for the slave's ability to survive." ... Genovese ... held that historians and sociologists had misunderstood the nature of the slave family.... The record of evidence, he contended, showed that "slaves created impressive norms of family life."

Fogel and Engerman subsequently argued that "slave owners were averse to breaking up black families." Genovese even claimed that masters "saw some advantage in strengthening the power of the male in the household." Therefore, "the essential story of black men in slavery lay with the many who overcame every possible hardship and humiliation to stand fast to their families."[1]

When they rejected the previous family paradigm, the dissidents also threw out earlier findings about the impacts of slave trading. In the 1930s, Bancroft contended that "slave rearing became the source of the largest and often the only regular profit of nearly all slaveholding farmers and of

many planters in the Upper South." Consequently, "the selling singly of
young children privately and publicly was frequent and notorious." In the
1950s, Stampp argued that "slaves were raised with an eye to marketabil-
ity." Conrad and Meyer contended that breeding returns were necessary
to ensure profits to the slaveholders of the border states. Since it was difficult to hypothesize stable nuclear families against such arguments, the
dissenters questioned previous findings about the extent of slave trading. Fogel and Engerman stressed strong kinship ties and functional
household structures as evidence that "it was to the economic interest
of planters to encourage the stability of slave families." They claimed that
only one out of every twenty-two slaveholders sold a slave in any given
year. In their estimation, 13 percent or less of the interregional sales
destroyed marriages, only 2 percent of the masters' migrations caused
family disruptions, and less than 10 percent of all sales were children
under thirteen. In his most recent work, Fogel contended that "interstate
slave trading could not have accounted for a significant fraction of the
profits of the slaveowning class."[2]

Sounding very much like an antebellum Southern novelist, Genovese
claimed that "an impressive number of slaveholders took losses they could
ill afford in an effort to keep families together. For the great families, from
colonial times to the fall of the regime, the maintenance of family units
was a matter of honor." With respect to white sexual exploitation of slave
women, Genovese offered four generalizations:

Much of the plantation miscegenation occurred with single girls under circumstances that varied from seduction to rape and typically fell between the two.
Married black women and their men did not take white sexual aggression lightly
and resisted effectively enough to hold it to a minimum. Most of the miscegenation in the South occurred in the towns and cities, not on the plantations or even
farms. . . . Typically the slaveholders could not take their black "wenches" without
suffering psychic agony and social opprobrium.

The dissidents also popularized the notion that it was economically
rational for owners to provide adequate survival needs to their slaves.
Genovese contended that "the overwhelming majority of masters gave
their slaves enough to eat." Fogel remains convinced that the food, clothing and shelter provided to most slaves was calorically adequate and
"better than what was typically available to free urban laborers at the
time."[3]

The protesters achieved what they set out to do politically. By posit-
ing the counterimage of a stable nuclear slave family, they added fuel
to the controversy over the state of the contemporary black family that
had been triggered by the Moynihan Report. In a 1997 monograph,

Berlin and Rowland pledged their allegiance, as do most contemporary scholars, to the "accepted wisdom" about the African-American slave family.

Slaves based their family life on the marriage compact. They courted according to customs of their own choosing and selected partners according to rules of their own making.... Once married, most slave husbands and wives honored their vows with lifelong fidelity.... Within the slave household, husbands and wives played distinct and complementary roles.... Most slave children were born into two-parent households.... Many slaves named their children after their parents, grandparents, aunts, and uncles; few named them after their owners. Husbands and wives divided the labor of childrearing among themselves.... Fathers also played an important role in the lives of slave children, and, perhaps, to strengthen the more distant tie, children were more often named for their fathers than their mothers.... Slaves recognized that their owners had an interest in maintaining a modicum of family stability on the plantation.[4]

Even though many of its generalizations sound more like a Disney script than scholarly research, the Gutman-Fogel paradigm is now so deeply entrenched and respected that writers like me are now dissidents from the mainstream.

Even though there is little empirical research to support their generalizations, many slavery specialists embrace romantic cliches about small plantations and the Upper South. According to Berlin, slaves on large plantations "worked longer, harder, and with less control over their own lives" than did slaves on plantations where there was a "mixed labor force of slaves, servants, and wage workers." That notion probably derives from the popular misperception that Upper South slavery was more benign. Frazier presumed that ex-slaves who had lived on small plantations had enjoyed a more stable family life than blacks on larger plantations. Others have argued that "smaller slaveholdings led to more intimacy and greater personal regard between owner and owned."[5]

Challenging the Dominant Paradigm

The dominant paradigm is handicapped by three fundamental methodological weaknesses. First, Gutman and others began with the presumption that the contemporary African-American family is more stable than Moynihan argued. Therefore, they reasoned, the slave household must also have been more like white nuclear families than Moynihan assumed. They made their second methodological blunder by drawing generalizations from sources that are not representative of a majority of U.S. slaves (i.e., data about large plantations and about the Lower South). Third, those who support the dominant paradigm have been preoccupied with slave selling as the major threat to the stability of families. As a result, they have either ignored or underestimated the destabilizing effects of slave hiring, of owner assignments to distant work sites, of abroad marriages, and of owner migrations.

Since 1980, four important investigations have called into question the dominant paradigm. Crawford and Patterson contend that size of plantation is a major determinant of the quality of slave life, but not in the manner that popular mythology would lead us to predict. Patterson argued that worldwide, over time, small slaveholdings have always been more brutal in living conditions. Using the WPA slave narratives, Crawford found that there were many more female-headed households, more severe punishment, greater malnutrition, and higher fertility on small plantations. By studying slave trader records, Tadman established that one of every three Upper South slave marriages was broken by a master's intervention, one in every five disruptions being caused by a sale. Moreover, one-half of the sales involved the separation of children from their parents. Most recently, Stevenson made a strong case that Upper South slave households were women and children, not the stable nuclear arrangements described by Gutman.

Taken altogether, the evidence overwhelmingly supports the conclusion that matrifocality was a fundamental characteristic of most slave families, even when fathers lived locally. Matrifocal families were not inherently problematic, structurally or functionally. The day-to-day absence of a father from a slave family did not necessarily mean that there were not other males available to take on some, if not all, of the socializing responsibilities, nurture, discipline, emotional commitment, and even protective stances that slave fathers ideally provided.... Of course those "surrogate" fathers were much more available within larger communities than smaller ones, especially since those holdings with fewer slaves had a decided absence of males in their population. Children being raised under those conditions had m[any] fewer options for daily, familial-like contact with adult male slaves than those who lived among larger numbers of men generally found in more populous quarters.[6]

This research builds upon the work of those four writers, but it also breaks new ground because it tests the thesis of the dominant paradigm that a majority of U.S. slaves lived in stable, nuclear families. In the Mountain South, masters threatened the persistence of enslaved households in three significant ways. First, masters routinely interfered in marriage formations and child rearing, weakening the bonds between family members and causing high child and maternal mortality. Second, owners repeatedly disrupted households, as they removed members and structured the absence of adult males. On the one hand, "abroad" spouses, children, and other kin kept dropping into and out of households, as they moved to and from hire-outs or neighboring owners. On the other hand, frequent sales and high mortality rates meant that household composition altered every few years. High death rates and forced labor migrations necessitated the absorption of unrelated persons or extended kin whose former households had disintegrated. Mountain slaveholders placed black families at risk in a third way. Owners expropriated most of the production, allocating to their slaves survival rations below the actual subsistence requirements of household members. To maximize profits, mountain masters externalized to slave households (a) most of the costs of their food, clothing, and health care as well as (b) the costs associated with reproducing surplus laborers for export.[7]

The myth of the stable nuclear slave family was derived from analysis of conditions that are representative of only a small minority of U.S. slaves. Since I do not want to replicate Gutman's methodological error, I am not suggesting that we make the theoretical quantum leap of generalizing family patterns for all U.S. slaves from another restricted sample. What I am arguing is that the findings about the Mountain South vary so dramatically from the accepted wisdom that we have strong indicators that the dominant paradigm is *just flat wrong* about a majority of U.S. slave families! On the one hand, this study documents broad variation from the dominant paradigm for 215 counties in six Upper South states and thirty-eight counties in three Lower South states. Since findings about this large diverse region contradict most of the accepted family theses, we have strong justification for questioning the universal applicability of the dominant paradigm. On the other hand, the life situation of slaves in the Mountain South was more similar to that of a majority of U.S. slaves than were those Lower South large plantations on which supporters of the dominant paradigm have grounded their generalizations. Southern Appalachia is not just a regional peculiarity, for my findings are in line with other studies about small plantations and about the Upper South. It is clear from my research and from the work of Patterson, Crawford, Tadman, and Stevenson that the three best predictors of slave family instability and disruption are

• ownership by a small slaveholder,
• residence of the slave in a slave-selling region, and
• frequent slave hiring for distant nonagricultural occupations.

All three of those risk factors were at play in the Mountain South, a slave-selling region characterized by small holdings, with about one-quarter of its black laborers assigned to nonagricultural occupations. In short, what we have learned about the Mountain South provides more reliable clues about threats to the persistence of a majority of U.S. slave families than does the dominant paradigm. Like black Appalachians, a majority of

U.S. slaves were threatened by one or more of these disruptive factors by 1820.[8]

Since the Mountain South was typical of enslavement circumstances for a majority of U.S. slaves, several findings of this study call into question the most important theses of the dominant paradigm.

- Slave trading occurred much more frequently than has been assumed and was more economically significant to slaveholders than Fogel contended. A majority of family disruptions were caused by sales that permanently severed kinship ties, and nearly two-thirds of all Appalachian slave sales separated children younger than fifteen from parents and siblings.[9]
- Breakup of slave families by masters and the structured absence of black fathers occurred much more often than is portrayed by the dominant paradigm. Only one-fifth of the Appalachian slave households were complete families in which parents and children resided together, and female-headed households occurred four times more often than Gutman claimed.
- Though not permanent separations, abroad marriages, hire-outs, and work assignments to distant sites disrupted slave families and endangered women to a much greater extent than Gutman presumed.[10]
- Contrary to the claims of the dominant paradigm, masters routinely interfered in marriage formation, child-bearing practices, breastfeeding decisions, and child care.
- Mountain masters pressured women to reproduce younger and to maintain higher fertility rates than has been assumed to be characteristic of large plantations.
- Mountain masters structured chronic hunger and malnutrition and required a majority of slave households to supplement rations through household production. As a result of shortfalls in basic survival needs and masters' exploitative reproductive strategies, a mountain slave was 1.4 times more likely to die than other U.S. slaves, enslaved adult women experienced a higher mortality rate than males, and more than one-half of all slave children died before age ten.

This study also challenges the claims of the dominant paradigm with respect to the state of the African-American family at emancipation. Gutman and Genovese agree that ex-slaves "entered the postwar social system with a remarkably stable base." Gutman argued that "fewer than one in ten lived apart from an immediate family" during Reconstruction. He also claimed that, when emancipated, most ex-slave families had two parents and that most older couples had lived together in unbroken long-term relationships. Supposedly, "the black family that emerged from slavery already had a distinct and quite simple nuclear structure."

By 1866, he postulated, two-thirds of all spouses had reunited. Crawford claimed that 80 percent of ex-slaves were reunited after emancipation and that, when freed, two-thirds of black youngsters were already living with both parents. Another generalization that pervades the field is the notion that, after emancipation, adult women stopped working in the fields and ended their employment outside their households.[11]

Even if these optimistic generalizations provide an accurate assessment of those ex-slaves who had lived on large Lower South plantations, these generalizations certainly do not reflect the experiences of ex-slaves who were emancipated in the Upper South or those who lived on small holdings. To a much greater extent than occurred in the Lower South, the Civil War disrupted Upper South slave families through military labor impressment, contraband migrations, an increased incidence of sales and owner migrations, and mistreatment of black soldier families. Moreover, Union policies slowed emancipation in Upper South counties with low black population densities. When we consider those dangers in addition to antebellum risk factors, we can see that the optimistic findings of the dominant paradigm simply cannot be true. Because of interstate slave trading, an Upper South slave suffered a one-in-three chance of being permanently removed from family, and one of every four marriages was broken by interstate slave sales. Moreover, small plantations had a higher incidence of one-parent households and of children separated from their parents. Southern mountain slaves were permanently separated from families and lived in one-parent households more frequently than other Upper South blacks. Two-thirds of the Appalachian ex-slaves were separated from their parents during their childhood, and women headed more than half the households. Consequently, it is likely that half or more of Upper South slave families began the Reconstruction period as broken marriages and that a majority were decomposed kinship units from which children and extended family were permanently lost. Since women headed about half of those households, earlier claims have seriously overstated the extent to which emancipated females stopped working outside their homes. During Reconstruction, African-American families were further threatened by deep poverty exacerbated by debt peonage systems, continuing illiteracy, and racial violence.[12]

Revisiting the Slave-Breeding Debate

While not orchestrating barnyard breeding methods, mountain plantations did indeed structure an exploitative reproductive system aimed at generating surplus slaves whose labor could be sold or hired. On the one hand, many Appalachian slaveholders profited at least as much from an enslaved woman's reproduction of surplus laborers as they did from her production of market crops. On the other hand, mountain masters treated enslaved women and children as "resources to be optimally manipulated for productive ends," so they restructured the most fundamental aspects of childbirth and parenting. Owners' control of breastfeeding and child rearing weakened the woman's role as mother and established her children as bonded property. Such reproductive interference was "designed to teach both of them their place in the patriarchal system." After their children reached age ten, Appalachian slave mothers lost two of every five of them through sales or other forced labor migrations.[13]

However, these mothers lost an even higher percentage of their offspring to premature deaths. Attenuated breastfeeding, mothers' early ages at first births, and ecological risks caused high infant mortality rates. Malnutrition, environmental hazards, and occupational accidents also took a high toll of black children between ages one and ten. Paradoxically, that high child mortality spurred *increased fertility* among slave women, a pattern that parallels contemporary population trends in several poor countries. When the first child died before age one, four-fifths of the mountain slave women were pregnant again within less than two years. After 1800, infant and child mortality rose steadily on Appalachian plantations, in exactly the same historical era when the number of slave exports to the Lower South was peaking. As the market demand for slaves escalated, the reproductive rates of Appalachian slave women increased, as did the mortality rates among slave children. It is not just coincidental that Appalachian slave women began to reproduce at younger ages or that they shortened the waiting periods between pregnancies. Far from being natural or the result of women's unilateral decisions, such high fertility was imposed on mountain slave women, to no less degree than frequent pregnancies were inflicted upon the wives of slaveholding males. Rising mortality spurred significant declines in the mothers' average age at first birth and in the amount of time women spaced between live births. Consequently, the number of children born to slave women increased over time, as a result of earlier ages at first birth and shorter average spacing between pregnancies.[14]

To offset the dampening economic effect of high child mortality on their slave exports, mountain masters *externalized* to enslaved women the responsibility for producing adequate numbers of surviving children. Appalachian slave women were deprived of autonomy in motherhood roles through their masters' structural interference in pregnancy, breastfeeding, and child rearing. Affluent white parents celebrated and mourned deaths of their own children, but they rarely noted with any empathy the mortality toll that took one-half or more of the black children they owned.

While reeling under the emotional strains of childhood deaths in their own families, Appalachian masters burdened their enslaved women with repeated incidents of emotional and psychological distress associated with the removal of their offspring. Even though they were economically valuable to their masters, mountain slave women "were viewed with disdain as persons." Thus, an above-average incidence of white male sexual exploitation was also foisted upon mountain slave women. By blaming mothers, Appalachian masters "ideologically camouflaged" the degree to which their malnutrition, reproductive, and overwork strategies caused the ill health or deaths of children. Because black women experienced a higher incidence of miscarriages than whites, owners often accused expectant mothers of destroying the fetuses. If babies died prematurely of SIDS, owners indicted the mothers for infanticide. By bestializing the mountain slave mother in these ways, the Appalachian master received community legitimation for his structural interference in slave reproduction. By violating the only areas of possible reproductive autonomy enjoyed by the enslaved mother, the mountain master cemented his structural dominance over the slave family.[15]

Mountain masters may not have engaged in direct breeding practices, but they did *commodify* the sexuality of mountain slave women. In an attempt to maximize profits from all levels of slave women's labor, Appalachian masters extended their power over the black woman's body so that they controlled her both as an *asexual labor unit* and as a *reproductive laborer*. Consequently, Appalachian masters externalized to enslaved women unmanageable structural tensions among their different work roles. In their daily lives, mountain slave women juggled the conflicting labor demands associated with market commodity production, subsistence production for their own families, manufacture of goods consumed by their masters' households, and reproduction of the labor force. On the one hand, slave girls reached puberty one to three years earlier than boys because of their high-fat diets. At the same time that girls were undergoing the added physical stress of heavier chores, they were reaching menarche. However, females were probably fed less well due to their lower sales value. Simultaneously, mountain masters shifted teenage girls to harder physical labor and began to pressure them to reproduce. Because of the health risks associated with their conflicting productive and reproductive roles, mountain slave girls were more likely than boys to be underweight, and they experienced a rising mortality rate after fifteen. On the other hand, the duties associated with reproduction and child care did not relieve women from other work. Pregnant women and nursing mothers continued their long hours of evening household production.

In addition, there was a complex relation between annual cycles of crop production, hiring contracts, pregnancies, and deliveries. The agricultural cycle of production and the regimen of annual hires were deeply intertwined with the biological cycle of reproduction. One-third of all pregnancies began in the months after the harvest, so many women faced the final trimester of pregnancy at a time when their labor would be of greatest value in the fields or at hired locations. The woman's advanced stage of pregnancy did not usually release her from much of her normal workload. In short, women gave birth in a strong seasonal pattern during the months of highest labor demand and greatest health risk from lowered food supplies and epidemics. To complicate matters, those newborns needed to be weaned to a controlled feeding schedule in time for the mothers to return to fall harvests. Consequently, conception, pregnancy, birth, and breastfeeding often conflicted with the seasonal cycles of productive labor. That structural tension between *reproductive* and *productive* labor increased the incidence of maternal and infant mortality. That increased child mortality, in turn, kept mountain slave women trapped by their owners in a vicious cycle of early weaning, high child mortality, and high fertility. Perhaps one mistress explained the paradox most aptly. In order to secure his economic "station," she wrote, the slaveholder had to be "master in all things on his plantation, everything, nothing excepted."[16]

Was There an Independent Slave Economy?

Fox-Genovese was conceptually wrong when she argued that slave households "did not provide stable units of production or reproduction" and "were not essential units of income-pooling." In peripheries throughout the capitalist world economy, nonnuclear households, like those of Appalachian slaves, have persisted over long historical periods. Even when members are not all biologically related or may not share a common residence, such composite households aggregate their livelihoods from a variety of strategies. Despite their structural instability and their historical fragility, mountain slave households formed resource pools – material, spiritual, and cultural – upon which people could count for support during crises. Unstable and decomposed kinship units though they were, Appalachian slave households kept alive family histories and myths about the African diaspora, organized day-to-day resistance, nurtured a counter-hegemonic culture, and practiced a liberation theology. Resource pooling provided those households a mechanism for persistence in the wake of inadequate allocations of basic survival needs and frequent family disruptions. Thus, households were *sustenance pooling structures* through which slaves organized self-provisioning, confronted external threats, and ensured the short-term survival and intergenerational reproduction of laborers.[17]

Did household subsistence production generate an *independent slave economy?* Over the last two decades, several scholars have argued that slaves "took control of a large part of their lives, by producing food for themselves and for others, tending cash crops, raising livestock, manufacturing finished goods, marketing their own products, consuming and saving the proceeds." Supposedly, "access to garden plots and foraging and fishing rights provided an essential foundation for economic independence" and opened a window of autonomy that slaves would not otherwise have enjoyed. If I were to follow this recent tendency to describe garden parcels, craft production, and self-hiring strategies as part of an independent economy, I would assign to these subsistence activities a romanticized academic idealization with which Appalachian slaves did not agree. In the attempt to recognize agency, Michael Gomez has cautioned, researchers must be careful "not to over-emphasize the options of the slave, nor to exaggerate her ability to negotiate her life's parameters. For in the end, the land used for subsistence farming, the skills required for moonlighting, and the time to pursue either had to be sanctioned or provided by the slaveholder." That the slaves were enterprising, resilient, and creative is clear; but there is no evidence that their cash-earning or subsistence endeavors gave them autonomy from their owners' regulation. To use an antebellum Appalachian expression, they were "makin' do and gettin' by." They were engaging in *self-exploitation* in order to generate their own survival resources.[18]

Rather than feeling liberated by their subsistence production, mountain slaves recognized the harsh realities of their *super-exploitation*. Like most other Appalachian ex-slaves, William Brown remembered that he was always tired and hungry; he did not state that he felt liberated or empowered by the added labor of household production. "When I began work in the morning," he said, "I could usually see a little red in the east, and I worked till ten before eating: at two I would eat again, and then work ... until ten at night." After working twelve hours for the master, John Day's father worked "till midnight" in the blacksmith shop of his Sequatchie Valley plantation, in order to earn a little cash. On such a day, he would have been lucky to sleep five hours. A middle Tennessee woman responded to the work bell at 4:00 A.M., and she described her life as "hard times. From the time [she] got up until bed-time [she] didn't have no time to eat idle bread." Another middle Tennessee slave recalled that they "didn't have time to study 'bout nothing but work," and he added "stock would be treated better sometimes." According to a northern Alabama slave, they "didn't know nothen but to work," and "the' warn't no good times there." With family subsistence production facing them in the evenings, Anna Lee recalled that they "just generally fell in at the door cause [they] would be so tired when [they] came in at night from [their] days work out in the field." At the end of his work day, "lots of times" John Finnely was "so tired [he] couldn't speak for to stop de mule, [he] jus' have to lean back on de lines." Ruben Woods, Sarah Wilson, Oliver Bell, and Frank Menefee expressed the same sense of blinding, endless labor. Frank knew that "iffen you didn't wuk, dey tended to you." Because the slaveholder "never had no mercy fer nobody," Oliver described enslavement as "skeery times." Physical exhaustion – not economic independence – permeated the life histories of mountain slaves, for days and nights were circumscribed by "jus work, eat and sleep." How could nighttime work for their own families have been anything other than sheer drudgery, punctuated by the powerful recognition that "you couldn't git out o' dat," if there were to be enough food and clothing for the members of your own household? Two mountain slaves provide the most accurate evaluations. Aunt Clussey focused on "de voices of de tired folks a comin' home singing atter de sun done sunk behin' de mountain." In order to subsidize their master's ration shortfalls, however, these families had to exacerbate their fatigue with extended evening hours of family work. "When a slave gets grown," Thomas Cole commented, "he is jest lak a mule, dey works fer der grub and a few clothes and works jest as hard as a mule."[19]

To claim that the added burden of extra evening and weekend work made Appalachian slaves feel "independent," we would have to silence such voices of people who experienced the actual circumstances, and we would, thereby, romanticize their super-exploitation as benign. To overstate the liberating effect of family parcels or cash earning is to ignore the reality that such overwork was necessitated by the capitalist's inhumane profit maximizing. With relatively few exceptions, it was the obligation of the mountain slave household to feed and clothe itself. To accomplish that, black Appalachians were burdened with day labor in the master's enterprises and night work to accumulate the resources upon which household survival hinged. A Caribbean slave family might have been able to amass $300 to $500 from subsistence cultivation and livestock raising, but the typical mountain slave household was lucky to acquire enough extra for a few items of clothing, food, or shoes. Moreover, Appalachian slaves were removed from town markets by considerable distances, and most accumulated only limited reserves of foodstuffs for periods of scarcity. Barickman has observed that slave household production served the economic and management interests of owners.

When and where provision grounds existed, they benefitted chiefly and even exclusively the planters, who freely manipulated the size of the plots and the time allotted to slaves to work in them according to their own interests. To the slaves, access to a plot of land for a garden may have represented not so much a 'right' or a privilege as an additional burden.

Household subsistence production relieved the owner of the expense of providing adequate survival investments in laborers; therefore, slaves were working for their masters on their own time, as well as his.[20]

Even if market exchanges brought to slaves the degree of economic autonomy described by several recent writers, only a minority of North American slave families ever benefited. Less than one-third of the U.S. slave population earned cash or participated in monetary transactions of any kind. In comparison to the Caribbean and other parts of the New World, marketing by slaves was generally more limited in mainland North America. According to Berlin and Morgan:

The vastness of the land, the absence of towns, and – most significantly – the competition of non-slaveholding whites constrained the slaves' ability to trade independently. Only in towns – like the rice ports of the Carolina and Georgia lowcountry or the small riverine villages of the Louisiana sugar country – did mainland North-American slaves create Sunday markets approximating those further south. Instead, the plantation itself became the great entrepot for slave-grown produce on the mainland, with planters buying the slaves' produce for their own use, factoring the slaves' sales and purchases, or establishing stores at which slaves could buy and sell. Beyond the boundaries of the plantation itinerant peddlers – often immigrants – and white store keepers became the most important trading partners for mainland slaves, purchasing their produce and selling them liquor and other contraband goods.

For these reasons, marketing and property accumulation by North American slaves were meager in comparison to other parts of the New World. Caribbean laws mandated one day every two weeks for households to work their own crops. However, American South masters regimented the few leisure hours of slaves by requiring them to use their own time for household production, thereby binding them to the geographical space of the owner's plantations.[21]

Opportunities were even more limited in the Mountain South. In fact, other U.S. slaves earned cash nearly three times more frequently than Appalachian slaves. Even though the vast majority engaged in garden cultivation and household production, less than 12 percent of mountain slaves earned cash or participated in monetary transactions. Caribbean laws may have set aside provision grounds for slaves, but the household production of Appalachian slaves occurred at the mercy and the whim of the owners. The garden parcel and hunting and fishing rights could be withdrawn at any time, and the master could deny permission to go to town, to market goods, or to hire one's evening labor to neighbors. According to Patterson, owners held ultimate control over the slave's *peculium*, which is "the investment by the master of a partial, and temporary, capacity in his slave to possess and enjoy a given range of goods." The *peculium* was always tenuous, for it was a privilege that the owner could withdraw at any time, and the master always reserved a claim on the possessions of the slave. In short, owners recognized their slaves' property accumulation only to the extent those holdings affirmed their own domination. Because the slave never legally owned anything they produced, their economic activities could not be independent from their masters. Masters "proscribed the goods slaves could buy and sell freely, constrained their right to hire their own time and collect overwork and, if given the opportunity, denied slaves the property they had earned on their own, thus enforcing their claim to the slaves' entire being and its product." Rather than making them more economically independent, subsistence production made slaves complicit in their own oppression. To the extent slaves succeeded in feeding themselves and earning a surplus, masters reduced rations and expanded the laborers' work to include the use of their limited leisure hours to produce their own survival resources. In addition, Appalachian plantations, commercial enterprises, and industries held tight rein over the manner in which their slaves disposed of their petty commodities. Most slave households traded their surpluses through transactions with their own masters or employers. Rather than operating independently, mountain slaves depended on white collaboration, and that cooperation could not be taken for granted or relied upon absolutely.[22]

Why Would Owners Risk Slave Investments?

Supporters of the dominant paradigm have assumed that "most masters attempted to sustain, if not enhance, the material well-being of their human property." Mortality and nutritional evidence about the Mountain South calls into question this overused generalization. Appalachian slaves experienced chronic hunger and malnutrition twice as often as other U.S. slaves, and they were much more likely to die than their Lower South counterparts. Moreover, women of childbearing age and children experienced the worst shortfalls in basic needs and the highest mortality risks. The scholarly presumption has been that slaves were "capitalized labors ... whose value declined if their nutritional status was allowed to diminish significantly." However, it has never been established that a malnourished slave had a lower market value. Indeed, Upper South slaves sold in interstate transactions were shorter than slaves born in the Lower South, probably reflecting inadequate nutrition and a higher incidence of nonagricultural occupations. Furthermore, a long-term strategy of investing in the survival needs of slaves was predicated upon the economic stability of the owner. Such a long-term investment strategy would have required a profit margin that was wide enough and consistent enough over several years to permit investments in human property from which there would be little monetary return. However, small plantations – especially those in the Mountain South – experienced numerous financial crises and recessions that forced them to make decisions to meet immediate, short-range cash flow problems.[23]

What was a rational economic decision for a large Lower South plantation would have brought financial disaster to most Appalachian masters. On mountain plantations, cash shortfalls occurred almost annually, and debt crises occurred about every three years. Thus, malnutrition and inadequate provision of basic survival needs were cost-informed decisions and rational, profit-maximizing strategies. Why did mountain slaveholders distribute weekly rations of cornmeal and the fattest cuts of pork while withholding wheat flour, lean pork, and beef? First, Appalachian masters withheld from slave diets those crops that were produced for export. Because Appalachian flour was prized in western Europe, South America, and the West Indies, owners were not willing to allocate these profitable commodities to laborers. By 1860, Appalachian counties were exporting nearly 6.5 million bushels of wheat and 1.2 million barrels of flour. While withholding wheat from slaves, the typical small mountain plantation exported 5.4 barrels of flour every year. Beef and lean pork brought the highest prices at distant cities, so masters profited by omitting these meats from the diet of slaves.[24]

However, there is evidence that Appalachian slaves did not even receive adequate rations of corn and meal, commodities that were not nearly so profitable. By 1860, mountain plantations were processing more than one-third of their corn output to produce meal and whiskey for distant markets. Appalachians were exporting more than 1.6 million barrels of meal, a staple food that provisioned the laborers on plantations in the Lower South, the West Indies, and South America. By 1860, Appalachia exported more than four million gallons of grain alcohol. While providing inadequate corn allocations to its slaves, the typical mountain plantation was exporting to distant markets 8 barrels of meal and 26 gallons of whiskey.[25]

Second, Appalachian slaves competed for food with livestock. Before they were driven to market in the fall, mountain plantations used corn to fatten cattle and hogs. In 1860, Appalachians exported more than a million hogs and nearly half a million cattle. In addition, Appalachian farms were using more than one-fifth of their corn production to feed itinerant drives at commercial livestock stands and drover inns. However, there was another livestock export that drained corn from the food supply of mountain slaves, to an even greater degree than did hogs and cattle. As cotton production expanded throughout the Lower South, the demand and the market prices for work animals rose and remained relatively stable. Between 1840 and 1860, mule and horse exports nearly tripled, and the Mountain South produced more work stock than any other region of the United States. By 1860, Appalachia was sending to the Lower South more than ninety thousand work animals every year, and those work animals were heavily concentrated into large herds owned by slaveholders.[26]

Why would masters risk slave child investments? Until about age ten, youngsters did not produce enough to cover their maintenance costs. Operating on a narrow profit margin, mountain masters rationed survival needs in relation to productivity and in relation to income that could be generated from hire or sale of the slave. Appalachian owners rarely hired slaves before the age of ten, and a slave younger than ten had a market value only one-third of the value of an eighteen-year-old. Improvement in diet and growth spurts coincided with the age at which children entered the labor force and the age at which their market value increased dramatically. After they began to assume adult work roles, slaves experienced "catch-up growth," reflecting higher protein intakes. At age ten, an Appalachian slave child faced only about half the risk of mortality that characterized the first few years of life. In that same time frame, the market value of that child increased 143 percent. By age nineteen, an Appalachian slave was only half as likely to die as a ten year old. Between the ages of ten and nineteen, slave prices more than doubled again. In short, masters increased their distribution of nutrients, clothing, and shoes in relation to labor output and market value of slaves.[27]

We can see the profit-maximization strategy most clearly when we examine slave child malnutrition against the backdrop of production of work animals. While swine and cattle foraged in the woods and mountain meadows for most of their diet, work animals consumed large amounts of grains, peas, pumpkins, and sweet potatoes. In fact, mountain masters allocated three times more corn weekly to a mule than they provided to each slave. These were not irrational economic decisions. By 1840, market prices for young mules and slave children were about the same, or mules were actually more valuable. At ages two and five, mules sold at higher prices than slaves of the same age. Most graziers marketed their animals at age two, but yearlings could be sold without health risk. Cotton planters preferred to purchase young mules that had not been broken to draft because a "coltish demeanor" was "evidence of youth." Mules were at peak demand between October and early December, allowing mountain masters to export them before they incurred expensive winter feeding. In contrast to slave children, mules had an extraordinary immunity to disease, and few foals were stillborn or died from exposure to bad water or ecological hazards.[28]

By age two, the mule was trainable, and it was ready to assume a peak work load by age three. To reach maximum labor output of slave children, owners must feed, shelter, clothe, and discipline them until about age fourteen. It was cheaper to feed a mule than a slave child, for the animal's diet could be supplemented with woodland foraging, pastures, fodder, corn cobs, wheat straw, or rotting vegetables. To feed slave children their daily mush, owners incurred the added expense of processing the corn into meal or hominy. Gross as it seems, slave children on small Appalachian plantations competed with young mules and horses for the calories they needed to grow and survive. If the net upkeep of a slave equaled or exceeded his or her market value, there was little incentive for the owner to practice humane nutrition. As a short-term profit-maximizing strategy, mountain masters allocated more of their scarce corn toward the nurture of export livestock. Appalachian slaves comprehended that they were treated as though they were less valuable than their owners' animals. Except for a few skilled artisans and wagoners, slaves were not permitted to use mules for distant errands. "You couldn' get a horse an' ride. You walk," Fountain Hughes recalled. Robert McFalls thought that western North Carolina masters "fed the animals better" and "didn't half feed" their slaves. Thomas Cole agreed, saying that some Jackson County, Alabama, slaves "didn't have as easier time as de mules, fer de mules was fed good and de slaves laks ter have starved ter death." Human malnutrition was a rational profit-maximizing strategy in another way, for Appalachian masters externalized to slave women and their households many of the costs associated with feeding and maintaining the slave children they owned.[29]

Toward a New Paradigm of the U.S. Slave Family

In his 1989 capstone study, Fogel argued that enslavement was morally reprehensible because owners denied to African-Americans freedom from domination, economic opportunity, citizenship, and cultural self-determination. It is disturbing that Fogel excluded from his moral indictment the forcible removal of kin and masters' disruptions of black households. While I strongly endorse his call for an "effort to construct a new paradigm on the slave family," I would hope to see writers assign greater priority to the human pain of family separations than has occurred over the last three decades. Celebration of resistance and cultural persistence to the exclusion of investigations of those forces that broke families will not advance a new school of thought in directions that are any more accurate and reliable than previous generalizations. As we move toward a new paradigm, we need to follow nine lines of new inquiry.[30]

- We need new research that documents slave family life in institutional arrangements that represent the residential and work circumstances of a majority of African-Americans. That requires directing greater attention to plantations smaller than fifty, to the Upper South and slave-selling areas, and to nonagricultural laborers.
- We need to make realistic assessments of all labor migrations. Adherents to the dominant paradigm have been preoccupied with slave selling and have presumed that permanent separations were not caused by hire-outs, migrations with owners, slave inheritance within the owner's family, and assignment to distant work sites. However, it is clear in the slave narratives that all these forced migrations severed kinship ties, threatened marriages, generated great numbers of female-headed households, and weakened bonds between children and fathers.
- New research needs to reevaluate the strengths and weaknesses of *abroad marriages* because scholars have tended to presume that such relationships were more stable than they actually were. Such arrangements left women to generate the survival needs of their households and to protect children without the daily support of husbands or other adult males. Moreover, masters withdrew family visits so routinely that households could not count on regular reunions of spouses or of parents and children.
- In future approaches, we need to define family disruption more broadly. Marriage breakups are only one indicator. Loss of children occurred much more frequently, breaking ties between parents and offspring and between siblings. Moreover, few African-Americans maintained long-term connections with extended kin.
- Taking into account variations by size of slaveholding, by subregion, and by type of production, we need to reexamine threats to family persistence caused by inadequate nutrition, shortfalls in basic survival needs, and ecological conditions.
- Scholars need to abandon the myth that family stability is measured in terms of the presence of a *nuclear family*. First, such a family construct did not characterize antebellum white households, and it is doubtful that this ideal type has ever typified Americans. Second, stability

characterizes nonnuclear family constructions in many nonwestern societies. Third, the absence of adult males was not a cultural choice because enslaved women were never in a structural position to control household composition without owners' intervention. Fourth, many enslaved women pooled survival resources by relying on support from other females.

- We need to learn from contemporary demographic trends in many poor countries where high infant mortality rates fuel population growth. On a different conceptual plane than has typified earlier discussions, we need to rethink the connection between high slave child mortality and fertility patterns of enslaved women.

- We need to investigate threats to slave families that occurred during the Civil War and the emancipation process. Families were separated, often permanently, by military labor impressments, enlistment of black soldiers, and the removal of kin to contraband camps. There was an increased incidence of Upper South slave selling and owner migrations throughout the war, magnifying the chances that a slave would be permanently separated from kin. Emancipation came slower in the Upper South, particularly in those counties with large numbers of pro-Union slaveholders or low black population densities. After liberation, most ex-slaves remained with former owners two years or longer, continuing to reside in the same cabins they had occupied during enslavement. Reconstruction labor policies worked against family rebuilding and increased the likelihood of new family disruptions (e.g., indenturement of children to former owners).

- Finally, scholars need to take a fresh look at the historical overlap between African and indigenous enslavement. First, the import of Africans did not trigger so abrupt an end to Native American enslavement as historians have claimed. Second, researchers have ignored hardships for ethnically mixed slave families caused by forced removals of indigenous peoples from the U.S. Southeast. Third, there was a higher incidence of Native American heritage among southwestern African-Americans who were more often owned by or interacted frequently with Indians.

While Fogel stresses "the critical importance of quantitative consideration," I argue that integrating the perspective of the affected slaves is even more crucial. Even though the existing paradigm is heavily grounded in cliometrics, demography, and sophisticated economic projections, it has still failed to capture the diversity of slave family life on different sized plantations and in different sections of the American South. What we need in the future are approaches that triangulate quantitative analyses with slave accounts to draw comparisons between subregions of the American South, between different parts of the world, and between large and small plantations. The best rationale for a new paradigm can be heard in the painful voices of African-Americans. Elderly ex-slaves mourned the loss of parents, spouses, children, siblings, and grandparents. Even when they had been separated from kin at very early ages, they sensed that a significant element of their souls had been wrenched from them. A mountain slave says it best: "We never met again. . . . That parting I can never forget." In the minds of black Appalachians, poverty, illiteracy, and racial inequality were not the worst legacies of enslavement. Bad as those structural factors were, it was the forced removals of family that broke their hearts and generated a community wound that was not healed by liberation. Moreover, half the Appalachian ex-slaves carried into the twentieth century the structural impacts of past diasporas, exacerbated by new family separations borne of a chaotic war and an inhumane emancipation process.[31]

Notes

These locator codes are used to refer to the collections of slave narratives. See the bibliography for complete citations. Each locator code is followed by volume number and page numbers. For example, *Slave* 6 (a): 382 should be read *Slave*, vol. 6, part a, p. 382.

CWVQ	*The Tennessee Civil War Veterans Questionnaires*
Fisk	Eqypt, Masuoka, and Johnson, "Unwritten History of Slavery," Fisk University Archives
Great Slave Narratives	Bontemps, *Great Slave Narratives*
Slave	Rawick, *The American Slave*
Slave I	Rawick, *The American Slave: Supplement I*
Slave II	Rawick, *The American Slave: Supplement II*
Slavery Time	Killion and Waller, *Slavery Time*
Slave Testimony	Blassingame, *Slave Testimony*
website	http://scholar.lib.vt.edu/vtpubs/mountain_slavery/index.htm
Weevils	Perdue, Barden, and Phillips, *Weevils in the Wheat*

INTRODUCTION

1. Opening quote is from *Slave I*, 1: 151. UK, "Slave Narratives, Notes and Data," p. 11, J. Winston Coleman Papers. *Slave I*, 12: 335, 257. *Slave*, 2 (a): 23. *Weevils*, pp. 159–60.
2. Fogel and Engerman, *Time*, vol. 1, pp. 49–51. Fogel, *Without Consent*, pp. 69, 142–50, 181–82. Gutman, *Black Family*, pp. 11–28, 164, 304–05, 602–03. *Families and Freedom*, pp. 7–9.
3. Fogel and Engerman, *Time*, vol. 1, p. 132, claimed that only one of every ten U.S. slaves was a mulatto. Fogel, *Without Consent*, pp. 55, 125, 147–49. Steckel, "Peculiar Population," 738–39.
4. Gutman, *Black Family*, p. 102. Fogel, *Without Consent*, pp. 178–82. *History*, vol. 1, pp. 530–31. Genovese, *Roll*, p. 7. Steckel, "Slave Mortality," p. 91.
5. Patterson, *Slavery*, p. 206. Crawford, "Quantified Memory," pp. 149–55. Crawford, "Slave Family," pp. 336–37. Berlin and Morgan, *Cultivation*, p. 21. Steckel, "Peculiar Population," 738–39.
6. Patterson, *Slavery*, pp. 164–65. Brazil, Cuba, Puerto Rico, and the Dutch colonies were the only other New World nations that did not abolish slavery

before 1860; see Fogel, *Without Consent*, pp. 65, 270. Watkin, *King Cotton*, p. 195. Dew, *Review*. Wickliffe, "Speech," p. 14. Analysis of state and national totals, U.S. Census Office, *Population of the U.S. in 1860*. Tadman, *Speculators*, pp. 19–20. Sutch, "Breeding," pp. 174–75.

7. Tadman, *Speculators*, pp. 45, 5, 70, 122. Gutman, *Black Family*, p. 151. Stevenson, *Life*, pp. 112–18. Wallerstein, "American Slavery," p. 1209. Genovese, *Roll*, p. 5. Sutch, "Breeding," p. 198, Table 2.

8. Patterson, *Rituals*, p. 29; he cites Kolchin, "Reevaluating," p. 581 and Parish, *Slavery*, p. 76. Kolchin, *American Slavery*, pp. 137–38. Berlin and Morgan, *Cultivation*, pp. 76–79.

9. *Families and Freedom*, pp. 7–9. For the WPA collection as a whole, 51 percent of the ex-slaves reported family breakups; see Crawford, "Slave Family," p. 333. Berlin and Morgan, *Slaves' Economy*, pp. 1–21. In a previous book, I analyzed resistance and countercultural activities among mountain slaves; see Dunaway, *Slavery*, Chs. 6 and 7.

10. Genovese, *Roll*, p. 7. Crawford, "Quantified Memory."

11. Wallerstein, *Modern World-System II*, pp. 167, 233–34. Dunaway, *First American Frontier*, pp. 11–12.

12. Dunaway, *First American Frontier*, pp. 196–97. Regarding other peripheries, see Wallerstein, *Modern World-System III*.

13. Dunaway, *First American Frontier*, pp. 196–97.

14. One of every 2.8 ridge-valley laborers was enslaved. Dunaway, *First American Frontier*, pp. 87–122. Phillips, "Incorporation," p. 802. Table 1.3, website.

15. For conceptualization of a *slave society*, see Berlin, *Many Thousands*, pp. 8–10. Findings about mountain slavery are derived from Dunaway, *Slavery*. Regarding Civil War trends, see McKinney, *Southern Mountain*, pp. 70–71. For Southern trends, see Wilson and Ferris, *Encyclopedia*, p. 21; Anderson, *Race and Politics*, p. 25.

16. Dunaway, *Slavery*.

17. Fogel, *Without Consent*, p. 193.

18. Berlin, *Many Thousands*, p. 107.

19. For extensive discussion about the debates over regional definition, see Dunaway, "Incorporation," pp. 989–91. For explanation of Appalachian terrain types, see Appalachian Regional Commission, *Appalachia*, pp. 17–28. Regarding terrain as precluding slavery, see Gray, *History*, vol. 1, pp. 308–10.

20. No other scholar has collected or analyzed an antebellum Appalachian statistical data set as massive or as chronologically extensive as mine. I have previously published the only region-wide economic history of antebellum Southern Appalachia that exists to date; see Dunaway, *First American Frontier*. In response to an inquiry from an Appalachian scholar, I counted the number of citations I selected from planters. There are fifteen for Thomas Jefferson and twenty-three from other planters. In contrast, there are ninety-six for small and middling slaveholders.

21. Berlin, *Many Thousands*, p. 97. McKinney, *Southern Mountain*, pp. 53–62.

22. For details, see "Methodological Issues," website. Trouillot, *Silencing*, pp. 149, 153, 26. Published sources of slave narratives are *Slave*, *Slave I*, *Slave II*, and *CWVQ*. The Fisk collection is archived as FUA, Egypt, Masuoka, and Johnson, "Unwritten History of Slavery." The Kentucky collection is archived

as UK, "Slave Narratives, Notes and Data," Typescripts, J. Winston Coleman Papers. A detailed discussion and the list of Appalachian slave narratives is available at the website.

23. Yetman, "Background," pp. 534–35. Woodward, "History," p. 472. Narratives were located for Appalachian counties of Alabama (32), Georgia (45), Kentucky (26), Maryland (13), North Carolina (13), South Carolina (2), Tennessee (57), Virginia (80), and West Virginia (25).

24. Fisk, p. 143. Trouillot, *Silencing*, pp. 26, 29, 49. Woodward, "History," p. 475.

CHAPTER 1

1. Opening quote is from UK, Amelia Jones narrative, J. Winston Coleman Papers. Wallerstein, *Modern World-System III*, p. 167. Potts, *World Labour*, Chs. 1 and 2. Fogel, *Without Consent*, pp. 63–65, 70. Patterson, *Slavery*, pp. 164–65. Watkin, *King Cotton*, p. 195. Dew, *Review*. Wickliffe, "Speech," p. 14. Analysis of state and national totals, U.S. Census Office, *Population of the U.S. in 1860*. Tadman, *Speculators*, pp. 19–20. Sutch, "Breeding," pp. 174–75.

2. Table 5.1, website. Tadman, *Speculators*, pp. 19–20. Sutch, "Breeding," pp. 174–75. During this same period, the rest of Southern Appalachia grew in population by little more than 54 percent. Analysis of aggregated county totals in U.S. Census Office, *Compendium* and U.S. Census Office, *Population of the U.S. in 1860*.

3. Table 5.2, website. The Upper South counties of the Mountain South were the Appalachian counties of Kentucky, Maryland, North Carolina, Tennessee, Virginia, and West Virginia. The Lower South counties of the Mountain South were the Appalachian counties of Alabama, Georgia, and South Carolina.

4. Tables 5.3 and 5.4, website. Regarding agricultural and extractive exports to the Lower South, see Dunaway, *First American Frontier*, pp. 225–48. Collins, *Domestic Slave Trade*, pp. 39, 50, 62, estimated that 40 percent of all slaves transferred between states were moved by traders. Fogel and Engerman, *Time*, p. 79, claimed that "only 16 percent of the interregional movement of slaves took place through market trading." Tadman, *Speculators*, p. 45n. Between 1840 and 1860, 502,500 slaves were transferred between regions; see Evans, "Some Economic Aspects," p. 333.

5. Table 5.5, website. Tadman, *Speculators*, pp. 45, 5; p. 7, provides a map showing that northern Alabama and northern Georgia were importing slaves. Stevenson, *Life*, p. 399n. Sweig, "Northern Virginia," p. 259. Dunaway, *First American Frontier*, pp. 71–73.

6. Dunaway, *First American Frontier*, pp. 208–14, 305–07. Rose, *Documentary History*, p. 341.

7. Ambler, *History*, p. 212. Morgan, *Emancipation*, p. 36. Turner, "Railroad," p. 242. *Slave II*, 9: 3639, 12: 136. Illustration 5.1, website.

8. For a description of a Richmond slave yard by an Appalachian slave sold there, see Hughes, *Thirty Years*, pp. 7–12. *Slave*, 11 (a): 167. DPL, letter dated 17 December 1821, Thomas Lenoir Papers.

9. *Slave*, 6: 9, 16: 67. Conner, "Slave Market," pp. 49–58. Wickliffe, "Speech," p. 14. Coleman, "Lexington's Slave Dealers," pp. 19–20. Shillitoe, "Journal," p. 461. *Slave*, 6:9. Illustration 5.2, website.

10. Table 5.6, website. Phifer, "Slavery," pp. 153–54. Inscoe, *Mountain Masters*, p. 84. Bancroft, *Slave Trading*, pp. 115–17. SHC, letter dated 15 December 1859, James Gwyn Papers. SHC, letter dated 9 December 1842, Thomas George Walton Papers. Betts, *Jefferson's Farm Book*, p. 13.

11. Policies and rates for slave insurance, UVSC, Lynchburg Hose and Fire Company in McCue Family Papers. For discussion of trading hubs to which Appalachians exported commodities, see Dunaway, *First American Frontier*, pp. 195–224.

12. Tadman, *Speculators*, p. 49. Stampp, *Peculiar Institution*, p. 216. VS, Slaves Condemned, Executed, and transported, 1783–1865, Virginia. HPL, Ellen Afto Manuscript.

13. *Virginia Northwestern Gazette*, 15 August 1818. *New Orleans Picayune*, 4 January 1860. Bancroft, *Slave Trading*, pp. 25–26n. *Slave*, 7 (a): 213. Stephenson, *Isaac Franklin*, pp. 26–27, 44–50, 103–09, 223. St. Abdy, *Journal*, 2: 209–10.

14. *Cumberland Advocate*, 28 October 1826. *Maryland Journal and True American*, 14 February 1832, 8 January 1833. Illustration 5.3, website.

15. *American State Papers: Indian Affairs*, vol. 2, p. 651. *Winchester Republican*, 23 June and 18 August 1826. *Monongalia Farmer*, 15 February 1834. UK, "Slave Interviews," p. 24, and typed working notes, J. Winston Coleman Papers. *Slave I*, 11: 20, 5 (b): 321–22, 12: 257. Dunn, *Abolitionist*, pp. 195, 199, 211. Illustration 5.4, website.

16. WV, letter dated 17 December 1846, George W. and Lewis Summers Papers. UVSC, letter dated 6 June 1837, Walker Family Papers. UVSC, letter dated 22 April 1833, Wallace Family Papers. UVSC, letter dated 18 January 1850, Rives Family Papers. UVSC, letter dated 30 June (no year), Blackwell Family Papers.

17. *Slave II*, 9: 3872, 3: 800.

18. *Slave I*, 7: 690–91. *Slave*, 14 (a): 354–55.

19. Tables 5.6 and 5.7, website. Slave trading entries were found in the following Appalachian attorney records and correspondence: UT, O. P. Temple Papers; UVSC, Callohill Mennis Papers; WV, 1800–20 records of James Wilson in Wilson-Stribling Families Papers; WV, Lewis Maxwell Papers; WV, George W. and Lewis Summers Papers; WV, David Goff Papers; WV, L. J. Forman Papers; WV, Andrew Nelson Campbell Papers; WV, Lewis Bennett Papers; WV, John Bassel Papers. See, for example, several entries in FC, Mason County, Kentucky, Account Book.

20. Stevenson, *Life*, p. 178. DPL, Diary and Accounts, 1839–41, William Holland Thomas Papers. *Slave I*, 12: 257. SHC, letter dated 5 June 1838, Hamilton Brown Papers. DPL, F. L. Whitehead and N. Loftuss Accounts of Slave Trading and UVSC, letters dated 14 March 1837 and 15 May 1839, Floyd L. Whitehead Papers.

21. SHC, letters dated 7 May 1845, 4 and 12 February 1846, 14 December 1846, 18 and 19 August 1849, 12 May 1858, 18 August 1859, 25 January

1863, 2 June 1859, 11 June 1859, 4 July 1859, 10 October 1857, James Gwyn Papers.

22. UVSC, letter dated 8 February 1858, McCue Family Papers. *Maysville Eagle*, 6 November 1849. WV, 1844 letter (date illegible), Wilson-Lewis Family Papers.

23. The phrase "the abominable traffic" is from Wickliffe, "Speech," p. 14. Stroud, *Sketch of Laws*, pp. 108, 167, 219, 232. Govan and Livingood, *Chattanooga*, p. 147. *Calendar of Virginia State Papers*, 8: 255. Trowbridge, *Desolate South*, p. 125. *Chattanooga Gazette*, 16 February 1849. *Chattanooga Advertiser*, 8 January 1857. *Daily National Intelligencer* (Washington, D.C.), 7 November 1836, 21 October 1837. *Lexington Gazette* (Virginia), 2 and 9 August 1860. Dew, *Bond of Iron*, p. 279. *Raleigh News and Observer*, 26 July 1925. DPL, many letters between 1835 and 1845, Tyre Glen Papers. SHC, letters dated 9 June 1862, 25 June 1862, 30 January 1863, 5 April 1863, Calvin J. Cowles Papers. SHC, letter dated 2 March 1835, Hamilton Brown Papers. Seals, *History*, p. 58.

24. Veney, *Narrative*, p. 27. *Huntsville Democrat*, 30 December 1835, 14 April 1841. Fisk, p. 166. *Slave*, 7: 141. UK, "Slave Interviews," J. Winston Coleman Papers, p. 34. Hamilton, "Minutes," p. 36. "Letters of B. Hawkins," pp. 242, 313.

25. *Slave I*, 8: 128.

26. SHC, letters dated 18 November 1835, 20 December 1836, 13 September 1837, Hamilton Brown Papers. SHC, letter dated 29 December 1845, James Gwyn Papers.

27. Pease, "Great Kanawha, " p. 198. *Staunton Spectator*, 3 February 1858. *Slave*, 11 (a): 47, 16 (a): 2, 13 (a): 118. SHC, entry dated 14 August 1851, James Gwyn Diary, p. 271, James Gwyn Papers. *Slave I*, 5: 461, 10: 2175, 12 (a): 196, 9: 1419–20. *Slave II*, 1: 68. NA, Records of Cherokee Agency, 29 July 1805, 18 August 1805.

28. *Alexandria Gazette and Daily Advertiser*, 8 August 1818. Pease, "Great Kanawha," p. 198. UK, Eaves narrative, J. Winston Coleman Papers. Coleman, *Slavery Times*, p. 211. *Western Citizen*, 30 April and 3 May 1848. *Asheboro Southern Citizen and Man of Business*, 6 May and 3 June 1837. Franklin, *Free Negro*, p. 54. *Slave Life in Georgia*, pp. 49–50.

29. Tadman, *Speculators*, ch. 3. Ingraham, *Southwest*, vol. 2, p. 238. Weld, *American Slavery*, pp. 76, 69–70. WV, letter dated July 1836, Wilson-Lewis Family Papers. Andrews, *Slavery*, pp. 140, 142–43, 148. *Kanawha Register*, 5 February 1830.

30. Hale, *Early History*, p. 44. Featherstonhough, *Excursion*, vol. 1, pp. 169. Illustration 5.5, website.

31. Tables 5.8 and 5.15, website. About 10 percent of all Upper South slaves through age twenty-nine, 5 percent of those in their thirties, and 2 percent of those older than thirty-nine were traded locally each year. See Tadman, *Speculators*, p. 45.

32. UVSC, "Negro Book, 1858–1862," Nelson County Business Ledgers. UVSC, Callohill Mennis Papers, 1830–50. WV, letter dated 17 December 1846, George W. and Lewis Summers Papers. UT, letters dated 11 July

1858, 11 February 1859, 30 April 1860, 17 October 1859 in O. P. Temple Papers.

33. See, for example, 1846 bill of sale for a young boy sold at auction for $500; the document is signed by Asa Holland, Sheriff, UVSC, Holland Family Papers. *Weevils*, p. 60. *Alexandria Gazette and Virginia Advertiser*, 10 January 1858. These two towns advertised frequent auctions in regional newspapers. See Warrenton's *Palladium of Liberty*, 15 January 1819. *Winchester Republican*, 23 June and 18 August 1826. *National Intelligencer*, 2 July 1833. *Alexandria Gazette and Virginia Advertiser*, 6 January 1858.

34. Rose, *Documentary History*, p. 341. *Chattanooga Advertiser*, 8 January 1857. *Rome Southerner and Advertiser*, 26 August 1860. Featherstonhough, *Excursion*, vol. 1, pp. 36–37. *Slave I*, 7: 688, 12: 335–36.

35. *East Tennessean*, 7 March 1840. *Kentucky Gazette*, 27 September 1788. UK, "Slave Interviews, Notes and Data on Kentucky Slavery," J. Winston Coleman Papers. *Slave II*, 9: 3880. Tilley, "Journal," p. 500. Beeman, "Trade," p. 187. Lambert, *Undying Past*, p. 64. Hoskins, *Anderson County*, p. 37. Seals, *History*, p. 58. SHC, letter dated 9 November 1848, Thomas George Walton Papers.

36. For the national average, see Fogel and Engerman, *Time*, vol. 1, p. 56. Table 5.9, website. For example, UVSC, lists of slaves for hire, 1856–60, Folly Farms Papers; UVSC, 1802–22 hirings in Edmund Bacon Memoranda Book; UVSC, 1803 rental of wagon driver, Page-Walker Family Papers; UVSC, 1848–57 documents detailing slave hiring by A. T. M. Rust, Rust Family Papers; UVSC, 1831 estate account of Lawrence Washington, Virginia Letters Collection; UVSC, 1796–1826 documents itemizing slave hires in Gen. Joel Leftwich Papers; UVSC, many examples in James McDowell Family Papers; UVSC, several letters dated between 1830 and 1839, Byers Family Papers; UVSC, 1787 promissory note and 23 December 1835 letter, John Hook and Bowker Preston Papers; UVSC, slave hired to Fauquier resort, Keith Family Papers; UVSC, letter dated 5 December 1863, William D. Cabell Papers; DPL, 22 March 1844 letters, Francis Thomas Anderson Papers; UT, many entries in O. P. Temple Papers; WV, 1800–20 records of James Wilson in Wilson-Stribling Families Papers; WV, several entries in Lewis Maxwell Papers, George W. and Lewis Summers Papers, David Goff Papers, L. J. Forman Papers, Andrew Nelson Campbell Papers, Lewis Bennett Papers, John Bassel Papers, McNeill Family Papers; and WV, 1810–21 entries in William Sommerville Papers. The narratives of twenty-eight Appalachian slaves appear in Still, *Underground Railroad*; seven of them reported they had been hired out. Analysis of NA, 1860 manuscript Slave Schedules, McMinn County, Tennessee, and Loudon County, Virginia. Hire-outs were not systematically enumerated in the census manuscripts for any other Appalachian counties.

37. Bancroft, *Slave Trading*, pp. 147–48. For example, an eastern Tennessee attorney collected commissions for arranging slave hires; see UT, letters dated 14 June 1856, 6 September 1856, 17 October 1859 in O. P. Temple Papers. SHC, letters dated 29 December 1845, 20 December 1845, 29 December 1845, James Gwyn Papers. UVSC, Negro Book, 1858–62, Nelson County

Business Ledgers. See also WV, 1810–21 entries in William Sommerville Papers. *Slave*, 10 (a): 192. *Virginia Free Press* (Charleston, WV), 10 December 1840.

38. UK, letter dated 1 November 1860, Hunt-Morgan Family Papers. DPL, letter dated 3 November 1853, William Weaver Papers. UVSC, letter dated 29 December 1855, Weaver-Brady Iron works and Grist Mill Papers. VS, letter dated 15 December 1848, Tredegar Letterbook. *Louisville Daily Democrat*, 20 December 1855. *Richmond Whig*, 24 December 1841. *Richmond Enquirer*, 18 January 1855. SHC, letters dated 22 January 1839, 15 December 1841, Hamilton Brown Papers.

39. *Winchester Virginian*, 20 December 1838; also a page of slave-hiring ads in that issue. *Lynchburg Virginian*, 13 December 1838. NC, entries dated 1 July 1855, 1 July 1861, Account Book, David L. Swain Papers. SHC, letters dated 15 November 1853, 26 December 1862, Hamilton Brown Papers.

40. Table 5.10, website. Tadman, *Speculators*, p. 112. Analysis of Appalachian slave narratives. Fogel, *Without Consent*, pp. 54–56. Twelve of twenty-eight Appalachian narratives in Still, *Underground Railroad*, report that slaves ran away to circumvent impending sales. *Slave*, 4: 92, 74. *Slave I*, 3: 94. *Slave II*, 9: 3872.

41. Table 5.11, website. Tadman, *Speculators*, pp. 113, 129. *Slave I*, 14: 79. Chambers, *Things*, pp. 273–74.

42. *Slave*, 16: 77, 8 (a): 105. *Slave II*, 3: 791. UVSC, letter dated 2 August 1859, Weaver-Brady Iron Works and Grist Mill Papers. WV, letter dated 8 January 1835, George W. and Lewis Summers Papers. SHC, letter dated 9 February 1865, Calvin J. Cowles Papers. Dew, *Bond of Iron*, pp. 134–35. SHC, letters dated 12 December 1864 and 9 February 1863, Lenoir Family Papers. WV, letter dated 14 November 1855, Andrew Nelson Campbell Family Papers.

43. SHC, letter dated 6 February 1859, Thomas George Walton Papers. Dew, *Bond of Iron*, pp. 253–56, 279–80. *Abingdon Democrat*, 20 February 1857. SHC, letter dated 8 December 1864, Jones and Patterson Family Papers. *Slave*, 16 (b): 13. Betts, *Jefferson's Farm Book*, p. 19.

44. *Lexington Observer and Reporter*, 18 October 1845. Clay, *Memoirs*, vol. 1, p. 559. *The Liberator* (Richmond, Kentucky), 2 May 1845.

45. SHC, letter dated 2 March 1835, Hamilton Brown Papers. DPL, letter dated 11 March 1864, Alfred W. Bell Papers.

46. SHC, letter dated 10 June 1856, James Gwyn Papers. Betts, *Jefferson's Farm Book*, pp. 31–32.

47. For an extensive analysis of these practices, see Savitt, "Use," pp. 331–48. *Richmond Enquirer*, 8 May 1860. *Lexington Observer and Reporter*, 20 November 1847. *Charleston Mercury*, 12 October 1838. Savitt, "Use," pp. 337. *Milledgeville Statesman and Patriot*, 16 August 1828. *Richmond Daily Dispatch*, 21 July 1854. Martineau, *Retrospect*, vol. 1, p. 140.

48. WV, estate appraisement of John Fairfax, Ralph Fairfax Records. *Huntsville Democrat*, 16 August 1825. *Montgomery Advertiser*, 28 December 1853. *Slave II*, 5: 1866. Coombs, *America Visited*, p. 234.

49. UVSC, indenture dated 29 October 1847, Holland Family Papers. WV, letter dated 23 August 1836, Wilson-Lewis Family Papers. UVSC, 1796–1826

entries, Gen. Joel Leftwich Papers. VHS, John Dawson Letters, 1788–94. UVSC, Several 1827–28 letters from Sidney Reese in Lewis, Anderson, and Marks Family Papers. "Letters of A. D. Kelly," p. 30. Entry of 16 May 1792 in Hendrix, *Pendleton County. Tennessee Gazette*, 13 April 1803. *Weevils*, p. 161.

50. Ford, *Writings*, vol. 4. pp. 416–17. Betts, *Jefferson's Farm Book*, pp. 12–14. UVSC, letter dated 4 December 1791, Thomas Jefferson Papers. Ellis, "Jefferson's Cop-out," p. 49. To estimate how frequently Jefferson sold slaves, I scrutinized all 1787–1820 entries in the University of Virginia Library, "Calendar of Thomas Jefferson Papers," an inventory that permits easy identification of entries reporting slaves sales.

51. VHS, letters dated July, 1847, 20 November 1847, 1 December 1847, 2 March 1848, William Macon Waller Papers.

52. SHC, letters dated 22 July 1833 and 20 January 1834, Hamilton Brown Papers. DPL, William Holland Thomas Diary, 17 August 1858, William Holland Thomas Papers. SHC, letters dated 4 July 1842, 20 March 1848, Thomas George Walton Papers. "Letters of A. D. Kelly," pp. 27–33. *Slave I*, 7: 687–88.

53. Table 5.12, website. Regarding agricultural output, see Dunaway, *First American Frontier*, 131–42.

54. Tables 5.13 and 5.4, website. SHC, letter dated 10 May 1859, James Gwyn Papers. Wallerstein, *Modern World-System III*, p. 166.

55. Dunaway, *First American Frontier*, pp. 79, 290. Fogel and Engerman, *Time*, vol. 1, p. 56, claimed that 7.5 percent of Lower South slaves were hired out annually. Appalachian owners frequently commented in letters about the long-range "investment value" of slaves and included slaves as part of the marriage dowries of their daughters. Tadman, *Speculators*, p. 117.

56. Betts, *Jefferson's Farm Book*, pp. 161–62. Rose, *Documentary History*, p. 204–05. UT, Caswell Diary, 31 December 1856. WV, letter dated 18 November 1840, Wilson-Lewis Family Papers.

57. Table 5.14, website. For conventional view, see Blackmun, *Western North Carolina*, vol. 1, p. 132.

58. Table 5.15, website. Stealey, "Salt Industry," pp. 234–45. Fogel, *Without Consent*, pp. 64, 69. Dunaway, *First American Frontier*, pp. 287–322.

59. Phillips, *American Negro Slavery*, pp. 373–75. NC, letter dated 3 January 1842, David L. Swain Papers. SHC, letter dated 5 September 1844, Lenoir Family Papers. Olmsted, *Back Country*, p. 253. Fogel and Engerman, *Time*, vol. 1, p. 54.

60. Tables 5.16 and 5.17, website. For Southern trends, see Fogel and Engerman, *Time*, vol. 1, p. 48.

61. For detail about Appalachia's antebellum industrial and manufacturing development, see Dunaway, *First American Frontier*, pp. 157–94.

CHAPTER 2

1. Opening quote is from *Slave I*, 12: 335. Cather, *Sapphira*, p. 7. Inscoe, *Mountain Masters*, p. 90. SHC, letters dated 28 January 1854, 1 March 1854, Hamilton Brown Papers. *Monongalia Farmer*, 9 August 1834.

2. SHC, James Hervey Greenlee Diary, pp. 157–58.
3. Randolph, *Cabin and Parlor*, p. 31. Patterson, *Slavery*, p. 208. Betts, *Jefferson's Farm Book*, p. 21. Inscoe, *Mountain Masters*, p. 90.
4. Wallerstein, *Historical Capitalism*, p. 102. "Address of James Barbour" is an 1825 presidential address to the Agricultural Society of Albermarle County, Virginia. McDonald, *Woman's Civil War*, p. 247. *Slave*, 10 (a): 192.
5. DPL, letters dated 20 February 1836, 30 December 1839, John Warfield Johnston Collection. DPL, letter dated 22 January 1842, Bedinger-Dandridge Letters. UVSC, letter dated 17 February 1819, Graham Family Papers. SHC, letter dated 9 January 1819, Lenoir Family Papers. SHC, Lucilla Gamble McCorkle Diary, 17 December 1846. Eastman, *Aunt Phillis's Cabin*, pp. 213–15. Van Evrie, *Negroes*, pp. 230–32, 242–43. UVVS, Memoir of Alansa Rounds Sterret, p. 3.
6. Table 7.1, website. Crawford, "Slave Family," p. 346. Fogel, *Without Consent*, p. 179. Fogel, *Without Consent*, p. 183. For examples, see *Slave*, 1: 425; *Slave I*, 3: 96; *Slave II*, 1: 115; *Slave Testimony*, p. 738; *Great Slave Narratives*, p. 207; *Slavery Time*, p. 100; *Weevils*, pp. 165–66, 264–65; Veney, *Narrative*, p. 10; Fisk, pp. 2, 54–55, 116, 141, 156, 205, 238; Drew, *North-side View*, pp. 45, 281; Hughes, *Thirty Years*, pp. 6–12.
7. Gutman, *Black Family*, p. 153. Estimates of the proportion of slave sales that caused spouse separations range from 13 percent to 23 percent; see Fogel and Engerman, *Time*, vol. 1: 48–52; Tadman, *Speculators*, p. 300; Gutman, *Black Family*, pp. 141–52. Frazier, "Slave Family," p. 236. Marriage breakup estimates were derived from analysis of 171 incidents in the Appalachian slave narratives. For example, see UVSC, letter dated 5 January 1822 in Carr Family Papers. Illustration 7.1, website.
8. Table 7.1, website. UVSC, letter dated 18 September 1863, William Cabell Papers. UK, "Slave Interviews," J. Winston Coleman Papers, p. 38. Fogel and Engerman, *Time*, vol. 1, p. 49. *Slave II*, 5: 1791, 1: 94, 3: 671. For family separations due to migrations, see *Slave*, 12: 239, 7: 138, 4 (a): 274, 13: 127; *Slavery Time*, p. 100; *Great Slave Narratives*, p. 207; Veney, *Narrative*, p. 10. SHC, letter dated 26 January 1853, Hamilton Brown Papers.
9. Table 5.6, website. UVSC, letter dated 5 January 1822, Carr Family Papers. Weld, *American Slavery*, p. 179. See also p. 52 for separation of an Augusta, Virginia, slave family. *Slave*, 10 (b): 222. *Slave II*, 6: 2273. UVSC, letter dated 10 November 1847, Wright Family Papers.
10. *Slave I*, 5: 298. DPL, letter dated 27 June 1859, William Weaver Papers. McDonald, *Woman's Civil War*, pp. 82–84.
11. SHC, letter dated 4 November 1847, Lenoir Family Papers. NC, letter dated 21 August 1843, David L. Swain Papers. Fisk, p. 141. *Slave II*, 9: 3639. Rose, *Documentary History*, p. 151. Illustration 7.2, website.
12. Table 7.1, website, and Dunaway, *Slavery*, Ch. 5. Patterson, *Slavery*, pp. 337–38. Tadman, *Speculators*, p. 217. Van Evrie, *Negroes*, pp. 230–32, 242–43. *Slave I*, 12: 335, 257. *Weevils*, p. 277.
13. Table 7.1, website. Censer, *North Carolina Planters*, p. 140. SHC, will dated 4 April 1842, Thomas George Walton Papers. "Letters of A. D. Kelly," p. 29. *Slave*, 10 (a): 41. Ellis, "Jefferson's Cop-out," p. 53. *Slave*, 13 (a): 268. Brabson, *John Brabson*, 22–23. *Slave II*, 3: 803–04.

14. Letter n.d. 1859, Letters. SHC, wills dated 3 February 1812, 20 February 1829, Hamilton Brown Papers. *Slave,* 11 (b): 148. UVVS, Robert Christian Will, 16 December 1858. UVVS, Mary M. Burton Will, 20 August 1859. UVVS, Mary G. Calhoon Will, 24 October 1859.

15. Gutman, *Black Family,* p. 131. *Slave,* 10 (a): 42. SHC, James Hervey Greenlee Diary, vol. 1, p. 185.

16. DPL, letter dated 29 November 1859, William Weaver Papers. *Slave II,* 6: 2282–83. *Slave I,* 12: 329.

17. Fisk, p. 4. *Slave,* 2 (a): 39. UVSC, letter dated 20 April 1807, Thomas Jefferson Papers. *Lexington Gazette* (Virginia), 6 February 1851. Bancroft, *Slave Trading,* pp. 215–16.

18. Table 7.1, website. Lewis, *Coal,* p. 163. *Slave,* 3 (a): 34. *Slave II,* 4: 1098. Rose, *Documentary History,* pp. 329–30.

19. Crawford, "Slave Family," pp. 333–34. Fogel, *Without Consent,* p. 150. Gutman, *Black Family,* pp. 9–21. Tadman, *Speculators,* pp. 211–12.

20. Table 7.2, website. Analysis of Lewis, *Coal,* p. 166. Gutman, *Black Family,* pp. 9–15.

21. Table 7.3, website. Fauve-Chamoux, "Household Forms," pp. 135–56. Little, "Ethnicity," pp. 289–302. Robles and Watkins, "Immigration," pp. 191–212. Stevenson, *Life,* p. 222 . Fox-Genovese, *Plantation Household,* p. 374. *Slave II,* 3: 669. Only 6.5 percent of the Appalachian ex-slaves saw their fathers as the authority figure. Slave child discipline estimated using ninety-three incidents from the Appalachian slave narratives; findings total more than 100 percent since several respondents described more than one disciplinary action.

22. *Pennsylvania Freedmen's Bulletin,* March 1867, pp. 15–16. Patterns of maternal residence were dervied from analysis of Appalachian slave narratives. *Slave II,* 3: 672. Stevenson, *Life,* p. 179. Fox-Genovese, *Plantation Household,* p. 49.

23. Elkins, *Slavery,* pp. 49–50. Andrews, *Slavery,* p. 102. MC, letter dated 7 January 1856, Jordan and Davis Papers. *Slave,* 12: 238.

24. *Slave,* 19 (a): 42. *Slave II,* 9: 3878. Fisk, p. 94. *Slave I,* 4: 658.

25. Table 7.3, website. UK, Carl Hall interview, J. Winston Coleman Papers. *Slave I,* 7: 689.

26. Betts, *Jefferson's Farm Book,* 26 March 1792. Russell, *Free Negro,* p. 131. Stampp, *Peculiar Institution,* pp. 96–97. McKivigan, *Roving Editor,* p. 207. Catterall, *Judicial Cases,* vol. 4, p. 63; vol. 2, p. 502. *Staunton Spectator,* 2 December 1857, 23 August 1859.

27. Dunaway, *First American Frontier,* pp. 287–322. *Weevils,* p. 276. *Slave II,* 3: 669. Perusal of numerous slave inventories in family records of Appalachian slaveholders. *Slave,* 7: 138, 10 (b): 128, 10 (a): 40, 100, 10 (b): 128. *Slave I,* 1: 144, 3: 94.

28. *Slave,* 7: 138, 108, 12: 136. *Slave II,* 3: 914.

29. Fogel and Engerman, *Time,* vol. 1, pp. 49–50. Child separations from families were derived from analysis of 171 incidents in the Appalachian slave narratives. Fogel, Galantine, and Manning, *Without Consent,* p. 258. SHC, letters dated 15 April 1844, 1 January 1846, 16 September 1846, James Gwyn Papers. In the 19 December 1838 issue of the *Alexandria Gazette,* for

example, Kephart announced: "I will give the highest cash price for likely negroes, from 10 to 25 years of age." For example, UVSC, 1846 bill of sale for a young boy sold by the sheriff on the auction block, Holland Family Papers. Fisk, p. 116. Drew, *North-side View*, p. 45. *Slave II*, 9: 3880. *Slave I*, 7: 688, 12: 335–36. *Weevils*, p. 166.

30. SHC, letter dated 9 February 1863, Lenoir Family Papers. *Slave II*, 4: 1242. Fisk, p. 130. *Slave I*, 14: 79, 12: 328. Drew, *North-side View*, 46. *Weevils*, p. 264. SHC, James Hervey Greenlee Diary, 4 May 1847. SHC, letter dated 17 January 1837, Hamilton Brown Papers.

31. Dill, "Fictive Kin," p. 154. Washington, *Up from Slavery*, p. 4. *Slave*, 7: 172, 4 (a): 274, 13 (a): 264, 10 (a): 40. *Slave II*, 2: 77. *Slave I*, 1: 361, 1161, 8: 1215.

32. Morrissey, *Slave Women*, p. 50. "Address of James Barbour," p. 291. *Slave*, 4 (b): 36. *Slave I*, 3: 271–72. UK, letter dated 29 January 1841, Scott Family Papers. *Slave II*, 10: 4275. Betts, *Jefferson's Farm Book*, p. 77.

33. Rawick, *From Sundown*, p. 93. *Slave I*, 12: 335, 8: 913. *Slave*, 12 (a): 196, 7 (a): 345–47.

34. *Slave*, 12: 240, 1: 426. *Weevils*, p. 81.

35. *Slave I*, 5 (a): 212. *Slave*, 7: 138–39, 3 (b): 110, 10 (a): 287. Fisk, p. 155. *Slave II*, 3: 671. *Great Slave Narratives*, pp. 207–08.

36. Analysis of Appalachian slave narratives.

37. SHC, letter dated 9 February 1863, Lenoir Family Papers. *Slave II*, 4: 1242. Fisk, p. 130. *Slave I*, 14: 79, 12: 328. Drew, *North-side View*, 46. *Weevils*, p. 264. SHC, James Hervey Greenlee Diary, 4 May 1847. SHC, letter dated 17 January 1837, Hamilton Brown Papers.

38. Drew, *North-side View*, p. 45. *Slave*, 4 (a): 290, 6: 268, 11 (b): 207, 16: 67. *Slave II*, 5: 1554, 1: 347–48. *Weevils*, p. 265. *Slave I*, 1: 149–50.

39. WV, Hannah Valentine letter dated 1 November 1837, Andrew Nelson Campbell Family Papers. *Slave*, 10 (a): 192, 10 (b): 255, 7: 138–39, 16: 78, 12: 136. *Slave I*, 11: 17, 5 (b): 293.

40. Stevenson, *Life*, p. 249.

41. Slave child discipline was estimated using ninty-three incidents from the Appalachian slave narratives; findings total more than 100 percent because several respondents described more than one disciplinary action. Stroyer, *My Life*, pp. 119–21.

42. Lane, *Narrative*, p. 18. *Great Slave Narratives*, p. 208. Veney, *Narrative*, pp. 7–8. *Slave*, 12: 241. *Slave I*, 5 (b): 448. Illustration 7.3, website.

43. *Slave*, 12: 240–41. King, "'Suffer,'" p. 154.

44. Stevenson, *Life*, p. 249.

45. King, " 'Suffer,' " p. 154. *Slave II*, 9: 3875. *Slave*, 7 (a): 34.

46. Table 7.3, website. *Slave*, 10 (a): 40, 10 (b): 254, 12: 238, 7: 151. *Slave II*, 10: 4272. Attitudes of children toward fathers were derived from analysis of Appalachian slave narratives.

47. *Slave*, 16 (b): 13, 13 (a): 73, 269. *Slave I*, 14: 352.

48. *Slave*, 14 (a): 101, 16 (b): 13. *Slave I*, 12: 330.

49. Regarding emasculation of slave males, see Fox-Genovese, *Plantation Household*, pp. 49–50, 373–74. *Slave I*, 9: 1524. *Slave* 10 (a): 43, 12: 309–10. *Great Slave Narratives*, p. 211.

50. *Slave*, 4 (a): 225, 10 (b): 254. *Slave II*, 3: 784. *Slave I*, 9: 1524, 3: 94.
51. Tables 7.2 and 7.3, website. Fox-Genovese, *Plantation Household*, pp. 297, 299.
52. Table 7.2, website, and Dunaway, *Slavery*, Ch. 6. Most Appalachian ex-slaves reported family losses. WV, Hannah Valentine Letter, Slave Letter, 2 May 1838, Andrew Nelson Campbell Family Papers. DPL, Vilet Lester to Patsy Patterson, 29 August 1857, Joseph Allred Papers. Fisk, p. 2.
53. *Slave II*, 3: 805. *Slave I*, 14: 356.
54. *Slave I*, 5 (a): 293, 12: 328–29. Patterson, *Slavery*, p. 7. Gutman, *Black Family*, pp. 146, 148. Brown, *Narrative*, p. 51. Ramsey, *Been Here*, pp. 33, 114. I previously documented slave family history preservation as antisystemic resistance. See Dunaway, *Slavery*, Ch. 7.

CHAPTER 3

1. Opening quote is from *Slave*, 16 (b): 12. Steckel, "Peculiar Population," p. 733. Savitt, *Medicine*, pp. 67–68, 147. For detailed information about the slave illnesses and deaths recorded for two Appalachian plantations, see UVSC, Slave Record Book, 1836–65, Massie Account Book, Massie Family Papers. U.S. Census, *Mortality Statistics*, p. 44. Health patterns calculated using 297 newspaper advertisements for slaves who ran away from masters who lived in the Appalachian counties of North Carolina and Virginia. These ads were found in Meaders, *Advertisements*, and Parker, *Stealing*.
2. Table 6.1, website.
3. Clothing and shoe estimates were derived from analysis of Appalachian slave narratives. *Slave I*, 5 (b): 218, 297, 305–06, 3: 478–79. Cade, "Out of Mouths," pp. 327–28. *Slave II*, 3: 791, 6: 2274. *Slave*, 13: 76, 16: 67, 87–88, 18. *Weevils*, p. 82.
4. Fogel, Galantine, and Manning, *Without Consent*, p. 356. Ramsey, *Been Here*, p. 96. 182 Appalachian slave narratives provide discussion of clothing and shoe allotments. Findings total more than 100 percent because most respondents listed two or more complaints. *Slave*, 3 (b): 75.
5. *Slave I*, 12: 328. *Slave II*, 5: 1555. Starobin, *Industrial Slavery*, pp. 55–58. Dew, *Bond of Iron*, pp. 69–70, 76, 82, 111, 270–72. *Slave*, 16: 81. VHS, January 1813, David Ross Letterbook.
6. Fisk, pp. 56, 216. Gurney, *Journey*, pp. 53–54. *Slave*, 16 (b): 1–2, 12: 347. *Slave I*, 1: 293. *Slave II*, 3: 791. *Alexandria Gazette and Daily Advertiser*, 24 July 1817. Song from John Jackson, "The Devil Wore Hickory Shoes," sound recording.
7. *Slave I*, 5 (b): 305–06. *Slave*, 11 (b): 207. Starobin, *Industrial Slavery*, pp. 54–59. Dew, *Bond of Iron*, p. 111. DPL, letters dated 21 September 1860, 15 March 1861, William Weaver Papers.
8. Oral histories collected by the author. *Slave*, 12: 308–09. Fisk, p. 6. *Weevils*, p. 224. *Slave I*, 3: 94, 1: 151. *Slave II*, 3: 785. Savitt, *Medicine*, pp. 188–90.
9. Fisk, pp. 5, 14. *Slave I*, 11: 18, 8: 1216, 919, 3: 618. UVSC, letter dated 21 December 1851, John Buford Papers. *Slave*, 6 (a): 278, 12: 347. AL, B. Smith letter dated 15 August 1844. Betts, *Jefferson's Farm Book*, pp. 25, 55.

10. Kelso, "Archaeology," pp. 5–14. The types of slave living quarters were calculated from Appalachian slave narratives. For North American slave housing, see Singleton, "Archaeology," pp. 123–24, 127–28, and Cade, "Out of
the Mouths," pp. 295–97. *Slave*, 6: 154, 4 (b): 35, 1: 425, 12: 240. Smith,
First Forty Years, p. 67. *Slave I*, 3: 481. Gruber, "Archaeology," pp. 2–7.
Andrews and Young, "Plantations," pp. 7–8. *Slave II*, 3: 670. Fisk, p. 13.
Illustration 6.1, website.

11. NA, Manuscript Slave Schedules for Appalachian counties. Andrews and
Young, "Plantations," p. 8. SHC, James Hervey Greenlee Diary, 18 January
1847. *Slavery Time*, p. 98. Fisk, p. 13. *Slave*, 6: 1, 154–56, 425, 4 (a): 225,
275, 179, 14 (a): 354, 12: 136, 307, 8 (a): 324, 13: 74, 16: 15, 7: 45. Andrews,
"Spatial Analysis," pp. 22–33. *Slave I*, 3: 272, 481, 12: 334. *Slave II*, 10: 4273,
6: 2273, 5: 1553–54, 6: 2273, 9: 3638, 3: 673. *Weevils*, pp. 81–82, 98.

12. Starobin, *Industrial Slavery*, pp. 57–59. Salmon, *Washington*, p. 58. SHC, letter dated 8 January 1832, Hamilton Brown Papers. Bryan, "Letters," p. 343.
Carolina Watchman, 18 May 1844. Silliman, "Remarks," pp. 104–05. *Slave I*,
8: 912. *American Journal of Science*, 13 (1828): 208. Catterall, *Judicial Cases*,
vol. 2, pp. 243–44. Ramsey, *Been Here*, p. 46. Dew, *Bond of Iron*, p. 76.

13. Fogel and Engerman, *Time*, vol. 1, p. 115. Slave housing trends derived from
analysis of manuscript slave schedules for Appalachian counties. White and
Cherokee housing estimates derived from analysis of a systematic sample of
3,447 farm households; for methods, see Dunaway, *First American Frontier*,
pp. 326–39. NA, Manuscript Census Roll, 1835, of the Cherokee Indians.
Herman, "Slave Quarters," p. 273. Jefferson, *Notes*, p. 152. Harrison,
"Memories," p. 247. Scholars have argued that slave cabins were no worse
than poor white housing; see, for example, Fogel and Engerman, *Time*,
vol. 1, pp. 115–17.

14. *Slave*, 7 (a): 345, 13: 73, 12: 309, 16 (a): 2, 19: 205, 11 (b): 147. Fisk,
pp. 216–17. VHS, letter dated 22 March 1809, Holburn Letterbook.
Starobin, *Industrial Slavery*, p. 138. Pease, "Great Kanawha," pp. 199–200.
Washington, *Up from Slavery*, p. 26. Mosby, "Salt Industry," p. 48. Stealey,
"Salt Industry," p. 399. *Weevils*, p. 155. HPL, L. Allan Letter, 13 August 1859.
UVSC, letter dated 9 September 1834, John Hook and Bowker Preston Papers. UVSC, letter dated 28 March 1856, Nathaniel Beverly Tucker Papers.
SHC, letter dated 7 December 1834, Hamilton Brown Papers. SHC, let-
ter dated 27 October 1858, James Gwyn Papers. Dew, *Bond of Iron*, pp. 272,
326. McGee and Lander, *Rebel*, p. 91. Betts, *Jefferson's Farm Book*, pp. 18–19,
27–28, 32, 39, 57, 305, 505. Savitt, *Medicine*, pp. 292–95, 55.

15. Kiple and King, *Another Dimension*, p. 13–44. Savitt, *Medicine*, pp. 292–95,
59–61, 55. Dew, *Bond of Iron*, p. 326. SHC, James Hervey Greenlee Diary,
28 December 1847. Betts, *Jefferson's Farm Book*, pp. 28, 39, 18–19, 243, 505.
For examples, see SHC, letter dated 7 December 1834, Hamilton Brown
Papers, and UVSC, letter dated 28 March 1856, Nathaniel Beverly Tucker
Papers. Dew, *Bond of Iron*, p. 326. McGee and Lander, *Rebel*, p. 91. Bryan,
"Letters," p. 343.

16. Savitt, *Medicine*, pp. 59, 64–65. Bear, *Family Letters*, p. 21. Kelso,
"Archaeology," pp. 16–17. Andrews, "Spatial Analysis," pp. 67–69. Bryan,

"Letters," p. 343. *Hillborough Recorder*, 20 May 1829. Starobin, *Industrial Slavery*, p. 138. Pease, "Great Kanawha," pp. 199–200. Washington, *Up from Slavery*, p. 26. Mosby, "Salt Industry," p. 48. Stealey, "Salt Industry of Great Kanawha," p. 399. *Weevils*, p. 343. *Kanawha Banner*, 25 October 1832, 31 July 1834. WV, Luke Willcox Diary, 30 May 1849, 29 June 1849, 13 July 1849, 21 August 1849, 5 July 1850.

17. Betts, *Jefferson's Farm Book*, p. 76. Crosby, *The Columbian Exchange*, p. 209. Kiple and King, *Another Dimension*, p. 75. Fisk, p. 115. *Slave*, 12 (a): 198. Kelso, "Archaeology," p. 124. *Slave I*, 5 (a): 213. Janney and Janney, *Janney's Virginia*, pp. 35, 41. Savitt, *Medicine*, pp. 173–76. Kelso, "Archaeology," p. 14. Breeden, *Advice*, p. 130.

18. Affleck, "Hygiene," pp. 429–36. *Slave I*, 9: 1526. *Slave*, 13: 73. Grandy, *Narrative*, p. 8. Savitt, *Medicine*, p. 59. Illustration 6.2, website.

19. Dunaway, *First American Frontier*, pp. 276–83. Mathew, *Agriculture, Geology*, pp. 284–86. *Medical Repository* 4 (1805): 105. *Hillsborough Recorder*, 20 May 1829.

20. *Slave II*, 5: 1864, 3: 796–97. *Slave I*, 3: 481. Fisk, pp. 13, 10. *Slave*, 12: 307. McKivigan, *Roving Editor*, pp. 124–26.

21. Janney and Janney, *Janney's Virginia*, pp. 181–89. *Slave*, 12: 316. *Slave I*, 3: 98. Kelso, "Archaeology," p. 9. Ramsey, *Been Here*, p. 98. Fisk, pp. 216–17. VHS, letter dated 22 March 1809, Holburn, Taylor Papers, Letterbook. *Slave II*, 6: 2257.

22. Table 3.2, website, and Dunaway, *Slavery*, Ch. 3. Starobin, *Industrial Slavery*, p. 63. *Richmond Enquirer*, 2 January 1855. For example, the Kanawha Slave Insurance Company and the Albermarle Insurance Company; see Catterall, *Judicial Cases*, vol. 2, p. 22. *Staunton Republican Vindicator*, 30 April 1859. UVSC, letter dated 7 December 1853, McCue Family Papers.

23. *Richmond Daily Whig and Public Advertiser*, 6 June 1846. Washington, *Up from Slavery*, p. 38. Stampp, *Peculiar Institution*, p. 108. VHS, letter dated 16 September 1813, David Ross Letterbook. Catterall, *Judicial Cases*, vol. 1, pp. 181–82; vol. 2, p. 559. Lewis, *Coal*, pp. 154–55. Starobin, *Industrial Slavery*, pp. 46–47. WV, Luke Willcox Diary, vol. 1, 9 January 1844. WV, Train Deposition, 18 December 1852, Beeson vs. Ruffner, Circuit Superior Court, 1846, Kanawha County Court Records.

24. SHC, James Hervey Greenlee Diary, 4 April 1849. Dew, *Bond of Iron*, p. 78. Bryan, "Letters," p. 343. Catterall, *Judicial Cases*, vol. 2, p. 112. Savitt, *Medicine*, pp. 107–08. St. Abdy, *Journal*, vol. 2, p. 326. DPL, letter dated 11 November 1857, William Weaver Papers.

25. *Lynchburg Daily Virginian*, 11 September 1852, 11 October 1854. Olmsted, *Back Country*, pp. 271–74. UVSC, letter dated 18 April 1854, John Buford Papers. Noe, *Southwest Virginia's Railroad*, p. 83. Savitt, *Medicine*, pp. 109–10. *Slave*, 3: 70. *The South*, pp. 312, 319. UK, letters dated 22 and 28 December 1860, Hunt-Morgan Family Papers. UVSC, letter dated 3 January 1850, Hubard Papers. Illustration 6.3, website.

26. Weld, *American Slavery*, pp. 27–35. Fogel and Engerman, *Time*, vol. 1, pp. 109–17. Steckel, "Slave Height," pp. 363–80. Margo and Steckel, "Heights," pp. 516–38. Sutch, "Treatment," pp. 335–438. Sutch, "Care," pp. 231–301. Owens, *This Species*, pp. 50–69. Savitt, *Medicine*, pp. 86–98.

Kiple and King, *Another Dimension*, pp. 149–51. Steckel, "Peculiar Population," pp. 732–36. Fogel, Galantine, and Manning, *Without Consent*, pp. 292, 306.

27. Fogel, *Without Consent*, pp. 134, 137.

28. Table 6.2, website. Fogel, Galantine, and Manning, *Without Consent*, pp. 301, 305, 368. Betts, *Jefferson's Farm Book*, pp. 144–48. For antebellum food allowances, see Dunaway, *First American Frontier*, pp. 329–30.

29. Table 6.3, website. Douglass, *My Bondage*, p. 253. About 16.8 percent of U.S. ex-slaves reported that their food supply was inadequate; see Fogel, Galantine, and Manning, *Without Consent*, pp. 305, 334. However, 36.3 percent of Appalachian narratives reported inadequate food. Starobin, *Industrial Slavery*, pp. 11–12, 50. Illustration 6.4, website.

30. Analysis of Appalachian slave narratives. Savitt, *Medicine*, pp. 99, 100–03. McKivigan, *Roving Editor*, p. 156. Salmon, *Washington*, p. 58. *Harper's* 32 (1866): 35. Lewis, *Coal*, pp. 117–18, 153. Young, "Slave Subsistence." Gruber, "Archaeology," pp. 2–9. Andrews and Young, "Plantations," pp. 7–8. Kelso, "Archaeology," pp. 11, 16. Singleton, "Archaeology," pp. 126–28. Fisk, pp. 10–11. *Slave*, 4 (a): 274, 16: 30, 11–12. Kiple and King, *Another Dimension*, p. 82. SHC, James Hervey Greenlee Diary, 13 July 1847.

31. Analysis of Appalachian slave narratives. *Slave*, 13: 75–76, 16: 11, 45–46, 7: 172, 12: 146, 4 (a): 274, 10 (b): 128–29. *Slave I*, 3: 479, 7: 172, Hughes, *Thirty Years*, pp. 10–11. Betts, *Jefferson's Farm Book*, p. 185. Ferguson, *Uncommon Ground*, pp. 100–06. UVSC, letter dated 3 March 1855, Silas McDowell Papers. Illustration 6.5, website.

32. *Slave II*, 3: 788–89, 9: 3871–72. Fisk, pp. 155–56. *Slave*, 13: 128, 2 (a): 95. Betts, *Jefferson's Farm Book*, p. 185. *Slave I*, 7: 695. *Weevils*, p. 160. "Address of James Barbour," p. 290. Owens, *This Species*, pp. 62–63.

33. Only two masters described in Appalachian slave narratives broke with the regional slave diet customs in this manner. *Slave*, 4 (b): 75, 7: 141–42. Of other U.S. slaves, 51.6 percent received regular rations; 48.4 percent supplemented rations with their own food sources. In contrast, 93.3 percent of all Appalachian slaves supplemented masters' rations with their own food sources. U.S. estimates are from Fogel, Galantine, and Manning, *Without Consent*, pp. 305, 334. Appalachian estimates are derived from analysis of regional slave narratives.

34. *Slave*, 12: 317. *Slave II*, 3: 789. *Slave I*, 7: 689, 3: 617. Ferguson, *Uncommon Ground*, p. 94. Chambers, "He Gwine Sing," p. 85.

35. *Slave*, 3: 87–88, 2 (a): 244, 2 (b): 46, 12: 316–17. *Slave II*, 5: 1555, 11: 17. *Slave I*, 1: 151–52. Illustration 6.6, website.

36. Steckel, "Work," p. 494. *Slave II*, 3: 808. *Slave I*, 12: 337–39. VHS, letter dated 25 August 1853, David Ross Letterbook. Starobin, *Industrial Slavery*, pp. 52–54. DPL, letters dated 1 December 1828, 31 December 1828, 29 March 1829, 11 August 1829, 2 April 1860, 28 May 1860, William Weaver Papers. *Early and Wife*, vol. 1, pp. 230, 243, 275. Salmon, *Washington*, p. 58.

37. Fisk, pp. 141, 6, 216. Genovese, *Roll*, p. 10. UK, J. Winston, Coleman Papers, pp. 12, 61. *Slave*, 10 (a): 189, 211, 16: 11, 45–46, 67, 7: 162. *Slave I*, 12: 328, 1: 19, 5 (b): 304. *Slave Testimony*, p. 737. *Weevils*, p. 81.

38. VHS, entries dated August 1813, Ross Letterbook. Dew, *Bond of Iron*, p. 111. *Slave II*, 9: 3871, 3: 916. Janney and Janney, *Janney's Virginia*, pp. 19–34. Savitt, *Medicine*, pp. 101–02. *Slave I*, 3: 101, 786, 1: 293. UT, grocery order dated 1836, Caldwell Papers. *Slave*, 6: 269–70, 10 (b): 101. Kelso, "Archaeology," p. 16. Table 2.3, website, and Dunaway, *Slavery*, Ch. 3.

39. About 5.5 percent of U.S. ex-slaves reported food stealing; see Fogel, Galantine, and Manning, *Without Consent*, pp. 305, 334. However, 17.3 percent of Appalachian narratives reported food stealing. Betts, *Jefferson's Farm Book*, p. 10. *Slave*, 7: 141–42, 4 (a): 117–18, 197–98.

40. Drew, *North-side View*, p. 280. *Weevils*, p. 155. *Slave I*, 8: 1217. *Slave*, 1: 425, 2 (a): 46, 16: 15–16. UK, J. Winston Coleman Papers, p. 40.

41. Ferguson, *Uncommon Ground*, p. 95. Affleck, "Hygiene," p. 431. Owens, *This Species*, pp. 57–58.

42. Owens, *This Species*, pp. 57–65. Kiple and King, *Another Dimension*, p. 72. Genovese, *Political Economy*, pp. 44–46. Calculated using 297 newspaper advertisements for slaves who ran away from masters who lived in the Appalachian counties of North Carolina and Virginia. These ads were found in Meaders, *Advertisements*, and Parker, *Stealing. Slave*, 2 (a): 90.

CHAPTER 4

1. Opening quotes are from Betts, *Jefferson's Farm Book*, p. 43 and *Weevils*, pp. 159–60. McKitrick, *Slavery Defended*, pp. 37–38. Mercer, *Popular Lectures*, pp. 49–51. Turrentine, *Romance*, p. 27. Fox-Genovese, *Plantation Household*, p. 195. Stevenson, *Life*, p. 39.

2. *American Ladies Magazine* 8 (5) (May 1836), p. 286. Fox-Genovese, *Plantation Household*, pp. 99, 17–18, 276–78. Stevenson, *Life*, pp. 116–18, 136–37, 10. McMillen, *Motherhood*, pp. 32–33, 165–78. SHC, letters dated 10 November 1843, 27 December 1843, Lenoir Family Papers.

3. Stevenson, *Life*, pp. 101–03. McMillen, *Motherhood*, pp. 189, 79–110. Leavitt, *Brought to Bed*, p. 67. Newell, "Effect," p. 533. Folger, *Family Physician*, p. 244. Gunn, *Domestic Medicine*, p. 342. Simons, *Planter's Guide*, p. 71.

4. McMillen, *Motherhood*, pp. 57–64, 189. UVSC, letters dated 14 and 21 July 1821, 21 July 1817, Graham Family Papers. SHC, letters dated 19 February 1837, 31 March 1837, 20 May 1842, Winter 1832, 9 April 1837, 11 May 1837, Lenoir Family Papers. WV, letter dated 10 February 1857, Andrew Nelson Campbell Family Papers. SCH, Lucilla Gamble McCorkle Diary, Summer and Fall 1847. Thompson, "Cases," pp. 340–43.

5. Fogel and Engerman, *Time*, vol. 1, p. 127. Plowden C. J. Weston, "Plantation Instructions."

6. Table 8.1, website. *Slave*, 4 (a): 80, 11 (a) 167, 8 (a): 324, 1: 425, 6: 155–56. Blassingame, *Slave Community*, p. 167. *Slave II*, 3: 673, 9: 3874, 10: 4274. Fisk, p. 217. Day and Hook, "Short History," pp. 57–58. Poor Europeans and Americans (including the Irish and the British working class) utilized the same wedding ceremony; see Gutman, *Black Family*, pp. 275–77, 281–83.

7. *Slave*, 14 (a): 101. *Slave I*, 3: 273. *Slave II*, 6: 2282–83. SHC, slave marriage license dated 26 December 1848, Thomas George Walton Papers. SHC,

slave marriage license dated 7 June 1846, Hamilton Brown Papers. Veney, *Narrative*, p. 18.

8. Regarding Broad River churches, see Logan, *Sketches*, p. 38.

9. *Slave*, 8 (a): 105. Coombs, *America Visited*, p. 233. *Slave I*, 5 (b): 299.

10. Still, *Underground Railroad*, p. 260. *Slave II*, 9: 3880, 5: 1556. Fisk, p. 1. *Weevils*, p. 161.

11. *Slave II*, 3: 786, 806. *Slave*, 4 (a): 228. Fisk, p. 5. *Weevils*, p. 265.

12. Veney, *Narrative*, p. 26.

13. Table 7.3, website, and Dunaway, *Slavery*, Ch. 6. Fogel and Engerman, *Time*, p. 133, claimed that only 4.5 percent of the WPA narratives report white fathers. Crawford, "Slave Family," p. 337, argued that 5.7 percent of the slave narratives report white fathers. *Slave*, 4 (b): 35. Fox-Genovese, *Plantation Household*, p. 294.

14. Fisk, pp. 1–2, 8. Stevenson, *Life*, p. 239. *Slave*, 16: 31. UK, Carl Hall narrative, J. Winston Coleman Papers. *Weevils*, pp. 300–01. Illustration 8.1, website.

15. Fisk, pp. 55–56. *Slave*, 12: 239.

16. *Slave Testimony*, pp. 475–87. For a summary of the scholarly debates about the Jefferson–Hemings relationship, see Gordon-Reed, *Jefferson*.

17. Sutch, "Breeding," p. 181.

18. Table 8.2, website.

19. McManus, *Black Bondage*, pp. 36–40. *New York Gazetteer*, 16 November 1784. *Pennsylvania Gazette*, 21 May 1767, 26 February 1767. *New York Weekly Post-Boy*, 17 May 1756, 28 November 1765. *New England Weekly Journal*, 6 June 1738. *Boston Gazette*, 25 June 1754. Greene and Harrington, *American Population*, p. 101.

20. Table 8.2, website. U.S. Census Office, *Statistical View*, p. xxxix.

21. Table 8.2, website. Butlin, *Antebellum Slavery*, pp. 32, 40.

22. Average age at first pregnancy was calculated from a systematic sample of 2,692 African-American mothers who were selected from the 1870 Census of Population manuscripts for Appalachian counties. These estimates are conservative because older children were much more likely to be missing from their mothers' households in 1870, causing an overestimation of the mother's age at first pregnancy. *Slave I*, 1: 153. Trussell and Steckel, "Age of Slaves," p. 504. Stevenson, *Life*, pp. 246–50. Similar patterns are evident in the slave lists recorded for some Appalachian plantations.

23. Fogel, *Without Consent*, pp. 181–82. *Slave*, 6 (a): 280. Although these statistics may seem astonishing, they are not peculiar to Appalachia. A decade later, African-American women were still rejecting the early childbearing practices that had characterized the slavery years. Throughout the 1870s, a high percentage of African-American women delayed reproduction and marriage into their twenties. See Gutman, *Black Family*, pp. 635–36, n13.

24. *Slave*, 12 (a): 136, 10 (b): 128, 16 (b): 13. *Slave II*, 9: 3637–38, 6: 2273, 3: 669. *Slave I*, 5: 461, 9: 1524.

25. Table 8.3, website. Because of the high incidence of family disruptions, plantation slave lists and census slave schedules are corrupted by the same types of inaccuracies. Slave lists reported only those children residing in the household with the mother, often omitting preteens who were hired out or assigned to

a distant work site. When offspring married, owners began to report them as separate households and did not often record their ties to mothers. Using slave lists, one researcher estimated that Loudoun County, Virginia, slave women averaged only five to seven children throughout their reproductive years. Such slave lists cause an undercount because they did not report offspring who had been relocated or who had died before their teens. See Stevenson, *Life*, p. 404, n54.

26. U.S. trends from Fogel, *Without Consent*, p. 149.

27. Fogel, *Without Consent*, p. 153. Steckel, *Economics*, pp. 203–06, 226–32. Crawford, "Slave Family," p. 346. Klein and Engerman, "Fertility," p. 373. Fogel, *Without Consent*, pp. 179, 183. Betts, *Jefferson's Farm Book*, pp. 45–46.

28. Trussell and Steckel, "Age of Slaves," p. 496–99. Dreizen, Spirakis, and Stone, "A Comparison," pp. 256–63. Malcolm, *Growth*, pp. 51–55. Frisch and McArthur, "Menstrual Cycles," pp. 949–51.

29. *Letters of William Lee*, 2: 363–64. "Address of James Barbour," pp. 290–91. Betts, *Jefferson's Farm Book*, pp. 43, 45–46.

30. There is scant evidence in the Appalachian slave narratives of masters who engaged in forced breeding techniques. Eastern Kentucky slave Carl Hall claimed that: "Only the strong healthy women were allowed to have children, and often were not allowed to mate with their own husbands, but were bred like livestock to some male negro who was kept for that purpose because of his strong phisique, which the master wished to reproduce, in order to get a good price for his progeny." The owner of the privileged stockman "charged a fee of 1 out of every 4 of his offspring for his services." A Pickens County, South Carolina, slave also remembered that some male slaves were kept for forced mating. According to her, a neighboring slaveholder "would rent the stockman and put him in a room with some young woman he wanted to raise children from." For these instances, see UK, "Slave Interviews," J. Winston Coleman Papers, and *Slave*, 10 (b), 222–23. UK, Mandy Gibson narrative, J. Winston Coleman Papers. *Slave I*, 1: 432. *Slave*, 7 (a): 345, 11 (a): 46. Kotlikoff, "Quantitative Description," pp. 49–51. Tadman, *Speculators*, p. 126.

31. Fox-Genovese, *Plantation Household*, p. 293. Smith, *Mastered*, pp. 119–20. Betts, *Jefferson's Farm Book*, p. 43. Newell, "Effect," p. 535. Falkner, *Infant*, pp. 4–6. Campbell, "Work," pp. 800–01, 811. McMillen, *Motherhood*, pp. 39–42.

32. *Slave II*, 3: 785. Steckel, "Work," p. 145. Fogel, "Overwork" p. 321. Payne, "Report," p. 204. *Slave*, 16 (b): 13–14.

33. Brown, "Midwifery," p. 460. *Slave II*, 9: 3640. *Slave*, 19: 215, 16: 45. Midwife practices derived from analysis of Appalachian slave narratives. Bickley, "Midwifery," pp. 55–67. For slave midwives, see *Slave*, 12 (a): 199, *Slave I*, 3: 95. Southern trends from McMillen, *Motherhood*, p. 189. Appalachian trends from analysis of eighty-one slave narratives. For a mistress who delivered slave babies, see *Slave*, 7: 24. For physician treatment of Appalachian slave women, see SHC, doctor visits, 1843–57, Attachment to Estate Settlement of Margaret Brown, Hamilton Brown Papers. SHC, doctor's statement dated 16 December 1857, James Gwyn Papers. DPL, doctor's statement dated 17 November 1864, Alfred W. Bell Papers.

34. Table 8.3, website. *Slave II*, 11: 41–42.
35. Falkner, *Infant*, pp. 32, 38–39. Steckel, "Women," p. 55. Cody, "Seasonality," pp. 61–78. Leavitt, *Brought to Bed*, pp. 68–70. SHC, letter dated 20 September 1843, Hamilton Brown Papers.
36. Meigs, *Females*, p. 315. "Letters of 1831–32," p. 225. Warrington, *Obstetric Catechism*, p. 176. Stevenson, *Life*, pp. 104, 250. Potts, *World Labour*, p. 50. *Slave*, 1: 425–26, 3: 498, 796, 4 (b): 75–6. Appalachian masters probably followed lay-in customs that were common throughout the U.S. South; see Campbell, "Work," p. 807. Fogel, *Without Consent*, p. 28. Owens, *This Species*, p. 40. Poor white mill women returned to work a few days after delivery; see Falkner, *Infant*, pp. 4–6. VHS, letter dated 9 January 1813, David Ross Letterbook. *Ferry Hill*, xvi–xviii. Olmsted, *Seaboard*, p. 190. Falkner, *Infant*, p. 51. Fogel, Galantine, and Manning, *Without Consent*, p. 311.
37. Table 8.4, website. Geggus, "Slave," p. 268. Lantz, "Family," p. 671. For examples of childbirthing deaths, see *Slave*, 7: 138, 10 (a): 100, 12: 136, 274, 16: 77; *Slave I*, 1: 144, 8: 1221; *Slave II*, 3: 914. Jacobs, *Incidents*, pp. 60–61.
38. Riordan and Auerbach, *Breastfeeding*, pp. 105–34. Stuart-Macadam and Dettwyler, *Breastfeeding*, p. 25. Lawrence, *Breastfeeding*, p. 312.
39. Stevenson, *Life*, p. 98. Fox-Genovese, *Plantation Household*, p. 279. McMillen, "Sacred Duty," pp. 336–49. Sigourney, *Letters*, p. 29. Gunn, *Domestic Medicine*, pp. 66–78. Sunley, "Literature," pp. 153–55. Janney and Janney, *Janney's Virginia*, p. 15. SHC, letter dated 12 April 1845, Undated letter from Mrs. L. E. Lenoir, Lenoir Family Papers.
40. Riordan and Auerbach, *Breastfeeding*, pp. 476–80. Raphael, *Breastfeeding*, p. 190. Falkner, *Infant*, pp. 109–11, 211, 2, 4–7. Lawrence, *Breastfeeding*, pp. 186, 303–04. Apple, *Mothers and Medicine*, p. 180. Maher, *Anthropology*, p. 5. *Slave II*, 3: 797. *Slave*, 12: 309, 13 (a): 149, 4 (b): 75. Smith, *Mastered*, p. 134. *Southern Cultivator* 2 (10 July 1844), p. 107. Bruce, *New Man*, p. 14. Fisk, p. 117. *Slave I*, 9: 1526. Illustration 8.2, website.
41. *Slave I*, 1: 426. *Slave*, 19: 215, 16: 58–59. Greene, *Diary*, pp. 496, 919.
42. Before six months, an infant lacks the digestive enzymes needed to process solid foods, and its tongue cannot move food around in its mouth. Lawrence, *Breastfeeding*, pp. 314–20. Riordan and Auerbach, *Breastfeeding*, pp. 109–11. Stevenson, *Life*, p. 109. Falkner, *Infant*, p. 182. Lawrence, *Breastfeeding*, p. 319. SHC, letters dated 24 April 1844, 13 June 1844, Lenoir Family Papers.
43. Falkner, *Infant*, p. 110. Hull and Simpson, *Breastfeeding*, p. 8. Menard, "Maryland," pp. 29–54. Bush-Slimani, "Hard Labour," pp. 89–90. McDonald, *Economy*, p. 38. Smith, "Family Limitation," pp. 40–57. Lewis and Lockridge, "Sally," p. 22. Golden, *Social History*, p. 25. Stevenson, *Life*, pp. 247–48.
44. Fogel, Galantine, and Manning, *Without Consent*, pp. 598–99. Wet nursing patterns derived from analysis of Appalachian slave narratives. SHC, letters dated 28 April 1836, 25 September 1842, 27 August 1845, Lenoir Family Papers. UVSC, letter dated 12 December 1859, McCue Family Papers.
45. Fox-Genovese, *Plantation Household*, p. 137. SHC, Lucilla Gamble McCorkle Diary, 2 June and 6 July 1846. UVSC, letters dated 1 January 1858,

12 December 1859, McCue Family Papers. *Slave*, 13: 74–75. *Slave II*, 6: 2241. *Slave I*, 1: 144, 9: 1421–22.

46. *Slave II*, 2: 45, 9: 3879, 6: 2275, 3: 804–05. *Slave*, 4 (b): 74, 107.

47. McMillen, "Sacred Duty," pp. 336–49. Fox-Genovese, *Plantation Household*, pp. 280, 137–38. Patterns of white child nursing derived from analysis of Appalachian slave narratives. *Slave*, 3 (b): 273, 16: 79, 67, 8 (a): 324, 11 (a): 47, 10 (a): 287. *Slave I*, 5: 461. Betts, *Jefferson's Farm Book*, p. 77. *Weevils*, pp. 243, 345. Illustration 8.3, website.

48. Steckel, "Slave Mortality," pp. 86–114. Steckel, "Work," pp. 490–95. Illustration 8.4, website.

49. Table 2.2, website. Slave child mortality rates calculated from published county totals in U.S. Census, *Mortality Statistics*, pp. 191–93, 255–57, 259–61, 249–51, 285–87, 289–91. Because the published census did not disaggregate black mortality by age, we must estimate the mortality rates for black Appalachian children. National trends were applied to the mortality rates that characterized white Appalachians. However, the mortality rate for adult Appalachian slaves was 1.4 times the national average, so this adjustment was also made. For U.S. trends, see Steckel, "Slave Mortality," pp. 86–114. Kiple and Kiple, "Slave Child," p. 299. The high mortality of Appalachian slave children has also been documented by Sweig, "Northern Virginia, p. 107, and by Stevenson, *Life*, pp. 248–49. Savitt, *Medicine*, pp. 148–53. Early childbearing practices derived from analysis of Appalachian slave narratives.

50. Hull and Simpson, *Breastfeeding*, pp. 6–7. Fogel, *Without Consent*, p. 146. McMillen, "Sacred Duty," pp. 341–42. Kiple and Kiple, "Slave Child," pp. 299, 290–91.

51. Medical care patterns derived from analysis of Appalachian slave narratives. *Slave II*, 1: 281. *Slave*, 10 (a): 101. Still, *Underground Railroad*, p. 549. *Slave I*, 14: 354.

52. Savitt, *Medicine*, pp. 107–08. *Ferry Hill*, p. 55. Catterall, *Judicial Cases*, vol. 2, pp. 112, 153. Washington, *Up from Slavery*, 38–39.

53. *Slave I*, 8: 1216, 14: 354, 8: 216–17. *Slave*, 12: 137, 309, 16: 23, 46, 10 (b): 218, 19: 206. Child clothing and shoe allotments derived from analysis of Appalachian slave narratives. Kiple and Kiple, "Slave Child," pp. 284–307. Still, *Underground Railroad*, p. 549. *Weevils*, p. 81. Berlin, Favreau, and Miller, *Remembering*, p. 289.

54. Food patterns derived from analysis of Appalachian slave narratives. Deetz, *Small Things*, pp. 52–53. *Slave*, 12: 308, 7: 172, 10 (a): 181. *Slave I*, 9: 1523, 8: 913, 13 (a): 192, 16: 22, 9: 1523. *Slave II*, 3: 670. Fisk, pp. 97, 114. Still, *Underground Railroad*, p. 549. Yetman, *Life*, p. 265.

55. Fisk, pp. 11–14. *Slave I*, 5 (a): 218, 11: 17, 7: 688–89. *Slave*, 3 (b): 13. *Weevils*, p. 81.

56. *Slave*, 16: 11, 10 (a): 189, 3 (a): 261, 11 (a): 168, 13: 149, 128. *Slave I*, 1: 187, 152, 14: 353–54, 12: 147. Fisk, pp. 156, 144–45. *Slave II*, 6: 2258, 3: 917. Washington, *Up from Slavery*, pp. 9–10.

57. Kiple and Kiple, "Slave Child," pp. 296–98, 284–309. Steckel, "Work," pp. 500, 504. Falkner, *Infant*, pp. 161–62, 209, 218–20. Lawrence, *Breastfeeding*, p. 657. Hull and Simpson, *Breastfeeding*, pp. 46–47. Boulton, Laron, and Rey, *Long-Term*, pp. 8, 35–54. Steckel, "Peculiar Population," p. 738.

58. *Slave I*, 8: 913, 9: 1422. DPL, Hannah Valentine letter dated 2 May 1838, Campbell Family Papers. Gutman, *Black Family*, p. 288. *Slave*, 10 (b): 254, 1: 57. *Slave II*, 3: 801. Fisk, pp. 216, 13–14.

CHAPTER 5

1. Opening quote is from *Slave*, 19: 214–15. Smith, Wallerstein, and Evers, *Households*, pp. 259–61. Deere, "Rural Women's Subsistence," p. 9. Thompson, "Structures," p. 410. Lim, "Capitalism," p. 77. Veltmeyer, "Surplus Labor," p. 222. Marx, *Capital*, vol. 1, pp. 431, 599, 602. Ware, *Notes*, pp. 201–02. Von Verlhof, "Women's Work," p. 22. McGuire, Smith, and Martin, "Patterns," p. 89.

2. For antebellum food allowances, see Dunaway, *First American Frontier*, pp. 329–30. *Slave*, 16 (a): 31. About 16.8 percent of U.S. ex-slaves reported that their food supply was inadequate; see Fogel, Galantine, and Manning, *Without Consent*, pp. 305, 334. However, 36.3 percent of Appalachian narratives reported inadequate food. Fisk, p. 107. *Slave II*, 3: 672. Smith, "Historical Geography," pp. 98–99. About 5.5 percent of U.S. ex-slaves reported food stealing; see Fogel, Galantine, and Manning, *Without Consent*, pp. 305, 334. However, 17.3 percent of Appalachian narratives reported food stealing.

3. Table 2.3, website. *Slave*, 4 (b): 35. For the average field-work week, see Fogel, *Without Consent*, p. 28. For the notion of self-exploitation, see Medick, "Proto-Industrial Family," p. 300.

4. *Slave*, 10 (a): 182, 12 (a): 313, 199, 81, 139, 16 (b): 24, 47, 90, 35, 33, 19: 214, 13: 94, 129, 14 (a): 355, 1: 56, 19: 214. Fisk, pp. 217–18, 100, 108. Savitt, *Medicine*, pp. 171–86. *Slave I*, 4: 429, 5: 462, 8: 913, 12: 257, 3: 98–99. Hudson, *To Have*, pp. 110–11. *Slave II*, 5: 1564, 6: 2282, 2284, 3: 673–74. Betts, *Jefferson's Farm Book*, p. 44. Janney and Janney, *Janney's Virginia*, pp. 47–48. Krochmal, Walters, and Doughty, *Guide*. Wiggington, *Foxfire Book*, pp. 230–48.

5. Fisk, pp. 11, 237–38. *Slave*, 16: 87. *Slave I*, 5 (b): 448. *Slave II*, 3: 791, 785. *Richmond Daily Dispatch*, 18 February 1858. Singleton, "Archaeology," pp. 124–25. WV, letter dated 5 November 1855, Andrew Nelson Campbell Family Papers. "William Walrond," pp. 23–25. Bouwman, *Traveler's Rest*, pp. 166–67. Dew, *Bond of Iron*, pp. 181–83.

6. Langhorne, *Southern Sketches*, pp. 116–17. Janey and Janney, *Janney's Virginia*, p. 89. *Slave*, 6: 154, 13, 86, 268, 4 (b): 76, 3: 785. VS, Legislative Petitions, Loudoun 1836, in Legislative Papers. Letter dated 5 November 1855, WV, Andrew Nelson Campbell Family Papers. *Slave I*, 10: 4345. *Great Slave Narratives*, p. 212. *Slave II*, 10: 4345. Embree, *Emancipator*, p. 79. Epstein, *Sinful Tunes*, pp. 181–82.

7. *Slave*, 4 (b): 76, 13: 80, 16: 87. *Slave II*, 3: 672–73, 5: 1525, 10: 4345–46. Fisk, pp. 107, 11. SHC, James Hervey Greenlee Diary, 12 February 1849, 11 December 1849, 6 January 1851.

8. *Slave*, 1: 427, 4 (b): 76, 6: 154, 268–69. *Slave II*, 2: 45, 4: 1163, 3: 785–91, 10: 4345, 5: 1525. SHC, James Hervey Greenlee Diary, 2 January 1850,

1 October 1850. Fisk, pp. 130, 89, 107–08. *Slave I*, 10: 4345, 3: 482. *Great Slave Narratives*, 212. Janney and Janney, *Janney's Virginia*, p. 82. Shuptrine, *Home to Jericho*, p. 102.

9. Fisk, p. 131. *Slave II*, 1: 355, 9: 3638. *Slave*, 10 (b): 218, 16: 77, 17: 229. *Ferry Hill*, p. 129. Letter dated 5 November 1855, WV, Andrew Nelson Campbell Family Papers. Catterall, *Judicial Cases*, vol. 1, p. 220, vol. 2, p. 559. *Alexandria Gazette and Virginia Advertiser*, 20 December 1856. *Niles Register*, 7 August 1830. Illustration 9.1, website.

10. Regarding overwork practices, see Dew, *Bond of Iron*, pp. 151, 162, 181–83. Jackson, *Free Negro Labor*, pp. 180–81. UVSC, letter dated 2 December 1857, Southside Virginia Family Papers. *Alexandria Gazette*, 4 January 1859. Lewis, *Coal*, pp. 119–26, 159–62. VHS, letter dated 14 January 1813, David Ross Letterbook. UVSC, Etna Furnace Negro Books, 1854–61, 1852–60, and Buffalo Forge Negro Book, 1850–58, Weaver-Brady Iron works and Grist Mill Papers. Hopkins, *Hemp Industry*, pp. 135–37. UVSC, 1830–41 Journal, Weaver-Brady Iron Works and Grist Mill Papers. Olmsted, *Cotton Kingdom*, p. 48. *Early and Wife*, vol. 1, p. 245, 276. WV, Luke Willcox Diary, vol. 1, p. 17. Bradford, "Ironworker," pp. 199–200. *Slave*, 2 (b): 7, 13 (a): 266, 16: 30, 71. *U.S. Telegraph*, 11 November 1826. *Harper's Monthly* 32 (1866): 35. *Slave I*, 1: 19. *Slavery Time*, p. 99. Wade, *Slavery in Cities*, p. 53. SHC, letter dated 1 March 1836, Hamilton Brown Papers. Redpath, *Roving Editor*, p. 183. VS, Cyrus H. McCormick Letter, 2 December 1854. DPL, letter dated 24 October 1859, William Holland Thomas Papers. SHC, letter dated 22 February 1843, Thomas George Walton Papers. SHC, letters dated 20 December 1832, 2 March 1835, 6 December 1835, 1 March 1836, 6 June 1836, 23 July 1836, 24 August 1840, 13 December 1845, 15 January 1847, Hamilton Brown Papers. McKivigan, *Roving Editor*, p. 188. WV, Capehart vs. Norton and Coleman, Circuit Superior Court, 1846, Kanawha County Court Records.

11. SHC, letter dated 4 July 1859, James Gwyn Papers. Veney, *Narrative*, pp. 131–32. For a similar example, see Fisk, p. 9. Lerner, *Black Women*, pp. 33–34.

12. Cash earning patterns derived from analysis of Appalachian slave narratives. Dunaway, *First American Frontier*, pp. 78–79. Berlin and Morgan, *Slaves' Economy*, pp. 17–23. Wood, *Women's Work*, pp. 184–85.

13. Fisk, pp. 11, 107–08, 130. *Slave*, 4 (b): 76, 13: 80, 16: 87, 1: 427. *Slave II*, 3: 672–73, 791, 793, 5: 1525, 10: 4345, 9: 3879. SHC, James Hervey Greenlee Diary, 12 February 1849, 6 January 1851. Wood, *Women's Work*, p. 181. Scholars have identified this pattern in other regions as well. See Olwell, "Reckoning," p. 37; McDonald, *Economy*, pp. 151–62; Berlin and Morgan, *Slaves' Economy*, p. 12.

14. *Slave*, 16: 13. Furman, *Slavery*, p. 18. *Slave II*, 3: 786. UVSC, Negro Book, 1852–62, Nelson County Business Ledgers. See, for example, UVSC, Negro Book, 1830–40, Buffalo Forge, Weaver-Brady Iron Works and Grist Mill Papers.

15. Mullin, *Africa in America*, pp. 153–55. Catterall, *Judicial Cases*, vol. 3, p. 198. *Laws*, p. 39. Beeman, "Trade," p. 175. *Harper's Monthly* 40 (1869), p. 827.

Stroud, *Laws*, pp. 57–83. Henry, "Slave Laws," pp. 179–88. McDougle, "Slavery," p. 245. Wade, *Slavery in Cities*, pp. 106–10.

16. Catterall, *Judicial Cases*, vol. 2, p. 597. *Laws*, p. 9. *Slave*, 12: 348–49. I found no slave, free black, or female accounts in manuscript store accounts, except the payroll accounts for black employees of company stores. All transactions in company stores were charged against wages or overwork, so there was no actual extension of credit without collateral. Slaves were typically identified in company store accounts as "negro," so I presumed that independent stores would have followed this custom. Because there were so few free blacks in Appalachian communities, it was easy to cross-match their surnames in census manuscripts with names in these independent store accounts: WV, Fairmont General Store Records; UK, Graham Account Book; DPL, William LaPrade Account Books; and with company store records in WV, Winifrede Mining and Manufacturing Company Documents; WV, Donnally and Steele Kanawha Salt Works Records; and WL, Etna Furnace Company Account Book. McCurry, *Masters*, pp. 96–98, found similar credit biases in the South Carolina Low Country. Patterson, *Negro*, p. 51. Mooney, *Slavery*, pp. 33–34. McDougle, "Slavery," p. 245. *Laws*, pp. 24–25. Schweninger, "Slave Independence," pp. 101–25. *Richmond Daily Dispatch*, 18 February 1858. VS, Legislative Petitions, Loudoun 1836, in Legislative Papers. Beeman, "Trade," 175. *Harper's Monthly* 40 (1869), p. 827.

17. Table 3.3, website. Eslinger, "Liquor Reform," pp. 172–73. *Ferry Hill*, p. 11. Jackson, *Free Negro Labor*, p. 101. Woodson, "Washerwoman," pp. 269–77. Analysis of NA, 1860 Census of Population manuscripts, Sullivan County, Tennessee; Botetourt County, Virginia; Knox County, Tennessee. Ebert, "Window," p. 50. UVSC, Phoebe Jackson Account Book.

18. *Slave II*, 10: 4345. *Slave*, 3: 785.

19. Walsh, "Slave Life," pp. 186–87. Fogel and Engerman, *Without Consent*, pp. 139–44. Berlin and Morgan, *Cultivation*, pp. 19–20. Fogel, *Without Consent*, p. 51.

20. Tables 6.3 and 9.1, website.

21. Wiggington, *Foxfire 3*, p. 75–78, 163n. SHC, entries dated 16 January 1851, 10 February 1851, 15 May 1851, James Hervey Greenlee Diary.

22. Margo, "Civilian Occupations," pp. 176–77. Throughout the Americas, slaveholders assigned a greater percentage of slave women to field work. In Jamaica, 90 percent of the women and 57 percent of the men did field work; in the United States, 69 percent of the women and 58 percent of the men were assigned to field work. See Fogel, *Without Consent*, p. 46. Illustration 9.2, website.

23. Fox-Genovese, *Plantation Household*, p. 195. Wallerstein, *Historical Capitalism*, p. 25. Kotlikoff, "Quantitative Description," pp. 31–53.

24. Table 7.3, Illustration 9.3, website. For polarization of reward, see Wallerstein, *Historical Capitalism*, p. 72.

25. Table 9.1, website. Smith, Wallerstein, and Evers, *Households*, pp. 81–82. *Slave I*, 11: 18, 16, 9: 1419. Fox-Genovese, *Plantation Household*, p. 172. Joyner, *Riverside*, pp. 75–76. Craton, *Empire, Enslavement*, p. 138. Clark, *History*, vol. 1, pp. 149, 195. Pinchbeck, "Virginia Artisan," p. 42. Betts,

Jefferson's Farm Book, p. 77. Fogel, Galantine, and Manning, *Without Consent*, p. 76. WV, Marmaduke Dent Farm Journal, vol. 15, p. 129. *Slave*, 6 (a): 25–26. Hill, *Weaving*, pp. 152–54.

26. *Slave*, 2 (a): 71, 4 (b): 75. SHC, James Hervey Greenlee Diary, 10 and 22 January, 10 February, 15 May 1851. Fisk, p. 130. Fox-Genovese, *Plantation Household*, p. 181. *Slave I*, 11: 138.

27. *Slave I*, 14: 353, 1: 432, 3: 101, 5 (a): 214, 9: 1526, 12: 256. *Slave II*, 5: 1557, 6: 2280, 2258. *Slave*, 12: 138, 147, 13: 80. Fisk, p. 132. *Weevils*, p. 276. Illustration 9.4, website.

28. *Slave*, 4 (b): 76, 16: 30, 11–14. *Slave I*, 8: 324, 1216, 11: 18, 5 (a): 220, 214. *Slave I*, 3: 482, 5 (a): 214. Fisk, p. 58. Fox-Genovese, *Plantation Household*, pp. 185–86, 120–24, 434n63, 179. SHC, James Hervey Greenlee Diary, January through March, 1847. Wiggington, *Foxfire 8*, pp. 82–88. Ferguson, *Uncommon Ground*, p. 47. Joyner, *Riverside*, p. 75. Fogel and Engerman, *Without Consent*, vol. 1, p. 139. Betts, *Jefferson's Farm Book*, pp. 55–57. *Weevils*, p. 81. *Slave II*, 2:45, 3: 497.

29. *Slave*, 15 (b): 129, 12: 308–09, 16: 46, 87–88, 7: 172. Fisk, pp. 57–58, 149. Fox-Genovese, *Plantation Household*, p. 180. *Weevils*, p. 6. Clark, *History*, vol. 1, pp. 441, 223, 542, 399, 552. *Slave I*, 5 (a): 220, 5 (b): 297, 12: 335, 255, 3: 478. *Slavery Time*, p. 99. *American State Papers: Finance*, vol. 4, p. 142; vol. 2, p. 691. WV, Marmaduke Dent Farm Journal, 21 August 1869. Pinchbeck, "Virginia Artisan," pp. 41–42. *Alexandria Gazette and Daily Advertiser*, 19–24 December 1816, 12 June 1817. *Slave II*, 4: 1099, 5: 1555. Inscoe, *Mountain Masters*, p. 195. *Kentucky Gazette*, 5 September 1809.

30. *Slave I*, 5 (b): 298, 297, 7: 689, 11: 131. Irwin, *Alex Stewart*, p. 126. Fisk, pp. 91, 149. Wiggington, *Foxfire 2*, pp. 184–255. *Slave*, 4 (b): 75. *Slave II*, 10: 4273.

31. *Slave*, 6 (a): 90–91, 16 (b): 12–14, 14 (a): 353, 12: 144. *Slave I*, 3: 478, 7: 695, 5 (b): 297, 11: 131–32. *Slave II*, 3: 671. Fisk, p. 56. King, "Suffer," p. 156. *Weevils*, pp. 88–89. Illustration 9.5, website.

32. *Slave*, 13 (a): 267, 6: 155, 12: 308. *Slave I*, 5 (b): 297, 3: 478–79, 5 (a): 256, 8: 1216. *Slave II*, 5: 1555–56.

33. *Slave I*, 7: 689, 11: 17–18, 132, 5 (a): 256, 461, 3: 97, 272, 12: 334. *Slave*, 8 (a): 46, 6 (a): 90, 12: 144, 13 (a): 267, 16: 45. *Weevils*, pp. 81, 6. *Slave II*, 3: 671. Irwin, *Alex Stewart*, p. 126. Fisk, p. 56. For detail about weaving, see Wiggington, *Foxfire 2*, pp. 172–255, and *Foxfire 8*, p. 52.

34. Once a year, the seamstress made a pattern for each adult slave, by having the person lie on old newspaper. With a pencil, she traced the human shape and size, allowing a little growing room. *Slave*, 12: 144, 312, 13: 76, 16: 30, 78, 87, 67; 9 (b): 151, 2 (b): 114, 10 (b): 166, 6 (a): 47, 7: 46. *Slave I*, 7: 689, 11: 17–19, 5 (a): 256. *Slave II*, 3: 67, 791, 1: 347–48. Kelso, "Archaeology," p. 15. Fisk, p. 146.

35. *Slave*, 16 (b): 14, 17: 230, 2 (a): 71, 15 (b): 129. *Slave I*, 12: 335, 11: 18, 3: 272.

36. Table 7.3, website. Use of cash derived from analysis of Appalachian slave narratives and from perusal of slave accounts at several company stores. UVSC, Negro Books, 1854–61, Etna Furnace, Weaver-Brady Iron Works and Grist Mill Papers. *Early and Wife*, vol. 1, p. 276. Dew, *Bond of Iron*, pp. 151,

181–83. Olmsted, *Cotton Kingdom*, p. 48. Lewis, *Coal*, pp. 126, 159–62. Dew, *Bond of Iron*, p. 162.

37. Washington, *Up from Slavery*, pp. 9–10. *Slave*, 6: 195, 7: 35, 13: 80. *Slave I*, 12: 334. Fisk, p. 108.

CHAPTER 6

1. Opening quote is from Fisk, p. 144. McKinney, *Southern Mountain*, pp. 22–26. Even though the map shows a few counties in eastern Kentucky and West Virginia free of warfare and guerilla activity, it is likely that every county of the Southern Appalachians (with the exception perhaps of western Maryland) was disrupted by sporadic foraging raids and retaliatory conflicts between Unionists and Confederates. *Slave*, 4 (a): 291–92. Hearn, *Six Years of Hell*, pp. 78–90. O'Brien, *Mountain Partisans*, pp. 114–15. McKinney, *Southern Mountain*, pp. 23–24.

2. *Slave II*, 3: 808. Dew, *Bond of Iron*, p. 295. *Slave*, 7 (a): 21, 16: 57, 6 (a): 381. *Slave I*, 12: 258, 337–39. *Freedom*, vol. 2, p. 526.

3. *Slave*, 10 (a): 188, 12: 313–14. Berlin, Favreau, and Miller, *Remembering*, p. 240. *Freedom*, vol. 2, pp. 399–402.

4. *Slave I*, 5 (b): 316, 309–13, 1: 433, 5 (a): 213. *Slave*, 5: 449, 4 (b): 1527, 7 (a): 21, 16: 57, 10 (a): 100, 6 (a): 381. Jordan, *Black Confederates*, pp. 133–34.

5. *Slave*, 6 (a): 280, 12 (a): 313–14, 200, 4 (b): 78, 16 (b): 14–15. Fisk, pp. 14, 58. *Lexington Valley Star* (Virginia), 30 May, 6 June 1861. *Slave I*, 8: 1222, 14: 387–88, 12: 258. *Slave II*, 10: 4274.

6. Sitterson, *Secession*, pp. 220–21. *Freedom*, vol. 2, p. 430. SHC, letter dated 15 April 1861, Theodore Morrison Papers. Dew, *Bond of Iron*, pp. 294–95. Letter dated 4 April 1861, Hairston Papers. SHC, James Gwyn Diary, 4 May 1861, James Gwyn Papers.

7. Fisk, pp. 59, 4. *Slave*, 16 (b): 14–15. *Families and Freedom*, p. 41.

8. *Slave II*, 3: 808. *Freedom*, vol. 2, p. 379. Jordan, *Black Confederates*, pp. 40–48, 79. Inscoe, "Confederate Opportunists," pp. 84–95. UVSC, Nancy Emerson Diary, 8 January 1863. *Slave I*, 12: 258. Buck, *Sad Earth*, p. 144. Illustrations 13.1, 13.2, and 13.3, website.

9. Analysis of Appalachian slave narratives. *Slave I*, 1: 152–53.

10. Jordan, *Black Confederates*, pp. 55, 58–61, 66–67, 125, 205, 321. Fisk, p. 55. *Slave*, 11 (a): 168. *Slave II*, 5: 1866. Illustration 13.4, website.

11. *Slave I*, 5 (b): 307. Berlin, Fields, Miller, Reidy, and Rowland, *Slaves No More*, pp. 206–07. Analysis of Appalachian slave narratives. *Freedom*, vol. 2, p. 213.

12. There were few black military laborers in Maryland, and Union impressment of slaves began later in Virginia, Georgia, and North Carolina; see *Freedom*, vol. 2, p. 486. *Slave II*, 3: 816–18.

13. *Freedom*, vol. 2, pp. 630–31, 366, 396–99, 659–61, 378. Illustration 13.5, website.

14. *Families and Freedom*, pp. 22–23. *Slave*, 14 (a): 80–81.

15. *Freedom's Soldiers*, pp. 11–14. *Slave*, 7 (a): 21, 10 (a): 306, 189, 4 (b): 38–39, 11 (a): 255. Fisk, p. 218. *Slave I*, 5 (a): 212–13, 8: 1222–23.

16. Table 13.1, website. *Freedom's Soldiers*, pp. 16–17. *Freedom*, vol. 2, pp. 485–86.
17. Slave military service was derived from analysis of Appalachian slave narratives. *Freedom's Soldiers*, pp. 6n, 21, 26, 42. Franklin, *Diary*, pp. xxvii–xxxi. *Freedom*, vol. 2, p. 378, 396–97. *Slave I*, 11: 121, 14: 357. *Slave II*, 3: 816–20.
18. Berlin, Fields, Miller, Reidy, and Rowland, *Slaves No More*, p. 180. Analysis of county totals from U. S. Census Office, *Population in 1860*. *Freedom*, vol. 2, pp. 376–77. *CWVQ*, p. 1233. *Slave II*, 3: 816. *Weevils*, pp. 168–69. *Freedom's Soldiers*, pp. 122–23. Fisk, p. 150.
19. Franklin, *Diary*, pp. xvii, 5, 46–47, 43. *Slave I*, 5 (b): 315. *Freedom*, vol. 2, pp. 377, 145.
20. Jordan, *Black Confederates*, pp. 245, 213, 223, 196–97. *Slave I*, 12: 336. *Slave*, 13 (a): 272.
21. *Slave*, 7: 173–74, 16 (b): 12, 6: 270–71. *Weevils*, pp. 167–68. Jordan, *Black Confederates*, pp. 283–85. *Freedom*, vol. 2, pp. 406–407, 456–58.
22. Fisk, pp. 150, 218. Jordan, *Black Confederates*, p. 281. *Freedom's Soldiers*, pp. 134–35.
23. *Families and Freedom*, pp. 137–38. *Black Military Experience*, pp. 154–58, 160, 170, 271, 290–94, 314–15, 338–39, 341. With similar racial discrimination, the Confederate Army withheld pay, uniforms, and provisions from the Cherokee soldiers in William Holland Thomas's western Carolina regiment; see DPL, letter dated 8 July 1864, William Holland Thomas Papers. *Freedom*, vol. 2, p. 700. Jordan, *Black Confederates*, pp. 272, 132.
24. *Freedom's Soldiers*, p. 43.
25. *Freedom*, vol. 2, pp. 112, 156–57. *Slave Testimony*, pp. 735–36.
26. *Families and Freedom*, pp. 116–17, 109.
27. *Slave I*, 12: 331. *Slave*, 10 (a): 177. *Weevils*, p. 162 . *Freedom*, vol. 2, pp. 449, 526–29.
28. *Freedom*, vol. 2, pp. 168–69, 682. *Families and Freedom*, pp. 137–38.
29. *Freedom*, vol. 2, pp. 635, 671–73, 685, 689–90, 693.
30. *Freedom*, vol. 2, pp. 125–26. *Families and Freedom*, pp. 125–26.
31. *Freedom*, vol. 2, pp. 384, 458, 460–61, 475, 444, 127, 131–34, 136–40, 178–79. Illustration 13.6, website.
32. *Freedom*, vol. 2, p. 157. McDonald, *Woman's Civil War*, pp. 64–65.
33. *Freedom*, vol 2, pp. 200, 227, 162. *Slave I*, 14 (a): 80–81. Illustration 13.7, website.
34. Berlin, Fields, Miller, Reidy, and Rowland, *Slaves No More*, p. 192. *Families and Freedom*, p. 119. *Freedom*, vol. 2, pp. 424, 664–65. Illustration 13.8, website.
35. *Freedom*, vol. 2, pp. 143, 183, 648, 127. *Families and Freedom*, pp. 125–26.
36. *Freedom*, vol. 2, pp. 476, 442, 148–49, 435–39. Illustration 13.9, website.
37. *Freedom*, vol. 2, pp. 226–27, 95, 124, 230, 441–42. Berlin, Fields, Miller, Reidy, and Rowland, *Slave No More*, pp. 162–63. *Families and Freedom*, p. 138.
38. *Freedom*, vol. 2, pp. 666–67, 33, 408–11, 144–45, 147.
39. *Freedom*, vol. 2, pp. 438, 681, 694–95, 440. *Families and Freedom*, pp. 122–25. Illustration 13.10, website.

40. *Families and Freedom*, pp. 121–22, 126. *Freedom*, vol. 2, pp. 691, 466–67, 460, 694. Berlin, Fields, Miller, Reidy, and Rowland, *Slaves No More*, p. 180.

CHAPTER 7

1. Opening quote is from Brown, *Crossing*, pp. 65–66. Table 14.1, website. *Slave I*, 5 (a): 354. *Freedom's Soldiers*, p. 6 n 10. *Freedom*, vol. 2, p. 11. *Families and Freedom*, pp. 26, 33–34, 69, 71–72.

2. SHC, James Gwyn Diary, 31 July 1865, James Gwyn Papers. Clemson, *Rebel*, pp. 92–93. VHS, letter dated 5 June 1865, Holburn Letterbook. Bouwman, *Traveler's Rest*, p. 193. *Freedom*, vol. 2, pp. 528–29. Illustration 14.1, website.

3. Gutman, *Black Family*, pp. 375–79. *Freedom*, vol. 2, pp. 625–38. SHC, James Hervey Greenlee Diary, 9 and 13 May, 14 June, 8 October 1865.

4. SHC, entries dated 13 February, 25 August, 20 November 1865, 24 February 1866, James Gwyn Diary, James Gwyn Papers. Clemson, *Rebel*, pp. 92–93.

5. *Slave*, 4: 78–79, 6 (a): 280–81. *Slave II*, 9: 3877.

6. *Freedom*, vol. 2, pp. 474–77. *Slave*, 10 (a): 304. *Weevils*, p. 275. *Slave II*, 3: 674. *Slave I*, 12: 336–38. *Families and Freedom*, pp. 177, 248n16. Illustration 14.2, website.

7. *Slave*, 16: 79, 24. Harlan and Blassingame, *Washington Papers*, vol. 1, pp. 13–14. *Weevils*, pp. 180, 58–59.

8. Brown, *Crossing*, pp. 65–66. More than one-quarter of the regional narratives were collected by black interviewers.

9. *Slave*, 3 (b): 119, 4 (b): 78–79. *Slave I*, 5 (a): 215. *Slave II*, 6: 2260–61.

10. *Slave II*, 6: 2285–86, 10: 4275. *Families and Freedom*, p. 119.

11. Table 14.2, website.

12. Tables 14.3 and 14.4, website. Johnson and Campbell, *Black Migration*, pp. 43–56. Anderson, *American Census*, p. 80. One-third of white Union soldiers died; see *Encyclopedia of American History*, p. 292. However, the death rate for black soldiers was higher because of the lack of equitable medical care; see *Freedom*, vol. 2, p. 424. At least one-third of black Appalachian males aged sixteen to forty-five enlisted as Union soldiers; see Table 13.1, website. Slave narratives, archival sources, and published primary sources document the presence of labor recruiters in Appalachian counties after 1880. See WV, Marmaduke Dent Farm Journal, vol. 7, p. 105; vol. 13, p. 10; vol. 14, p. 19; vol. 16, p. 126; vol. 18, p. 60. *Slave*, 11 (a): 69, 8 (a): 62, 8 (b): 231. *Slave I*, 5: 204–05, 11: 305–06. Langhorne, *Southern Sketches*, pp. 17, 114. *Slave II*, 4: 1434–35.

13. *Slave*, 7: 163, 11 (a): 211, 4 (b): 78–79. "Evelyn Williams." Fisk, pp. 129–31. *Slave II*, 6: 2260–61, 4: 1167.

14. Berlin, Fields, Miller, Reidy, and Rowland, *Slaves No More*, pp. 171–72. Letters and orders dated 15 June 1865, 4 November 1865, 24 April 1865, General Order 11, Assistant Superintendent Records. Orser, *Material Basis*, pp. 139–40. *Slave II*, 6: 2288. Illustration 14.3, website.

15. *Slave I*, 2: 283, 5: 462, 1: 433, 8: 918–19. *Slave II*, 6: 2287–88. *Slave*, 7: 163, 10 (a): 178, 8 (a): 105. *Freedom*, vol. 2, pp. 75–76, 472–73n. UVSC, William T. Gordon Diary, 7 August 1865.

16. Berlin, Favreau, and Miller, *Remembering*, p. 321. *Slave*, 16: 24, 43–44. *Greenville Mountaineer*, 14 February and 18 July 1867.

17. Dunaway, *First American Frontier*, p. 87–122. Morgan, *Emancipation*, p. 153. *Slave*, 16: 68, 8 (a): 106. *Slave II*, 4: 1103–05. *Slave I*, 12: 338–39, 1: 20, 5 (b): 308, 3: 483. Fisk, p. 133.

18. *Slave*, 7: 26. *Slave I*, 1: 144, 153. *Slave II*, 9: 3875, 3: 818–19. *Southern Railroad*, pp. 50–51. Taylor, *Negro*, p. 31.

19. *Freedom*, vol. 2, pp. 702–03. *Families and Freedom*, p. 120.

20. *Families and Freedom*, pp. 127–30, 139, 209–10. *Slave I*, 8: 1223–24. *Freedom's Soldiers*, pp. 159–60.

21. Buck, *Sad Earth*, pp. 287–88. Veney, *Narrative*, p. 41. Trowbridge, *Desolate South*, pp. 62–64. McKinney, *Southern Mountain*, pp. 30–61. SHC, James Hervey Greenlee Diary, 25 May 1865. James Gwyn Diary, 31 July 1865, James Gwyn Papers. Clemson, *Rebel*, p. 93–96, 105.

22. Dunaway, *First American Frontier*, pp. 133–52. SHC, letter dated 30 August 1865, Hamilton Brown Papers. Langhorne, *Southern Sketches*, pp. 4–5.

23. Dunaway, *First American Frontier*, pp. 305–12. Clemson, *Rebel*, p. 107. SHC, letters dated 4 and 14 March 1866, Hamilton Brown Papers. SHC, James Gwyn Diary, 5 May 1865, James Gwyn Papers. SHC, James Hervey Greenlee Diary, 15 September and 21 December 1865. Langhorne, *Southern Sketches*, p. 52. *Slave II*, 10: 4347–48.

24. *Slave*, 13: 93, 11 (a): 169, 16: 39, 8 (a): 106. *Slave II*, 3: 823.

CHAPTER 8

1. Opening quote is from *Slave II*, 5: 1565–67. Tables 14.6 and 14.7, website. NA, 1870 Census of Population enumerator manuscripts, Floyd County, Georgia. WV, Marmaduke Dent Farm Journal, 14 June 1860, 1 January, 10 March, 31 December 1867, 22 March 1869, 28 January and 30 July 1868, 22 June 1869, 1 January 1870, 31 December 1879, 24 May 1882. Smith, *Wealth of Nations*, especially pp. 66–88, 304–09, 427–46. UVSC, Louisa H. A. Minor Diary, December 1865. Illustration 14.4, website.

2. Table 14.5, website. Names of black farmers or farm laborers in the sample of households were cross-checked against the 1870 Census of Agriculture enumerator manuscripts. SHC, James Hervey Greenlee Diary, 20 October, 10 November 1866, 21 February, 4, 10, 11, 20, 21 May, 3, 4, 21, 27 June, 9, 11, 29 July, 28 August, 5, 17 September, 1, 22 October, 1, 17, 18, 21, 26 November, 4, 14 December 1867.

3. *Slave*, 12: 244, 314, 8 (a): 106, 16: 47, 2 (a): 292, 13 (a): 272, 10 (a): 45. SHC, Account Book, 1 June 1865 through 31 December 1867, James Gwyn Papers. *Slave II*, 6: 2285.

4. Tables 14.6 and 14.7, website. *Slave*, 10 (a): 102, 1: 57. *Slave I*, 12: 339, 5 (a): 215–16. *Slave II*, 6: 2287, 4: 1104. Moore, *Mountain Voices*, p. 101.

5. Morgan, *Emancipation*, p. 152. *Slave*, 10 (b): 129, 4 (b): 79, 10 (a): 189–90. NA, Records Relating to Court Cases, Shenandoah County, Virginia, 30 November 1866. *Slave II*, 3: 675. SHC, James Hervey Greenlee Diary, comparison of 1867, 1877, 1878 entries.

6. Tables 14.8 and 8.6, website. WV, Marmaduke Dent Farm Journal, 11 and 31 January 1867, 2 July 1870, 31 January 1874. *Slave I*, 7: 699–700.

7. Tables 3.4, 3.5, and 14.5, website.

8. *Slave II*, 3: 499. *Slave*, 16: 13. The number of black laborers dropped dramatically at one southwestern Virginia iron works; see UVSC, 1865–72 ledger, Weaver-Brady Iron Works and Grist Mill Papers. Langhorne, *Southern Sketches*, p. 105. Wright, *Racial Violence*, p. 38. Montell, *Saga*, pp. 166, 252. Taylor, *Negro*, pp. 142–43. Millner, "Conversations," pp. 213–22. Bailey, "Judicious Mixture," pp. 117–32. Trotter, *Coal, Class and Color.*

9. Langhorne, *Southern Sketches*, p. 17. *Weevils*, p. 8. Wright, *Racial Violence*, p. 144. WV, Henri Jean Mugler Diary, vol. 20, pp. 21–49. *Slave*, 13: 90–91. Morgan, *Emancipation*, p. 194. *Greenville Mountaineer*, 14 February 1867. Illustration 14.6, website.

10. Ward, *Southern Railroad*, pp. 50–62. Bell also reported that "the Chinese were turned loose without being paid in full."

11. Wish, *George Fitzhugh*, p. 333. *Slave II*, 5: 1566.

12. *Slave Testimony*, pp. 737–38.

13. Knoxville Industrial Association, "Facts and Figures, 1869." McKinney, *Southern Mountain*, pp. 30–61. Cooling, "People's War," pp. 124, 132. Sarris, "Shot," pp. 31–44. Fisher, "Definitions," pp. 89–112.

14. *Louisville Courier-Journal*, 5 December 1878, p. 3. Disney, "Mountain Feuds," p. 10. Klotter, "Feuds," pp. 290–317. Warner, "Comments," p. 270. Fleming, *Civil War*, pp. 279–81, 265. Trowbridge, *Desolate South*, pp. 232–33. *Slave*, 13: 90. Ward, *Southern Railroad*, pp. 53–54. *New York Times*, 11 February 1866, p. 12. NA, Assistant Superintendents Records, Virginia, Letters dated 30 March and 30 May 1868.

15. Table 14.9, website. For example, one writer has claimed that "Appalachians have not been saddled with the same prejudices about black people that people of the Deep South have;" see Jones, "Appalachian Values," p. 514. Recent revisionist research supports these trends for the Reconstruction era. There was a greater per-capita incidence of lynchings in Southern states with smaller black populations; see Tolnay and Beck, *Festival*, pp. 37–38. After 1880, a black Appalachian was more likely to be lynched than a black non-Appalachian in the same states. In the late 1880s and early 1890s, there were twice as many lynchings in the Appalachian counties of Virginia as there were in the Tidewater, and a northern Georgia black was twice as likely to be lynched as a southern Georgia black; see Brundage, *Lynching*, pp. 142, 270–83.

16. Table 14.10, website. Between 1865 and 1870, Klan and mob violence against black Union soldiers and their families was common throughout the South. See *Families and Freedom*, p. 121; *Black Military Experience*, pp. 808–09. *Freedom's Soldiers*, p. 173. *Slave II*, 3: 818–19. NA, Records Relating to Court Cases, Montgomery County, Virginia, 25 July 1866.

17. Conway, *Reconstruction*, p. 68. Coulter, *Georgia*, p. 371. Grant, *Way It Was*, pp. 125, 159, 160, 164. *Slave*, 12: 351. *Slave I*, 4: 430.

18. Stagg, "Problem," pp. 303–18. *Slave*, 3 (a): 16, 248, 2 (b): 250–55, 120, 12 (b): 200, 2 (a): 46. *Greenville Mountaineer*, 18 July 1867. Clemson, *Rebel*, p. 95. *Greenville Mountaineer*, 26 October 1870.

19. Analysis of Klan incidents, Fleming, *Civil War*, p. 703. *Slave II*, 3: 824–28. *Slave*, 1: 57–58. Ward, *Southern Railroad*, pp. 57–58.

20. WV, Ku Klux Klan, Monongalia County Manuscripts. This 1868 collection includes a list of members, the oath, and the constitution for the organization. *Slave II*, 5: 1568–69. NA, Records of the Education Division, Monthly Reports, Kentucky, Letter dated 13 October 1868. Wright, *Racial Violence*, pp. 307–11, 26, 38–41, 148–49, 307–23. *Slave I*, 8: 919. Patton, *Sketches*, p. 46. NA, Records Relating to Murders and Outrages, North Carolina.

21. NA, Records Relating to Murders and Outrages, Virginia, February and April 1868. SHC, letter dated 18 May 1868, Hamilton Brown Papers. *Slave*, 16: 68. *Slave II*, 6: 2285. *Slave I*, 5 (a): 77.

22. Tables 14.10 and 14.11, website. In NA, Records Relating to Murders and Outrages, 401 of the 1,162 incidents reported in Appalachian counties were raids on black political meetings, assaults on voters or political candidates, destruction of black churches and schools, assaults on black ministers or teachers, and assaults on whites who supported black organizations. *Slave II*, 5: 1568–69. Olson, "Race Relations," pp. 154–55.

23. *Freedom's Lawmakers*, p. 75; this collection includes no lists of black officers for Kentucky and Maryland.

24. *Slave*, 7: 163, 2 (b): 120–21, 3 (b): 216–17, 10 (b): 224. *Slave I*, 11: 23.

25. Such violence was so pervasive throughout the Southern Mountains that it is impossible to mention every incident, so I have selected only a few typical cases. Table 14.10, website. Analysis of NA, Records Relating to Murders and Outrages. Grant, *Way It Was*, p. 228. *Slave*, 12: 243. Stowell, "Negroes," pp. 76–78. Fleming, *Civil War*, p. 626. Jordan, *Black Confederates*, p. 105.

26. Wright, *Racial Violence*, pp. 36–37. DDC, Alice Williamson Diary, 2 May through 15 May 1864. NA, Monthly Report, June 1868, West Virginia, District of Columbia, Records of the Education Division, District of Columbia, Monthly Reports, Maryland, June 1868.

27. Dunaway, *First American Frontier*, pp. 292–93. Fisk, p. 218. NA, Records of the Education Division, District of Columbia, Monthly Reports, West Virginia, March and June 1868. WV, Marmaduke Dent Farm Journal, vol. 10, p. iii.

28. Trowbridge, *Desolate South*, p. 262. Freedmen's schools operated in the Alabama counties of Jefferson and Talladega; the Georgia counties of Chattooga, Cherokee, and Floyd; Madison County, Kentucky; the North Carolina counties of Buncombe and Burke; the Tennessee counties of Coffee, Franklin, Hamilton, Jefferson, Knox, Sullivan, and Warren; plus the Virginia counties of Amherst, Bedford, Botetourt, Franklin, Frederick, Montgomery, Nelson, Rappahannock, Roanoke, Rockbridge, Rockingham, Shenandoah, and Washington. All three western Maryland counties and the West Virginia counties of Berkeley, Jefferson, Harrison, Ohio, and Wood operated public black schools. For a diary that documents such erratic circuit trips to schools in Appalachian Virginia, see Horst, *Fire*, pp. 138–59. The black colleges were Christiansburg Normal Industrial Institute (Montgomery County, Virginia), Quaker Freedmen's Normal Institute (Maryville, Tennessee), Howard School (Chattanooga), Knoxville College (Tennessee), Stover College (West

Virginia), and Talladega College (Alabama). Stokely and Johnson, *Encyclopedia*, pp. 80–81, 274, 315. Peck, *Berea's First*, p. 38. Taylor, *Negro*, pp. 172–73. *Christiansburg Herald* 1 (1) (1999), p. 1. King, *Southern States*, vol. 1, p. 343. NA, Monthly Reports, West Virginia, February and March 1868, Records of the Education Division, District of Columbia. Stover College Records.

29. NA, Records of the Education Division, District of Columbia, Letters dated 1 and 2 September 1867, Monthly Reports, West Virginia, March and June 1868. Monthly Report, Maryland, March 1868.

30. Table 14.12 and 14.6, website.

31. *Slave*, 13: 93, 16: 24, 13, 47, 72, 10 (a): 182. *Slave I*, 8: 1161, 2: 74, 5 (a): 216. Fisk, p. 129.

32. Horst, *Fire*, pp. 39, 44–47, 53, 138–49. Jones, *Soldiers*, pp. 31–68.

33. Table 14.12, website. Berlin, Favreau, and Miller, *Remembering*, p. 321. *Slave*, 10 (b): 166. *Slave I*, 5 (b): 29.

34. Tables 13.1 and 14.13, website. NA, Assistant Superintendent Records, Monthly Reports, Montgomery County, Virginia, March 1866. deForest, *Union Officer*, pp. 36–37.

35. Tables 14.13 and 8.2, website.

36. Morgan, *Emancipation*, pp. 172–73. *Slave*, 3 (a): 261. *Slave I*, 9: 1423. Jordan, *Black Confederates*, pp. 302–03. Fisk, pp. 88, 94.

37. Tables 8.1 and 14.6, website. Analysis of 1866 Marriage Registers for Nelson, Rockbridge, and Montgomery Counties, Virginia, as reported in Gutman, *Black Family*, p. 12.

38. Drew, *North-side View*, p. 45. *Slave II*, 10: 4342. Veney, *Narrative*, pp. 41–42.

39. *Slave*, 11 (b): 209–10. WV, Marmaduke Dent Farm Journal, 20 January 1867, 17 May 1870.

40. deForest, *Union Officer*, pp. 97–99. *Slave*, 7: 138, 143, 16 (b): 34–35. *Slave I*, 5 (b): 318.

41. Table 14.13, website. Gutman, *Black Family*, pp. 415–17, 420. *Slave*, 2 (b): 9. Randolph, *Sketches*, pp. 89–91.

42. UH, unsigned 1869 letter to Laura Spicer, Mintz, "Excerpts." Fisk, p. 58. Illustration 14.7, website.

43. Table 14.14, website. Gutman, *Black Family*, pp. 167–68. *Families and Freedom*, pp. 185–87. WV, Marmaduke Dent Farm Journal, 22 March 1869, 14 April and 3 June 1867.

44. *Freedom*, vol. 2, p. 524. Gutman, *Black Family*, pp. 402–11.

45. *Slave I*, 2: 74, 9: 1527–29. Godbold and Russell, *Confederate Colonel*, p. 130. Illustration 14.8, website.

46. NA, Assistant Superintendents Records, Virginia, 20 May 1866. NA, Records Relating to Court Cases, Virginia, 30 September 1866.

47. *Slave*, 16 (b): 15, 22, 13, 4 (b): 34, 10 (a): 100–01. *Slave II*, 3: 500, 4: 1242, 10: 4275, 6: 2261. *Slave I*, 3: 102, 12: 339.

THEORETICAL REPRISE

1. Opening quote is from Tadman, *Speculators and Slave*, p. 133. Moynihan, *Negro Family*, pp. xi–xii. Gutman, *Black Family*, pp. 461–64, 644n1–2. Fogel, *Without Consent*, pp. 164–65; for additional personal discussion, see

pp. 389–90. Du Bois, *Negro American Family*, pp. 47–49, 152. Frazier, *Negro Family*, pp. 23–30. Stampp, *Peculiar Institution*, pp. 340–48. Phillips, *American Negro Slavery*, p. 369. Collins, *Domestic Slave Trade*, p. 74. Fogel and Engerman, *Time*, vol. 1, pp. 49–52. Genovese, *Roll*, pp. 453, 489, 485–86.

2. Bancroft, *Slave Trading*, pp. 68, 208. Stampp, *Peculiar Institution*, pp. 245, 251. Bancroft and Stampp argued against the earlier slave trading views of Phillips, *American Negro Slavery*, and Collins, *Domestic Slave Trade*. Conrad and Meyer, *Economics*, pp. 80–85. Fogel and Engerman, *Time*, vol. 1, pp. 5, 53, 79. Fogel, *Without Consent*, pp. 392, 69.

3. Genovese, *Roll*, pp. 415, 424, 453, 486, 489. Fogel, *Without Consent*, pp. 391, 134. Southern novels portray a paternalistic mystique in which slaveholders embraced a "sentiment of honor," which demanded that slaves only be "purchased to remain in the district." Though a few slaves had to be sold away from their families because of their unruliness, southern writers claimed that such occurrences "were very uncommon." Any disadvantages of such forced migrations were minimized because the slave's "strongest affection" was believed to be "love of master, his guide, protector, friend," not ties to black kin. Slaves were not supposed to establish the same kinds of family feelings as whites, so any disruption would be ameliorated by quick remarriage. See Randolph, *Cabin and Parlor*, p. 3, and Eastman, *Aunt Phillis's Cabin*, pp. 213–15.

4. *Families and Freedom*, pp. 7–9.

5. Berlin, *Many Thousands*, p. 106. Frazier, "Slave Family," p. 236. Inscoe, *Mountain Masters*, pp. 104–06. Neither Gutman, *Black Family*, p. 338, nor Fogel, *Without Consent*, pp. 152–53, support such notions about small plantations.

6. Crawford, "Quantified Memory." Patterson, *Slavery*, pp. 218–30. Tadman, *Slaves and Speculators*, pp. 211–12. Stevenson, *Life*, p. 222.

7. Thompson, "Structures," p. 414. Wallerstein, *Modern World-System II*, p. 241.

8. Gutman, *Black Family*, pp. 11–28, 164, 304–05, 602–03. Crawford, "Quantified Memory." Patterson, *Slavery*, pp. 218–30. Tadman, *Slaves and Speculators*, pp. 211–12. Stevenson, *Life*, p. 222.

9. Fogel and Engerman, *Time*, vol. 1, pp. 5, 53, 79. Fogel, *Without Consent*, pp. 392, 69.

10. Gutman, "Persistent Myths," pp. 181–210.

11. Ibid. Genovese, *Roll*, pp. 450–52. Gutman, *Black Family*, pp. 9, 12, 141, 167–68, 146. Crawford, "Slave Family," pp. 333–36.

12. Tables 8.2 and 8.3, website. Gutman, *Black Family*, pp. 9, 12, 141, 167–68, 146. Crawford, "Slave Family," pp. 333–36. Tadman, *Speculators*, p. 174.

13. Patterson, *Slavery*, pp. 5–9. Gutman, *Black Family*, pp. 75–76. Maher, *Anthropology*, p. 24.

14. Steckel, "Slave Mortality," pp. 100–01. Stevenson, *Life*, pp. 245–48. Maher, *Anthropology*, p. 164.

15. For the notion of ideological camouflage, see Patterson, *Slavery*, p. 229. For examples of slaveholder reaction to child deaths, see DPL, letter dated 13 November 1856, John L. Bailey Collection; SHC, letter dated 8 July 1825, Lenoir Family Papers; SHC, Lucilla Gamble McCorkle Diary. Savitt,

Medicine, p. 119. VHS, letter dated 9 January 1813, David Ross Letterbook. UVSC, letter dated 15 December 1841, Hubbard Family Papers. When a new infant died "sometime in the night" on a Nelson County, Virginia, plantation, the master reported in his journal that Matilda had "over laid" a baby that "was well and hearty when she went to bed." When her newborn died under similar circumstances, Marietta was found guilty of infanticide by the Loudoun County court and ordered deported to the Lower South. See *Loudoun Democratic Mirror*, 11 November 1858.

16. Bush-Slimani, "Hard Labour," p. 84. Boydston, "Daily Bread," p. 22. Steckel, "Women," pp. 44–56. Cody, "Seasonality," pp. 72–73. Lumpkin, *Making*, p. 22. Regarding early menarche and high-fat diets, see Chapter 4, and Frisch and McArthur, "Menstrual Cycles," pp. 949–51.

17. Regarding mountain slave diaspora myths, resistance, and culture, see Dunaway, *Slavery*, Chs. 6 and 7. Fox-Genovese, "Antebellum Southern Households," pp. 248–49. Wallerstein and Smith, "Core-Periphery," pp. 259–61. Thompson, "Structures," pp. 403, 417. Lim, "Capitalism," pp. 76–77.

18. Gomez, *Exchanging*, p. 222.

19. Berlin and Morgan, *Slaves' Economy*, p. 1. Tomich, "Contested Terrains," p. 254. Schlotterbeck, "Internal Economy," p. 178. Drew, *North-side View*, p. 280. *Slave*, 4 (a): 302, 4 (b): 36, 6 (a): 279, 7 (a): 346, 1: 58, 16: 12. Fisk, pp. 214–16. *Slave I*, 1: 149–51, 21, 10: 4273. *Slave II*, 6: 2280, 10: 4273, 3: 785. For discussion of the concepts of *self-exploitation* and *super-exploitation*, see Smith, Wallerstein, and Evers, *Households*, pp. 259–61; Deere, "Rural Women's Subsistence," p. 9; and Marx, *Capital*, vol. 1, pp. 431, 599, 602.

20. Morrissey, *Slave Women*, p. 53. Barickman, "A Bit," pp. 651–52. Olwell, "Reckoning," p. 39. Sanford, "Archaeology," p. 119. *Slave*, 16: 30. SHC, James Hervey Greenlee Diary, 24 December 1843.

21. For a summary of literature taking this view, see Barickman, "A Bit," p. 649n1. Berlin and Morgan, *Slaves' Economy*, pp. 1–27, 131–81. Cardoso, "Peasant Breach," pp. 49–57. Turner, *From Chattel*, pp. 241–57. Crawford, "Quantified Memory," p. 547. Berlin and Morgan, *Slaves' Economy*, p. 12. Mullin, *Africa in America*, pp. 137–38. Mintz, *Origins*, pp. 47–53.

22. Mintz, *Origins*, pp. 47–53. Patterson, *Slavery*, pp. 185–86. Berlin and Morgan, *Slaves' Economy*, p. 20.

23. Komlos and Coclanis, "Puzzling Cycle," p. 443–44, 452. Tadman, *Speculators*, pp. 111–32. Analysis of Appalachian slaveholder records. Dunaway, *First American Frontier*, pp. 294–98.

24. Dunaway, *First American Frontier*, pp. 139–50. Gawalt, "James Monroe," p. 267.

25. Dunaway, *First American Frontier*, pp. 148–52.

26. Ibid., pp. 139–42, 151–53, 386n9. Lamb, "Mule," p. 24.

27. Fogel and Engerman, *Time*, p. 76. Steckel, "Work," pp. 498–501. Calculated using statistics in Sutch, "Breeding," Table 3, and Steckel, "Peculiar Population," Table 4, p. 739.

28. Table 8.5, Illustration 8.5, website. Betts, *Jefferson's Farm Book*, p. 138. Gray, *History*, vol. 1, pp. 563–64. Dunaway, "Incorporation," pp. 1029–31. Analysis

of Appalachian slave narratives. Phillips, *Life and Labor*, p. 134. Lamb, "Mule," pp. 18, 29.

29. Lamb, "Mule," pp. 18, 29. Berlin, Favreau, and Miller, *Remembering*, p. 289. *Slave*, 16 (b): 12. *Slave II*, 3: 785.
30. Fogel, *Without Consent*, pp. 167, 393–98.
31. Hughes, *Thirty Years*, p. 6. Illustration 14.9, website.

Bibliography

ARCHIVAL COLLECTIONS UTILIZED

AL: ALABAMA DEPARTMENT OF ARCHIVES AND HISTORY, MONTGOMERY, ALABAMA

George Brewer, "History of Coosa, Alabama," Typescript
Montevallo Coal Mining Company Records
Pardons, Paroles, and Clemency Files, 1821–53
B. Smith Letter, 15 August 1844

CWM: COLLEGE OF WILLIAM AND MARY LIBRARY, WILLIAMSBURG, VIRGINIA

Brown, Coalter, and Tucker Family Papers

DDC: DIGITIZED COLLECTIONS, DUKE UNIVERSITY, DURHAM, NORTH CAROLINA

Alice Williamson Diary, http://Scriptorium.lib.duke.edu

DPL: WILLIAM L. PERKINS LIBRARY, DUKE UNIVERSITY MANUSCRIPTS, DURHAM, NORTH CAROLINA

Thomas Adams Account Books, 1768–1808
Joseph Allred Papers
Francis Thomas Anderson Papers
John L. Bailey Collection
Daniel Baker Papers
Bedinger-Dandridge Letters
Alfred W. Bell Papers
N. L. Blakemore Papers
James Blanton Papers
William Bolling Papers
Bryarly, Samuel, Richard, and Rowland Papers
Campbell Family Papers
Clement Claiborne Clay Papers
Samuel Smith Downey Papers

Mary D. Fraser Papers and Account Books
Tyre Glen Papers
William H. Hatchett Papers
John Warfield Johnston Collection
Michael Kidwiler Papers
Henry Clay Krebs Papers
William LaPrade Account Books, 1839–60
William Law Papers
Thomas Lenoir Papers
Joseph Long Papers
Henry Kent McCay Papers
James McDowell Papers
Mary Singleton McDuffie Papers
Hugh Minor Notebooks
Charles Ellis and George Wythe Munford Papers
Battaile Muse Papers
John Quincy Adams Nadenbousch Papers
John M. Orr Papers
Green W. Penn Papers
Benjamin Pennybacker Daybook
Poor Relief Records, Augusta County, Virginia, 1791–1822
H. I. Rhodes Memorandum Book
John Rutherford Papers and Letter Books
Richard W. Sanders and John W. Greene Papers and Notebooks
Samuel P. Sherrill Account Book
Staunton, Virginia, Poor Records, 1770–1872
Vincent Tapp Papers
Augustin Louis Taveau Papers
Cabell Tavenner and Alexander Scott Withers Papers
William Holland Thomas Papers
John W. Timberlake Papers
Michael H. Turrentine Papers
William Weaver Papers
F. L. Whitehead and N. Lofftus Accounts of Slave Trading
Philip J. Winn Collection

ET: EAST TENNESSEE HISTORICAL SOCIETY, KNOXVILLE, TENNESSEE

Knoxville Industrial Association, "Facts and Figures, 1869," trade pamphlet

FC: FILSON CLUB, LOUISVILLE, KENTUCKY

Willis and Lafayette Green Papers, 1818–60
Edward Harris Letter, 1797
Willard R. Jillson, "A History of the Coal Industry in Kentucky," paper read
    before the Filson Club, 7 November 1921, Typescript

Mason County, Kentucky, Account Book, 1797–99
Frank B. Russell Papers, 1849–60
Peyton Skipwith Papers
John Wallace Journal
Warrick-Miller Papers

FHC: FAMILY HISTORY CENTER, CHURCH OF JESUS CHRIST OF THE LATTER
DAY SAINTS, SALT LAKE CITY, UTAH

Bradley County, Tennessee Poor Commission Records
County Tax Lists for North Carolina, Virginia, and West Virginia
Claiborne County, Tennessee, Livestock Brands, 1853–79
Claiborne County, Tennessee, Stage Coach Book

FUA: FISK UNIVERSITY ARCHIVES, NASHVILLE, TENNESSEE

Ophelia Egypt, H. Masuoka, and C. S. Johnson, comp., "Unwritten History
    of Slavery: Autobiographical Account of Negro Ex-slaves," Social Science
    Document No. 1 (1945), Mimeographed Typescript

HPL: HANDLEY PUBLIC LIBRARY, WINCHESTER, VIRGINIA

Ellen Afto Manuscript
L. Allan Letter
Allen Family Papers
Rebecca Ebert, "A Window on the Valley," Typescript
Market Street United Methodist Church Records, 1842–60

HSP: HISTORICAL SOCIETY OF PENNSYLVANIA, PHILADELPHIA,
PENNSYLVANIA

Elihu Embree Papers

HUL: HARVARD UNIVERSITY LIBRARY, CAMBRIDGE, MASSACHUSETTS

Brainerd Journal, American Board of Commissioners for Foreign Missions
    Papers

LC: LIBRARY OF CONGRESS, WASHINGTON, D.C.

American Colonization Society Papers

MC: MCCORMICK COLLECTION, STATE HISTORICAL SOCIETY OF
WISCONSIN, MADISON, WISCONSIN

Jordan and Davis Papers

MSA: MARYLAND STATE ARCHIVES, ANNAPOLIS, MARYLAND

Frederick County, Maryland Livestock Brand Registry, 1851–53, County Land
    Records

NA: NATIONAL ARCHIVES, WASHINGTON, D.C.

Assistant Superintendents Records, Records of the Assistant Commissioner for
    the State of Virginia, Bureau of Refugees, Freedmen, and Abandoned Lands,
    1865–68, Record Group 105, M784, M1246
Census Roll, 1835, of the Cherokee Indians East of the Mississippi
Federal Writers Project, "Slave Narratives, A Folk History of Slavery in the
    United States from Interviews with Former Slaves," Typewritten Records,
    1941
Freedmen Labor Contracts, Records of the Assistant Commissioner for the State
    of Tennessee, Bureau of Refugees, Freedmen, and Abandoned Lands, 1865–
    68, Record Group 105, M999, Roll 20
Records of the Cherokee Indian Agency in Tennessee, 1801–35
Records of the Education Division, Bureau of Refugees, Freedmen, and
    Abandoned Lands, 1865–68, Record Group 105, Pub. No. 803, Roll 16
Records Relating to Court Cases Involving Freedmen, Records of the As-
    sistant Commissioner for the State of Virginia, Bureau of Refugees,
    Freedmen, and Abandoned Lands, 1865–68, Record Group 105, M1048,
    Reel 59
Records Relating to Murders and Outrages, Bureau of Refugees, Freedmen, and
    Abandoned Lands, 1865–68, Record Group 105, M798, Roll 32; M843,
    Rolls 31–33, 39; M869, Roll 34; M999, Roll 34; M1048, Reel 59
U.S. Census Office, Census Enumerator Manuscripts for Appalachian Counties
    were utilized for these censuses:
        Census of Agriculture, 1860
        Census of Agriculture, 1870
        Census of Population, 1860
        Census of Population, 1870
        Census of Manufacturing, 1860
        Slave Schedules, 1840–60
U.S. Congress, Report No. 39, Twenty-Second Congress, First Session

NC: NORTH CAROLINA DEPARTMENT OF ARCHIVES AND HISTORY, RALEIGH,
NORTH CAROLINA

Walter Clark Papers
David L. Swain Papers

SHC: SOUTHERN HISTORICAL COLLECTION, UNIVERSITY OF NORTH
CAROLINA, CHAPEL HILL, NORTH CAROLINA

Walter Alves Papers

John McPherson Berrien Papers
John Houston Bills Papers
John Luther Bridges Papers
Hamilton Brown Papers
Farish Carter Papers
Calvin J. Cowles Papers
William G. Dickson Papers
H. B. Eiler Letter Book
George Phifer Erwin Papers
Peachy R. Grattan Papers
James Hervey Greenlee Diary, 1848–53
James Gwyn Papers
Peter Wilson Hairston Papers
Stephen B. Heard Papers
Hoke Papers
Nathaniel Hunt and Company Papers
Gen. Edmund Jones Papers
Jones and Patterson Family Papers
Lenoir Family Papers
James Lee Love Papers
Lucilla Gamble McCorkle Diary, William McCorkle Papers
Silas McDowell Papers
Peter Mallett Papers
James Mallory Diary
Theodore Morrison Papers
Pettigrew Family Papers
George Wesley Race Diary
Jacob Siler Papers
Thomas George Walton Papers
Plowden C. J. Weston, "Plantation Instructions"
Martha Ann Hancock Wheat Diary, 1850–66
Willis R. Williams Papers
Benjamin Cudworth Yancey Papers

TROY: TROY STATE UNIVERSITY LIBRARY, TROY, ALABAMA

John Horry Dent Farm Journals and Account Books, 1840–92

TS: TENNESSEE STATE LIBRARY AND ARCHIVES, NASHVILLE, TENNESSEE

Knox County Road Commissioners Minutebook, 1808–19
Chris D. Livesay Papers

UH: DIGITIZED COLLECTIONS, UNIVERSITY OF HOUSTON, HOUSTON, TEXAS

Mintz, Steven, ed., "Excerpts from Slave Narratives," http://vi.uh.edu/pages/
  mintz/primary.htm

UK: UNIVERSITY OF KENTUCKY SPECIAL COLLECTIONS, LEXINGTON, KENTUCKY

Buckner Family Papers
William Calk Papers
Diary of Judge Cabell Chenault, Chenault-Bowmar Family Papers
J. Winston Coleman Papers on Slavery, Typescripts
Forsythe Family Papers
Francis M. Goddard Diary, 1834–50
Graham Account Book
John Halley, "Journal of Trips to New Orleans"
Halley Family Papers
Hilton Family Diaries
Hunt-Morgan Family Papers
Kentucky House Journal (1838–39)
Joseph and Archibald Logan Papers
Means-Seaton Papers
National Society of the Colonial Dames, "Old Furnaces of Kentucky," Typescript
Scott Family Papers
Cyrenius Wait Papers
Wickliffe-Preston Papers

UT: UNIVERSITY OF TENNESSEE SPECIAL COLLECTIONS, KNOXVILLE, TENNESSEE

Caldwell Papers
"Diary of William R. Caswell, 1856," Typescript
John Sevier Papers
O. P. Temple Papers

UVSC: SPECIAL COLLECTIONS DEPARTMENT, ALDERMAN LIBRARY, UNIVERSITY OF VIRGINIA, CHARLOTTESVILLE, VIRGINIA

Charles J. Affleck Papers
Edmund Bacon Memoranda Book
Barbour Family Papers
Barringer Family Papers
Baumgardner Family Papers
Bell Family Papers
Berkeley Family Papers
Blackwell Family Papers
James Breckenridge Papers
Breckinridge Family Papers
Broad Run Baptist Church Minutes, 1762–1859
Austin Brockenbrough Papers
Bruce Family Papers
Buck Family Papers
John Buford Papers

Byers Family Papers
William D. Cabell Papers
Calendar of Thomas Jefferson Papers
Carr Family Papers
E. G. Chapman Farm Journal
Chestnut Grove Baptist Minute Books, 1773–1860
Christ Episcopal Church, Parish Register, 1830–65
William W. Davis Iron Manufacturing Company Papers
Nancy Emerson Diary, Emerson Family Papers
Etna Furnace Papers
Folly Farms Papers
Richard Foster Papers
Goose Creek Baptist Church Records, 1775–1853
William T. Gordon Diary, Gordon Family Papers
Graham Family Papers
Grinnan Family Papers
Holland Family Papers
John Hook and Bowker Preston Papers
Hubard Family Papers
Phoebe Jackson Account Book
James River and Kanawha Canal Company Papers
Thomas Jefferson Papers
Keith Family Papers
Kelly-Norris Papers
Kohler Papers
Gen. Joel Leftwich Papers
Lewis, Anderson, and Marks Family Papers
McCue Family Papers
McDowell Family Papers
Massie Family Papers
Mathews-Dundore Papers
Socrates Maupin Papers
Callohill Mennis Papers
Louisa H. A. Minor Diary, 1855–66
Mount Ed Baptist Church Minute Book
Nelson County Business Ledgers
New Hope Baptist Church Minute Book, Thomas S. Bobcock Papers
Wilson Cary Nicholas Papers
Page-Walker Family Papers
Perry, Martin, and McCue Family Papers
Preston-Davis Family Papers
Randolph Family Papers
Register of Free Blacks, Washington County
Rives Family Papers
Rust Family Papers
Southside Virginia Family Papers
Alexander H. H. Stuart Letters
George Thrift Papers, 1844–58

Trist, Burke, and Randolph Family Papers
Nathaniel Beverly Tucker Papers
Virginia Letters Collection
Walker Family Papers
Wallace Family Papers
Watson Family Papers
Weaver-Brady Iron Works and Grist Mill Papers
Weaver-Brady Records
White Family Papers
Floyd L. Whitehead Papers
Wilson, Whitehead, and Houston Family Papers
Wise Family Papers
Wright Family Papers

UVVS: VALLEY OF THE SHADOW, ELECTRONIC TEXTS, INSTITUTE FOR
ADVANCED TECHNOLOGY IN THE HUMANITIES, UNIVERSITY OF VIRGINIA,
CHARLOTTESVILLE, VIRGINIA

http://jefferson.village.virginia.edu/vshadow2
B. S. Brooke Letter, 14 November 1859
Mary M. Burton Will
Mary G. Calhoun Will
Robert Christian Will
Henry Kenneday Will
Memoir of Alansa Rounds Sterrett

VHS: VIRGINIA HISTORICAL SOCIETY, RICHMOND, VIRGINIA

Campbell-Preston Papers
Caperton Family Papers
John Dawson Letters
Ellzey Family Papers
John E. Fletcher Papers
Holburn Letterbook, Taylor Papers
James Lawrence Hooff Diary
James River and Kanawha Company Papers
David Ross Letterbook, 1812–13
William Macon Waller Papers

VP: VIRGINIA POLYTECHNIC INSTITUTE AND STATE UNIVERSITY LIBRARY,
BLACKSBURG, VIRGINIA

Virginia and Tennessee Railroad Minutes, Virginia and Tennessee Railroad
    Collection

VS: VIRGINIA STATE LIBRARY AND ARCHIVES, RICHMOND, VIRGINIA

Bethel Baptist Church Character Certificates, Garnett Ryland Collection

Legislative Papers, a Collection of 25,000 Petitions Sent to the Legislature of
    Virginia, 1775–1860
Lewis Medical Account Book
Loudoun County Court Records
Cyrus H. McCormick Letter, 2 December 1854
Mountain Plain Baptist Church Minute Book, 1833–69
Registers of Death, 1853–60
Roanoke District Baptist Association Records
William Henry Ruffner Papers
Slaves Condemned, Executed, and Transported, 1783–1865, Records Group 48,
    Auditor of Public Accounts
Tredegar Letterbook, Tredegar Company Records
Virginia Board of Public Works Reports, Legislative Documents
Virginia Executive Papers, Letters Received, 1750–1835
Zion Hill Baptist Church Records

WL: WASHINGTON AND LEE UNIVERSITY LIBRARY, LEXINGTON, VIRGINIA

Etna Furnace Company Account Book, 1854–57

WV: WEST VIRGINIA COLLECTION, WEST VIRGINIA UNIVERSITY LIBRARY,
MORGANTOWN, WEST VIRGINIA

Baltimore and Ohio Railroad Records
Barbour County Manuscripts and Articles
Barbour County, Miscellany Papers # 1115
Barbour County Typescript
John Bassel Papers
Alfred Beckley Papers
Louis Bennett Papers
Daniel Boardman Papers
Arthur I. Boreman Papers
Brooke County Archives
James M. Burnside Papers
Andrew Nelson Campbell Papers
Charles L. Campbell Typescripts
Chapin Family Papers
John P. Clarke Papers
Coal River and Kanawha Mining and Manufacturing Company Account Books
Justus Collins Papers
Courtney Family Papers
James M. Crump Typescript
Ruth Woods Dayton Papers
Deakins Family Papers
Marmaduke Dent Papers
J. Q. Dickinson and Company Papers
Donnally and Steele Kanawha Salt Works Records, 1813–15

William Henry Edwards Papers
Stephen B. Elkins Papers
William Ewin Papers
Ralph Fairfax Records
Fairmont General Store Records
Fleming Family Papers
L. J. Forman Papers
Free Negro Register, Monroe County Archives
Freeman Family Papers
M. J. Garrison and Company Records
A. C. L. Gatewood Papers
David Goff Papers
Great Kanawha Coal, Oil and Metallurgic Company Papers
Jacob Guseman Records
Harrison Hagans Papers
William Hall Papers
Felix G. Hansford Papers
Harper's Ferry Typescript
Harrison County Tax Book, 1831–32
R. H. Hendershot Shipping Bills
Henderson-Tomlinson Families Papers
Adolphus P. Howard Papers
Alfred Hughes Stock Certificates
Ice's Ferry Typescripts
Iron Furnaces Typescript
George W. Johnson Papers
Kanawha County Archives
Kanawha County Court Records
John Pendleton Kennedy Papers
Ku Klux Klan, Monongalia County Manuscripts
Peter T. Laisley Papers
Frederick B. Lambert Papers
Legislative Petitions of Kanawha County
Eugene Levassor Papers
Lewis Family Papers
Lightburn Family Papers
John R. Lynch Papers
John McClaugherty Papers
McCoy Family Papers
Isaac McNeel Papers
McNeill Family Papers
John Williamson Marshall Papers
Marshall County Archives
John D. Martin Papers
Mason County Court Records
Lewis Maxwell Papers
Maysville, Kentucky, Papers
Edward E. Meredith Papers

H. E. Metheny Papers
Henry O. Middleton Correspondence
Charles C. Miller Farm Records
William D. Mintz Papers
R. Emmett Mockler Papers
Monogalia County Land and Legal Papers, 1783–1859
Monroe County Archives
Monroe County Road Records, 1812–62
James Rogers Moreland Papers
Henri Jean Mugler Diary
William P. L. Neale Manuscript
Fred T. Newbaugh Papers
Bradford Noyes Recollections
Lawrence William Nuttall Papers
Ohio County, West Virginia, Brand Registration, 1772–1935
Parkersburg Town Council Journals, 1855–62
Carleton Custer Pierce Papers
George McCandless Porter Papers
Preston County Papers, 1775–1918
William Price Papers
Raleigh County Archives
Rathbone Family Papers
Thomas P. Ray Diary, 1829–52
C. R. Rector Typescript
John Rogers Papers
Ruffner-Donally and Company Records
Salt Sulphur Springs Records
James B. Shahan Letter
Samuel W. Shingleton Records
"Salt Manufacturing in Mason County, West Virginia," Typescript
Sloan Brothers Papers
George W. Smith Papers
William Sommerville Papers
Stover College Records
George Cookman Sturgiss Papers
George W. and Lewis Summers Papers
Summers County Archives
Sweet Springs Records
Talbott-Tolbert Family Papers
Taverns Typescript
Roy Thistle Papers
Samuel D. Thorn Ledger
William Tompkins Papers, Roy Bird Collection
White Sulphur Springs Company Records
Luke Willcox Diary, 1853–54
Nathaniel V. Wilson Correspondence
Wilson-Lewis Family Papers
Wilson-Stribling Families Papers

Winifrede Mining and Manufacturing Company Documents
Woodbridge-Blennerhassett Papers
William Gordon Worley Papers

PUBLISHED PRIMARY SOURCES

"Address of James Barbour," *American Farmer* 7 (December 1825): 287–92.

Affleck, Thomas. "On the Hygiene of Cotton Plantations and the Management of Negro Slaves." *Southern Medical Reports* 2 (1850): 429–36.

American State Papers. 38 vols. Washington, DC: Gales and Seaton, 1831–60.

Andrews, E. A. *Slavery and the Domestic Slave Trade in the United States*. Boston: Light and Stearns, 1836.

Appalachian Regional Commission. *Appalachia: A Reference Book*. Washington, DC: Government Printing Office, 1979.

Bear, James A., ed. *The Family Letters of Thomas Jefferson*. Columbia: University of Missouri Press, 1978.

Beeman, Richard R., ed. "Trade and Travel in Post-revolutionary Virginia: A Diary of an Itinerant Peddler, 1807–1808." *Virginia Magazine of History and Biography* 84 (1976): 174–88.

Betts, Edwin M., ed. *Thomas Jefferson's Farm Book with Commentary and Relevant Extracts from Other Writings*. Princeton, NJ: American Philosophical Society, 1953.

The Black Military Experience: A Documentary History, edited by Ira Berlin, Joseph P. Reidy, and Leslie Rowland. New York: Cambridge University Press, 1982.

Blassingame, John W., ed. *Slave Testimony: Two Centuries of Letters, Speeches, Interviews and Autobiographies*. Baton Rouge: Louisiana State University Press, 1977.

Bontemps, Arna, ed. *Great Slave Narratives*. Boston: Beacon Press, 1969.

Breeden, James. O., ed. *Advice among Masters: The Ideal in Slave Management in the Old South*. Westport, CT: Greenwood Press, 1980.

Brown, W. A. "Midwifery in a Country Practice." *Nashville Journal of Medicine and Surgery* 7 (1854): 459–63.

Brown, William W. *Narrative of William Wells Brown, A Fugitive Slave*. Boston: Antislavery Office, 1847.

Bruce, H. C. *The New Man: Twenty-Nine Years a Slave, Twenty-Nine Years a Free Man*. York, PA: Anstadt and Sons, 1895.

Bryan, T. Conn, ed. "Letters Concerning Georgia Gold Mines." *Collections of the Georgia Historical Society* 39 (1955): 401–09; 44 (1960): 338–46.

Buck, William P., ed. *Sad Earth, Sweet Heaven: The Diary of Lucy Rebecca Buck during the War between the States*. Birmingham, AL: Cornerstone, 1973.

Calendar of Virginia State Papers and Other Manuscripts, edited by W. P. Palmer. Richmond, VA: State of Virginia, 1875–93.

Cather, Willa. *Sapphira and the Slave Girl*. New York: Knopf, 1940.

Catterall, Helen T., ed. *Judicial Cases Concerning American Slavery and the Negro*, 4 vols. Washington, DC: Carnegie Institution, 1926–37.

Chambers, William. *Things as They Are in America*. Philadelphia: Lippincott, Grambo and Co., 1854.

Clay, Cassius M. *Cassius Marcellus Clay: Memoirs, Writings and Speeches,* 2 vols. Cincinnati, OH: J. Fletcher Brennan and Co., 1886.

Clemson, Floride. *A Rebel Came Home,* edited by Charles M. McGee and Ernest M. Lander. Columbia: University of South Carolina Press, 1961.

Coombs, Edith I. *America Visited: Famous Travellers Report on the United States in the 18th and 19th Centuries.* New York: Book League of America, 1908.

deForest, John W. *A Union Officer in the Reconstruction,* edited by James H. Croushore and D. M. Potter. New York: Oxford University Press, 1948.

Dew, Thomas R. *Review of the Debate in the Virginia Legislature of 1831 and 1832.* Richmond, VA: T. W. White, 1832.

Douglass, Frederick. *My Bondage and My Freedom.* New York: Orton and Mulligan, 1855.

Drew, Benjamin. *A North-side View of Slavery.* Boston: John P. Jewett, 1856.

Dunn, Durwood, ed. *An Abolitionist in the Appalachian South: Ezekiel Birdseye on Slavery, Capitalism, and Separate Statehood in East Tennessee, 1841–1846.* Knoxville: University of Tennessee Press, 1997.

Early and Wife v. Friend et. al.: An Appeal from the Circuit Court of Kanawha, 2 vols. Lewisburg, VA: William F. Parish, Printer, 1857.

Eastman, Mary H. *Aunt Phillis's Cabin, or Southern Life as It Is.* Philadelphia: Lippincott, Grambo & Co., 1852.

Embree, Elihu. *The Emancipator.* 1820. Reprint. Nashville: B. H. Murphy, 1932.

"Evelyn Williams." Video directed by Anne Lewis. Whitesburg, KY: Appalshop Film and Video, 1996.

Families and Freedom: A Documentary History of African-American Kinship in the Civil War Era, edited by Ira Berlin and Leslie S. Rowland. New York: New Press, 1997.

Featherstonhough, G. W. *Excursion through the Slave States, From Washington on the Potomac to the Frontier of Mexico, With Sketches of Popular Manners and Geological Notices,* 2 vols. 1844. Reprint. New York: Negro Universities, 1968.

Ferry Hill Plantation Journal: Life on the Potomac River and Chesapeake and Ohio Canal: 4 January 1838–15 January 1839, edited by Fletcher M. Green, Thomas F. Hahn, and Nathalie W. Hahn. Shepherdstown, WV: American Canal and Transportation Center, 1975.

Fitzhugh, George. *Sociology for the South, or the Failure of Free Society.* 1854. Reprint. New York: Negro Universities Press.

Folger, Alfred M. *The Family Physician, Being a Domestic Medical Work Written in Plain Style.* Spartanburg, SC: Cottrell, 1845.

Ford, Paul L. *The Writings of Thomas Jefferson.* New York: Putnam and Sons, 1892–99.

Fox, Dixon R. *Harper's Atlas of American History.* New York: Harper and Brothers, 1920.

Franklin, John H., ed. *The Diary of James T. Ayers, Civil War Recruiter.* 1947. Reprint. Baton Rouge: Louisiana State University Press, 1999.

Freedom: A Documentary History of Emancipation, 1861–1867, edited by Ira Berlin, Steven F. Miller, Joseph P. Reidy, and Leslie S. Rowlands, 3 vols. Cambridge: Cambridge University Press, 1985–93.

Freedom's Lawmakers: A Directory of Black Officeholders during Reconstruction, edited by Eric Foner. Baton Rouge: Louisiana State University Press, 1996.

Freedom's Soldiers: The Black Military Experience in the Civil War, edited by Ira Berlin, Joseph P. Reidy, and Leslie Rowland. New York: Cambridge University Press, 1998.

Furman, Jan, ed. *Slavery in the Clover Bottoms: John McCline's Narrative of His Life during Slavery and the Civil War.* Knoxville: University of Tennessee Press, 1998.

Grandy, Moses. *Narrative of the Life of Moses Grandy, Late a Slave in the United States of America.* London: C. Gilpin, 1843.

Greene, Jack P., ed. *The Diary of Colonel Landon Carter of Sabine Hall, 1752–1778.* Charlottesville: University of Virginia Press, 1965.

Gunn, John C. *Gunn's Domestic Medicine; or Poor Man's Friend, Shewing the Diseases of Men, Women and Children.* Madisonville, TN: By Author, 1834.

Gurney, Joseph J. *A Journey in North America: Described in Familiar Letters to Amelia Opie.* Norwich, CT: J. Fletcher, 1841.

Hamilton, Kenneth G., ed. "Minutes of the Mission Conference Held in Spring Place." *Atlanta Historical Bulletin* 14 (Winter 1970): 42–69.

Harlan, Louis, and John W. Blassingame, eds. *The Booker T. Washington Papers,* 14 vols. Urbana: University of Illinois Press, 1972.

Hendrix, GeLee C., comp. *Pendleton County, South Carolina Deed Book A and B.* Greenville, SC: By Author, 1980.

Horst, Samuel L. *The Fire of Liberty in Their Hearts: The Diary of Jacob E. Yoder of the Freedmen's Bureau School, Lynchburg, Virginia.* Richmond: Library of Virginia, 1996.

Hughes, Louis. *Thirty Years a Slave: From Bondage to Freedom.* 1897. Reprint. New York: Negro Universities Press, 1969.

Ingraham, Joseph H. *The Southwest by a Yankee,* 2 vols. New York: Harper and Brothers, 1835.

Jackson, John. "The Devil Wore Hickory Shoes." Song 1 in "I Believe in Angels Singing: Songs from the Underground Railroad Era," compiled by Augusta Heritage Arts Center. Elkins, WV: Unity Productions, 1996 [sound recording].

Jacobs, Harriet A. *Incidents in the Life of a Slave Girl Written by Herself,* edited by Jean F. Yellin. 1861. Reprint. Cambridge, MA: Harvard University Press, 1987.

Janney, Werner, and Asa M. Janney, eds. *John Jay Janney's Virginia: An American Farm Lad's Life in the Early 19th Century.* McLean, VA: EPM Publications, 1978.

Killion, Ronald, and Charles Waller, comp. *Slavery Time When I Was Chillun Down on Marster's Plantation.* Savannah, GA: Beehive Press, 1973.

Kimzey, Herbert B., comp. *Early Genealogical and Historical Records: Habersham County, Georgia.* Athens, GA: By author, 1988.

King, Edward. *The Southern States of North America: A Record of Journeys,* 2 vols. London: Blackie and Son, 1875.

Lane, Lunsford. *The Narrative of Lunsford Lane.* Boston: J. G. Torrey, 1842.

Langhorne, Orra. *Southern Sketches from Virginia, 1881–1901,* edited by Charles E. Wynes. Charlottesville: University Press of Virginia, 1964.

Laws of the Cherokee Nation Adopted by the Council at Various Periods. Tahlequah, OK: Cherokee Advocate Officer, 1852.

Lerner, Gerda, ed. *Black Women in White America: A Documentary History.* New York: Pantheon Books, 1972.

"Letters of 1831–32 about Kentucky." *Filson Club Historical Quarterly* 16 (1942): 220–27.

"Letters of Alexander D. Kelly," *William and Mary Quarterly* 17 (1908): 27–33.

"Letters of Benjamin Hawkins," *Georgia Historical Collections* 9 (1924): 238–50, 310–29.

Letters of William Lee, edited by W. C. Ford. Brooklyn, NY: Historical Printing Co., 1891.

Logan, John R. *Sketches, Historical and Biographical, of the Broad River and King's Mountain Baptists Associations from 1800 to 1882.* Shelby, NC: By Author, 1887.

Lumpkin, Katherine D. *The Making of a Southerner.* Westport, CT: Greenwood Press, 1971.

McDonald, Cornelia P. *A Woman's Civil War: A Diary with Reminiscences of the War, from March 1862,* edited by Minrose C. Gwin. Madison: University of Wisconsin Press, 1992.

McGee, Charles M., and E. M. Lander, eds. *A Rebel Came Home: The Diary and Letters of Florida Clemson, 1863–1866.* Columbia: University of South Carolina Press, 1989.

McKitrick, Eric, ed. *Slavery Defended: The Voices of the Old South.* Englewood Cliffs, NJ: Prentice-Hall, 1963.

McKivigan, John R., ed. *The Roving Editor or Talks with Slaves in the Southern States, by James Redpath.* University Park: Pennsylvania State University Press, 1996.

Martineau, Harriet. *Retrospect of Western Travel.* London: Saunders and Otley, 1838.

Mathew, William M., ed. *Agriculture, Geology and Society in Antebellum South Carolina: The Private Diary of Edmund Ruffin, 1843.* Athens: University of Georgia Press, 1992.

Meaders, Daniel, ed. *Advertisements for Runaway Slaves in Virginia, 1801–1820.* New York: Garland Publishing, 1997.

Meigs, Charles D. *Females and Their Diseases: A Series of Letters to His Class.* Philadelphia: Lea & Blanchard, 1848.

Mercer, Margaret. *Popular Lectures on Ethics or Moral Obligation.* Petersburg, VA: Edmund and Julien C. Ruffin, 1841.

Newell, Franklin S. "The Effect of Overcivilization on Maternity." *American Journal of the Medical Sciences* 136 (1908): 533–41.

The Cotton Kingdom: A Traveller's Observations on Cotton and Slavery in the American Slave States, edited by Arthur M. Schlesinger. New York: Knopf, 1953.

A Journey in the Back Country, 1853–1854. New York: Mason Brothers, 1860.

Journey in the Seaboard Slave States with Remarks on Their Economy. New York: Dix and Edwards, 1856.

Page, Thomas N. *Social Life in Old Virginia before the War.* New York: Charles Scribner's Sons, 1897.

Parker, Freddie L., ed. *Stealing a Little Freedom: Advertisements for Slave Runaways in North Carolina, 1791–1840.* New York: Garland Publishing, 1994.

Payne, Alban S. "Report of Obstetrical Cases." *Steth.* 3 (1853): 204–05.

Perdue, Charles L., T. E. Barden, and R. K. Phillips, eds. *Weevils in the Wheat: Interviews with Virginia Ex-slaves.* Charlottesville: University Press of Virginia, 1976.

Ramsey, Frederic. *Been Here and Gone.* New Brunswick, NJ: Rutgers University Press, 1960.

Randolph, J. T. *The Cabin and the Parlor or Slaves and Masters.* Philadelphia: T. B. Peterson, 1852.

Randolph, Peter. *Sketches of Slave Life.* Boston: By Author, 1855.

Rawick, George P., comp. *The American Slave: A Composite Autobiography,* 19 vols. Westport, CT: Greenwood Press, 1972.

The American Slave: A Composite Autobiography, Supplement I, 12 vols. Westport, CT: Greenwood Press, 1977.

The American Slave: A Composite Autobiography, Supplement II, 10 vols. Westport, CT: Greenwood Press, 1979.

Redpath, James, *The Roving Editor or Talks with Slaves in the Southern States.* 1859. Reprint. New York: Negro Universities Press, 1968.

Rose, Willie Lee, ed. *A Documentary History of Slavery in North America.* New York: Oxford University Press, 1976.

St. Abdy, Edward. *Journal of a Residence and Tour in the United States of America, from April, 1833 to October, 1834.* London: John Murray, 1835.

Shillitoe, Thomas. "Journal of the Life, Labours and Travels of Thomas Shillitoe." *Friends Library* 3 (1839): 74–86.

Sigourney, Lydia H. *Letters to Mothers.* Hartford, CT: Hudson and Skinner, 1838.

Silliman, Benjamin. "Remarks on Some of the Gold Mines and on Parts of the Gold Region of Virginia, Founded on Personal Observations, Made in the Months of August and September, 1836." *American Journal of Science* 32 (1837): 98–130.

Simons, John H. *The Planter's Guide and Family Book of Medicine.* Charleston, SC: By Author, 1848.

Slave Life in Georgia: A Narrative of the Life of John Brown, edited by L. A. Chamerovzow. Freeport, NY: Books for Libraries Press, 1971.

Smith, Margaret B. *The First Forty Years of Washington Society.* New York: Charles Scribner's Sons, 1906.

The South: A Collection from Harper's Magazine. New York: Gallery Books, 1990.

Still, William. *The Underground Railroad: A Record of Facts, Authentic Narratives and Letters.* Philadelphia: Porter and Coates, 1872.

Stroud, George M. *A Sketch of the Laws Relating to Slavery in the Several States of the United States of America.* Philadelphia: H. Longstreth, 1856.

Stroyer, Jacob. *My Life in the South.* Salem, MA: Salem Observer Book, 1888.

The Tennessee Civil War Veterans Questionnaires, compiled by Gustavus W. Dyer and John T. Moore. Easley, SC: Southern Historical Press, 1985.

Thompson, George. "Cases of Puerperal Convulsions." *Western Journal of Medicine and Surgery* 8 (1851): 340–43.

Tilley, Nannie M., ed. "Journal of the Surry County Agricultural Society." *North Carolina Historical Review* 24 (1947): 494–531.

Trowbridge, John T. *The Desolate South, 1865–1866: A Picture of the Battlefields and of the Devastated Confederacy*, edited by Gordon Carroll. 1867. Reprint. New York: Duell, Sloan and Pearce, 1956.

Turrentine, Samuel B. *A Romance of Education: A Narrative Including Recollections and Other Facts Connected with Greensboro College*. Greensboro, NC: Piedmont Press, 1946.

United States Census Office. *Compendium of the Enumeration of the Inhabitants and Statistics of the United States*. Washington, DC: Thomas Allen, 1841.

Mortality Statistics of the Seventh Census of the United States, 1850. Washington, DC: A. O. P. Nicholson, 1855.

Population of the United States in 1860. Washington, DC: Government Printing Office, 1864.

Statistical View of the United States Being a Compendium of the Seventh Census. Washington, DC: A. O. P. Nicholson, 1854.

Van Evrie, John H. *Negroes and Negro "Slavery": The First an Inferior Race, The Latter Its Normal Condition*. Baltimore: J. D. Toy, 1853.

Veney, Bethany. *The Narrative of Bethany Veney: A Slave Woman*. Worcester, MA: A. P. Bicknell, 1890.

Ward, James A., ed. *Southern Railroad Man: Conductor N. J. Bell's Recollections of the Civil War Era*. DeKalb: Northern Illinois University Press, 1994.

Ware, Nathaniel. *Notes on Political Economy, As Applicable to the United States, by a Southern Planter*. New York: Leavitt, Trow and Co., 1944.

Warrington, Joseph. *The Obstetric Catechism: Containing 2,347 Questions and Answers on Obstetrics Proper*. Philadelphia: E. Barrington & G. D. Haswell, 1853.

Washington, Booker T. *Up from Slavery: An Autobiography*. New York: Association Press, 1901.

Weld, Theodore D. *American Slavery as It Is: Testimony of a Thousand Witnesses*. 1839. Reprint. New York: Arno Press, 1968.

Wickliffe, Robert. "Speech on Negro Law." Lexington, KY: Pamphlet, 1840. [Copy utilized from Wickliffe-Preston Papers, University of Kentucky Special Collections.]

Wiggington, Eliot, ed. *Foxfire Book*. Garden City, NY: Anchor Books, 1972.

Foxfire 2. Garden City, NY: Anchor Books, 1973.

Foxfire 3. Garden City, NY: Anchor Books, 1975.

Foxfire 8. Garden City, NY: Anchor Books, 1983.

"William Walrond: Settlement of Estate." *Virginia Appalachian Notes* 18 (1) (1994): 23–25.

Yetman, Norman R., ed. *Life under the "Peculiar Institution": Selections from the Slave Narrative Collection*. New York: Random House, 1970.

SECONDARY REFERENCES

Ambler, Charles H. *A History of West Virginia*. New York: Prentice-Hall, 1933.

Anderson, Eric. *Race and Politics in North Carolina, 1872–1901: The Black Second*. Baton Rouge: Louisiana State University Press, 1981.

Anderson, Margo J. *The American Census: A Social History.* New Haven, CT: Yale University Press, 1988.

Andrews, Susan C. "Spatial Analysis of an East Tennessee Plantation Houselot." M.A. thesis, University of Tennessee, 1992.

and Amy L. Young. "Plantations on the Periphery of the Old South: Modeling a New Approach." *Tennessee Anthropologist* 17 (1) (1992): 1–12.

Apple, Rima D. *Mothers and Medicine: A Social History of Infant Feeding, 1890–1950.* Madison, WI: University of Wisconsin Press, 1987.

Bailey, Kenneth R. "A Judicious Mixture: Negroes and Immigrants in the West Virginia Mines, 1880–1917." In *Blacks in Appalachia*, edited by William H. Turner and Edward J. Cabbell, pp. 117–32. Lexington: University Press of Kentucky, 1985.

Bancroft, Frederic. *Slave Trading in the Old South.* Baltimore, MD: J. H. Furst Co., 1931.

Barickman, B. J. "A Bit of Land Which They Call Roca: Slave Provision Grounds in the Bahian Reconcaro, 1780–1860." *Hispanic American Historical Review* 74 (4) (1994): 649–83.

Berlin, Ira. *Many Thousands Gone: The First Two Centuries of Slavery in North America.* Cambridge, MA: Harvard University Press, 1998.

and Philip D. Morgan, eds. *Cultivation and Culture: Labor and the Shaping of Slave Life in the Americas*, Charlottesville: University of Virginia Press, 1993.

and Philip D. Morgan, eds. *The Slaves' Economy: Independent Production by Slaves in the Americas.* London: Frank Cass, 1991.

Marc Favreau, and Steven F. Miller, eds. *Remembering Slavery: African Americans Talk about Their Personal Experiences of Slavery and Emancipation.* New York: New Press, 1998.

Barbara J. Fields, Steven F. Miller, Joseph P. Reidy, and Leslie S. Rowland. *Slaves No More: Three Essays on Emancipation and the Civil War.* New York: Cambridge University Press, 1992.

Bickley, Ancella R. "Midwifery in West Virginia." *West Virginia History* 49 (1) (1990): 55–67.

Blackmun, Ora. *Western North Carolina: Its Mountains and Its People to 1880.* Boone, NC: Appalachian Consortium Press, 1977.

Blassingame, John. *The Slave Community: Plantation Life in the Antebellum South.* New York: Oxford University Press, 1972.

Boulton, John, Zvi Laron, and Jean Rey. *Long-Term Consequences of Early Feeding.* Philadelphia: Lippincott-Raven, 1996.

Bouwman, Robert E. *Traveler's Rest and the Tugaloo Crossroads.* State of Georgia: Department of Natural Resources, 1980.

Boydston, Jeanne. "To Earn Her Daily Bread: Housework and Antebellum Working-Class Subsistence." *Radical History Review* 35 (1986): 19–38.

Brabson, Estalena, comp. *John Brabson I: Patriot of the American Revolution and Some of His Descendants.* Seymour, TN: Tricounty News, 1975.

Bradford, Sydney. "The Negro Ironworker in Antebellum Virginia." *Journal of Southern History* 25 (1959): 194–206.

Brown, Linda B. *Crossing over Jordan.* New York: Ballantine Books, 1995.

Brundage, W. Fitzhugh. *Lynching in the New South: Georgia and Virginia, 1880–1930.* Urbana: University of Illinois Press, 1993.

Bush-Slimani, Barbara. "Hard Labour: Women, Childbirth and Resistance in British Caribbean Slave Societies." *History Workshop Journal* 36 (1) (1993): 83–99.

Butlin, N. G. *Antebellum Slavery: A Critique of a Debate*. Canberra: 1971.

Cade, John B. "Out of the Mouths of Ex-Slaves." *Journal of Negro History* 20 (1) (1935): 294–337.

Campbell, John. "Work, Pregnancy and Infant Mortality among Southern Slaves." *Journal of Interdisciplinary History* 14 (4) (1984): 793–812.

Cardoso, Ciro F. S. "The Peasant Breach in the Slave System: New Developments in Brazil." *Luso-Brazilian Review* 25 (1): 49–57.

Censer, Jane T. *North Carolina Planters and Their Children*. Baton Rouge: Louisiana State University Press, 1984.

Chambers, Douglas B. "'He Gwine Sing He Country': Africans, Afro-Virginians, and the Development of Slave Culture in Virginia, 1690–1810." Ph.D. diss., University of Virginia, 1996.

Clark, Victor S. *History of Manufactures in the United States*. New York: Carnegie Institution, 1929.

Cody, Cheryll A. "Seasonality in Women's Lives on Low Country Plantations." In *More than Chattel: Black Women and Slavery in the Americas*, edited by David B. Gaspar and Darlene C. Hine, pp. 61–78. Bloomington: Indiana University Press, 1996.

Coleman, J. Winston. "Lexington's Slave Dealers and Their Southern Trade." *Filson Club Historical Quarterly* 12 (1938): 1–23.

Slavery Times in Kentucky. Chapel Hill: University of North Carolina Press, 1940.

Collins, Winfield. *The Domestic Slave Trade of the Southern States*. New York: Broadway Publishing, 1904.

Conner, Eloise. "The Slave Market in Lexington, Kentucky: 1850–1860." M.A. thesis, University of Kentucky, 1931.

Conrad, Alfred H., and John R. Meyer. *The Economics of Slavery and Other Studies in Econometric History*. Chicago: Aldine, 1964.

Conway, Alan. *The Reconstruction of Georgia*. Minneapolis: University of Minnesota Press, 1966.

Cooling, B. Franklin. "A People's War: Partisan Conflict in Tennessee and Kentucky." In *Guerillas, Unionists and Violence on the Confederate Home Front*, edited by Daniel E. Sutherland, pp. 113–32. Fayetteville: University of Arkansas Press, 1999.

Coulter, E. Merton. *Georgia: A Short History*. Chapel Hill: University of North Carolina Press, 1960.

Craton, Michael. *Empire, Enslavement and Freedom in the Caribbean*. Jamaica: Ian Randle Publishers, 1997.

Crawford, Stephen. "Quantified Memory: A Study of the WPA and Fisk University Slave Narrative Collections." Ph.D. diss., University of Chicago, 1980.

"The Slave Family: A View from the Slave Narratives. In *Strategic Factors in Nineteenth Century American Economic History*, edited by Claudia Goldin and Hugh Rockoff, pp. 331–50. Chicago: University of Chicago Press, 1992.

Crosby, Alfred. *The Columbian Exchange: Biological and Cultural Consequences of 1492*. Westport, CT: Greenwood Press, 1972.

Day, Randal, and Daniel Hook. "A Short History of Divorce: Jumping the Broom and Back Again." *Journal of Divorce* 10 (3/4): 57–63.

Deere, Carmen D. "Rural Women's Subsistence Production in the Capitalist Periphery." *Review of Radical Political Economics* 80 (1976): 9–18.

Deetz, James. *In Small Things Forgotten*. Garden City, NY: Doubleday, 1977.

Dew, Charles B. *Bond of Iron: Master and Slave at Buffalo Forge*. New York: W. W. Norton, 1994.

Dill, Bonnie Thornton. "Fictive Kin, Paper Sons and Compadrazgo: Women of Color and the Struggle for Family Survival." In *Women of Color in U.S. Society*, edited by Maxine B. Zinn and B. T. Dill, pp. 149–70. Philadelphia: Temple University Press, 1994.

Disney, Elijah F. "Mountain Feuds." *Berea Quarterly* 13 (April 1909): 10.

Dreizen, S., C. N. Spirakis, and R. E. Stone. "A Comparison of Skeletal Growth and Maturation in Undernourished and Well-Nourished Girls Before and After Menarche." *Journal of Pediatrics* 520 (1967): 256–63.

Du Bois, W. E. B., ed. *The Negro American Family*. Cambridge, MA: MIT Press, 1909.

Dunaway, Wilma A. *The First American Frontier: Transition to Capitalism in Southern Appalachia, 1700–1860*. Chapel Hill: University of North Carolina Press, 1995.

——— "The Incorporation of Southern Appalachia into the Capitalist World-Economy, 1700–1860." Ph.D. diss., University of Tennessee, 1994.

——— *Slavery in the American Mountain South*. Cambridge: Cambridge University Press, forthcoming.

Ebert, Rebecca A. "A Window on the Valley: A Study of the Free Black Community of Winchester and Frederick County, Virginia, 1785–1860." M.A. thesis, University of Virginia, 1986.

Elkins, Stanley M. *Slavery: A Problem in American Institutional and Intellectual Life*. Chicago: University of Chicago Press, 1959.

Ellis, Joseph J. "Jefferson's Cop-out." *Civilization* (December 1996/January 1997): 46–53.

Encyclopedia of American History, edited by Richard B. Morris. New York: Harper and Row, 1976.

Epstein, Dena J. *Sinful Tunes and Spirituals: Black Folk Music to the Civil War*. Urbana: University of Illinois Press, 1977.

Eslinger, Ellen. "Antebellum Liquor Reform in Lexington, Virginia." *Virginia Magazine of History and Biography* 99 (2): 163–86.

Evans, Robert. "Some Economic Aspects of the Domestic Slave Trade, 1830–1860." *Southern Economic Journal* 27 (1961): 329–37.

Falkner, Frank. *Infant and Child Nutrition Worldwide: Issues and Perspectives*. Boca Raton, FL: CRC Press, 1990.

Fauve-Chamoux, Antoinette. "Household Forms and Living Standards in Pre-Industrial France: From Models to Realities." *Journal of Family History* 18 (2) (1993): 135–56.

Ferguson, Leland. *Uncommon Ground: Archaeology and Early African America, 1650–1800*. Washington, DC: Smithsonian Institution Press, 1992.

Fisher, Noel C. "Definitions of Victory: East Tennessee Unionists in the Civil War and Reconstruction." In *Guerillas, Unionists and Violence on the Confederate Home Front*, edited by Daniel E. Sutherland, pp. 89–112. Fayetteville: University of Arkansas Press, 1999.

Fleming, Walter L. *Civil War and Reconstruction in Alabama*. Gloucester, MA: Peter Smith, 1949.

Fogel, Robert W. "Was the Overwork of Pregnant Women Profit Maximizing?" In *Without Consent or Contract: The Rise and Fall of American Slavery*, Vol. 3. *Evidence and Methods*, edited by R. W. Fogel, R. A. Galantine, and R. L. Manning, pp. 321–25. New York: W. W. Norton, 1992.

Without Consent or Contract: The Rise and Fall of American Slavery. New York: W. W. Norton, 1989.

and Stanley L. Engerman. *Time on the Cross: The Economics of American Negro Slavery*, 2 vols. Boston: Little, Brown and Co., 1974.

and Stanley L. Engerman, ed. *Without Consent or Contract: The Rise and Fall of American Slavery*. Vol. 1. *Technical Papers: Markets and Production*. New York: W. W. Norton, 1989.

Ralph A. Galantine, and Richard L. Manning, eds. *Without Consent or Contract: The Rise and Fall of American Slavery*. Vol. 3. *Evidence and Methods*. New York: W. W. Norton, 1992.

Fox-Genovese, Elizabeth. "Antebellum Southern Households: A New Perspective on a Familiar Question." *Review of the Fernand Braudel Center* 7 (1983): 215–54.

Within the Plantation Household: Black and White Women of the Old South. Chapel Hill: University of North Carolina Press, 1988.

Franklin, John H. *The Free Negro in North Carolina, 1790–1860*. Chapel Hill: University of North Carolina Press, 1943.

Frazier, E. Franklin. *The Negro Family in the United States*. Chicago: University of Chicago Press, 1939.

"The Negro Slave Family." *Journal of Negro History* 15 (1930): 198–259.

Frisch, Rose, and J. W. McArthur. "Menstrual Cycles: Fatness as a Determinant of Minimum Weight and Height Necessary for the Maintenance of Onset." *Science* 435 (1974): 949–51.

Gawalt, Gerard W. "James Monroe, Presidential Planter." *Virginia Magazine of History and Biography* 101 (2) (April 1993): 251–72.

Geggus, David P. "Slave and Free Colored Women in Saint Dominique." In *More than Chattel: Black Women and Slavery in the Americas*, edited by David B. Gaspar and Darlene C. Hine, pp. 259–78. Bloomington: Indiana University Press, 1996.

Genovese, Eugene D. *The Political Economy of Slavery: Studies in the Economy and Society of the Slave South*. New York: Random House, 1965.

Roll, Jordan, Roll: The World the Slaves Made. New York: Random House, 1974.

Godbold, E. Stanly, and Mattie U. Russell. *Confederate Colonel and Cherokee Chief: The Life of William Holland Thomas*. Knoxville: University of Tennessee Press, 1990.

Golden, Janet. *A Social History of Wet Nursing in America: From Breast to Bottle*. Cambridge: Cambridge University Press, 1996.

Gomez, Michael A. *Exchanging Our Country Marks: The Transformation of African Identities in the Colonial and Antebellum Period.* Chapel Hill: University of North Carolina Press, 1998.

Gordon-Reed, Annette. *Thomas Jefferson and Sally Hemings: An American Controversy.* Charlottesville: University Press of Virginia, 1997.

Govan, Gilbert E., and James W. Livingood. *The Chattanooga Country from Tomahawks to TVA.* 1952. Reprint. Knoxville: University of Tennessee, 1977.

Grant, Donald L. *The Way It Was in the South: The Black Experience in Georgia.* New York: Carol Publishing Group, 1993.

Gray, Lewis C. *History of Agriculture in the Southern United States to 1860,* 2 vols. Gloucester, MA: Peter Smith, 1958.

Greene, Evarts B., and Virginia D. Harrington. *American Population Before the Federal Census of 1790.* New York: Columbia University Press, 1922.

Gruber, Anna. "The Archaeology of Slave Life at Thomas Jefferson's Monticello: Mulberry Row Quarters r, s, t." *Archaeological Society of Virginia Quarterly Bulletin* 46 (1) (1990): 2–9.

Gutman, Herbert. *The Black Family in Slavery and Freedom, 1750–1925.* New York: Pantheon Books, 1976.

———. "Persistent Myths about the Afro-American Family." *Journal of Interdisciplinary History* 6 (1976): 181–210.

Hale, Will T. *Early History of Warren County.* McMinnville, TN: Standard Printing, 1930.

Harrison, Lowell H. "Memories of Slavery in Kentucky." *Filson Club History Quarterly* 47 (3) (1973): 242–57.

Hearn, Chester G. *Six Years of Hell: Harper's Ferry during the Civil War.* Baton Rouge: Louisiana State University Press, 1996.

Henry, H. M. "The Slave Laws of Tennessee." *Tennessee Historical Magazine* 2 (1916): 175–203.

Herman, Bernard L. "Slave Quarters in Virginia: The Persona behind Historic Artifacts." In *The Scope of Historical Archaeology: Essays in Honor of John L. Cotton,* edited by D. G. Orr and D. G. Crozie, pp. 253–83. Philadelphia: Temple University Press, 1984.

Hill, Sarah H. *Weaving New Worlds: Southeastern Cherokee Women and Their Basketry.* Chapel Hill: University of North Carolina, 1997.

A History of Etowah County, Alabama, 2 vols. Birmingham: Etowah County Centennial Commitee, 1968.

Hopkins, James F. *Hemp Industry in Kentucky.* Lexington: University of Kentucky Press, 1951.

Hoskins, Katherine B. *Anderson County.* Memphis, TN: Memphis State University Press, 1979.

Hudson, Larry E. *To Have and To Hold: Slave Work and Family Life in Antebellum South Carolina.* Athens: University of Georgia Press, 1997.

Hull, Valeria, and Mayling Simpson. *Breastfeeding, Child Health and Child Spacing.* London: Croom Helm, 1985.

Inscoe, John C. "Mountain Masters as Confederate Opportunists: The Profitability of Slavery in Western North Carolina, 1861–1865." *Slavery and Abolition* 16 (1995): 84–100.

Mountain Masters, Slavery, and the Sectional Crisis in Western North Carolina. Knoxville: University of Tennessee, 1989.

Irwin, John Rice. *Alex Stewart: Portrait of a Pioneer.* West Chester, PA: Schiffer Publishing, 1985.

Jackson, Luther P. *Free Negro Labor and Property Holding in Virginia, 1830–1860.* New York: D. Appleton-Century Co., 1942.

Johnson, Daniel M., and Rex R. Campbell. *Black Migration in America: A Social Demographic History.* Durham, NC: Duke University Press, 1981.

Jones, Jacqueline. *Soldiers of Light and Love: Northern Teachers and Georgia Blacks, 1865–1873.* Chapel Hill: University of North Carolina Press, 1980.

Jones, Loyal. "Appalachian Values." In *Voices from the Hills: Selected Readings of Southern Appalachia,* edited by Robert J. Higgs and Ambrose Manning, pp. 507–17. New York: Ungar, 1975.

Jordan, Ervin L. *Black Confederates and Afro-Yankees in Civil War Virginia.* Charlottesville: University Press of Virginia, 1995.

Joyner, Charles. *Down by the Riverside: A South Carolina Slave Community.* Urbana: University of Illinois Press, 1984.

Kelso, William M. "The Archaeology of Slave Life at Thomas Jefferson's Monticello: 'A Wolf by the Ears.' " *Journal of New World Archaeology* 6 (4) (1986): 5–20.

King, Wilma. " 'Suffer with Them Till Death': Slave Women and Their Children in Nineteenth-Century America." In *More than Chattel: Black Women and Slavery in the Americas,* edited by David B. Gaspar and Darlene C. Hine, pp. 147–68. Bloomington: Indiana University Press, 1996.

Kiple, Kenneth F., and Virginia H. King. *Another Dimension to the Black Diaspora: Diet, Disease and Racism.* New York: Cambridge University Press, 1981.

and Virginia H. Kiple. "Slave Child Mortality: Some Nutritional Answers to a Perennial Puzzle." *Journal of Social History* 10 (1977): 284–309.

Klein, Herbert S., and Stanley Engerman, "Fertility Differentials between Slaves in the United States and the British West Indies: A Note on Lactation Practices and Their Possible Implications." *William and Mary Quarterly* 35 (1978): 357–74.

Klotter, James C. "Feuds in Appalachia: An Overview." *Filson Club Quarterly* 56 (1982): 290–317.

Kolchin, Peter. *American Slavery, 1619–1877.* New York: Hill and Wang, 1993.

"Reevaluating the Antebellum Slave Community: A Comparative Perspective." *Journal of American History* 70 (3) (1983): 579–601.

Komlos, John and Peter Coclanis. "On the Puzzling Cycle in the Biological Standard of Living: The Case of Antebellum Georgia." *Explorations in Economic History* 34 (4) (1997): 433–59.

Kotlikoff, Laurence J. "Quantitative Description of the New Orleans Slave Market." In *Without Consent or Contract: The Rise and Fall of American Slavery.* Vol. 1. *Markets and Production: Technical Papers,* edited by Robert W. Fogel and Stanley L. Engerman, pp. 31–53. New York: W. W. Norton, 1992.

Krochmal, Arnold, Russell S. Walters, and Richard M. Doughty. *A Guide to Medicinal Plants of Appalachia.* Washington, DC: U.S. Department of Agriculture, 1969.

Lamb, Robert B. "The Mule in Southern Agriculture." *University of California Publications in Geography* 15 (1963).

Lambert, Darwin. *The Undying Past of Shenandoah National Park*. Boulder, CO: Roberts-Rinehart, 1989.

Lantz, Herman R. "Family and Kin as Revealed in the Narratives of Ex-Slaves." *Social Science Quarterly* 60 (4) (1980): 667–75.

Lawrence, Ruth A. *Breastfeeding: A Guide for the Medical Profession*. St. Louis: Mosby, 1994.

Leavitt, Judith W. *Brought to Bed: Childbearing in America, 1750 to 1950*. New York: Oxford University Press, 1986.

Lewis, Jan, and Kenneth A. Lockridge. "'Sally has been Sick': Pregnancy and Family Limitation among Virginia Gentry Women, 1780–1830." *Journal of Social History* 22 (1988): 1–23

Lewis, Ronald L. *Coal, Iron and Slaves: Industrial Slavery in Maryland and Virginia, 1715–1865*. Westport, CT: Greenwood Press, 1979.

Lim, Linda. "Capitalism, Imperialism and Patriarchy. In *Women, Men and the International Division of Labor*, edited by June Nash and Maria P. Fernandez-Kelly, pp. 70–92. Albany, NY: SUNY Press, 1983.

Little, J. I. "Ethnicity, Family Structure and Seasonal Labor Strategies on Quebec's Appalachian Frontier, 1852–1881." *Journal of Family History* 17 (3) (1992): 289–302

McCurry, Stephanie. *Masters of Small Worlds: Yeoman Households, Gender Relations, and the Political Culture of the Antebellum South Carolina Low Country*. New York: Oxford University Press, 1995.

McDonald, Roderick A. *The Economy and Material Culture of Slaves: Goods and Chattels on the Sugar Plantations of Jamaica and Louisiana*. Baton Rouge: Louisiana State University Press, 1993.

McDougle, Ivan E. "Slavery in Kentucky." *Journal of Negro History* 3 (3) (1918): 211–332.

McGuire, Randall H., Joan Smith, and William G. Martin. "Patterns of Household Structures and the World-Economy." *Review of the Fernand Braudel Center* 10 (1) (1986): 75–99.

McKinney, Gordon B. *Southern Mountain Republicans, 1865–1900*. Chapel Hill: University of North Carolina Press, 1978.

McManus, Edgar J. *Black Bondage in the North*. Syracuse, NY: Syracuse University Press, 1973.

McMillen, Sally G. *Motherhood in the Old South: Pregnancy, Childbirth and Infant Rearing*. Cambridge: Cambridge University Press, 1990.

"Mother's Sacred Duty: Breast Feeding Patterns among Middle and Upper-Class Women in the Antebellum South." *Journal of Southern History* 51 (3) (1985): 333–56.

Maher, Vanessa. *The Anthropology of Breastfeeding: Natural Law or Social Construct?* Oxford: Berg Publishers, 1992.

Malcolm, L. A. *Growth and Development in New Guinea: A Study of the Bundi People of the Mandang District*. Madang: Institute of Human Biology, 1970.

Margo, Robert A. "Civilian Occupations of Ex-Slaves in the Union Army, 1862–1865." In *Without Consent or Contract: The Rise and Fall of American Slavery*.

Vol. 1. *Markets and Production: Technical Papers*, edited by Robert W. Fogel and Stanley L. Engerman, pp. 170–85. New York: W. W. Norton, 1992.

and Richard H. Steckel, "The Heights of American Slaves: New Evidence on Slave Nutrition and Health." *Social Science History* 6 (Fall 1982): 516–38.

Marx, Karl. *Capital*, 3 vols. Chicago: Charles Kerr and Company, 1906.

Medick, Hans. "The Proto-Industrial Family Economy: The Structural Function of Household and Family during the Transition from Peasant Society to Industrial Capitalism." *Social History* 1 (1976): 291–315.

Menard, Russell. "The Maryland Slave Population, 1658 to 1730." *William and Mary Quarterly* 32 (1975): 29–54.

Millner, Reginald. "Conversations with the 'Ole Man': The Life and Times of a Black Appalachian Coal Miner." In *Blacks in Appalachia*, edited by William H. Turner and Edward J. Cabbell, pp. 213–22. Lexington: University Press of Kentucky, 1985.

Mintz, Sidney. *The Origins of the Jamaican Internal Marketing System*. New Haven, CT: Yale University Press, 1960.

Montell, William L. *The Saga of Coe Ridge: A Study in Oral History*. New York: Harper and Row, 1972.

Mooney, Chase C. *Slavery in Tennessee*. Bloomington: Indiana University Press, 1957.

Moore, Warren. *Mountain Voices: A Legacy of the Blue Ridge and Smokies*. Chester, CT: Globe Pequot Press, 1988.

Morgan, Lynda J. *Emancipation in Virginia's Tobacco Belt, 1850–1870*. Athens: University of Georgia Press, 1992.

Morrissey, Marietta. *Slave Women in the New World: Gender Stratification in the Caribbean*. Lawrence: University Press of Kansas, 1989.

Mosby, Maryida W. "Salt Industry in the Kanawha Valley." M.A. thesis, University of Kentucky, 1950.

Moynihan, Daniel P. *The Negro Family: The Case for National Action*. Washington, DC: Department of Labor, 1965.

Mullin, Michael. *Africa in America: Slave Acculturation and Resistance in the American South and the British Caribbean, 1736–1831*. Urbana: University of Illinois Press, 1992.

Noe, Kenneth W. *Southwest Virginia's Railroad: Modernization and the Sectional Crisis*. Urbana: University of Illinois Press, 1994.

and Shannon H. Wilson, eds. *The Civil War in Appalachia: Collected Essays*. Knoxville: University of Tennessee Press, 1997.

O'Brien, Sean M. *Mountain Partisans: Guerilla Warfare in the Southern Appalachians, 1861–1865*. Westport, CT: Praeger, 1999.

Olson, Eric J. "Race Relations in Asheville, North Carolina: Three Incidents, 1868–1906." In *The Appalachian Experience: Proceedings of the Sixth Annual Appalachian Studies Conference*, edited by Barry M. Buxton, pp. 153–68. Boone, NC: Appalachian Consortium Press, 1983.

Olwell, Robert. "A Reckoning of Accounts: Patriarchy, Market Relations, and Control on Henry Laurens' Lowcountry Plantations, 1762–1785." In *Working Toward Freedom: Slave Society and Domestic Economy in the American South*, edited by Larry E. Hudson, pp. 33–52. Rochester, NY: University of Rochester Press, 1994.

Orser, Charles E. *The Material Basis of the Postbellum Tenant Plantation: Historical Archaeology of the South Carolina Piedmont.* Athens: University of Georgia Press, 1988.

Owens, Leslie H. *This Species of Property: Slave Life and Culture in the Old South.* New York: Oxford University Press, 1977.

Parish, Peter. *Slavery: History and Historians.* New York: Harper and Row, 1989.

Patterson, Caleb. *The Negro in Tennessee, 1790–1865.* New York: Negro Universities Press, 1968.

Patterson, Orlando. *Rituals of Blood: Consequences of Slavery in Two American Centuries.* New York: Basic Civitas, 1999.

  Slavery and Social Death: A Comparative Study. Cambridge, MA: Harvard University Press, 1982.

Patton, Sadie S. *Sketches of Polk County History.* Asheville, NC: Miller Printing Co., 1950.

Pease, Louise M. "The Great Kanawha in the Old South, 1671–1861." Ph.D. diss., West Virginia University, 1959.

Peck, Elisabeth S. *Berea's First Century, 1855–1955.* Lexington: University of Kentucky Press, 1955.

Phifer, Edward W. "Slavery in Microcosm: Burke County, North Carolina." *Journal of Southern History* 28 (2) (1962): 137–65.

Phillips, Peter D. "Incorporation of the Caribbean, 1650–1700." *Review of the Fernand Braudel Center* 10 (1987): 781–804.

Phillips, Ulrich B. *American Negro Slavery: A Survey of the Supply, Employment and Control of Negro Labor as Determined by the Plantation Regime.* Baton Rouge: Louisiana State University Press, 1966.

  Life and Labor in the Old South. New York: Grosset and Dunlap, 1929.

Pinchbeck, Raymond B. "The Virginia Negro Artisan and Tradesman." *Publications of the University of Virginia* 7 (1926): 1–146.

Potts, Lydia. *The World Labour Market: A History of Migration*, translated by Terry Bond. London: Zed Books, 1990.

Raphael, Dana, ed. *Breastfeeding and Food Policy in a Hungry World.* New York: Academic Press, 1979.

Raulston, J. Leonard, and James W. Livingood. *Sequatchie: A Story of the Southern Cumberlands.* Knoxville: University of Tennessee Press, 1974.

Rawick, George P. *From Sundown to Sunup: The Making of the Black Community.* Westport, CT: Greenwood Press, 1972.

Riordan, Jan, and Kathleen G. Auerbach. *Breastfeeding and Human Lactation.* Boston: Jones and Bartlett, 1993.

Robles, Aroyds, and Susan C. Watkins. "Immigration and Family Separation at the Turn of the Twentieth Century." *Journal of Family History* 18 (3) (1993): 191–211.

Russell, John H. *The Free Negro in Virginia, 1619–1865.* 1913. Reprint. New York: Negro Universities Press, 1969.

Salmon, John S. *The Washington Iron Works of Franklin County, Virginia.* Richmond: Virginia State Library, 1986.

Sanford, Douglas W. "The Archaeology of Plantation Slavery in Piedmont Virginia: Context and Process." In *Historical Archaeology of the Chesapeake,* edited by P. A. Shackel and B. J. Little, pp. 115–30. Washington, DC: Smithsonian Institution Press, 1994.

Sarris, Jonathan D. "'Shot for Bein Bushwhackers': Guerilla War and Extralegal Violence in a Northern Georgia Community, 1862–1865." In *Guerillas, Unionists and Violence on the Confederate Home Front*, edited by Daniel E. Sutherland, pp. 31–44. Fayetteville: University of Arkansas Press, 1999.

Savitt, Todd L. *Medicine and Slavery: The Diseases and Health Care of Blacks in Antebellum Virginia.* Urbana: University of Illinois Press, 1978.

"Use of Blacks for Medical Experimentation and Demonstration in the Old South." *Journal of Southern History* 48 (1982): 331–48.

Schlotterbeck, John T. "The Internal Economy of Slavery in Rural Piedmont Virginia." In *The Slaves' Economy: Independent Production by Slaves in the Americas,* edited by Ira Berlin and P. D. Morgan, pp. 150–71. London: Frank Cass, 1991.

Schweninger, Loren. "Slave Independence and Enterprise in South Carolina, 1780–1865." *South Cariolina Historical Magazine* 93 (2) (1992): 101–25.

Seals, Monroe. *History of White County, Tennessee.* Spartanburg, SC: Reprint Co. Publishers, 1974.

Shuptrine, Hubert. *Home to Jericho.* Birmingham, AL: Oxmoor House, 1978.

Singleton, Theresa A. "The Archaeology of Slavery in North America." *Annual Review of Anthropology* 24 (1) (1995): 119–40.

Sitterson, Joseph C. *The Secession Movement in North Carolina.* Chapel Hill: University of North Carolina Press, 1939.

Smith, Adam. *An Inquiry into the Nature and Causes of the Wealth of Nations.* 1776. Reprint. Edited by C. J. Bullock. New York: P. F. Collier and Sons, 1909.

Smith, Daniel S. "Family Limitation, Sexual Control and Domestic Feminism in Victorian America." *Feminist Studies* 1 (1) (1973): 40–57.

Smith, James L. "Historical Geography of the Southern Charcoal Iron Industry, 1800–1860." Ph.D. diss., University of Tennessee, 1982.

Smith, Joan. Immanuel Wallerstein, and Hans-Dieter Evers, eds. *Households and the World-Economy.* Beverly Hills, CA: Sage, 1984.

Smith, Mark M. *Mastered by the Clock: Time, Slavery, and Freedom in the American South.* Chapel Hill: University of North Carolina Press, 1997.

Stagg, J. C. A. "The Problem of Klan Violence: The South Carolina Upcountry, 1868–1871." *Journal of American Studies* 8 (1974): 303–18.

Stampp, Kenneth. *The Peculiar Institution: Slavery in the Antebellum South.* New York: Knopf, 1956.

Starobin, Robert S. *Industrial Slavery in the Old South.* New York: Oxford University Press, 1970.

Stealey, John E. "The Salt Industry of the Great Kanawha Valley of Virginia: A Study in Antebellum Internal Commerce." Ph.D. diss., West Virginia University, 1970.

"Slavery and the Western Virginia Salt Industry." *Journal of Negro History* 59 (1974): 105–31.

Steckel, Richard H. *The Economics of U.S. Slave and Southern White Fertility.* New York: Garland Publishing, 1985.

"A Peculiar Population: The Nutrition, Health, and Mortality of American Slaves from Childhood to Maturity." *Journal of Economic History* 46 (1986): 721–41.

"Slave Height Profiles from Coastwise Manifestos." *Explorations in Economic History* 19 (1979): 363–80.

"Slave Mortality: Analysis of Evidence from Plantation Records." *Social Science History* 3 (3) (1979): 86–114.

"Women, Work and Health under Plantation Slavery in the United States." In *More than Chattel: Black Women and Slavery in the Americas*, edited by David B. Gaspar and Darlene C. Hine, pp. 43–60. Bloomington: Indiana University Press, 1996.

"Work, Disease and Diet in the Health and Mortality of American Slaves." In *Without Consent or Contract: The Rise and Fall of American Slavery*. Vol. 2. *Technical Papers: Conditions of Slave Life and the Transition to Freedom*, edited by R. W. Fogel and S. L. Engerman, pp. 489–507. New York: W. W. Norton, 1992.

Stephenson, Wendell H. *Isaac Franklin: Slave Trader and Planter of the Old South.* Baton Rouge: Louisiana State University, 1938.

Stevenson, Brenda E. *Life in Black and White: Family and Community in the Slave South.* New York: Oxford University Press, 1996.

Stokely, Jim, and Jeff D. Johnson, eds. *An Encyclopedia of East Tennessee.* Oak Ridge, TN: Children's Museum, 1981.

Stowell, Daniel W. " 'The Negroes Cannot Navigate Alone': Religious Scalawags and the Biracial Methodist Episcopal Church in Georgia, 1866–1876." In *Georgia in Black and White: Explorations in the Race Relations of a Southern State, 1865–1950*, edited by John C. Inscoe, pp. 65–90. Athens: University of Georgia Press, 1994.

Stuart-Macadam, Patricia, and Katherine A. Dettwyler. *Breastfeeding: Biocultural Perspectives.* New York: Aldine de Gruyter, 1995.

Sunley, Robert. "Early Nineteenth-Century American Literature on Child Rearing." In *Childhood in Contemporary Cultures*, edited by M. Mead and M. Wolfenstein, pp. 150–67. Chicago: University of Chicago Press, 1955.

Sutch, Richard. "The Breeding of Slaves for Sale and the Westward Expansion of Slavery, 1850–1860." In *Race and Slavery in the Western Hemisphere: Quantitative Studies*, edited by S. L. Engerman and E. D. Genovese, pp. 173–210. Princeton, NJ: Princeton University Press, 1975.

"The Care and Feeding of Slaves." In *Reckoning with Slavery: A Critical Study in the Quantitative History of American Negro Slavery*, edited by Paul David, H. G. Gutman, R. Sutch, P. Temin, and G. Wright, pp. 231–300. New York: Oxford University Press, 1976.

"The Treatment Received by American Slaves: A Critical Review of the Evidence Presented in *Time on the Cross*." *Explorations in Economic History* 12 (1975): 386–94.

Sweig, Donald. "Northern Virginia Slavery: A Statistical and Demographic Investigation." Ph.D. diss., College of William and Mary, 1982.

Tadman, Michael. *Speculators and Slaves: Masters, Traders, and Slaves in the Old South.* Madison: University of Wisconsin Press, 1989.

Taylor, Alrutheus A. *The Negro in Tennessee, 1865–1880*. Washington, DC: Associated Publishers, 1941.

Thompson, Lanny. "The Structures and Vicissitudes of Reproduction: Households in Mexico, 1876–1970." *Review of the Fernand Braudel Center* 14 (3) (1991): 403–36.

Tolnay, Stewart E., and E. M. Beck. *A Festival of Violence: An Analysis of Southern Lynchings, 1882–1930*. Urbana: University of Illinois Press, 1992.

Tomich, Dale W. "Contested Terrains: Houses, Provision Grounds and the Reconstitution of Labour in Post-Emancipation Martinique." In *From Chattel Slaves to Wage Slaves: The Dynamics of Labour Bargaining in the Americas*, edited by Mary Turner, pp. 241–57. London: James Curry Ltd., 1995.

Trotter, Joe W. *Coal, Class and Color: Blacks in Southern West Virginia, 1915–32*. Urbana: University of Illinois Press, 1990.

Trouillot, Michel-Rolph. *Silencing the Past: Power and the Production of History*. Boston: Beacon Press, 1995.

Trussell, J., and Richard Steckel. "The Age of Slaves at Menarche and Their First Birth." *Journal of Interdisciplinary History* 8 (1978): 477–505.

Turner, Charles W. "Railroad Service to Virginia Farmers, 1828–1860." *Agricultural History* 22 (1948): 239–47.

Turner, Mary, ed. *From Chattel Slaves to Wage Slaves: The Dynamics of Labour Bargaining in the Americas*. London: James Curry Ltd., 1995.

Veltmeyer, Henry. "Surplus Labor and Class Formation on the Latin American Periphery." In *Theories of Development: Mode of Production or Dependency*, edited by Ronald H. Chilcote and Dale L. Johnson, pp. 201–30. Beverly Hills, CA: Sage, 1983.

Von Verlhof, Claudia. "Women's Work: The Blind Spot in the Critique of Political Economy. In *Women: The Lost Colony*, edited by Maria Mies, Veronika Bennholdt-Thomsen, and C. von Werholf, pp. 13–26. London: Zed Books, 1988.

Wade, Richard C. *Slavery in the Cities: The South, 1820–1860*. New York: Oxford University Press, 1967.

Wallerstein, Immanuel. "American Slavery and the Capitalist World-Economy. *American Journal of Sociology* 81 (1976): 1199–1213.

Historical Capitalism. London: Verso Editions, 1983.

The Modern World-System II: Mercantilism and the Consolidation of the European World-Economy, 1600–1750. New York: Academic Press, 1980.

The Modern World-System III: The Second Era of Great Expansion of the Capitalist World-Economy, 1730–1840s. New York: Academic Press, 1989.

and Joan Smith. "Core-Periphery and Household Structures." In *Creating and Transforming Households: The Constraints of the World-Economy*, edited by J. Smith and I. Wallerstein, pp. 253–62. London: Cambridge University Press, 1992.

Walsh, Lorena S. "Slave Life, Slave Society, and Tobacco Production in the Tidewater Chesapeake, 1620–1820." In *Cultivation and Culture: Labor and the Shaping of Slave Life in the Americas*, edited by Ira Berlin and Philip D. Morgan, pp. 170–99. Charlottesville: University of Virginia Press, 1993.

Warner, Charles D. "Comments on Kentucky." *Harper's New Monthly Magazine* 7 (21 February 1881): 270–71.

Watkin, James L. *King Cotton: A Historical and Statistical Review, 1790–1908.*
1908. Reprint. New York: Negro Universities Press, 1969.

Wayland, John W. *Twenty-Five Chapters on the Shenandoah Valley.* Strasburg, VA:
Shenandoah Publishing House, 1957.

Wilson, Charles R., and William Ferris, eds. *Encyclopedia of Southern Culture.*
Chapel Hill: University of North Carolina Press, 1989.

Wish, Harvey. *George Fitzhugh: Propagandist of the Old South.* Baton Rouge:
Louisiana State University Press, 1943.

Wood, Betty. *Women's Work, Men's Work: The Informal Slave Economies of Lowcountry Georgia.* Athens: University of Georgia Press, 1995.

Woodson, Carter G. "The Negro Washerwoman, a Vanishing Figure." *Journal of
Negro History* 15 (3) (1930): 269–77.

Woodward, C. Vann. "History from Slave Sources: A Review Article." *American
Historical Review* 79 (2) (1974): 470–81.

Wright, George C. *Racial Violence in Kentucky, 1865–1940: Lynchings, Mob Rule,
and "Legal Lynchings."* Baton Rouge: Louisiana State University Press, 1990.

Yetman, Norman R. "The Background of the Slave Narrative Collection."
American Quarterly 19 (3) (1967): 534–53.

 Life under the "Peculiar Institution": Selections from the Slave Narrative Collection.
New York: Holt, Rinehart and Winston, 1970.

Young, Amy L. "Slave Subsistence at the Upper South Mabry Site, East
Tennessee: Regional Variability in Plantation Diet of the Southeastern
United States." M.A. thesis, University of Tennessee, 1993.

Index

small, 1, 2–3, 5, 10, 11–12, 13–14,
15, 55, 60–61, 66, 70, 85, 87, 89,
90, 111, 127–28, 142, 146, 152,
169–70, 171, 175, 181, 186, 203,
213, 217, 219
Spring Hill, 45
Traveler's Rest, 153, 213
See also Overseer; Slaveholder
Pocohontas County, WV, 86
Polk County, NC, 248
Poor white
children, 251
laborers, 6, 129, 132, 136, 206,
233–34, 236, 239, 264; see also
tables 1.5, 2.2 (website)
living conditions, 10, 92, 243, 254,
301n13
slave trading, 31–32, 33
trading with slaves, 155
See also Bounty hunters; Race
relations; Slave trader names
Poor white names
Bell, N. J., 241–42
Brooks, B. W., 32
Chester, John P., 32
Hurd, Buck, 33
Jordan, Alex, 199
Population trends, 3, 8–10, 11–12,
18–20, 238–39, 244–45. See also
urbanization; tables 1.1, 1.2, 1.4,
14.3, 14.4 (website)
Pregnancy
ex-slave, 125, 211, 224, 225–26,
305n22, n23
poor white, 130, 131, 307n36
slave, 3, 43, 53, 64, 65, 88, 123–34,
141, 144, 275
slaveholder, 114–17, 275
teenage, 2, 119, 121, 125, 142, 276
See also Breastfeeding; Childbearing;
Fertility; Midwife
Punishment, 11–12, 65, 69–70, 71, 75,
77–78, 79–80, 105, 112, 147, 149

Quaker Freedmen's Normal Institute
318

Race relations
antebellum, see discussion 1 (website)
postbellum, 243–52; see also Violence

Racism, 52–53, 59, 118–19, 130,
213–14, 219, 236, 244, 247–48,
264
Railroad, 22, 30, 40, 87, 91, 96, 97, 99,
155, 187, 188–89, 192, 205,
225–26, 228, 238, 240–42, 247
Randolph County, WV, 31
Rappahannock County, VA, 318n28
Reconstruction, 16, 214, 220, 230–67,
268, 273–74, 286, 317n15
Reproductive exploitation, 114–49, 273,
274–77, 281–84. See also
Breastfeeding; Fertility; Nurses;
Pregnancy; Sexual exploitation
Resistance, 2, 11–12, 42, 61, 79, 81,
111, 136
Rice, 18, 110, 180
Richmond, VA, 22, 25, 31, 33, 34, 40,
41, 43, 44, 65, 68, 194, 195, 261,
291n8
Rivers, 10, 21, 22, 24, 25, 26, 29, 30,
34, 36, 38, 40, 62, 94, 95, 99, 107,
109, 119, 144, 169, 181, 189, 192,
195, 246, 280
Roads, 10, 21, 27, 28, 32, 34–35, 38,
66–67, 94, 118, 158, 187, 189,
199–200, 203, 213, 244, 246, 247,
250, 257
Roanoke County, VA, 37, 68, 111, 248,
318n28
Rockbridge County, VA, 53, 62, 183,
194, 259, 318n28. See also
Lexington
Rockingham County, VA, 318n28
Rome, GA, 22, 31, 37, 46, 57, 179,
236–37, 238, 245–46
Runaways, 2, 28, 30, 31, 32, 34, 37, 42,
61, 84, 113, 147, 185, 186, 192
Russell County, VA, 42, 225, 229
Rutherford County, NC, 33, 248

St. Clair County, AL, 244
Salisbury, NC, 22
Salt
manufacturing, 33, 47, 48, 87, 92,
93, 95, 98, 109, 155, 187, 196, 247
in slave diet, 103, 104, 105–106, 110,
113, 131, 150
Saltville, VA, 196–97, 198
Savannah, GA, 25, 31